Globalisation, Social Justice and Sustainable Development in India

Globalisation, Social Justice and Sustainable Development in India

Manish K. Verma

GYAN

First Published, 2017

Published by

Gyan Publishing House
5, Ansari Road
Daryaganj, New Delhi-110002
Phone: 9811692060
E-mail: books@gyanbooks.com

Printed at: G. Print Process, Delhi.

Cataloging in Publication Data—DK
Courtesy: D.K. Agencies (P) Ltd. <docinfo@dkagencies.com>

Globalisation, social justice and sustainable development in India /
Manish K. Verma.
pages cm
Contributed articles.
ISBN 9788121214155

1. Globalisation—Social aspects—India. 2. Globalisation—Economic aspects—India. 3. Globalisation—Environmental aspects—India. 4. Social justice—India. 5. Sustainable development—India. 6. Economic development—India. I. Verma, Manish Kumar, editor.

LCC HN690.Z9G56 2017 | DDC 338.954 23

Contents

List of Figures

List of Tables

Preface

The rapid pace of globalisation has augmented a process of swift industrialisation and urbanisation all over the world which has far reaching effect on various facets of human environment and society. As a process, globalisation has not only swept the entire planet in its strong currents but also attempted to integrate it socially, economically, culturally, politically, commercially and technologically up to a large extent. Initiated at the global level since 1980s (early 1990's in India) in terms of liberalisation, privatisation and globalisation (LPG), it has played a pivotal role in terms of unification of the world in general and market in particular.

India, being the fastest growing economy and largest democratic country having second largest population in the world, is also equally affected by the globalisation process. The transformation of society and its various parts due to the neoliberal globalisation process during last couple of decades are so swift and forceful that it astonished everyone including academicians, social scientists, policy-makers, planners and people at large. Therefore, the nature, scope, form and impact of globalisation are under intense debate in India as intelligentsia holds differing perspectives over its impact on environment and society. Down the line, it's a perennial issue of concern whether to consider globalisation processes benevolent and beneficial to human beings, or contrarily, detrimental due to being instrumental for environmental degradation and creating exclusion, pauperisation, marginalisation, deprivation and injustice, especially for those who are at the margins of the society. Scholars hold that neoliberal globalisation process in recent times has emerged as a primordial source of distress, disparity, discrimination, deprivation, marginalisation, exclusion, ecological imbalance and environmental catastrophe; culminating into deprivation of social justice for the masses and undermining the possibility of sustainable development.

Most recently noticing serious pitfalls in the magnitude, direction, scale and level, the deliberations on globalisation per se has been shifted on to examine the convergence and divergence between the issues and interests of globalisation, social justice and sustainable development. Now the focus shifted on to comprehend in what way and up to what extent globalisation is using nature and environment to meet their developmental prerequisites, and how depletion of scarcely available resources, environmental catastrophe and ecological imbalance is negating the possibility of environmental sustainability and sustainable development. Further, what is the exact outcome of the process of globalisation from the perspective of marginalised and deprived sections of population: is it proving benevolent or obstinately turning out to be detrimental to secure social justice and therefore hindering the prospect of a just social order with equity, equality, dignity and forbearance. In this regard, the Indian experience of neoliberal globalisation holds immense relevance and significance due to the country being home for a large number of marginal and excluded people living below poverty line.

Against this backdrop, the edited volume is initiated with a view to comprehend the process of globalisation and to assess the inter-linkages between globalisation, social justice and sustainable development by putting Indian experience at the centre-stage. The papers of this volume are crafted with the intent to examine and comprehend the issues and concerns underlining the process of 'Globalisation vis-à-vis Social Justice and Sustainable Development' which has caught the attention of the intelligentsia. For the convenience and thematic understanding, the papers of the volume are divided into three sub-themes apart from one introductory chapter in the beginning. Each section covers one important facet of globalisation, social justice and sustainable development linkages by focusing on the Indian experiences, viz. 'Globalisation and Social Justice', 'Socio-economic Aspects of Globalisation', and 'Globalisation, Environment and Sustainable Development'. First and third unit of the volume comprises six papers each, whereas, five papers are included in the second section. Papers of the book are organised to address the sub-themes to which they particularly pertain and are contributed by academicians and experts hailing from renowned universities and institutes.

Due to having broader canvass and inter-disciplinary nature of issues covered, the book is of immense significance for academicians, researchers, post-graduate and graduate level students of social sciences and development studies, policy-makers and NGOs working in the area of globalisation, environment, sustainable development and social justice.

Lastly, it is time to extend gratitude and acknowledge all those who stood by me for the completion of the edited volume. At the outset, I owe a deep sense of gratitude to all the contributors of the volume. Without their novel contributions, dedicated hard work and support, the edited volume on "Globalisation, Social Justice and Sustainable Development in India" would have been a distant dream. They have extended their full support, co-operation and forbearance at every stage of the completion of the book and shown intense willingness to help me in the editing work to make the volume a reality.

I am thankful to Professor Kameshwar Choudhary, my senior colleague in the Department of Sociology for providing all kinds of support and assistance in formulation and sketching of the book. I also express my deep sense of gratitude to Professor N.M.P. Verma, whose support and guidance proved extremely valuable. I am equally thankful to Office Assistant of the Department of Sociology Mr Ajay Kumar for providing secretarial assistance. The contribution of my Research Scholars Mr Narendra Kumar and Mr Raju Shah is quite appreciative in this regard.

It is high time to show my sincere gratitude towards my teachers. First of all I extend a deep sense of gratitude to eminent Sociologist, extremely noble man and most fortunately my revered teacher, legendary Prof. Yogendra Singh who always stood by me and showered his blessings despite all odds. Along the same line Professor K.L. Sharma, Professor T.K. Oommen, Professor Nandu Ram, Professor Anand Kumar and Professor Ehshanul Haque are foremost among my notable teachers. It is their teaching and blessings which strengthened me at every moment of life.

It will go without saying if I don't mention the contribution of my family members whose encouragement, cooperation and forbearance enormously helped me to complete the volume. It is the inspiration and blessings of my late grandfather S. D. Verma and late grandmother Kishori Devi that I am in this position to fulfil their dreams. Even from heavenly abode, their blessings are encouraging and motivating me to work diligently to come up to their expectations. I take this opportunity to thanks my parents Sri U. K. Verma and Smt Usha Kiran Verma, brother and sisters, in-laws etc. for their love and cooperation extended to me at every moment of my life. The cooperation, help and assistance extended by my wife Runu Verma and the patience of my beloved son Aradhya Dev is highly appreciable for the completion of this endeavour. I have no hesitation in admitting here that my thorough academic engagement for the timely completion of the volume undermined and diminished their share of time and space which they would have certainly spent with me and enjoyed. Therefore, without their sacrifice and forbearance, this work would not have taken a proper shape.

Finally, I owe a deep sense of gratitude to the entire team of Gyan Publishing House, New Delhi for taking personal interest in getting this volume out of the press with high level of efficiency and least amount of aberrations and errors.

In the last I must admit that I am extremely benefitted from the suggestions of many colleagues in the process of writing and editing this volume. However, the entire responsibility about the content and form of the edited volume is mine, and if there are shortcomings I alone am to be blamed.

Manish K. Verma

Professor and Head
Department of Sociology
Babasaheb Bhimrao Ambedkar University
(NAAC Accredited 'A' Grade Central University)
Vidya Vihar, Rae Bareli Road, Lucknow-226025

List of Contributors

1. **Manish K. Verma** is Professor and Head in the Department of Sociology, Babasaheb Bhimrao Ambedkar Central University, Lucknow.
2. **Jitendra Ram** is teaching as Assistant Professor at the Centre for Sociological Studies, School of Social Sciences and Policy (SSSP), Central University of South Bihar, Gaya, Bihar.
3. **Deep Shikha Karthik** is Assistant Professor at the Department of English, Pandit Ram Lakhan Shukla Govt. P.G. College, Alapur, Ambedkar Nagar, Uttar Pradesh.
4. **Minati Sahoo** is teaching as Assistant Professor of Economics at Central University of Orissa.

   Subrat Kumar Malik is Research Scholar at the Department of Economics, Babasaheb Bhimrao Ambedkar Central University, Lucknow.
5. **Saket Bihari** is Associate Professor at the Indian Institute of Public Administration, New Delhi.
6. **Bushra Wadood** is a faculty at Integral University, Lucknow.

   Amina Jafri is teaching as Assistant Professor at Integral University, Lucknow.
7. **Poornima Jain** is Professor and Head at the Department of Sociology and Social Work, Dayalbagh Educational Institute (A Deemed University), Agra.
8. **Pratick Mallick** is faculty in Political Science at Acharya Prafulla Chandra College (NAAC Accredited Grade 'A'), New Barrackpore, Kolkata.
9. **Arvinder A. Ansari** is Professor, Jamia Millia Islamia, New Delhi.
10. **Surendra Meher** is teaching as Assistant Professor at the Department of Economics, Babasaheb Bhimrao Ambedkar Central University, Lucknow.
11. **Ruchi Bhalla** is Research Scholar at the Department of Economics, Babasaheb Bhimrao Ambedkar Central University, Lucknow.

12. **Tapan R. Mohanty** is Professor and Chairperson, Centre for Socio-Legal Studies, National Law Institute University, Bhopal.

13. **Haresh Narayan Pandey** is Assistant Professor at the Centre for Sociological Studies, School of Social Sciences and Policy, Central University of South Bihar, Gaya Campus, Bihar.

14. **Nandkishor More** is Associate Professor, Department of Environmental Science, School of Environmental Sciences, Babasaheb Bhimrao Ambedkar Central University, Lucknow. He has been awarded United Nations University, Tokyo Fellowship in 2006 and is recipient of ICTP, Italy Fellowship in 2007, UNESCO and IRD France fellowship in 2015. He has extensively travelled worldwide to participate in international conferences at Denmark, Cyprus, Italy, Sri Lanka, Malaysia, Thailand, Canada, Morocco, France etc.

    Shashi Kumar is Associate Professor, Department of Human Rights, School for Legal Studies, Babasaheb Bhimrao Ambedkar Central University, Lucknow. He has been awarded fellowships from University Grant Commission (1993), the International Institute of Human Rights, Strasbourg France (2009) and Raman Post-doctoral Fellowship for USA (2015).

15. **Abhishek Pandey** is Assistant Professor, Department of Economics, Dr. Shakuntala Misra National Rehabilitation University, Lucknow.

16. **Ashish Saxena** is Professor and Head, Department of Sociology, University of Allahabad, Allahabad.

    Vijaylaxmi Saxena is Independent Researcher and Freelance Writer. She is teaching Sociology as Assistant Professor at the Department of Law, Faculty of Law, Nehru Gram Bharti Vishwavidalaya, Allahabad.

17. **Sutandra Singha** is Research Scholar at the Centre for Russian and Central Asian Studies, School of International Studies, Jawaharlal Nehru University, New Delhi.

18. **Sheetal J. Tamakuwala** teaches as Assistant Professor in MSW Programme at the Department of Sociology, Veer Narmad South Gujarat University, Surat, Gujarat.

19. **Ravindra Kumar** is Advisor, WWF-India, New Delhi; Member, Advisory Group (Water), DST-CPR, Babasaheb Bhimrao Ambedkar Central University, Lucknow. He was formerly with SWARA and UPIWRD, Government of Uttar Pradesh.

Chapter - 1

Introduction

—*Manish K. Verma*

The introductory chapter introduces the main theme of the book by delineating into conceptual understanding and theoretical debate on globalisation, social justice and sustainable development. Thereafter, it provides an analytical glimpse of the papers included in the edited book and tries to interlink them with the key indicators while placing them in the background of the sub-theme to which they specifically pertains.

***Key Words**: Globalisation, Social Justice, Sustainable Development.*

The last two decades of the twentieth century is historically discernible with the inundation of a new process of transformation, which the world had never seen before, named as globalisation. With the dawn of the new century and a new millennium, globalisation appeared to become a key to the future of mankind promising to usher an era of unprecedented progress and prosperity with the introduction of latest technological innovations, creation of a single borderless world diminishing the barriers of time and space, converting the globe into a single world with free market wherein capital, goods and services can flow without any restriction and hindrance. The shining contours of globalisation dazzled and mesmerised almost all the nations and their natives and it appeared as if all the tribulations of the world would be solved in as lesser time as possible. However, not more than a decade since the process of globalisation unearthed on the planet with great fanfare, it started getting realised by the nations especially the third world countries including India that 'all that glitters is not gold': the delusion started shattering by the awareness that the countless promises of globalisation has not been fulfilled and probably it would never be accomplished with the present state of being. Contrarily, the process accelerated unmasking of grater evils for the humanity: economic disparity between rich and the poor nations and the people further widened leading to large scale impoverishment of masses; discrimination based on caste, class, region, religion, sex, race, ethnicity etc. inflated to an unprecedented level; extreme cut-throat competition surfaced in the society eventually crippling the human values, ethical standards and moral aptitude; provided a congenial space for the emergence of neo-colonial activities wherein the dominant nations started exploiting the interests of the third world countries and literally harvested maximum benefits of globalisation in their own favour undermining the notion of sustainable development and the possibility of a just world order and, therefore, the global world and its citizens got united into hegemonic relations; most importantly, environmental destruction, depletion of natural resources, global warming and climate change reached to such a critical level from where human existence on the earth seems to be endangered and remain under constant threat of elimination.

The incessant process of globalisation and its present saga is creating serious doubt about its credentials and raises a question mark on the notion of sustainable development with equity and equality and eventually the possibility of bringing social justice unto the last. Even though, globalisation, sustainable development and social justice appear to be inextricably inter-related and theoretically move in a straight line, but on a pragmatic level they portray another side of the spectrum. In reality, at contemporary times, globalisation and sustainable development have taken position of two ends of the pole and subsequently social justice is struggling to find its position somewhere in between. Even though, theoretically speaking, globalisation is vying for sustainable development but practically it falls short of its aim and as a result undermining the possibility of a harmonious relation between nature and society and just social world with peaceful coexistence.

India, being the second largest populated country of the world, biggest democracy and fastest growing economy, right from 1990s (though the process of globalisation started in early 1980s at the global level but India joined the movement much later, in 1990s) onwards could not resist to get carried away with the wave of globalisation in order to garner its benefits for fulfilling the needs of its growing market demand of consumer products. Hence, India opened its market and extended red carpet welcome to the MNCs, industrialists and other stake holders to carry out business by creating favourable policies, allotting huge patches of land in scanty rates and providing tax heavens. The effort was done by the Indian Government in sheer negligence of the interests of the local land holders, small farmers, petty businessmen, marginalised communities and most importantly the common masses. Moreover, with these efforts in place, the pace of ecological imbalance and environmental destruction accelerated with far more speed than ever before. However, the recent trends evolved after advent of globalisation was not a new phenomenon in India. Much before the dawn of globalisation, "when the process of development formally got under way after Indian independence, it was viewed above all as a collective national endeavour to reduce the gap between India and the industrialised countries of the West. In the circumstances, any talk of ecological constraints to economic activity would have been regarded at best as irrelevant, and at worst, as a deviation from the primary task of rapid industrialisation.

In unanimously advocating large scale, rapid industrialisation, Indian economists have quarreled merely over the means to achieve these ends. Not surprisingly, their discussions have ignored the environmental consequences of economic growth as well as the finite nature of many natural resources" (Guha, 2008: 2-3). Therefore, globalisation has appeared as a new ray of hope for the Indian economists, planners and development practitioners. Hence, they perceived it as their greatest opportunity to garner the maximum potential of globalisation in order to cater their development needs. The mad race to meet the development endeavours of a growing population not only marred the interests of the weaker sections of the society in India but also created large scale social and economic rifts, ecological imbalance and environmental destruction. Slowly and gradually India has also witnessed similar social, economic, political, ecological and environmental backlashes which their Western counterparts were experiencing.

Comprehending globalisation project as problematic, Joseph Stiglitz drew attention towards the inherent discontent of globalisation in terms of its asymmetrical, hegemonic and devastating effect on society. Even though Stiglitz expressed his opinion in the context of USA and other Western countries, but the same viewpoint proves true in the Indian context as well. He warns against the extreme reform strategies adopted by governments which he calls, 'shock therapy' that have failed miserably. He opines, "government needs to–and can–adopt policies that help countries grow but also ensure that growth is shared more equitably". He further asserts that, "there are, of course, no magic solutions. But there are a multitude of changes to be made–in policies, in institutions, in the rules of the game, and in mindsets–that hold out the promise of helping make globalisation work better........." (Stiglitz, 2012: ix-xvi). In a similar fashion, much before Stiglitz writes, Wallerstein called "globalisation no more than a buzzword that describes the current situation in which the end of the 'cold war' has led to the emergence of a unipolar world with an unassailable supremacy of the USA both in global economy and geopolitics. To him, globalisation is meaningless as an analytical concept. The concept only serves primarily as a political prescription for the developing world to opt for all kinds of short cuts to integration with the capitalist global economy." (Dhanagare, 2012: 33). Therefore, sensing inherent tribulations, globalisation in its present form started getting disenchanted from the minds and lives of the nations and people around the globe.

Under the circumstances, Pieterse has rightly puts in, "the crisis of developmentalism as a paradigm manifests itself as a crisis of modernism in the West and the crisis of development in south. The awareness in ecological limits to growth is a significant part of modernism. New social movements in the West enunciate the end of linear progress. Modernity is viewed increasingly as a theory and practice that is more exclusive than inclusive. The charmed circle of achievement and success, which is glamorised in media and advertisements, exacts a high toll excludes and marginalises many". (Pieterse, 2006: 27). As a result, recent times has seen reverse movement against globalisation wherein even the most powerful countries like USA, UK, Canada and Germany are trying to shrink themselves in their own shelf by focusing on their primordial interests and keeping aside the global well being.

Based on the above discussion it is quite clear that since the days of its inception, globalisation not only attracted but also affected one and all in its ambit. Therefore, "due to its all pervasive impacts on the society, perhaps no other term has received as much scholarly and media attention in the last couple of decades as globalisation" (Verma, 2015: 2). Thus, Giddens has rightly called it as an inevitable force, transforming all aspects of contemporary society, politics and economy (Giddens, 1999).

Keeping apart the controversies associated with the buzzword globalisation, whatsoever is its present shape and whatever would be its future, it is undoubtedly interesting to trace, note and sketch its origin and evolution, comprehend its definition and meaning and understand different perspectives held by scholars across globe for its comprehensive understanding.

Globalisation: Origin and Evolution

Although globalisation has made waves in the intellectual parlance much recently, its foundation is deep rooted in history. An exploration of the origin of the highly deliberated epitome of modern days, we find that "although the word 'global' is over 400 years old, the common usage of such word as 'globalisation', 'globalise' and 'globalising did not begin until about 1960. In 1961, Webster became the first major dictionary to offer the definitions of globalism and globalisation" (Waters, 2001: 2). However, much before the word globalisation appeared formally among the intellectual discussion, historically its evidences are found in the writings of several classical thinkers, scholars and academicians. "Saint Simon noticed that industrialisation was inducing commonalities of practice across the disparate cultures of Europe. Seeking to hasten the process, he argued for a utopian internationalism that includes a pan-European government and a new and universalising humanistic philosophy. Saint Simon's ideas found their ways through Comte to Durkheim. Durkheim's genuine legacy to globalisation is his theories of differentiation and culture. He opined that industrialisation tends to weaken collective commitments and to open the way for dismantling the boundaries between societies" (Waters, 2001: 8). In a similar fashion, "where Durkheim identified structural specialisation, Weber finds rationalisation as the globalising solvent among all the Western cultures so as to set up an 'iron cage' for all moderns. Rationalisation, to him, implies that all the cultures will characterise by the depersonalisation of social relationships, the refinement of techniques of calculations, the enhancement of the importance of specialised knowledge, and the extension of technically rational control over both natural and social processes" (Verma, 2015: 3).

Going further deep into the issue, we notice that, "Karl Marx is probably the first classical theorist who most explicitly discussed about the impact of globalisation while discussing capitalism. In the opinion of Marx, globalisation caused an enormous increase in the power of the capitalist class because it opened up new markets for it. In so doing he identified an economic dimension of the process" (Verma, 2015: 3). "As early as in the mid nineteenth century Karl Marx had observed that capitalism as an economic system is by definition and necessarily an international economic system. In the 1960s, Andre Gunder Frank analysed the implication of the phenomena when advancing his thesis on 'capitalist accumulation' and the 'development of underdevelopment'. And, before the word 'globalisation' has acquired currency, Immanuel Wallerstein (1979) spoke of 'the capitalist world economy' and the 'world system theory'. Of course, it is not just the term that is new; what is new is the pervasiveness of the phenomena and the speed at which it has engulfed all parts of the world" (Jayaram and Rajasekhar, 2012: 2). "To the question of whether globalisation is truly metamorphosing economy in fundamental way, John Kenneth Galbraith, an eminent economist replied that 'such a reference to a new economy is just short of fraudulent. What was once termed capitalism is now being called a market economy or corporate system, i.e. profit maximisation through monopolies at any cost. But then the new expression 'market system' is preferred because it is seen as a more bland, ideologically neutral, and yet sophisticated way of describing the gory side of capitalism. Globalisation is, thus, yet another way of putting the fact that capitalist regime gets extended beyond political boundaries of nation state" (Verma, 2015: 3; Dhanagare, 2012: 33-34).

Globalisation: Definition and Meaning

In a monumental piece of work on modernity, Giddens elaborates on globalisation by stating that, "Globalisation can be defined as the intensification of the world-wide social relations which link distant localities in such a way that local happenings are shaped by events occurring many miles away and vice-versa. This is a dialectical process because such local happenings may move in an obverse direction from the very distanciated relations that shape them. Local transformation is as much a part of globalisation as the lateral extension of social connections across time and space" (Giddens, 1990: 64). In the definition of Giddens, the notion of time and space finds a central place. His emphasises on locality and territoriality is stressed through the process of globalisation. Here he emphasises not merely on grand events but also on the autonomisation of local lifeworlds. Globalisation therefore symbolises, for him, localisation also. Further, "while considering globalisation coterminous with modernisation, Giddens attributed four dimensions of it: the nation-state system, the world capitalist economy, the world military order and the international division of labour. Each of these four, according to him, is an extension of societal modernity" (Dhanagare, 2012: 30).

In another attempt to provide a comprehensive definition of globalisation, Friedman and Kalpan express it into, "the integration of everything with everything else. It is the process of integration of markets, finance and technology, especially information technology in a way that shrinks the world to a miniature in size and enables people from different parts of the globe to reach around the world faster, deeper and cheaper" (Friedman and Kaplan, 2002: 64). The definition of Friedman encircled, by and large, economic aspects by confining himself to market and economy alone while understanding globalisation. A more elaborate and comprehensive description of globalisation is given by E. Anitat which illustrates globalisation as "the process through which an increasingly free flow of ideas, people, goods and capital leads to the integration of economies and societies" (Anitat, 2002: 4). Anitat further puts in, "such global integration has boosted growth and incomes and has thereby helped to raise general standard of living in less developed and underprivileged parts of the world. With globalisation not only sophisticated technologies have become available to developing countries, but also marked improvements in average literacy, quality of health and general life expectancy and, above all, greater integration have taken place and these have promoted human freedom. This has been possible because information sharing and market expansion now provide increasing choices to people" (Anitat, 2002: 4).

Robertson, in a similar fashion holds that, "globalisation as a concept refers both to the compression of the world and the intensification of the consciousness of the world as a whole...both concrete global interdependence and the consciousness of the global whole" (Robertson, 1992: 8). Waters has given a more elaborate definition of globalisation by stating it to be, "A social process in which the constraint of geography on economic, political, social and cultural arrangements recede, in which people become increasingly aware that they are receding and in which people act accordingly" (Waters, 2001: 5). Therefore, it can be affirmed that "globalisation has changed the face of the world irrevocably: time has been compressed, communication revolutionised, the concept of self and community metamorphosed, and the idea of the state and its boundaries changed" (Jayaram and Rajasekhar, 2012: 2). "It has all pervasive impact on the lives and livelihood of the global citizens; at times it is positive and at other proves detrimental" (Verma, 2015: 5).

Therefore, based on the above discussion, it is evident that the process of globalisation envelopes all aspects of human society and plays key role in compression of the world into a single entity in terms of economic, political, social, cultural and technological perspectives. In a closer overview, the studies on globalisation in a broader perspective underlines five main analytical frameworks in which the nuances of globalisation can be understood. These are: Globalisation as internationalisation, Globalisation as liberalisation, Globalisation as universalisation, Globalisation as westernisation or modernisation and, finally, Globalisation as deterritorialisation.

Globalisation: Different Perspectives

The process of globalisation translating into social, economic, political and ecological alteration and transformation has attracted the attention of scholars, policy-makers, media and the people worldwide and thus remained the centre of attention, deliberations and dialogue during last couple of decades. "However, it is an important issue of concern whether to consider it benign and a blessing for the overall benefit of the humankind or a curse as it is causing environmental degradation and giving rise to upsurge of poverty, unemployment and discrimination" (Verma, 2015: vii).

Contemporary discourse on globalisation is centred on to comprehend its origin, trace the path of evolution and understand its nature and characteristics in a comprehensive manner. "There are scholars who perceive globalisation as historically rooted and originated, in some tacit form, during the early modern period. This perspective finds support in the writings of various classical thinkers such as August Comte, Hegel, Karl Marx, Max Weber, Emile Durkheim etc. who, in some form or other, discussed in detail the process of transformation of the traditional society into a modern industrial society and associated trends of rising complexity, rationalities and unemployment and, thus, various characteristics of globalisation in their writings. However, there is another school of thought which considers globalisation as a completely new and the latest phenomena the world has come across. According to them, it originated on the global level in the post-liberal era with liberalisation, privatisation and globalisation (LPG) format in the early 1990's and provided platform for the extra-ordinary growth of information and communication technologies (ICT) as well as played a significant role in terms of unification of the world in general and market in particular. Scholars like Joseph Stiglitz, Ronald Robertson, Anthony Giddens, Kaplan etc. provided substantial evidences through their writings in support of this viewpoint. However, it would be worth mentioning here that the idea and process of globalisation gathered momentum in actual sense due to three historical happenings in the 1980s. They were the collapse of the erstwhile Soviet Union, the demolition of the Berlin Wall and the advent of the world wide web (WWW)" (Verma, 2015: vii – viii).

At another level of discussion, the most important issue of contention amongst scholars is to consider globalisation as an extension of the modernisation process, or on the other hand, can it be called as a new model of development. In this regard, scholars used varying concepts to identify the process of globalisation. They named the phenomenon as - 'knowledge society', 'information society', 'reflex society', 'global village' etc. Contrarily, "there is another perspective which calls the globalisation process sponsored by the Western hegemonic drive wherein the developed, powerful and technological giant Western countries are using globalisation as a tool to augment their control over not only the distribution of scarce resources and goods all over the world but also the ecology, environment, economy, society and governance of the developing and under-developed countries. Thus, in a way, the Western countries are not only continuing with their age old colonial policy of drain of wealth but to extend it further and making the globalisation project more sharper, they are by and large intending to control knowledge, information, technology, economy, society and ultimately environment. The view of globalisation as a project of Western hegemony finds expression in the writings of scholars of 'world system theory', 'theory of development of under-development' and 'centre-periphery theory'" (Verma, 2015: viii).

Therefore, the manner in which the process of globalisation has worked out in the last couple of decades, it gives a clear signal that it is not rigid and fixed but an evolving reality which significantly changed its contours after its evolution and during diffusion at global level. The process of globalisation initiated by the developed nations as a hegemonic practice of flow of trade and commerce in a unilateral direction over the underdeveloped countries, it has now converted into a multilateral flow of investment and services in the backward direction as well. Hence, a summary of above discussion underlines that there are as many interpretations of globalisation, as many its interpreters and there should not be any surprise due to the multifaceted and dynamic nature and character it possess.

As of now, one of the most important issues of deliberation amongst intelligentsia is to ascertain the nature of globalisation, whether it is just and benign in nature or contrarily creates a destructive role and rifts apart the society based on power matrix. Moreover, in parlance with the main motto of the volume, social justice emanating from the globalisation process needs to be assessed. Therefore, to justify the necessity of the volume, let us dwell into the understanding of origin, evolution and conceptual framework of social justice.

Social Justice: Meaning, Origin and Evolution

The term 'Social justice' symbolises fair and just relation between the individual and society measured in terms of the distribution of wealth, opportunities and social privileges. The term initially coined by Jesuit priest Luigi Taparelli in the 1840s and it spread during the revolutions of 1848 with the work of Antonio Rosmini-Serbati. After the Renaissance and Reformation, the modern concept of social justice, as developing human potential, began to emerge through the work of a series of authors. Baruch Spinoza in, *On the Improvement of the Understanding* (1677) contended that the one true aim of life should be to acquire "a human character much more stable than [one's] own", and to achieve this "pitch of perfection... The chief good is that he should arrive, together with other individuals if possible, at the possession of the aforesaid character." During the enlightenment and responding to the French and American Revolutions, Thomas Paine similarly wrote in *The Rights of Man* (1792) society should give "genius a fair and universal chance" and so "the construction of government ought to be such as to bring forward...all that extent of capacity which never fails to appear in revolutions." In the late industrial revolution, progressive American legal scholars began to use the term, particularly Louis Brandeis and Roscoe Pound. Subsequently, in his writing in 1861, the influential British philosopher and economist, John Stuart Mill stated in *Utilitarianism* that "Society should treat all equally well who have deserved equally well of it, that is, who have deserved equally well absolutely. This is the highest abstract standard of social and distributive justice; towards which all institutions, and the efforts of all virtuous citizens, should be made in the utmost degree to converge." From the early twentieth century it got embedded in international law and institutions. In the late twentieth century, a number of liberal and conservative thinkers, notably Friedrich von Hayek rejected the concept by stating that it did not mean anything, or meant too many things. However, the concept remained highly influential, particularly with its promotion by philosophers such as John Rawls. In the later twentieth century, social justice is made central to the philosophy of the social contract, primarily by John Rawls in, *A Theory of Justice* (1971). In 1993, the Vienna Declaration and Programme of Action treat social justice as a purpose of human rights education. In later years, the writings of Martha Naussbaum and Amartya Sen continued the debates on the nature and scope of social justice. Sen tried to make social justice instrumental in solving the miseries of the society by stating that, "a theory of justice that can serve as the basis of practical reasoning must include ways of judging how to reduce injustice and advance justice, rather than aiming only at the characterisation of perfectly just societies- an exercise that is such a dominant feature of many theories of justice in political philosophy today" (Sen, 2009: ix).

Social Justice: Different Perspectives

The different concepts of justice, as discussed in ancient Western philosophy, are typically centered upon the community. Plato wrote in *The Republic* that it would be an ideal state that "every member of the community must be assigned to the class for which he finds himself best fitted." Similarly, Aristotle believed rights existed only between free people, and the law should take "account in the first instance of relations of inequality in which individuals are treated in proportion to their worth and only secondarily of relations of equality." Reflecting upon the time when slavery and subjugation of women was typical, ancient views of justice tended to reflect the rigid class systems that still prevailed. On the other hand, for the privileged groups, strong concepts of fairness and the community existed. Distributive justice is considered by Aristotle to require that people are distributed goods and assets according to their merit. Further, Socrates is attributed with developing the idea of a social contract, whereby people ought to follow the rules of a society, and accept its burdens because they have accepted its benefits. During the Middle Ages, religious scholars particularly Thomas Aquinas continued discussion of justice in various ways, but ultimately connected being a good citizen to the purpose of serving God.

However, the discourse on justice will not be complete if we do not discuss the divergent viewpoint adopted by scholars. "One approach concentrates on identifying perfectly just social arrangements and takes the characterisation of 'just institutions' to be the principal- and often the only identified- task of the theory of justice. Woven in different ways around the idea of a hypothetical 'social contract', major contributions are made in this line of thinking by Thomas Hobbes in seventeenth century, and later by John Locke, Jean-Jacques Rousseau and Immanuel Kant, among others. The contractarian approach has been the dominant influence in contemporary political philosophy, particularly since a pioneering paper (Justice as Fairness) in 1958 by John Rawls which preceded his definitive statement on that approach in his classical book, *A Theory of Justice.* In contrast, a number of other Enlightenment philosophers (Smith, Condorcet, Wollstonecraft, Bentham, Marx, John Stuart Mill, for example) took a variety of approaches that shared a common interest in making comparisons between different ways in which people's lives may be led, influenced by institutions but also by people's actual behaviour, social interactions and other significant determinants" (Sen, 2010: xvi).

To stress his standpoint, Sen in a subtle way rejected the ideas and notion of attaining justice devised by other scholars. He states, "many of the principle theories of justice concentrated overwhelmingly on how to establish 'just institutions', and give some derivative and subsidiary role to behavioural features. For example, John Rawls's rightly celebrated approach of 'justice as fairness' yields a unique set of 'principles of justice' that are exclusively concerned with setting up 'just institutions', while requiring that people's behaviour complies entirely with the demands of proper functioning of these institutions. In the approach to justice presented in this work, it is argued that there are some crucial inadequacies in this overpowering concentration on institutions (where behaviour is assumed to be appropriately compliant), rather than on the lives that people are able to lead" (Sen, 2010: xi).

Sen argues that justice is ultimately connected with the way people's lives go and not merely with the nature of the institutions surrounding them as advocated by John Rawls. Therefore, he strongly advocates for 'capability approach'- an approach which he devised following Martha Nussbaum.

"The capabilities approach considers that wellbeing must be evaluated in terms of the freedom and opportunities to be and to do that people have reasons to value. These freedoms to be and to do constitute the foundations of quality of life. Two main components of this approach are functioning and capabilities. Functioning is what a person achieves. To achieve a given level of well being, it is necessary to be able to perform correctly a certain number of vital functions, such as being able to move, to remain in good health, to have a balanced diet, to be socially recognised and respected, and to be able to take part in collective decisions. These functionings only represent well being in the form of its realisation. After this, the question of how this can be done arises. Thus, the idea of capability represents diverse combinations of the functioning (states and actions) that the person can achieve" (Ballet *et al.* 2013: 29). Therefore, the capabilities approach considers freedom to be both constitutive and instrumental for development. Freedom is the essential goal of development, but it is also the main means by which it is achieved. Hence, sent remarks powerfully in his book, *The Idea of Justice*, "what moves us, reasonably enough, is not the realisation that the world falls short of being completely just- which few of us expect-but that there are clearly remediable injustices around us which we want to eliminate" (Sen, 2009: vii).

With the above discussion on globalisation and social justice, we came down to the third and most relevant concept of the volume: sustainable development: a notion that, though of most recent origin, has made waves in recent intellectual discourse. For convenience of understanding, let us have a look at the concept of social justice.

Sustainable Development: Meaning, Origin and Evolution

Sustainable development can be called as the regulating principle for accomplishing the essential goals of human development. At the same time it tries to sustain the capability of natural systems to supply the natural resources and ecosystem services upon which depends the society, economy and other related aspects. The main aim of the effort is to create such a society wherein livelihood conditions and resource consumption continue to confer human requirements without compromising the natural resources reserve. Therefore, sustainability in this perspective can be explained in terms of the efforts to maintain production process indefinitely, both natural and human, by replacing resources consumed with resources of equivalent or greater worth without mortifying or compromising natural biotic systems. Hence, the process of sustainable development envelops the anxieties which we have for the carrying capacity of natural resources and try to blend it with the social, political, and economic milieu. In addition, it also highlights the responsibilities of the present generation to improve planetary resources and maintain their reserves so that the future generations about to come on earth can use it for their sustenance and survival.

The word sustainable development has its genesis in the idea of sustainable forest management. The perspective originated in Europe during the seventeenth and eighteenth centuries. While responding to the condition of depletion of timber assets in England, John Evelyn in his 1662 essay *Sylva* advocated that planting trees would be a national duty of all the land holders so as to prevent the destructive tendencies of misuse of natural resources. In 1713, Hans Carl von Carlowitz, a senior mining administrator in the service of Elector Frederick Augustus I of Saxony published his work *Sylvicultura Oeconomica on forestry.* Inspired from the thought of Evelyn and French minister Jean-Baptiste Colbert, von Carlowitz engineered the conception of managing forests for sustained yield. His monumental idea became source of inspiration to others, which included Alexander von Humboldt and Georg Ludwig Hartig. Eventually the idea finally got blossomed and culminated into science of forestry. This in turn further inspired many including Gifford Pinchot, first head of the US Forest Service, who tried to wisely use the forest resources as a ploy to forest management. Further, Aldo Leopold under the influence of their predecessors propounded land ethics which subsequently proved influential in the development of the 1960s environmental movement.

A major breakthrough in this direction took place following the publication of Rachel Carson's *Silent Spring* in 1962. Subsequently, the growing environmental movements focused on to the inter-linkages between economic growth, development and environmental degradation. One of the first uses of the word sustainable was done in the modern-days by the Club of Rome in 1972. It is a monumental testimony on the Limits to Growth, given by a cluster of scientists headed under Dennis and Donella Meadows hailing from Massachusetts Institute of Technology. Unfolding the necessity of global equilibrium, the authors wrote: "We are searching for a model output that represents a world system that is sustainable without sudden and uncontrolled collapse and capable of satisfying the basic material requirements of all its people."

Further, the International Union for the Conservation of Nature in the year 1980 published world conservation strategy by introducing the term "sustainable development" which referred sustainable development as a global priority. Subsequently, after two years, the United Nations World Charter for Nature advocated five basic principles of human conduct for conservation of nature. It gave way to the release in 1987, the most discussed United Nations World Commission on Environment and Development report commonly known as the Brundtland Report having blueprint for Our Common Future.

Sustainable Development: Recent Perspectives

The awareness about environmental protection and sustainable development is quite a latest phenomenon. Most recently, the environmental discourse has increasingly gained significance in formulating development theories, models, and policies, especially under the broader framework of 'sustainable development'. In the past, the mainstream theories and models of development had never given heed to address the criticality associated with ecological and environmental issues. As such, due to large scale unawareness and negligence about the importance of environmental protection and conservation of natural resources and also because of human beings continuous foreplay with the nature, ecology and environment; the environmental condition of planet earth reached to such a threshold level from where our serene existence on earth came under serious danger. Therefore, more recently, there emerged a worldwide consensus that the environmental and ecological concerns represent one of the most critical issues that humanity is confronted as on date. Subsequently, the discourse on environment has gained significant attention at almost all the important international forums of development. Eventually, the relationship between environment and development is being seriously taken into consideration and emerged as a focal issue in almost all the major theoretical debates and empirical policies. However, more recently the concept of 'sustainable development' has emerged as the most articulate and representative perspective to comprehend issues involved in the nexus between environment and development. "As a model, sustainable development has been articulated and popularised through a series of reports, conferences and symposia, for example, World Conservation Strategy: Living Resource Conservation for Sustainable Development (1980, IUCN), Our Common Future (WCED, 1987), the United Nations Conference on Environment and Development (1992), the Kyoto Conference (1997)" (Haque, 2000: 4) and many more at various international platforms.

Therefore, being emerged as an extremely complicated discipline amidst deep rooted environmental crisis, there are no unanimity among scholars about the nature and form sustainable development consists. Hence, sustainable development is seen by intelligentsia from varying perspectives. Scholars perceive it, "as 'injunction' that we should not satisfy ourselves by 'impoverishing our successors' (Solow, 1993); as a relationship between dynamic human economic system and larger ecological system that ensures the continuity of human life (Norton, 1992); as a management of ecological system for future generations based on open and multiple approaches to the valuation of ecosystem (Page, 1992); as an improvement in the quality of life without deteriorating natural resources (Pearce and Watford, 1993)." (Haque, 2000: 4)

However the most recent definition of sustainable development emerged in the meeting of the World Commission on Environment and Development commonly known as Our Common Future in the year 1987. The report is considered, as of now, one of the most widely recognised definitions of sustainable development. It states:

"Sustainable development is development that meets the needs of the present without compromising the ability of future generations to meet their own needs".

The definition contains two key concepts:

- The concept of 'needs', in particular, the essential needs of the world's poor, to which overriding priority should be given; and
- The idea of limitations imposed by the state of technology and social organisation on the environment's ability to meet present and future needs.

Since the days of Brundtland Report, the notion of sustainable development has reached beyond the initial intergenerational agenda to focus further on the objective of 'socially inclusive and environmentally sustainable economic growth'. The UN Conference held in 1992 on Environment and Development published the Earth Charter, which draw the objective of building of a just, sustainable, and peaceful global society in the twenty-first century. The action plan Agenda 21 for sustainable development identified information, integration, and participation as key ingredients to facilitate countries achieve development that recognises these interdependent pillars. The main emphasis lies here is that in sustainable development each one is a user and provider of information. It stresses the need to change from old sector-centered ways of doing business to new approaches that involve cross-sectoral co-ordination and the integration of environmental and social concerns into all development processes. Moreover, the main emphasis of Agenda 21 is on to involve broad public participation in decision making, which for them is a fundamental prerequisite for attaining sustainable development goals.

In the United Nations Charter, the Millennium Declaration identified principles and treaties on sustainable development which included social and economic development, along with environmental protection. Therefore from this perspective, in a broader sense, sustainable development symbolises a systematic approach to growth and development and to administer natural, produced, and social capital for the wellbeing of present as well as future generations. The way United Nations used the term sustainable development, it got a broader canvass wherein it addresses not only issues associated with land development but also human development concerns such as education, public health, and most importantly a suitable standard of living.

A study conducted in 2013 emphasised that the concept of sustainability should be restructured through four interconnected perspectives: ecology, economics, politics and culture. In September 2015, 2030 Agenda for Sustainable Development is formally adopted by the United Nations General Assembly which is based on a set of 17 Sustainable Development Goals (SDGs) on the principle of 'universal, integrated and transformative'. It is decided that the goals set forth in the summit are to be implemented from the year 2016 and all the countries of the world has to achieve it by 2030.

Despite large scale awareness programmes undertaken through summits and meetings and setting of manifold agendas throughout the world to accelerate sustainable development, howsoever, the concept of sustainable development has been—and still is—subject to criticism from various corners. The most pertinent question raised in this regard is that what exactly is to be sustained in sustainable development? The main argument contends that the sustainable use of a non-renewable resource is not possible. The critique argued that any positive rate of exploitation will eventually exhaust the finite stock of earth in the long run. Therefore, the viewpoint infers that the eighteenth century Industrial Revolution as a whole is unsustainable in nature. Critiques also argued that the connotation of the notion of sustainable development has opportunistically been expanded from 'conservation management' to 'economic development'. They also argued that the Brundtland Report is meant to serve the interests of business and hence promoted nothing but business by attaching ambiguous and insubstantial concept as a public relations slogan which is a common strategy adopted by the dominant countries of the world to meet their own development interests.

Globalisation, Social Justice and Sustainable Development: The Inter-linkages and Indian Milieu

Though globalisation, social justice and sustainable development are inextricably interconnected but their relationship is somewhat complex. Theoretically speaking, right from the days of the advent of globalisation on global level, it is advertently portrayed that very soon the miseries of the world will be a matter of history; by realising the fruits of the development engineered by globalisation not only countries of the world will come on a single level of development platform but also the disparities and discrimination deep embedded in the social and economic matrix will go away. Therefore, it is the duty of all the nations of the world to be part of the process as soon as possible. It appeared as if those who are not willing to join the race, will be missing a greater opportunity and shall lag behind other nations in attaining developmental goals and prosperity. As a result, nations and people joined the movement in a greater haste and in a temptation to attain prosperity in no lesser time started compromising the regional, national and global interest of sustainability, conservation of natural resources, ecological and environmental protection and most importantly protection of the interest of the people from marginal and deprived communities. Result is quite alarming and can be visualised by naked eyes. Our existence on planet earth is in danger now. Due to rampant environmental destructions and global warming, not only are the scarce natural resources on the verge of depletion but also led us to a threshold level. Therefore, the wave of globalisation quite effectively and dangerously marred the possibility of sustainable development. At the moment we are finding difficulties to sustain ourselves and fulfil our development requisites with the available natural resources, keep apart the interest of the forthcoming generations. Moreover, the possibility of a just society also became bleak as the days progressed. The promise of globalisation that it will bring prosperity on earth and everyone would draw its benefits also remained a myth. It is observed that the process of globalisation not only further consolidated the hegemonic relations between nations and between people within nation but also successfully created a greater divide in a black and white terms between rich and poor, powerful and powerless, high and low, to name a few. Therefore, the viewpoint that social justice can be equally accessed by all the citizenry of the world turned out to be mirage: though it appeared as if it is within the reach of everyone but in reality it remained a distant dream.

Therefore, in practical terms the trilogy of globalisation, social justice and sustainable development appeared to be in conflict with each other and at times tried to penetrate in the domain of each other to fulfill their sectoral interests. So the possibility of a harmonious relation between all the three seems to be missing as of now. Indian being the fastest growing economies in the world also tries to get hold of the most powerful process of the world called globalisation and at present juncture of time finding itself at the cross-roads. All the major problems, which the other part of the world is facing, are equally surfaced in India. Poverty, unemployment, population boom, illiteracy, food insecurity, health hazards, economic disparity, discrimination, rural-urban divide, formation of slums, environmental destruction, ecological imbalance are rampant in India. Therefore in the present context food, shelter, clothing, water, health, sanitation, quality education, livelihood, social security and most importantly, human dignity and social justice are slipping out of the hands of common man. Recently published Oxfam report titled 'An economy for the 99 per cent' rightly portrays Indian condition by underlining that, "in signs of rising income inequality, India's richest 1 per cent now hold a huge 58 per cent of the country's total wealth–higher than the global figure of about 50 per cent. On the other hand, the poorest 10 per cent have seen their share of income fall by more than 15 per cent" (The Hindu, 2017). Due to insatiable demand for land to meet globalisation, privatisation and industrialisation prerequisites–"some 60 million people have been displaced in India since independence" (Dubey, 2008: xv) according to one estimate causing widespread concern for development induced displacement. Paradoxically, 40 per cent of such displaced represent STs and 20 per cent hails from SCs- the most marginalised and vulnerable sections in India. Moreover, in 2012, the Indian government confirmed that 22 per cent of its population is below its official poverty limit. In 2015, around 170 million people, or 12.4 per cent lived in poverty defined as income of ₹ 123.5 a day. However, the Indian Government projected figure mismatch with the estimation of other agencies. The World

Bank, in 2011 based on 2005's PPPs International Comparison Program, estimated 23.6 per cent of Indian population, or about 276 million people, lived below $ 1.25 per day on purchasing power parity.

Hence, there should not be any problem in accepting that all is not well with India: so far as the present state of social, economic, ecological and environmental milieu is concerned. Despite 70 years long prolong journey performed by development planners in independent India, policy makers could not able to curb the menace of poverty and inequalities.

Structure of the Present Volume

At such a time when the galaxy of intelligentsia are grappling with the relation between globalisation and sustainable development, its impact on nature vis-à-vis marginalised and deprived sections and concern for promoting social justice in order to fathom a just social world, wherein not only the distribution of scarce goods, honour and justice is done on an egalitarian basis for the present generation but also due conservation is done for the future generations about to be born on earth, present volume is contoured by situating Indian experiences at the centre stage. Under this milieu, the volume is titled, *Globalisation, Social Justice and Sustainable Development in India.* It begins with the Introduction chapter which unfolds the theme of the book by delineating into conceptual understanding and theoretical debates on globalisation, social justice and sustainable development, their inter-linkages and significance by taking into account the views and standpoint of available scholarly works. Thereafter, it bestows an analytical portrayal of various papers covered in the edited book vis-à-vis their respective sub-themes to which they specifically pertains by assessing the convergence and divergence between issues and interests of globalisation, social justice and sustainable development by focusing Indian experience.

Now let me briefly provide a synoptic view of the volume which is divided into three parts for the convenience of comprehensive thematic discussion and understanding. Part I is captioned *Globalisation and Social Justice* and has a broad canvas. The section explores the inter-linkages between globalisation and social justice and examines whether the process is beneficial to all and inclusive in nature. Whether the advent of globalisation helped in establishing just and egalitarian society, or contrarily, it excluded the marginalised, deprived and vulnerable sections of society from the fruits of neoliberal development process is the focal point of understanding of this section. Further, the section also examines whether globalisation is responsible for amplification of disparity, discrimination and distress in society which is already having deep roots in social and economic structure.

In the first paper of the unit, 'Caste Hierarchy and Dalits in the Era of Globalisation' **Jitendra Ram** views the existential situation of Dalits in the state of Bihar after independence. He attempts to unravel the status of Dalits in the social hierarchy created by the Hindu caste system and their changing patterns and dynamics of relationship with different caste groups. The main thrust of the paper is to ascertain the impact of globalisation on the marginalised groups, especially the Dalits in Bihar by taking into consideration whether globalisation has accelerated social change among deprived sections and proved as boon or alternatively, it has aggravated their marginalisation and further broadened disparity among them. For the purpose of arriving at conclusions, various caste-based indicators were taken for consideration which includes caste composition, jajmani system, traditional occupation, class structure and social change among Dalits in Bihar. It is widely known and acknowledged that, the paper highlights, the society in Bihar is highly caste-ridden where caste affiliations plays crucial role in deciding the social status and position of an individual. From this perspective, caste as an institution still dominates the social system of Bihar, especially among the Hindus in continuity with other parts of India, despite the secular role played by other such institutions like education, economy, polity, etc. Most importantly, caste domination carries a broader canvass and is experienced not only in rural but also in urban areas. The conclusion drawn suggests that the traditionally dominant four upper castes: Brahmins, Rajputs, Bhumihars and Kayasthyas still enjoy caste-based supremacy, ritual superiority, better social status and most importantly politico-economic power than the rest of the Hindu castes in Bihar. These castes practice feudal behaviour which is institutionalised by the caste system and perpetuate the servility of the untouchable. The paper underlines that despite the wave of globalisation, the caste-based rigidity still remains here. Consequently, dominant castes as a whole still follow traditional norms and practices which percolated among them from previous generations, in some form or other, symbolising the subsistence of feudal social structure.

Deep Shikha Karthik in her scholarly work 'A Literary Analysis of Social Justice and Humanism in Joseph Conrad's Heart of Darkness and Mulk Raj Anand's Untouchable' analyses aspects of social justice and humanism through the lenses of literature and novel. She asserts that social justice is normally associated with the conception of equality and equal access in society. As an ideology it corroborates equal treatment of all human beings without any social distinction based on caste, colour, race, religion, sex and so on so forth. In a similar parlance, humanism envisages people's capability and responsibility to lead meaningful and honourable life. By asserting the self-respect and dignity of each human being, humanism beholds the maximisation of individual emancipation and prepares to take up the agreeable opportunities with social and global responsibility. It encourages the expansion of participatory democracy and further helps in amplification of such an open society which remains committed for human rights and social justice. By highlighting the core aspects of social justice and humanism, the paper examines and compares whether these notions are rooted in the novels of Joseph Conrad's *Heart of Darkness* (1899) and Mulk Raj Anand's *Untouchable* (1935). The findings emphasise that the Polish-born English novelist Joseph Conrad's *Heart of Darkness* and the great Indian novelist Mulk Raj Anand's novel *Untouchable* clearly define social justice as the core of humanism. *Heart of Darkness* is a captivating story about the racism in Africa as well as a symbol for social commentary on imperialism by Joseph Conrad. It is a literary masterpiece which embodies the essence of light contrasting with darkness. Joseph Conrad also presents the thought of human power, individual responsibility, and social justice by raising his voice against racism. Likewise, in *Untouchable* Mulk Raj Anand insists on the ideology of social justice and humanism by elevating the issue of untouchability and casteism in India. He believes in the dignity of every man without any discrimination on the basis of caste, creed or economy. Through his work, Mulk Raj Anand speaks against the hunger, exploitation, and the silent and intense suffering of vast number of untouchables, the destitute, the downtrodden, the beggars, the lepers, and countless oppressed ones including men, women and children. In ideological Convergence both *Heart of Darkness* and *Untouchable* believe in the possibility of achieving a better world order through the ideology of social justice and humanism. Although, both the authors come from entirely different nations and social background but still they evolve same sensibility and devotion to the concerns of mankind especially those who have been marginalised from the mainstream society. Therefore, through their works, both Joseph Conrad and Mulk Raj Anand expose the silent passions that burst in the hearts of the people who are forbidden to rise up and express themselves.

In the paper, 'An Analysis of Gender Neutrality of Mining Activities in Tribal District of Odisha', **Minati Sahoo and Subrat Kumar Malik** attempts to examine the notion of gender neutrality in the mining activities in the tribal districts of Odisha. By highlighting the financial contributions of mining sector to the economy of Odisha, the paper further attempts a comparative analysis of the impact of mining on local communities in general in terms of Human Development parameters and on women in particular in terms of Gender Development parameters in the tribal and non-tribal mining districts of Odisha. The findings of the paper highlights that despite significant monetary contributions by mining sector to the state economy, the state has failed miserably for the improvement and development of socio-economic conditions of the people in general and women in particular in tribal dominated mining district. It further emphasise that the tribal dominated mining district have lower Human Development Index and Gender Development Index than that of their non-tribal counterparts. The prime areas in which mining operations influence women disproportionately include health, education and livelihood. Therefore, the study recommends that a comprehensive mechanism needs to be devised by government through which revenues generated by mining could be used for the development of the local communities particularly women working in mining areas. The paper strongly advocated that some policy initiatives must be undertaken in order to enhance women's economic self-sufficiency, gender equality and wellbeing in the mining districts of Odisha.

Saket Bihari touch upon the issue of 'Gender and Globalisation' in his paper from the point of view of its policy implications. He opines that the understanding of globalisation would never be complete unless the issue of gender equity gets proper space in the fulcrum of development. There are reasons for this. One of the pertinent reasons is about locating the significance of 'female gender' at par with 'male' in terms of their participation in workforce. The paper argues that as the Indian economy is growing, the work opportunity among women appears to be vulnerable because of their marginalisation. Therefore, in order to promote the status of women in the country, the conception of gender budgeting has been initiated. But the expectation from gender budgeting that with its effective and focused agenda it will bring out desirable changes in the status of women could be fulfilled only partially due to lack of coordination between planning and implementation. Hence, a lot is needs to be done in a male dominated society which has apparently praised the work of women outside the household boundaries but within the four walls they have mostly been victimised with inhuman practices and atrocities. The need of the hour is to ensure a dignified space for women so that they can freely express their choices in terms of job selection and realistic aspirations. The paper further draws attention towards past by pointing that historically the builders and architects of modern India have always dreamt of the quest for social justice and equity in terms of women empowerment. Attempts have also been made in the past to sensitise about gender discourse and to put it into mainstream as well. But for all practical purposes, the plight of gender sensitisation has always remained critical due to reinforcement and re-assertion of male as the pivot in shaping and reshaping all structural configurations in the given social set up. Even after ample shed on gender, the conceptual construct of hoi polloi has not been flushed out from the stereotypical patterns. In all known human societies, gender has been orchestrated on power matrix where physical superiority has played an instrumental role to gain an edge and advantage. The physical superiority drove all epochs of history to finally take a turn as to where men and women are to be placed. The intricate emerging hierarchies within the gender framework demand serious and logical considerations. Thus, the paper aims at locating the issue of gender in the light of globalisation process at grass root level. To perpetually participate in globalisation is to appreciate the tenets of sustainable development fruitfully which requires the equal participation of the weaker sex. With the historical narration on gender, the paper with its effective arguments shows the social segment is needed to mainstream women in equitable gender discourse.

In their paper, 'The Praxis of Injustice' **Bushra Wadood and Amina Jafri** have done a glocal investigation of Indian culture and its women. They begins with the emphasis that India boasts of being one of the most ancient sites of culture and civilisation where women have been recognised as goddesses and been worshipped. But the paper takes a deeper look on the issues related to women in the wake of globalisation wherein India has emerged as a booming economic power in the world and tries to unravel the other side of the story. It raises a most pertinent question by pointing out that in the last couple of years, a number of revolutionary innovations and changes have transformed our lives. Have these changes impacted and brought light in the lives of women as well or are they still the victims of social exclusion and been marginalised from having positive changes in their lives? By examining the present state of women in India, the paper attempts to address those women issues which need immediate attention and action with an endeavour to focus on the ground realities of women and their social lives; how they have been perceived culturally and in what specific ways they have been portrayed in literature and media. Most importantly, how powerfully women have been protected and supported from Indian Legal Systems and, last but not the least, to evaluate the measures undertaken so far in order to bring major transformation in their lives.

In the last paper of the unit, 'Transgenders and Social Justice in the Era of Globalisation', **Poornima Jain** examines the current status of trans in Uttar Pradesh state of India by delineating into the kinds of abuse they are facing and most importantly, the forms of legal safeguards provided to them in India. She begins with the argument that inequality is a natural and universal phenomenon. There are various forms of inequality such as social, economic, political, cultural, technological and knowledge based, to name a few, deeply rooted in the society. Moreover, there are many basis of inequality like caste, class, region, physical fitness, education, and gender. The paper underlines that gender-based inequality has several implications on society and on all categories of gender. There is inequality between male and female genders, and also more significantly between male, female on the one hand and transgenders on the other. In this background the paper argues that from antiquity, transgenders have remained present in every society; nevertheless, they have always been excluded and marginalised from the larger society. Society considered them as significantly weak and as an object of pity, shame, stigma, curse, abuse, rejection and eventually exclusion from the mainstream. Subsequently, they face discrimination, harassment, and violence in many areas of their lives. Major reason for their pathetic condition is that from most developed nations like US to the developing nations like India or Bangladesh, most people lack an understanding of the meaning of transgender and have a negative attitude towards them. Consequently, trans people face a wide range of discriminating practices by the rest of the society which impedes the process of development of a nation. The persistent situation poses a serious problem of social injustice embedded in the social structure and India is also not untouched with it. Statistically speaking, at present India accounts for approximately 4,87,803 trans population out of whom 3,23,120 are in rural areas and 1,64,683 residing in urban. Uttar Pradesh has total trans population of 18,734 among them 14,828 are in rural and 3,906 are living in urban areas. Divided on other lines, according to Census 2011 figures of trans population, SCs constitute 26,404, STs 639, Literates 66,249, Illiterates 71,216, total workers 38,115 and non-workers 99,350. Moreover, despite manifold transformations and attitudinal changes brought about by the government towards the unattended sections in the wave of globalisation, still, the conditions of TGPs worldwide including India are below the satisfaction level. National Transgender Discrimination Survey conducted by the National Centre for Transgender Equality and the National Gay and Lesbian Task Force (2011) alarmingly found that; (1) Unemployment rate is double the population as a whole, (2) 90 per cent reported harassment on the job, (3) 47 per cent had experienced an adverse job outcome, such as being fired, not hired, or denied a promotion, (4) 15 per cent lived on $ 10,000 per year or less, double the rate of the general population. (5) Significant housing instability: 19 per cent were homeless, 11 per cent have faced eviction and 26 per cent forced to seek temporary space in accordance to the report of NCTE and NLGBTQ Task Force 2011. Existing pathetic situation of trans population needs immediate attention of governance and policy makers.

Part II of the book '**Socio-economic Aspects of Globalisation**' examines the popular debate in India whether the process of globalisation benefited all from social and economic point of view or it further widened the society on lines of caste, creed, religion and region on the one hand and amplified economic disparity by further pauperising the population by putting majority at the bottom of the pyramid. Therefore, the section interrogates the popular notion that globalisation has benefitted one and all especially in the developing country like India by unravelling the other side of the story.

First paper of the section, 'Smart City and the New Indian Middle Class' is contributed by **Pratick Mallick**. The paper begins by underlining that smart city is the newest term in the politics of Indian urbanisation oriented to ameliorate the environmental conditions of human beings and to ensure their survival. Smart city projects target the reduction of carbon footprint in the uses of different modern contrivances. Every-year *Conference of Parties* (CoP) summits held-up and takes pledge to reduce the environmental pollution across the world on an egalitarian basis. However, some provisions of privileges for the third world countries are made in terms of providing extra period for implementations of the decisions of those summits. The paper intends to demonstrate how such damage control mechanisms generate two separate challenges to domestic politics in India as a developing society. First, such preferences given to the developing and backward countries are sometimes criticised by thinkers of *state theories* and *post-neo-colonialist* in the age of globalisation for unbridled use of the communicative devices like computer, mobile phones, air conditioners etc. emitting Green House Gases. These gadgets have been the basic consumables to the Indian middle class, which is no more *only* representation of middle class but the *new* version of the Indian middle class. Due to continuous progress in the Tertiary sector of the economy and commercialisation of education, the New Indian Middle Class (NIMC) is continuously assuming numerical preponderance and psychological stronghold so much so that they have become almost both consumers as well as producers in the present globalised Indian market. Secondly, as already indicated, with an innate psychological intent for better life-styles and systemic alienation generated due to over indulgence in mechanical works, this class is indulging in the *politics of forgetting*. Subsequently, causing a steady transformation in the subaltern politics in India which includes the transformation in the nature of leadership as well as the policies being formulated remained highly NIMC centric.

In the paper on 'Globalisation and Withering of Handloom Industry', **Arvinder A. Ansari** highlights the findings of her comprehensive study of the weavers of Varanasi district of Uttar Pradesh. The paper begins with the emphasis that handloom is not only the means of livelihood for weaving community but is also a cultural tradition defining a way of life for Indian weavers that caters to the need of a diverse cultural ethos ranging from exquisite fabrics to popular items of mass production for daily use. The traditional 'Banarasi' weave has attained supremacy in weaving customs of India and is characteristically recognised for its auxiliary amplification, the accompanying weft, captivating over the accustomed weave for its finest fabrics like silk and the unbeatable designs that continue to be the part of learning skills from generation to generation. The best skilled Banarasi saree weavers in Varanasi are primarily Muslims belonging to Ansari Community, which use to be prosperous community prior to introduction of New Textile Policy 1985. During 1990s, the liberal policy of government on imports and the emergence of competition among imported and domestic products has led to competition in the sector, as a result, handloom sector lagged behind. Handloom sector based and dependent upon manual work whereas power loom involves machine work, which makes it cost efficient and cheaper, thereby leading to displacement of handlooms from the market. Due to globalisation, the power loom has taken the place of handlooms, subsequently; the art has come to an edge of extinction. Hence, bringing severe repercussions which include poverty and unemployment amongst most of the handloom weaving households. Moreover, as a consequence of globalisation, it gradually has been displaced from the country. Today, thousands of looms have been abandoned as inexpensive Chinese silk fabrics cascade Indian markets, throwing numerous weavers who used to make the iconic Banarasi silk saree, out of work. Weaving has been one of the most ancient occupations of the country and has been providing the employment to more than half of the population, after agriculture. For most of the families in the country, handloom weaving has been the source of livelihood and an art, which they have been preserving for generations. The concern of the government should be the protection and preservation of Banarasi Saree, which is not merely a piece of cloth, but also an ancient art and a way of living. It is in this light that the paper analyses the impact of trade liberalisation on the economic and social life of the weavers of Varanasi district.

Surendra Meher and Ruchi Bhalla submission on 'Globalisation and Economic Growth' ponders into the issue of its implications on employment and poverty in India. The authors accentuate that globalisation generally refers to social and economic integration among different countries in the world. It also implies the movement of capital, technology, people, and culture across countries. As a process it was initiated in India during early 1990s and was accompanied by other measures like liberalisation and privatisation. Number of policy measures was undertaken in post-globalisation period. One of the important implications of globalisation has been that economic growth accelerated at a faster rate especially after mid 1990s. A new kind of information revolution with increased density of market took place with the advent of globalisation. However, in most of the developing countries including India, a large section of population could not avail the desired benefit of such changes. There seems to be declining employment growth after 1990 with increased employment causalisation. Most of the workforce took shelter in the informal sector. The impoverisation of small and marginal farmers continued and we did not witness a significant decline in the poverty of the masses. In other words, the aspect of human development especially for the vulnerable sections of the society remained more or less untouched. With the background, the paper seeks to examine the different aspects of globalisation and economic growth and its implications on changes in employment pattern and poverty of the masses. The paper uses secondary data such as National Sample Survey Organisation, Statistical extracts, Census of India, National Accounts Statistics and other available documents to come to the conclusion.

Further in the section **Tapan R. Mohanty** explores the dimensions of equity, equality and excellence in his most noteworthy paper on 'Globalisation and Education'. He begins with the emphasis that at the turn of the twenty-first century, globalisation has emerged as the most pervasive process of social transformation. After industrial revolution and colonialism it is the globalisation that has brought a significant transformation into social and economic facets of the globe. Globalisation with its emphasis on economic integration and principle of free trade has not only altered the instruments and mechanisms of cultural exchange but has also significantly affected the delivery mechanism as well as value of social goods like education. In this paper an attempt has been made to provide a critical analysis of the impact of globalisation on education particularly of primary education. While doing so, the paper makes generalisations by critically analysing all levels of education to derive a comprehensive understanding. In fact, the study intends to highlight the fact that under the aegis of globalisation there has been increase in the number of private English medium schools which are trying to fulfill the educational demands of an aspiring middle class on increased commercialisation intent. On the other hand, the government schools suffer from low infrastructural facilities and poor quality of teaching due to negligence and lack of adequate funding. The article is divided into five subsections in the form of an introductory description of globalisation, role of state in the educational provisioning, marketisation of education and the balance between equity, equality and excellence. The paper concludes by underlining that despite the mushrooming growth of private schools and occasional islands of excellence, the quality of education in government primary schools is poor and is creating strong hurdle for poor, deprived and marginalised students to create a better future for them using educational tools as a means of socio-economic transformation.

'Globalisation and Town Identity' is the last paper of the section submitted by **Haresh Narayan Pandey**. Through his research paper, the author attempts to study the formation of cultural identity in the wake of globalisation in a multi castes and multi-religious town *Shamli* situated in Muzaffarnagar District of Uttar Pradesh by the use of techniques of data collection like observation, focus group discussion and interview schedule. The objectives of the paper is to understand formation of cultural identity in the town Shamli by delineating into the details like which aspect of globalisation- media or market is the most influential, what kind of new hybrid structures have emerged, and to record the kind of new social and cultural celebrations have started in Shamli in the contemporary times. To derive a comprehensive picture, blend of positivist, phenomenological and social anthropological category in an integrated fashion has been used for developing discussion around concept of various local, regional and national identities vis-à-vis globalisation. It is well understood that the process of Globalisation stems from technological revolution in communication and production processes, and viewed as homogenising and hybridising in nature, operating in the socio-cultural life of people. It also symbolised global circulation of dominant western socio-cultural products and practices resulting into spreading cultural imperialism of the West. The process led to the formation of a new social and cultural identity pattern in community or group which was comparatively far more complex in nature and conflicting with the local identity. As a result, people in the community or group feel lost their true identity and find themselves in some kind of identity conflict. As a result, people in town has experienced disintegration of collectivities, rise of individuality, tensions and conflict between the old and the new generations; emergence of manifold new socio-cultural celebrations, and rise of several hybrid structures in the areas of food, cloths, films, etc.

The concluding part III of the book, **'Globalisation, Environment and Sustainable Development'** ponders into the issue of globalisation and the question of environmental sustainability with a thrust on sustainable development. Scholars are grappling across globe to estimate the environmental consequences of globalisation and to evolve enduring conservation policies not only to safeguard planet earth from the wrath of environmental destructions but also to deduce strategies for sustainable development keeping in view the interests of the present as well as future generations to come who also have equal rights on the global resources. Therefore, in an intent to address the above debate, the papers included in the section interrogate the Indian panorama by divulging into the existing reality.

The section begins with the paper of **Nandkishor More and Shashi Kumar** on 'Globalisation, Climate Change and the Dynamics of Sustainable Development'. The authors underlines that even before the call of sustainable development much highlighted by Gro-Harlem Brundtland in *Our Common Future,* the land mark report submitted under the aegis of United Nations Conference on Environment and Development (UNCED) popularly known as Earth Summit, the process of globalisation of world economies and use of natural resources was already in place. The division of world into two major 'Blocks' representing Developed and Developing nations have introduced new dimensions of alignment: one with technology centric and the other conservation based but technology deficient. It thus appeared as if on the existence of former, the genesis of the later is dependent. However, those who contemplated the issues of sustainable development brought attention towards the most pertinent questions, development for whom? by whom? and how? The interesting dimension to the duo of Globalisation and Sustainable Development added another feather with the emerging threats of Climate Change directly affecting the society and indirectly to the forces which govern it. Thus, new dimension of Climate change as one of the most important global environmental challenges emerged with deep seated implication for food production, water supply, health, energy etc. Moreover, the heat of Climate Change has already started producing results having very real consequences on people's lives. Because of increase in surface temperature, melting of snow and rise in sea levels is rampant resulting into several climate related eventualities like flooding, droughts, cyclone etc. occurring in many parts of the world eventually affecting the socio-economic life of people. Rethinking of global development model, based on principles of scientific sustainability is an absolute necessity at present and the scientists are by and large convinced now that human beings have caused much harm to mother Earth by letting global warming over the last 60 years or so. The IPCC's Fifth Assessment Report (AR5) suggests that without additional efforts to reduce GHG emissions beyond those in place today, the global surface temperature towards the end of the twenty-first century will increase by 4.8°C, and sea levels could rise as much as 0.8 meters, compared to pre-industrial levels. Significantly, the adverse impact of climate change has hindered in accomplishing the task of protection and promotion of human rights of common masses. In this context, sustainable development has direct bearing on the concerns of human rights. Moreover, the environmental degradation and problem of climate change has given a new dimension to sustainable development by making it more complex and intriguing issue.

Subsequently in the most notable submission on 'Climate Change and Environmental Degradation' **Abhishek Pandey** critically evaluates the concern for sustainable development in India. The author begins with the emphasis that environmental degradation and climate change is the most pressing challenges facing humankind today. Science about climate change is quite convinced that its impacts are being felt across the globe with increasing temperatures, changing weather patterns, increasing frequency of extreme events, melting glaciers and rising sea levels. Almost all the countries are feeling the heat, though to a varying extents. As a fastest developing country, India's challenge is to meet its development aspirations in a carbon-constrained world. The challenges before developing country like India become more strenuous due to financial constraints and lack of expertise for adaptation and mitigation technology and therefore much more exposed to bear the brunt of climate change. Climate change is expected to boast far reaching implications for India due to its high dependence on natural resources and also the potential to violate constitutionally guaranteed rights to life and livelihood of the people. The efforts made by the UNFCCC and the Kyoto Protocol provisions are clearly inadequate to address the climate change challenges. The Supreme Court of India has issued principle guidelines in the past in some landmark cases that appears as a ray of hope to protect the potential violation of rights of people due to climate change. The highest issue of importance to developing countries are to reduce the vulnerability of their natural and socio-economic systems to the projected climate change. The wide ranging potential impacts of climate change on sustainable development and vice versa, suggest that the linkages between these two aspects need to be analysed critically in a developing country like India to realise the goal of sustained economic development. The paper concludes by underlining that the most effective way to address climate change is to adopt a sustainable development pathway by shifting to environmentally sustainable technologies and promotion of energy efficiency, renewable energy, forest conservation, reforestation, water conservation strategies etc.

Ashish Saxena and Vijaylaxmi Saxena in their paper titled, 'Religiousity, Environmental Strands and Social Justice' have done a multi-dimensional analysis of *Kumbh Mela* at Allahabad City of Uttar Pradesh.

The paper highlights that in recent global era, there has been a spectacular growth in public consciousness about the forms of environmental degradation in India. With an amazing but welcome rapidity, this awareness is being translated on the one hand into substantial media coverage, and on the other into the creation of new government departments concerned with different aspects of environment management. All over the world people from local to global level have been directly victimised by the depletion of natural resources due to the short-lived developmental activities initiated by the modern forms of state apparatuses are organised themselves to raise the voice against the over exploitation of natural resources. Departing from the conventional categorisation of social movements based on ethnic, class, gender differences, these new social movements attracted voice of the people from different parts of the world regardless of class, creed, colour or gender for a common cause called protection of our environment. The theory of Ecological Modernisation perhaps put forward a radical transformational phase as the way modern society grapples with the environment question. While coming down to Indian experience, religion is one of the most important facets of history and contemporary life. It may not be wrong to say that religion has been, and continues to be, a matter of absorbing interest for many in India still today. In former centuries no aspect of life was set apart from religion. All social relations were inevitably and legitimately suffused with religious ideas and acts. The possibility of religion in a modern world can be felt through altered functioning of religion. The marketisation of religion by religious gurus performing miracles and fascinating public, the involvement of religious organisations in the building up of hospitals and schools, working for the victims of natural disasters etc. and politicisation of religion by the outburst of fundamentalists reflect its altered character. Thus, in contemporary India, the impact of modernisation has led to the emergence of new religions, revivals, and reforms within the great traditions. In modern societies, with their complex fabric of social differentiations, not only among religion, but other groups and social activities, there appears a proliferation of rites. It is believed that during the auspicious astrological moment, the waters of the Ganges have the ability to wash away layer upon layer of karmic debt. Millions of Hindus have already started pouring into the northern Indian city of Allahabad for the *Kumbh Mela* festival. Such a large-scale event poses unfathomable challenges for organisers, especially when it comes to sanitation. Even if enduring hardship is integral to the act of pilgrimage and even if such hardships do not deter pilgrims from attending these various circumstances - unsanitary conditions, severe cold, dense crowding and intense noise - are all those that would be expected to be bad for well-being. But are they? We ask if, in the light of social psychological research identifying associations between involvement in social group-related activities and well-being, participation in this mass gathering could impact well-being positively. Thus, against the dysfunctionality of crowd of '*Mela*' as source of nuisance, mismanagement and cheats, this work humbly tries to explore the critical functionality of historical 'Prayag *Kumbh*'. It is observed that 'religious *Mela*' has a spread-effect of maintaining sanitation through collective participation. It is emphasised that socialisation of good sanitation practices to the pilgrims can be instrumental in carrying it further at far flung areas of diverse India and making clean and green India. To this end, the Indian government set up a special administration body about a year ago that is responsible for the smooth-running of the festival. But the people who make it work are the cleaners. They're the lowest paid, and they're working round the clock. There are thousands of street cleaners, then there's a smaller group that cleans the water. Further, by going through the factors responsible for the failure of Ganga Action Plan (GAP), the parliamentary standing committee on science and technology, environment and forests has doubts if the Prime Minister's mission of cleaning Ganga by 2020 will be accomplished.

Further in the paper 'Globalisation and Environmental Sanitation: Health Implications in India', **Sutandra Singha's** study offers a conceptual framework for the analysis of health implications of globalisation and related degradation in environmental sanitation in India. The framework is developed by identifying the main determinants which deteriorate environmental sanitation and the ways these factors are getting affected by globalisation process. The resulting conceptual model explicitly visualises that globalisation impacts land use activities and thereby affects the environmental determinants of human health in terms of air, water and soil pollution. The paper intends to examine two main mechanisms–urban industrialisation and green revolution, through which globalisation can lead to ecosystem degradation and consequent health hazards. Industrialisation in India has resulted into unplanned growth of cities, congestion, unhygienic situation and health problems. The urban-industrial environment poses risk of water-borne, vector-borne, respiratory and infectious diseases and also the urban heat island amplification of heat waves. As the number of urban consumers and their material expectations are on a rise symmetrically cities keep on contributing environmental degradation in order to meet steep rise in consumer goods. In the agricultural sector, the Green Revolution has transformed India into a self-sufficient country; however it is posing serious threat to human health in terms of increased incidence of cancer and biological toxicity due to excessive application of chemicals and pesticides in farming. In this background, the paper provides an account of government strategies undertaken in the era of globalisation to safeguard and promote environmental sanitation. Further, it also offers some practicable policy measures that can be adopted to combat the existing environmental health hazards.

The penultimate paper of the section 'Dialectics and Dynamics of the EIA Professional Groups in Transnational Global Villages' is submitted by **Shital J. Tamakuwala.** The prime emphasis of the paper is that professionalism is a key concept in the sociologies of work, occupations, professions and organisations. The author considers different ways in which professionalism is currently being interpreted while taking special reference to the emerging profession in the era of globalisation. Wickenden elaborates six characteristics of a profession in the form of: (a) renders a specialised service based upon advanced specialised knowledge and skill and dealing with its problems primarily on an intellectual plane rather than on a physical or a manual labour level. (b) Involves a confidential relationship between a practitioner and compensates a client or an employer. (c) Is charged with substantial degree of public obligation by virtue of its profession of specialised knowledge. (d) Enjoys a common heritage of knowledge, skill and status to the cumulative store of which professional men are bound to contribute through their individual and collective efforts. (e) Performs its services to a substantial degree in the general public interest, receiving its compensation through limited fees rather than through direct profit from the improvement in goods, services, or knowledge, which it accomplishes. (f) Is bound by a distinctive ethical code in its relationships with clients, colleagues, and the public. Under the backdrop, the paper attempts to configure the methodological framework to analyse the profession emerging out on environmental impact assessment. In addition, attempt has been made to understand the formation of the profession of EIA in India and its dynamics in the discursive practices of the post-structuralist and postmodern sociological jargons. With the help of literature, an assessment is made as to how this profession has emerged so far and to what extent it fulfills the credentials as mentioned above. For the purpose of deriving empirical data, the study considered study of professionals in 10 institutions/ institutes, 10 NGOs, and 10 EIA experts based at Surat, Gujarat. Data obtained was verified and compared with the blueprint of professional characteristics. Therefore, with the help of sociological imagination, the paper comes out with the interfaces of undercurrents that help enrich the discipline of environmental sociology.

The concluding paper of the section and the volume is submission of **Ravindra Kumar** on 'Equity and Social Justice in Large Public Irrigated Command' is an analysis of **Upper Ganga River Basin.** The author begins with a critical note that Land, Water, and Environment- the three pillars of ecological service providers, if degraded globally on the name of development, giving surge to rising temperature, pollution, no-flows in the rivers and poor health, what would happen to the concern of food security and poverty alleviation? While raising the most pertinent ecological issues, the paper further ponders into the question of water. The author assumes that the farmers are the best persons to provide the field view about the accessibility of irrigation water by delineating into questions of who gets water and who does not and; how water becomes accessible with what kind of instrumental means and ends. In view of this, a survey of farmers was conducted by WWF-India during

Jan-Feb 2016 in Lower Ganga Canal and March-April, 2016 in Upper Ganga Canal command areas to overview 150 years old public irrigation system (UGC commissioned since 1854 with cultural command area of 9 lakh ha and LGC commissioned since 1878 having CCA of 11.2 lakh ha). The research finds a significant decline in both designed irrigated area over time to about 6 lakh ha annually against their created irrigation potential of 8.37×10^5 ha and 8.72×10^5 ha respectively. It is estimated that water input is three- times higher over evapotransmision (Et) requirements of crops. Excessive use of ground water in canal commands by 88 per cent (UGC) to 95 per cent (LGC) by farmers has been found due to water guzzling cropping pattern and unreliable canal supplies, leading to excess energy consumption and over drawal of groundwater. Surprisingly, high crop yields have been seen in middle and tail ends of canal system during kharif and rabi respectively, but at increased cost of cultivation. Migration of young farmers from canal tail-ends in particular and from rural to urban areas in general is frequent in the area due to reasons of income and employment disparity. With the new land acquisition policy operative providing compensation @ 4 times higher than the market rate, most of the farmers would like to move out of agriculture for better incomes. At the same time, it provides an opportunity for intensive cropping and commercial agriculture with less land and water. On the basis of the findings, the paper suggests that canal supply could be regulated in a better way to match the irrigation demand, i.e., for improving dependability while reducing the surface water wastage. Judicious use of surface and groundwater is essential to meet the irrigation demand and to ascertain adequacy. Proper utilisation of groundwater potential could help in improving the cropping intensity. Alternatively, canal supplies could be curtailed on head and used to meet the tail-end requirements, i.e., to ascertain equity and to avoid environmental degradation in command areas.

References

Anitat, E. 2002. Surmounting the Challenge of Globalisation. Finance and Development. IMF, Washington D.C. March: 4-7.

Ballet, Jerome et al. 2013. Environment, Justice and the Capability Approach. Ecological Economics, Vol. 85, January 2013, pp. 28-34; http://www.science direct.com/science/article/pii/S0921800912004144 Accessed on 28/11/2016.

Dhanagre, D.N. 2012. Globalisation in Jayaram, N. and Rajasekhar, D. (ed.). Vulnerability and Globalisation: Perspective and Analysis from India, Jaipur, Rawat Publications.

Dubey, Muchkund. 2008. Preface. India Social Development Report 2008: Development and Displacement. Council for Social Development. New Delhi. Oxford University Press.

Friedman, T. and Kalpan, R. 2002. States of Discord (a debate). Foreign Policy. U.S.A. March-April: 64-70.

Giddens, Anthony. 1999. The Third Way: The Renewal of Social Democracy. Malden, Massachusetts. Polity Press.

Giddens, Anthony. 1990. The Consequence of Modernity. Cambridge. Polity Press.

Guha, R. (ed.). 2008. Social Ecology. Oxford University Press, New Delhi.

Haque, M. Shamsul. 2000. "Environmental Discourse and sustainable Development: Linkages and Limitations, Ethics and the Environment, 5(1): 2000, pp. 3-21.

Jayaram, N. and Rajasekhar, D. 2012. Vulnerability and Globalisation: Perspective and Analysis from India, Jaipur, Rawat Publications.

Pieterse, Jan Nederveen. 2006. Development Theory: Deconstruction / Reconstruction. Delhi. Sage India.

Robertson, R. 1992. Globalisation: Social Theory and Global Culture. London. Sage.

Sen, Amartya. 2010. The Idea of Justice. New Delhi. Penguin India.

Sen, Amartya. 2009. Identity and Violence: the Illusion of Destiny. New Delhi. Penguin India.

Stiglitz, Joseph. 2012. Globalisation and its Discontents. New Delhi. Penguin Books India.

The Hindu. 2017. Richest 1 per cent owns 58 per cent of total wealth of India: Oxfam. www.thehindu.com/business/Economy/Richest-1-own-58-of-total-wealth-in-India-Oxfam/article17044486.ece. Accessed on 05/03/2017.

Verma, Manish K. 2015. Globalisation and Environment: Discourse, Policies and Practices. New Delhi and Jaipur, Rawat Publications.

Waters, Malcolm. 2001. Globalisation. London. Routledge.

Wikipedia on Social Justice: https://en.wikipedia.org/wiki/Social_justice accessed on 04.07.2017.

Wikipedia on Sustainable Development: https://en.wikipedia.org/wiki Sustainable_development accessed on 04.07.2017.

Wikipedia on Poverty in India: https://en.wikipedia.org/wiki/Poverty_in_India accessed on 06.07.2017.

Unit - I

Globalisation and Social Justice

Chapter - 2

Caste Hierarchy and Dalits in the Era of Globalisation: A View from Bihar

—Jitendra Ram

The paper explores Caste hierarchy and status of Dalits in the era of Globalisation. The study attempts to unravel the status of Dalits in the social hierarchy created by the Hindu caste system and their changing patterns of relationship with different caste groups in the state of Bihar after independence. The main thrust of the paper is to ascertain the impact of globalisation on the marginalised groups, especially the Dalits in Bihar by taking into consideration whether globalisation has accelerated social change among deprived sections and proved as boon or alternatively, it has aggravated their marginalisation and further broadened disparity among them. For the purpose of arriving at conclusions, various caste based indicators were taken for analysis which includes caste composition, jajmani system, traditional occupation, class structure and social change among Dalits in Bihar. It is widely known and acknowledged that the society in Bihar is highly caste-ridden where caste affiliations plays crucial role in deciding the social status and position of an individual. From this perspective, caste as an institution still dominates the social system of Bihar, especially among the Hindus in continuity with other parts of India, despite the secular role played by other such institutions like education, economy, polity, etc. Most importantly, caste domination carries a broader canvass and is experienced not only in rural but also in urban areas. The conclusion drawn suggests that the traditionally dominant four upper castes: Brahmins, Rajputs, Bhumihars and Kayasthyas still enjoy caste based supremacy, ritual superiority, better social status and most importantly politico-economic power than the rest of the Hindu castes in Bihar. These castes practice feudal behaviour which is institutionalised by the caste system and perpetuate the servility of the untouchable. It is also observed that despite the wave of globalisation, the caste based rigidity still remains here. Consequently, dominant castes as a whole still follow traditional norms and practices which percolated among them from previous generations in some form or other symbolising the feudal social structure.

Key Words: *Globalisation, Dalits, Castes, Feudal, Hierarchy.*

Introduction

India's ex-untouchables, constitutionally known as Scheduled Castes (SCs) and self-acclaimed as Dalits, account for 16.20 per cent of the total population of the country, according to 2001 Census. The total population of SCs in the country is 166.63 millions. There is no Scheduled Caste in Nagaland, Andaman Nicobar Islands and Lakshadweep. The highest percentage (28.85 per cent) of the SCs population is in Punjab and the lowest (0.03 per cent) is in Mizoram. Historically, Dalits have been the most subordinated and poorest people in India. They have been subjected to various kinds of social discrimination and economic deprivation in the country. The present paper elucidates the hierarchy of caste system and placing of the Dalits in that in Bihar. In this, we would discuss the status of Dalits in the hierarchy of the Hindu caste system and the changing patterns of their relationship with the different castes groups, in the state, after Independence. It mainly includes the caste composition and the traditional Jajmani system as well as the traditional occupations of the Dalits, Era of Globalisation and changes in their status over all these years.

The society in Bihar is considered to be caste-ridden where caste plays very crucial role in social behaviour, interaction and social relations among people of the diverse socio-economic background. The members of four upper castes, i.e., Brahmin, Rajput, Bhumihar and Kayastha enjoy higher rather highest social status than members of the rest of the Hindu castes in the traditional Hindu social system. By tradition, they also enjoy ritual superiority and the highest social prestige and politico-economic power which provide legitimacy to their caste supremacy. In the past also, members of these castes practiced feudal behaviour which was institutionalised by the caste system and which perpetuated the servility of the untouchables, now Scheduled Castes or Dalits. It is also said that the members of these castes followed and are still following their traditional norms and values adopted from the Hindu religious scriptures whatsoever in forms these have percolated among them. They have, from generation to generation, been well-supported by the feudal social structure and, in this way, such a feudal social structure plays a very crucial role in the state of Bihar. It mainly deals with the dominant social position of a particular caste group in rural areas in the state. While after Independence some changes have occurred in their behaviour patterns as well as in the feudal or semi-feudal social structure in the state, but these are not much significant as is evident from the present social scenario. Hence, it is significant to observe the status of Dalits in the existing caste hierarchy and take note of changed, if any, in that in Bihar.

The Hierarchy of Caste System in Bihar

Before analysing structural arrangement of numerous castes in Bihar, it is necessary to have a brief look at the caste system and hierarchical arrangement of numerous castes as well as sub-castes in the country as a whole.

The institution of caste is all pervasive among the Hindus in India. According to Srinivas (1982:3), "caste is undoubtedly an all-India phenomenon in the sense that there are everywhere hereditary, endogamous groups which form a hierarchy and that each of these groups has a traditional association with one or two occupations". On the other hand, what Ambedkar stated about caste is that "caste in India means an artificial chopping off of the population in fixed and definite units, each one prevented from fusing into another through the customs and endogamy" (cited in Rodrigues, 2002:245). The conceptual and theoretical explanations of hierarchy vis-à-vis caste hierarchy derive primarily from the work of Louis Dumont. According to Dumont (1988:66), the hierarchy of caste system among the Hindus is based on ideology of purity and pollution. This concentration on ritual status is what makes the caste hierarchy a true hierarchy. Consideration of economic and political power is secondary in this scheme of things. Dumont argues that this hierarchy positions castes in such a way that the elements of parts (castes) are ranked in relation to the whole. Dumont further argues that all castes are placed in this hierarchy which has universal consensus within the Hindu society. The fundamental opposition in the caste hierarchy is between the pure Brahmin and the impure Untouchable. Such a hierarchy orders all the castes from Brahmin at the apex to the Untouchable at the bottom on a single continuous scale. Gupta (1984:127) also explains the distinction between the secular status and the ritual status. According to him, the secular status is based on wealth, education, occupation, etc., whereas the ritual status is based on the concept of purity and pollution, suggested by Louis Dumont, as stated earlier. The concept of secular status is universal, whereas that of the ritual status is a bye-product of Indian caste system. In India, particularly among the Hindus, it is believed that the birth, death, menstruation, etc. bring a sort of impurity or evil influence to the persons associated with them. This evil influence can be warded off by observing certain rituals, i.e., the prescribed forms of action, like bathing in the holy river, giving alms or special offerings made to the gods or to the priests.

Caste as an institution still dominates the social system, especially among the Hindus, in India, despite the secular roles of other institutions such as education, economy, polity, etc. Castes operate not only in rural but also in urban areas as is evident from a number of studies. Therefore, a person's caste status in the caste system is taken into account while measuring his/her social status. There are two schools of thought regarding determination of a person's status in the caste system. According to one school, Louis Dumont may be regarded as representative of this school, see especially his (1988), caste is an institution with a systemic form and person's status is based on his/her birth in a particular caste (*Jati*) which has a definite rank in the caste hierarchy. This is his/her 'ascribed status' with which he/she is born and dies. It is also viewed in terms of corporate group which is similar to his/her caste rank. The concept of 'ascribed status' is taken from Linton (1936) that deals with a person's status in a society. According to him, it is assigned to a person by the society, without regard for the person's unique talent or characteristics. It deals with one's occupation and general social standing which is determined at birth.

According to the second school, (Representative of this school are Marriott, 1959, 1968; Mandelbaum, 1972; and Barreman, 1971; 1979, Nandu Ram, 1988, caste system is a dynamic one, and one is subjected to a variety of changes, especially in urban areas. A person's status (also his/her caste rank) is determined on the basis of a number of attributes acquired by him/her and the interaction between him/her and others. Such interaction is also guided by a person's socio- economic status and power position. There are also other criteria for status determination of a person and these are ritual and pollution, caste calling, etc., which themselves is subjected to change. Thus, on the basis of change in the pattern of interaction with others, a person's status in the caste system is 'achieved' and remains changeable (Ram, 1988:1). In this sense, a person's status is his position which is accorded to or 'achieved' by him in the caste system, while rank of his caste is an order assigned to a caste in the caste hierarchy. In other words, the status is attributed to an individual, while rank is assigned to a caste as a corporate group. Status is changeable, while rank is almost fixed (Marriott, 1955, 1959). According to Nandu Ram, the caste system is very complex and dynamic that it continues to engage the attention of social Scientists. The traditional society in India was constituted of numerous castes and sub-castes functioning within the wider frame of the *Varna.* It is particularly considered as a Hindu society. The caste system was rigid in principle and it did not allow any person to accept membership of the other caste. Ritual and social distances were observed strictly through taboos on pollutary interactions and restrictions on inter-dining and intermarrying. Therefore, there were some channels built into the system, especially in the form of the *Jajmani* (patron-client) relations and the pursuit of occupations other than the caste specific one, through which members of all castes were related to one another. Thus, the system maintained an interdependence of the various castes through ritual obligations and through performance of roles assigned and sometimes unassigned to them.

Caste System and Class Structure in Bihar

If we see the statement given by Nandu Ram, as referred earlier, about caste system in India, we find the same complexity of Hindu caste system in Bihar. In the Hindu caste system, an individual is born, lives and dies within the limits of his caste, as stated earlier. Thus, a caste in contemporary rural Bihar is an endogamous group with a set of ritual practices which separate it from other castes. The caste of a person is determined by his /her birth. Thus, people belonging to a particular caste claim that the origin of their caste is different from that of other castes. This claim is legitimised on the basis of various myths of origin of their caste which constitute an important element of caste beliefs. People belonging to different castes create their internal hierarchies according to their myths and beliefs about the origin of their caste (Sahay, 1998:207). The simplest and universally acceptable categorisation of all the Hindu castes in Bihar is three-fold: Forward, Backward and Scheduled Castes. The Forward Castes (upper castes) are Brahmin, Bhumihar, Rajput and Kayastha, and these have been historically dominant and continue to be dominant in both rural and urban areas. The Backward Castes (lower and upper) are a heterogeneous category in between the upper castes and the Scheduled Castes. The Scheduled Castes are at the lowest level of the caste hierarchy. In addition to these three categories, there are also Muslims and a fifth category is Scheduled Tribes in Bihar (Gupta, 1994:84). If we see the caste composition among the people especially Hindus in Bihar, we find that they are divided into many caste groups. It mainly shows the dominance of a particular caste group in society. Srinivas (1991:308, see Gupta, 1991) has coined the concept of dominant caste in terms of numerical social, economic and political domination. According to him, a dominant caste plays a very crucial role in upholding the hierarchical arrangement of castes or status order in its territory even in the social order. If we look at the dominant caste in Bihar, we find the 'twice-born' consisting of the upper and the upper backward castes- Bhumihar, Rajput, and the Yadav, Kurmi and Koeri are to be the dominant castes in the sense of the term used by Srinivas, although Brahmin and Kayastha also act like dominant in their relation to the Scheduled Castes or Dalits in the state.

Bihar is one of those states where the upper castes, although numerically very small, have traditionally enjoyed ritual superiority and social prestige (Roy, 1970:229), as stated earlier in this paper. They constitute only 12.7 per cent of the total population of the state, but their dominance has been much greater than their number. Their limited numerical strength is compensated by their ritual status, social prestige and politico-economic power. In ritual matters, the Brahmins enjoy the predominant position, followed by the Bhumihars, Rajputs and Kayasthas. The second group of castes is that of backward castes (both lower and upper) that are considered as intermediary castes between the upper castes and the Scheduled Castes. Both the lower and upper backward castes constitute 30.2 per cent and 18.8 per cent respectively (see Blair, 1980:65). The backward castes mostly consist of tenants and agricultural labourers as two-third of the agricultural tenants in the state belongs to the upper backward castes like Yadavas, Kurmis and Koeris. Interestingly, a sizeable number of the upper backward castes have become landowners after abolition of the zamindari system and implementation of other land reform policies after Independence in the state. The Scheduled Castes or the Dalits constitute the third category of castes groups in the state and are 14.5 per cent of the total population of Bihar. The remaining population in the state constitutes of Muslims (12.2 per cent), Scheduled Tribes (8.9 per cent) and others (2.8 per cent). The status of Dalits in Bihar is, by and large, not different from that of the Dalits in other states in the country. They continue to be marginalised sections and subjected to exploitation and humiliation, as stated earlier. They form a large labour-force for the landowning upper and upper-middle level or backward castes. There are twenty-three castes in this group. The Chamars, Dusadhs, Mushars, Bhuiyas, Passis, Dobis are 87.67 per cent of the total Scheduled Castes population in the state (Kumar, 2002:41-45).

As the caste system is said to be manifested concretely or functions primarily through the jajmani system, it is necessary to have a close look at the structure and functions of and the changes occurred in the latter. Although the jajmani system died down, to a great extent, in many north Indian states, including Bihar, its reminiscences particularly at the relational level are still visible distinctly. Kolenda (1981:6) provides an empirical analysis of the Jajmani system. She notes that it is critical for understanding how the 'caste system works because caste-value of pollution and occupational division of labour, and the general cultural emphasis upon hierarchy and inequality are all tightly involved in the Jajmani system'. In the village, the jajmani system seems to have a labour-buyer/wage-earner relationship. In Bihar, there are three terms used to designate a person and these are involved in the Jajmani system: *Pauni, Purohit,* and *Mahabrahman.* The term *jajman* designates a person who buys the labour power of the pauni, purohit and Mahabrahman. In this way, pauni, purohit and Mahabrahman provide services to the jajman. But they provide different services. For instance, Purohit performs rituals and worships deities for the jajman. In turn, jajman pays him in both cash and kind. Similarly, Pauni performs manual works like washing clothes, shaving, cutting hair and the like for jajman (Sahay, 1998:213).

In Bihar, Paunis belong to more than one caste such as the Nau, Dhobi, Lohar, Mallah and Bari. Apart from these castes, there are some other castes like Chamar, Pareri, Kohar, Dusadh and a few others whose members perform their traditional caste occupations and provide services to the jajman of the other castes. According to Sahay (*ibid.*: 218-220), they are not puani in real sense of the term because, after receiving their services, the jajmans pay them the required wage. It actually depends on the amount of the services they provide. Therefore, he also states about the relationship between various castes in selected villages like Unwas, Basantpur, Bishrampur and Bharchakia in Buxar district of Bihar. He also explains the change taking place in the jajmani system in Bihar. As he notices that the service castes people have stopped providing their caste services to the jajmans and the caste based occupations no longer exist in the villages. This is substantiated by the fact that a large majority of families belonging to the category of pauni do not perform their caste occupations. It also shows that the caste system as well as jajmani system in contemporary rural Bihar has undergone notable changes, especially in regards to the linkages between caste and occupation.

Wiser (1958) had made the first analytical study of the Jajmani system and delineated advantage and disadvantage of the system. Today, this system seems to more disadvantageous for the service castes. Anyway, according to him, the Jajmani system has remained a very important institution which deals with the social relationship among the people of different castes in villages with its network of mutual services. The Brahmin, Sonar, Lohar. Barhi, Hajjam, Mali, Dom, Dhobi and the Chamar are the castes which have been serving their clients belonging to the other castes. In return for their services, they have been paid yearly, half-yearly at a piece rate. The rate of payment has remained fixed customarily and this has not changed over decades. In the case of jajmani system in Bihar, Sachchidananda (1983:12-13) has said that as income derived from *Jajmani* obligation is insufficient for their subsistence of families of the service castes, because the patron castes, except the Brahman, sell their goods in market, the service castes work as agricultural labourers. Similarly, services of the Dom, Chamar, Hajjam and Dhobi are taken only on ceremonial occasion of the birth, marriage and death. Due to the influence of the market, the *Jajmani* system is not followed so vigorously as before and if anybody goes out of the system, hardly any penalty or punishment is given. Similarly, Singh (2005:3167) reports that the village of Dhampur is inhabited by 13 castes where caste boundaries are still strong in the sense that relations are more intimate within a caste than between castes. The upper castes and the Scheduled Castes or Dalits have had close relations in the village through the jajmani as well as non-jajmani relations. The Chamars dispose of dead cattle and handled most of the child-birth cases in the village and other Scheduled Castes or Dalits were related through non-jajmani ways in the patron-client relations. But now, in this social organisation, most of the Dalits do manual labour and provide the labour pool for agriculture and other activities. This type of social network is also related to the status of a person in the traditional Hindu caste system.

Contrary to this class structure is portrayed nationally as a parallel social structure to be found even in a developing society like India. The term class or class structure in the Indian context, unlike that in the Western societies, is not completely devoid of the primordial (such as caste, tribe, religion, gender, etc.) linkage of its members or the people. This is equally true in the case of both urban and rural areas, although a number of social scientists have attempted to situate class in Indian context and classify the population accordingly. Such attempt has been made by a few scholars in the case of Bihar also. Bihar is predominantly a rural society. It has 67,546 villages and 220 towns. By definition a town is one where

(1) the population is less than 5,000 persons;

(2) density of population is not less than 1,000 persons per square mile; and

(3) At least three-fourths of the adult male population is engaged in non-agricultural pursuits.

(See *Census of India*, 1971, Series-4, Bihar, Part VI-A, p. 28)

The growth of cities has been slow. Hence, the class structure in Bihar it has to be studied differently for both rural and urban areas. One finds different type of classes, with different characteristics, in rural and urban areas. Beteille (1974:126) divides the rural population of India into four or five main socio-economic groups according to their position in the system of production and puts them into three classes of upper, middle and lower in each caste. In Bengal, there are the *Zamindars, the Judders* (most often big tenants), the *bargadars* (share- croppers), and the *Khetimajdurs*. There are also merchant and artisans. In rural Bihar, land is still the basic source of livelihood. Hence in the case of rural Bihar, Max Harcourt (1977:324) distinguishes *ashraf* (landlord), *bakal* (village shopkeepers), *Pawania* (artisans), *jatiya* (small peasants directly cultivating their land), and a class of low castes at the local level. There are a large number of small and marginal farmers also in Bihar, like in the other state in the country. They usually possess not more than five acres of land. They have sufficient surplus labour and tools of production and also work as share-croppers. They mainly employ what is called family labour on their own farms and are essentially self-producers without hired labour. Occasionally, they hire labour to work on their behalf. Because they have little land and cultivate others' lands and are called tenants (Singh, 1990:55-56). There are also agricultural labourers who possess little or no land. Despite this, there are unskilled manual labourers. Most of them are poor and socially and educationally backward. They all have specific roles, and positions within the system such as casual and unskilled labourers, tenants, share-croppers, artisans, etc. (Joshi, 1978:7). The upper and upper-middle class in Bihar is comparatively small in number or in size of its members. The upper-middle class includes big businessmen and industrialists, senior bureaucrats, and the *Zamindars,* although the zamindari system has largely been abolished. The *Zamindars* are certainly Bihari in origin, but most of the industrialists are from Gujarat, Rajasthan and the Punjab (*ibid.*: 58-59). This class of people is not active in any political party, though they extend their support to it from the outside and enjoy power as a ruling class in Bihar. In urban areas, there is a large working class. In fact, in the industrial sector there has emerged a new class which may be termed as an urban working class. This class includes the skilled and unskilled or semi-skilled industrial workers, fourth grade employees in the government and semi-government offices, and employees in private establishments. In Bihar, a new class has recently emerged which is composed of government contractors, besides the already existing class of the senior bureaucrats and technocrats. Some landlords and rich peasants may also be included in this class. They have given up their old feudal ways and have invested their income in small-scale industries, buses and cinema houses. They enjoy economic and political domination and are considered as a ruling class Bihar (Singh, 1990:58).

On the other hand, Sharma (1996:62-63) explains about seven classes existing in Bihar, which may be regarded as descriptive categories. These have been identified on the basis of generation of surplus value in agriculture and its appropriation through the labour processes. These classes are:

(i) *The tied agricultural wage labour*-those households who are hired out as agriculture wage labour and are tied to an employer-land owner-cultivator through loan and or patch of land, regardless of other activities rendered or performed by them.

(ii) *Untied Agricultural wage labour*-those households who are hired out as agricultural wage labour, but are not tied with any employer or cultivator, regardless of other activities performed by them.

(iii) *Poor-Middle Peasants*- those who are cultivating their own land, but do not hire in or out agricultural wage, nor do they *lease* out their land to others.

(iv) *Middle Peasants*-Cultivating and not hiring-out, but occasionally hiring-in of wage labour, not leasing out their land, both males and females working on own land.

(v) *Big Peasants*-Cultivating, not hiring-out, but hiring-in of wage labour; not leasing-out their land, only male household members working on own land.

(vi) *Landlords* (including gentlemen farmers)- Landlords are those leasing-out land, and gentlemen farmers are those who are cultivating land by themselves but supervisory works only, not hiring-out but hiring in wage labour, not leasing out land.

(vii) *Non-agriculturalists*-all remaining households who are not dependent on agriculture; mostly include artisan castes.

Here, it may be pointed out that this classification of population into various classes both in rural and urban areas, which does not depend directly on land owned or cultivated by them but also is based on the different types of occupations of the people is not totally free from their primordial-caste, religion, etc., linkages. This means, the rich peasants and the big landlords, the upper and upper middle classes in urban areas are mostly from the upper castes besides a few Muslims, the middle level peasants are from the middle level or backward castes, and majority of the wage labour are from the lower or the Dalits castes. There are some anomalies in the classification. For instance, those who are forced to lease out their land because of age or illness and this prevent them from cultivating it will be classified as landlords. This may be correct upto a appoint but this is only half of the story. Households with no female members of working age cannot, by definition, be classified as middle peasants. This supports our argument given at the outset of this section. In the following section, we would discuss the traditional caste system and hierarchical arrangement of occupations of the different caste groups in the state of Bihar. It also includes their ritual status and their domination in rural areas.

Dalits in Bihar

There is also a common belief that in the traditional caste system, there is a hierarchy of traditional professions or occupations with a distinct gradation as high or low in the social as well as ritual contexts (Gupta,1984:38). It is said that in the beginning, division of the Hindu population was based on the assignment of a particular social function or occupation to each caste, namely Brahmins (the priestly class), Kshatriyas (the warriors' class), the Vaishyas (the commercial and agricultural community), and the Sudras (those engaged in menial services) and it went on very well. At the empirical level, Lynch (1974) explains that Dalits, along with agriculture or agricultural labour, independently pursue the traditional caste occupations. They are leather workers, weavers, fisher folk, scavengers, basket makers, etc. A few of them, particularly leaders of the workers, have improved their economic condition by improving and marketing their products. He cites the case of Jatavs or Chamars in Agra. He also deals with the negative aspect of change in their social status because they still suffer from the stigma of being untouchables. Similarly, a few studies on scavengers show that their conditions have not improved and their occupation continues to be looked down upon as polluted. On the other hand, Isaacs (1965) highlights that in urban areas, Dalits are engaged in both the organised and unorganised industrial sectors as petty shopkeepers, small entrepreneurs, scavengers, and are also in white-collar occupations mainly in the public sectors. Though there are a number of studies on multiple problems of workers in organised and unorganised sectors, but most of these do not focus exclusively on Dalit workers in these sector. Isaacs' study also reveals how the Dalit white-collar employees, irrespective of their positions in the administrative hierarchy, suffer from untouchability and the various forms of discrimination, including humiliation or looking down upon by their colleagues.

In Bihar, a large majority of Dalits have been assigned to their traditional occupations. They have particular type of occupation which is embedded in their particular caste. Here, the five castes- the Chamar, Dusadh, Dhobi, Pasi and Musahar are mentioned whose members have been pursuing their traditional occupations both in rural and urban areas. The question of who the Dalits or Scheduled Castes are in Bihar can be appreciated historically. For instance, in 1901, Risley, the then Census Commissioner of India, attempted, for the first time, to classily the Hindu castes according to their social standing. This, according to Mitra (*Castes and Tribes of West Bengal*, 1951, p.1), resulted in "incidentally showing the dragon's tooth of the 'depressed' and 'Scheduled' Castes". Risley divided the Hindu population into seven categories: (1) Brahman, (2) Castes other than Brahman, who rank above clean Sudras, (3) Clean Sudras, (4) Clean castes served by degraded Brahmans, (5) Castes other than group whose water was not accepted, (6) Unclean Sudras, and (7) Unclean feeders. In the next Census (1911), an enquiry was instituted to ascertain the castes which suffered specific religious and social disabilities. Only 12 of the present-day Scheduled Castes in Bihar were mentioned in the list. These were Bhuiya, Chamar, Dhobi, Dusadh, Dom, Musahar, Pasi, Rajwar, Hari, Bauri, Bhumij, and Pan. Now, there are 23 Scheduled Castes in the state (Haldar, 1976:74).

The Chamar is one of the most ancient castes of India and Bihar and its members are scattered in different parts of the state. The Chamars are the largest Scheduled Caste in Bihar and form 29 per cent of the population of Scheduled Castes in the state. Traditionally, they have been dealing with hides and skins of dead animals, and are making and repairing shoes. When a cattle dies, it is the Chamar's duty to take the cattle out of the village and do the rest. Some literate or even educated Chamars take out such dead cattles on contact. The Chamar contractors ask their caste-fellows to take away the dead cattle and take-off the skin. The contractors fix up some percentage with the co-workers for taking away the dead cattle from the demarcated areas. But in Bihar as well as in other parts of India a substantial percentage of their population has taken to cultivation and agricultural labourer (Sachchidananda, 1977:16; Benjamin, 1989:109). Many women of the Chamar community perform the traditional job of mid-wife of the other caste women during their delivery time in the village. The work they do is called '*parsuti*' in the village. Women who are involved in this type of work are called *'Chamaiens'*. They act as a lady doctor. The Chamaien goes to the household of the pregnant woman to delivering her child and does all types of work during the delivery and after. Sachchidananda (1977:16-24) argues that most of the women among them supplement their family income by working as midwife. As a matter of fact, in most of the villages they are the only specialists available at the time of a child birth. Both for the supply of the shoes as well as for the services at a child birth, the Chamars are closely related with the other castes or communities in the village through the Jajmani system.

Then, the Dusadhs are the second largest caste or community among the Scheduled Castes in Bihar and form 26 per cent of the Scheduled Castes population in the state. They are largely concentrated in Muzaffarpur and Darbhanga districts in North Bihar and Patna, Gaya and Monghyr in South Bihar. They are also found in other districts in the state. They are regarded as extremely useful as they are considered to be very good agricultural labourers, and they also rear cattle as well as pigs. Traditionally, they had almost monopolised the post of the village watchmen or *chawkidars* in different parts of the state. They claim to have descended from Dussashan, the brother of Kaurava prince Duryodhan. They are also divided into many sub-castes in Bihar. They primarily burn the dead and perform *Shradh.* They eat pork and do not hesitate in taking drinks. They work as grooms, elephant drivers, grass and wood cutters, etc.

The Dhobi or washerman caste accounts for 5 per cent of the Scheduled Castes population in the state. Both men and women wash dirty clothes of people of other castes in the village and are regarded as unclean. Some of them have shifted to urban centres and taken up laundry as their occupation. They are relegated to a low status in the caste hierarchy on account of their occupation and ritual pollution. They are also related with jajmani system in the villages. They have always been associated with the donkey which they keep to take their bag of clothes for washing on the river-bank or to the pond. Further, Pasi is another major Scheduled Caste in Bihar. The word 'Pasi' is derived from the word 'pasa' meaning a noose, 'aloop' or a rope belt (Kumar, 2002:147). They constitute four per cent of the Scheduled Caste population in the state. They are the traditional toddy-tappers and take out juice from the palm and dates trees. This has remained the main traditional occupation of Pasis in Bihar. They live in the thatched huts and their main source of livelihood is the sale of fermented palm and Khajur dates juice. They also make mats and containers with palm and date-palm leaves. They worship Hindu gods and goddesses and observe all the Hindu festivals.

Still, Musahars are another Scheduled Caste in Bihar and form 15 per cent of the Scheduled Castes population in the state. They have traditionally been known as rat-eaters (Das, 1992:7). There are some who believe that the term Musahar is the combination of two words, i.e., Musa+Ahar, meaning one who catches and eats rats (Vidyarthi and Mishra, 1977:16). They are also known as Buiyan in some parts of the state. They are mostly concentrated in the districts of Darbhanga, Saharsa, Purnea and Monghyr. They rear pigs and poultry and relish rats and snails. Their common recreations are drinking and gambling. They are divided into sub-caste in Bihar like Magahiya and Tirhutia, etc. (Sachchidananda, 1977:21).

Social Change among Dalits in Bihar

Here, we shall look at the social change among the Dalits in terms of changing their relationship with other castes in the state of Bihar. It also includes some reference models in the context of social change adopted by the Dalits in the state. According to Vidyarthi and Mishra (1977:209-10), the relationships of Dalits with higher castes in Bihar are on the verge of change. They argue that the enforcement of the Indian Constitution and Untouchability Offences Act 1955 along with the SC and ST (Prevention of Atrocities) Acts 1989, is being responsible for such change. Nowadays, a person belonging to a higher caste may be seen eating in the house of a Chamar, or Rajwar or Dusadh or Musahar. Earlier, the Dalit communities were not allowed to use utensils of a higher caste and also eat in his house. But now, they eat in the same utensils in which a higher caste person eats. They also mention that earlier the Chamars, the Rajwars, the Dusadhs or the Musahars were not allowed to fetch water from the well of the higher castes; but nowadays, they fetch water from any well or pond of the village. People belonging to the higher castes are aware that if they do not give brotherly treatment to the people of Scheduled Castes, they may lose their land due to land-grabbing movement or the other changed circumstances. Now, a Brahmin can be seen reciting from the Hindu Scriptures and Epics at the residence of a person of the Dalit community and the *Prasad* is distributed among all those present there, irrespective of their caste backward. It is still to be noted that the Prasad is prepared only by a man of higher caste for this purpose and not by member of Dalit community. The latter would not touch it unless it has been distributed first among members of the higher castes. These days, children of the higher castes sit together with children of the Scheduled Castes in the same classroom. Due to industrialisation, educational progress, and modern means of communication, some change has taken place in the Hindu caste system also. Hence, people of the upper castes are not as allergic today to the Scheduled Castes as they had been in the past, though there still exist antagonistic relations of one type or the other between them. They are slowly but gradually shielding their irrational and traditional prejudices and inhibitions towards the Scheduled Castes or the Dalits even in villages.

The concept of Sanskritisation, as formulated by M. N. Srinivas in Sociology, refers to "A process by which a 'low' Hindu caste or tribe or other group changes its custom, ritual, ideology, and way of life in the direction of a high, and frequently, 'twice born', caste. Generally, such changes are followed by a claim to a higher position in the castes hierarchy than that traditionally conceded to the claimant caste by the local community" (Srinivas, 1982:6). Srinivas further adds that though all lower or non-twice born caste want to sanskritise themselves, only some of them, whose economic and political conditions have improved, succeeded in it. To quote him, "while the sources of mobility lay in the political and economic systems, sanskritisation provided a traditional idiom for the expression of such mobility" (Srinivas, 1991:315, for details, see Gupta, 1991). Therefore, the concept of Sanskritisation is based on the understanding that in the caste hierarchy, lower or 'non-twice born' castes do not value their own customs, rituals, ideologies, styles of life, etc. That is why, they always try to give them up by imitating the customs, rituals, ideologies and ways of life of a higher 'twice' born caste.

Looking empirically, it seems that the process of Sanskritisation has been active among a few Scheduled Castes and lower castes people in some parts of Bihar. The adoption of this process has been recorded by Sachchidananda (1977) in four villages where Dalits have been eager to uplift themselves upto the standard of the higher castes. According to him, the Dusadhs claim themselves to be Kshtriyas. They relate themselves with the king Dushasan (a King mentioned in the *Mahabharatha*). Some members of the Dusadh caste have started using the title 'Singh' (a Rajput title). The Rajwar also claim that they are Kshatriyas. Thus, a number of the Dusadhs, Rajwars, Chamars and Musahars have begun to wear sacred thread (a cultural symbol of the upper castes). Interestingly, 30 per cent families of each of these castes in his studied villages have accepted the *Kabir Panth* and have become completely vegetarian. It is also seen that a member of the Dusadh caste likes to call himself a Dushasan Kshatriya, Paswan or Singh, as stated earlier. Similarly, a member of the Rajwar caste likes to call himself *Raj-Vanshi*, and a member of the Chamar caste likes to call himself *Ravidas* or *Arya,* etc. (*ibid.*:190-91). Their growing literacy, withdrawal from their traditional dirty occupations, and adoption of the dresses and customs of the higher castes show that the process of Sanskritisation is active in these villages. This also means the changing life pattern of the Dalits in the rural areas. Such is also the case of Dalits living in urban areas in the state.

Era of Globalisation

After discussing about social change among Dalits in Bihar, it is necessary to look at status of Dalits in the era of Globalisation briefly. But before doing so, as we know that Globalisation is a complex process by which the world is becoming a highly interconnected world through economic, social, political, educational and cultural contacts by suggesting a world full of movement of persons and mixture, contact, linkage, persistence cultural interaction and exchange. Thus, the world is shrinking in terms of time and space making the world feel closer, smaller and distances shorter (Jogdand and Michael, 2003:1). Globalisation also has brought lots of change in the context of science, knowledge, technology, innovative production, agriculture, communication, education, economy, health, etc. But there is no empirical evidence by which it can be said that globalisation has accelerated social change among deprived sections of society in India in general and in Bihar in particular.

Here, Nagla points out that some groups or sections are highly affected or marginalised due to globalisation in the name of development in Indian society. He, further, explains that "more than one-fifth of India's population does not have access to safe drinking water; nearly half of our population is illiterate, nearly two-thirds of our population lacks basic sanitation; nearly 40 per cent of our population lives in poverty" (Nagla, 2014:48). By considering his argument, we may say that landless labourers, marginal farmars, daily wage labourers, small agricultural sectors, Dalits, Tribals have been largely affected by globalisation in India in particular. In the case of Bihar, for example, Dalits have been the worst sufferers in the exploitative social order or in the system of hierarchical social order in the state in both rural and urban Bihar compared to other states. They also have been segregated from the main village or locality where twice-born lives in. In a similar way, Lal (1997) illustrates the economic, political and social exploitation of the Dalits done by the upper strata of society in Bihar. Not only that but Dalits are also the worst sufferer than any other community and their suffering is deeply embedded in the institution of Hindu caste system. In this context, we may assume that Globalisation has not broken the hierarchical order of caste system in Bihar so far. Caste still remains the fundamental determinant of social inequality of Dalits where 'social construction' based on justice, equality, liberty and fraternity are conveniently undermined and ignored (Ram, 1995:83).

Conclusion

We have analysed the hierarchy of caste system and placing of Dalits in that in Bihar. We have also discussed and the changing patterns of their relationship with the different caste groups in the state, especially after Independence. It mainly includes the caste composition and the traditional jajmani system as well as the traditional occupation of the Dalits and changes in their status over all the years. In Bihar, a sizeable section of Dalits are accorded with their own traditional occupations which are associated the high ritual pollution and low social prestige in society. However, the traditional occupation of Dalits in the state has changed to a large extent. Now, a large majority of them do not pursue their traditional occupation in villages. Due to industrialisation, educational progress and modern means of communication, they have shifted from their traditional occupations to new occupations like petty-business, jobs in public and private sectors, driving auto-vehicles, pulling rickshaws, *thelus* doing manual works, etc. mostly in urban areas. The Dalits in Bihar have followed, since the early time, the reforms movements like that of Arya Samaj, Kabirpanth and others. Even the social processes like Sanskritisation and Westernlisation or modernisation have played somewhat significant role in bringing the socio-political consciousness among them and changing their status in the state. Under the influence of Kabirpanth, a large number of Scheduled Caste people have changed their food habits. They, now, take vegetarian food, instead of non-vegetarian one. They are better economically, politically and socially somewhat better compared to what they were fifty years ago. This shows a drastic change among the Scheduled Castes in Bihar.

References

Benjamin, Joseph. 1989. *Scheduled Castes in Indian Politics and Society*, New Delhi: ESS, ESS Publications.

Beteille, Andre. 1974. *Studies in Agrarian Social Structure,* New Delhi: Oxford University Press.

Blair, Harry. W. 1980. 'Rising Kulaks and Backward Classes in Bihar', *Economic and Political Weekly*, Vol. 15. No. 2, January. 2:64-74.

Das, Arvind N. 1992. *The Republic of Bihar*, New Delhi: Penguin Books.

Dumont, Louis. 1988. *Homo Hierarchicus: The Caste System and its Implications*, New Delhi: Oxford University Press.

Gupta, A.R. 1984. *Caste Hierarchy and Social Change,* New Delhi: Jyotsna Prakashan.

Gupta, Dipankar (ed.). *Social Stratification,* New Delhi: Oxford University Press.

Gupta, Shaibal. 1994. 'Caste, Class and Landholding in the Analysis of Technology and Agricultural Production in Bihar', in K. L. Sharma (ed.), *Caste and Class in India*, Jaipur and New Delhi: Rawat Publications.

Haldar, A. K. 1976. 'The Scheduled Castes of Bihar: Their Distribution and Relative Concentration', *Journal of Social Research*, Vol, 19, No, (1): 74-84.

Harcourt, Max. 1977. 'Kisan Population and Revolution in Rural India', in D.V. Low, (ed.), *Congress and the Raj,* Colombia: South Asia Books.

Isaacs, Joseph R. 1965. *India's Ex-Untouchables*, Bombay: Asian Publishing House.

Joshi, P.C. 1978. 'Organizing Rural Poor: Some Basic Issues', *Mainstream* (New Delhi), 12. August, 7-12.

Kolenda, P. 1981. *Caste, Cult and Hierarchy: Essays on the Cultures of India*, Meerut: Folklore Institute.

Kumar, Rabindra. 2002. *Impact of Rural Development on Scheduled Castes*, New Delhi: Anmol Publications.

Lal, A.K. 1997. *Dalits in Action: An Evaluation of Bihar Dalit Vikas Samiti,* New Delhi: Concept Publishing Company.

Linton, Ralf. 1936. *The Study of Man: An Introduction*, New York: Appleton-Century-Crofts.

Lynch, Owen M. 1974. *The Politics of Untouchability,* New Delhi: National Publishing House.

Ram, Nandu. 1988. *The Mobile Scheduled Caste: Rise of a New Middle Class*, Delhi: Hindustan Publishing Corporation.

Ram, Nandu. 1995. *Beyond Ambedkar: Essays on Dalits in India,* New Delhi: Har-Anand Publications.

Rodrigues, Valerian. (ed.). 2002. *The Essential Writings of B. R. Ambedkar*, New Delhi: Oxford University Press.

Roy, Ramashray. 1970. 'Caste and Political Recruitment in Bihar', in Rajni Kothari (ed.), *Caste in Indian Politics*, New Delhi: Orient Longman.

Sachchidananda. 1977. *The Harijan Elite*, Delhi and Faridabad: Thomson Press (India) Limited.

Sachchidananda. 1983. 'Agrarian Relation: A Case Study of Purnea in Bihar', *Man in India*, Vol, 63, No, 1 March.

Sahay, Gaurang Ranjan. 1998. 'Caste System in Contemporary Bihar: A Case Study of Selected villages', *Sociological Bulletin*, 47(2), September: 207-220.

Sharma, Alakh N. 1996-96. 'Caste and Class in Rural Bihar', *Journal of Social and Economic Studies*, Vol, 12-13: 61.

Singh, Shashi Bhushan. 2005. 'Limits to Power: Naxalism and Caste Relations in a South Bihar Village', *Economic and Political Weekly*, July 16:3167-175.

Singh, Shyam Nand. 1990. *Reservation, Problems and Prospects,* New Delhi: Uppal Publishing House.

Srinivas, M. N. 1972. *Social Change in Modern India*, Delhi: Orient Longman.

Srinivas, M. N.1991. 'The Dominant Caste in Rampura' in Dipankar Gupta (ed.). *Social Stratification,* New Delhi: Oxford University Press.

Vidyarthi, L. P. and N. Mishra. 1977. *Harijan Today*, New Delhi: Classical Publications.

Wiser, W. H. 1958. *The Hindu Jajmani System*, U.P.: Lucknow Publishing House.

Chapter - 3

A Literary Analysis of Social Justice and Humanism in Joseph Conrad's *Heart of Darkness* and Mulk Raj Anand's *Untouchable*

—Deep Shikha Karthik

Social justice is normally associated with the conception of equality and equal access in society. As an ideology it corroborates equal treatment of all human beings without any social distinction based on caste, colour, race, religion, sex and so on so forth. In a similar parlance, humanism envisages people's capability and responsibility to lead meaningful and honourable lives. By asserting the self-respect and dignity of each human being, humanism beholds the maximisation of individual emancipation and prepares to take up the agreeable opportunities with social and global responsibility. It encourages the expansion of participatory democracy and the amplification of such an open society which remains committed for human rights and social justice. In this backdrop, the paper examines and compares the notion of social justice and humanism in the novels of Joseph Conrad's Heart of Darkness *(1899) and Mulk Raj Anand's* Untouchable *(1935). The Polish-born English novelist Joseph Conrad's* Heart of Darkness *and the great Indian novelist Mulk Raj Anand's novel* Untouchable *clearly define social justice as the core of humanism.* Heart of Darkness *is a captivating story about the racism in Africa as well as a symbol for social commentary on imperialism by Joseph Conrad. It is a literary masterpiece which embodies the essence of light contrasting with darkness. Joseph Conrad also presents the thought of human power, individual responsibility, and social justice by raising his voice against racism. Likewise, in* Untouchable *Mulk Raj Anand insists on the ideology of social justice and humanism by elevating the issue of untouchability and casteism in India. He believes in the dignity of every man without any discrimination on the basis of caste, creed or economy. Through his work, Mulk Raj Anand speaks against the hunger, exploitation, and the silent and intense suffering of vast number of untouchables, the destitute, the downtrodden, the beggars, the lepers, and countless oppressed ones including men, women and children. In ideological Convergence both* Heart of Darkness *and* Untouchable *believe in the possibility of achieving a better world order through the ideology of social justice and humanism. Although, both the authors come from entirely different nations and social background but still they evolve same sensibility and devotion to the concerns of mankind especially those who have been marginalised from the mainstream society. Therefore, through their works, both Joseph Conrad and Mulk Raj Anand expose the silent passions that burst in the hearts of the people who are forbidden to rise up and express themselves.*

Key Words: *Humanism, Social Justice, Untouchables, Racism, Casteism.*

The present paper explores and examines the notion of injustice or discrimination and its treatment by the perception of social justice and humanism by adopting a cross-cultural perspective with reference to analysis of racial discrimination in Joseph Conrad's novella, *Heart of Darkness* and Mulk Raj Anand's portrayal of caste discrimination in his novel, *Untouchable*. Prejudice or discrimination on the basis of caste or colour has been a universal practice by human race. The discrimination on each basis generates similar repercussions. It entwines the tale of wretchedness, sufferings, pain and agony in the life of an individual. It can be anecdotal that racism and casteism are sheer naught as they are simply social hypothesis. But, this social malevolence can only be exterminated from society when we behave toward every human being uniformly. Social vices like racism and casteism are mended into the same composition of discrimination. However, Joseph Conrad and Mulk Raj Anand both induce optimism in reader and admit the existence of social justice for human rights on the base of essential goodness of humankind irrespective of caste, race, or creed.

Social justice is normally associated with the conception of equality or equal prospect in society. It is an ideology which stands for the equal treatment of all human beings without any social distinction based on caste, colour, race, religion, sex and so on. Likewise, humanism is a sensible system of thought which establishes people's capability and responsibility to lead meaningful and honourable lives. By asserting the self-respect and dignity of each human being, it holds up the maximisation of individual emancipation and opportunity agreeable with social and global responsibility. It encourages the expansion of participatory democracy and the elaboration of the open society, standing for people's human rights and social justice. In the chapter entitled "Searching for the Meaning of Social Justice" of the work called *Social Justice and Social Work: Rediscovering a Core Value of the Profession*, Michael J. Austin, Christina Branom, and Bryn King state some definitional complexity in describing the term social justice:

> The definitional complexity can be seen in the following examples of efforts to define social justice: Social justice can refer to a system of belief (liberal and conservative), a substitute for the term social justice

> (oppression, discrimination, exploitation, etc.) a form of advocacy or intervention (doing social justice work), a value of a profession, and / or an organisation (social justice non-profit).(1)

It is imperative to recognise that why literature matters for social justice as literature holds uniquely transformative possibilities for altering our psychological configuration–generating new schemas that readers will remain to use. This involvement is one way the humanities can influence our day-to-day lives. Besides, literary scholars who have expanded elaborated schemas for comprehending literary works can have an actual effect on helping readers identify and take out the layers of meaning and culture in a piece of literature in addition to people and experiences they keep on to encounter. Literary scholars have the prospect to enlighten alternative ideas that can oppose ideologies which are adverse to people of colour, or women, or any subordinated people. Keeping in a different way, literary scholars understand literature better when they relate imaginary stories or characters with real social issues. In the chapter called "Social Justice from a Humanities Perspective: A Synthesis to Inform Practice" of the work entitled *Social Justice and Social Work: Rediscovering a Core Value of the Profession* by the authors Bryn King and Michael J. Austin, the function and involvement of literary theory and literary theorists in social justice is clearly provided. In this chapter it is noticeably expressed that how literature and literary theory raise awareness and consciousness about social justice in a socicty:

> Similar to the discipline of history, literary theorists provide another approach to engaging and promoting social justice. The systematic approach of literary scholars to promote social change involves exposing the values inherent in literature and its potential for challenging dominant ideologies ... literary theorists define themselves in terms of the goal of improving the human condition and addressing different forms of oppression. As Fitzgerald notes, focus approaches to literary theory can be identified to help define the form of oppression, namely, social class, gender, colonial power, and heteronormativity.(87)

As social transform sets in motion with individuals, literature and literary evaluation that have the power to reveal and alter the complex world people construct every day. New understanding of alternative ideas encourages social justice and humanism by expanding readers' intelligences and allowing them to be aware of future experiences in a more toned and compassionate way. Literature shapes people's perspectives, and how they perceive their world can in fact create a discrete reality or picture of society. If literary authors can offer readers the implements they need to better comprehend works by marginalised groups that show social injustice – such as natives, blacks, women, transgender, eunuchs, etc–then these works have a better possibility of being accepted into the standard. As David Miller visibly states the purpose of social justice in a society in the chapter entitled "The Scope of Social Justice" of the work *Principles of Social Justice*:

> Society is viewed as an organism in which the flourishing of each element requires the cooperation of all the others, and the aim of social justice is to specify the institutional arrangements that will allow each person to contribute fully to social well-being ... Social justice requires the notion of a society made up of interdependent parts, with an institutional structure that affects the prospects of each individual member, and that is capable of deliberate reform by an agency such as the state in the name of fairness.(4)

A Polish-born English novelist Joseph Conrad's novella, *Heart of Darkness* (1899) and the great Indian novelist Mulk Raj Anand's novel *Untouchable* (1935) clearly define the subject of social justice as the foundation of humanism in the world. Joseph Conrad brought up in the Polish Ukraine, a huge, productive plain between Poland and Russia. It was a diverse land, with four languages, four religions, and with various different social groups of people. A portion of the Polish-speaking population, comprising Conrad's family unit, belonged to the "szlachta" category, a traditional class in the aristocracy on the societal hierarchy, intermixing qualities of upper class and nobility. They had political authority, in spite of their underprivileged condition.

Joseph Conrad's father, Apollo Korzeniowski is known for his poetic temperament and passionate patriotism. His literary and political activities, his variety of plays and social satires are even if little known but they have tremendous influence on Apollo's son. Joseph Conrad granted British nationality in 1886. He has written several novels such as starting from his first novel, *Almayer's Folly* (1895), then, *An Outcast of the Islands* (1896), *The Nigger of the 'Narcissus'* (1897), *Heart of Darkness* (1899), *Lord Jim* (1900), *The Inheritors* (1901), *Typhoon* (1902, begun 1899), *The End of the Tether* (1902), *Romance* (1903), *Nostromo* (1904), *The Secret Agent* (1907), *Under Western Eyes* (1911), *Chance* (1913), *Victory* (1915), *The Shadow Line* (1917), *The Arrow of Gold* (1919), *The Rescue* (1920), *The Nature of a Crime* (1923), *The Rover* (1923), and *Suspense: A Napoleonic Novel* (1925) which is his unfinished novel and published posthumously. Joseph Conrad has also written several remarkable essays like "Autocracy and War" (1905), "The Mirror of the Sea" (1906) is a collection of autobiographical essays first published in various magazines 1904–6), "A Personal Record" (1912), "The First News" (1918), "The Lesson of the Collision: A monograph upon the loss of the 'Empress of Ireland'" (1919), "The Polish Question" (1919), "The Shock of War" (1919), "Notes on Life and Letters" (1921), "Notes on My Books" (1921), "Last Essays" which is edited by Richard Curle in 1926, and "The Congo Diary and Other Uncollected Pieces" (1978), edited by Zdzis³aw Najder.

Apart from these works, several film adaptations and operas in various genres and media have been based on, or inspired by, Conrad's writings.

Joseph Conrad is regarded as an early modernist, even if his works still inhibit fundamentals of nineteenth-century realism. His narrative technique and anti-heroic characters way of stories have inclined a number of authors, including T. S. Eliot, William Faulkner, Graham Greene, and more lately Salman Rushdie. A Polish literary historian, critic, and political activist known as Najder Zdzis³aw writes about Joseph Conrad's passion related with politics in his work entitled *Joseph Conrad: A Life*. He also quotes a British writer who is best known for his 1917 novel *South Wind* called George Norman Douglas' remark on Joseph Conrad as a politician in this work:

> Conrad was passionately concerned with politics. This is confirmed by several of his works, starting with *Almayer's Folly*...*Nostromo* revealed his concern with these matters more fully; it was, of course, a concern quite natural for someone from a country (Poland) where politics was a matter not only of everyday existence but also of life and death. Moreover, Conrad himself came from a social class that claimed exclusive responsibility for state affairs, and from a very politically active family. Norman Douglas sums it up: "Conrad was first and foremost a Pole and like many Poles a politician and moralist malgré lui (French: "in spite of himself"). These are his fundamentals. "Conrad sees political problems in terms of a continuous struggle between law and violence, anarchy and order, freedom and autocracy, material interests and the noble idealism of individuals ... was Conrad's historical awareness. His Polish experience endowed him with the perception, exceptional in the Western European literature of his time, of how winding and constantly changing were the front lines in these struggles.(352)

The most creative phase of Conrad's career spanned from 1897 to 1911, during this time he composed many works including *Heart of Darkness*. Joseph Conrad has received his inspiration to write *Heart of Darkness* after carrying out his journey to the Congo in 1890. The story of *Heart of Darkness* deals with a British man's expedition deep into the Congo of Africa, where he encounters the brutal and mysterious Kurtz, a European trader who has proved himself as a monarch of the native people there. This novel essentially contains vivid conflicts and clashes between human characters and the brutal forces of nature; and themes of selfishness, the violent part of human nature, racial prejudice and ultimately, social justice. Conrad was concerned in screening "psycho-political" states of affairs that drew parallels between the internal lives of single characters and the broader zoom of human history.

The tale of *Heart of Darkness* is set largely in Africa and the narrator is of European lineage, so of course there is an aspect of race and colonialism in this story. The protagonist of the novel, a thirty-two-year old British sailor

Charlie Marlow presents his experiences in the Congo about the violence, injustice, and cruelty performed by Europeans to natives there. It is a recurring character of Joseph Conrad's itself in this novel. Marlow points out a prevailing attitude of racism by showing how the whites consistently pass on to the black Indigenous people with pejorative and ugly names. On the other hand, Marlow feels a thrum of association to these wild, dancing, gesticulating people.

In *Heart of Darkness*, there is a sense of discrimination, exploitation, subjugation, colonisation that how the whites see the blacks merely as undeveloped or uncivilised people where everything they have to scorn and disrespect and nothing to particularly admire or appreciate. This is excellently shown in one incident when Marlow eagerly wants to give a dying black man a biscuit and then heedlessly dismissing the death of his black steersman as a savage who was no more account than a grain of sand in a black Sahara.

Although, he overlooks the man's task on his ship, he does not mourn for the man's death because he is black and consequently not worth mourning. Paradoxically, of course, a lot of the black natives are more moral and honest people, in spite of their savage ways, than the white, imperialist invaders. The subject of race, humanity, and human value is one of the other themes in this story. Ultimately, *Heart of Darkness* exhibits the quest for truth and social justice among the so many issues such as corruption, deception, communication, and violence. Marlow is looking for something essential, true and worthy of being every person equal and also something morally perfect and righteous against the others who have imposed their imperial will on the natives. Joseph Conrad's treatment of social justice and humanism is illustrious in this novel as he has great sympathy for the downtrodden people as innocent natives under the realm of British. In this respect he sometimes reminds readers strongly of Mulk Raj Anand or Charles Dickens whose novels too had been prompted by their sympathy for the browbeaten members of society. Similar to Mulk Raj Anand's or Charles Dickens' criticism of social evils in society, Joseph Conrad raises the question on the issue of harsh racism, injustice, and oppression faced by the colonised in the name of coloniser's civilising mission.

Certainly, the intention of his quest is Kurtz, a European trader but what he eventually discovers is that Kurtz is more wicked, greedy, and cruel than anyone else Marlow has encountered or even heard about. This exposure is devastating, for he realises that the core, the self, the heart, of everything "leads into the heart of an immense darkness" (Conrad, 76).

Another important idea that Joseph Conrad builds on is the subject of personal power and individual responsibility. *Heart of Darkness* has all the frills of the traditional adventure narrative–mystery, exotic setting, escape, suspense, unexpected attack along with the African history and racism towards the African people. Joseph Conrad writes that, "They passed me with six inches, without a glance, with the complete, deathlike indifference of unhappy savages"

(Conrad, 19). Conrad employs Marlow, the central character in the novel, as a speaker so he himself can enter the story and advise it through his own philosophical mind. Conrad writes explicitly about the hunger, sufferings, and pain of African people. On leading at the first station, Marlow comments what he observes that, "They were dying slowly–it was very clear. They were not enemies, they were not criminals, they were nothing earthly now, nothing but black shadows of disease and starvation lying confusedly in the greenish gloom" (Conrad, 20).

Marlow feels sympathy toward the natives as he states that the natives aren't criminals or lawbreakers but are being treated as if they are. Conrad displays that how the Africans are shown inferior and doomed people by whites. He raises the issue of racism and social injustice but not exposed himself as a racist.

The end result of *Heart of Darkness* has been concluded Conrad's divisions of the social world into two disconnect categories: 'us,' the Europeans, and 'them,' the Africans natives. As Frances B. Singh writes in *The Colonialistic Bias of Heart of Darkness* about how the colonialistic approach taken to the novel that, "Heart of Darkness was written, consciously or unconsciously, from a colonialistic point of view" (Singh, 278). In the novel, the author Joseph Conrad illustrates how racist the Europeans are toward blacks not only because they are turned into slaves but also it is seen how the European people seem to think the Africans are not equal level to them. There are several cases of discrimination and injustice towards woman in this story when women are looked down and they are considered to be worth less than men, or yet not as valuable. Injustice, exploitation, and racism can be seen all over in this novel.

There several critics as well as readers who have found Joseph Conrad himself as a complete racist because he has made some remarks about blacks that are very disturbing. For example, one of this type is when he comments that, "...the thought of their humanity-like yours...Ugly" (Conrad, 23). This just sets off to show how Conrad is an absolute racist. The notion of a black man's humanity being measured up to Conrad's is just plain revolting to Conrad. But, when he raises the issue of racism or seems like racist himself, simultaneously Conrad demands for social justice to blacks as well. As it is clearly shown that how the Europeans are racist toward blacks or how the European people seem to think the Africans are not equal to them because their black. This whole theory of story claims a justice and acceptability for Africans itself from its readers. Therefore, social justice and humanism both are questioned in *Heart of Darkness*.

Mulk Raj Anand was born in 1905 in Peshawar, India which is now in Pakistan and died September in 2004. He is known as prominent Indian author of novels, short stories, and critical essays in English, who is acknowledged for his realistic and sympathetic portrayal of the deprived in India. He is believed as an originator of the English-language Indian novel. After doing graduation with honours in 1924 from Punjab University in Lahore, Mulk Raj Anand pursued additional studies at the University of Cambridge and at University College in London. Even as in Europe, he turned out to be politically active in India's struggle for autonomy and shortly from then on he wrote a series of miscellaneous books on facets of South Asian ways of life, comprising *Persian Painting* (1930), *Curries and Other Indian Dishes* (1932), *The Hindu View of Art* (1933), *The Indian Theatre* (1950), and *Seven Little-Known Birds of the Inner Eye* (1978). As a creative writer, Anand first achieved wide recognition for his novels *Untouchable* (1935) and *Coolie* (1936), both of which scrutinised the predicaments of deprived people in Indian society. In 1945 he revisited to Bombay, now Mumbai to crusade for national reforms. Among his other major works are novels such as *Two Leaves and a Bud* (1937), *The Village* (1939), *Across the Black Waters* (1939), *The Sword and the Sickle* (1942), *The Big Heart* (1945), *The Private Life of an Indian Prince* (1953), and *The Road* (1961). Autobiographies which he has written are *Seven Summers* (1951) and *Morning Face* (1968) for that he won the Sahitya Academy Award as Best Literature award in India. Anand has written other novels and short-story collections and in addition edited several magazines and journals, together with *MARG*, an art quarterly that he established in 1946.

Mulk Raj Anand is one such personage, who is globally recognised as a distinguished novelist. Mulk Raj Anand's *Untouchable* and *Coolie,* R.K. Narayan's *Swami and Friends* and *The Bachelor of Arts*, Raja Rao's *Kanthapura* celebrate the commencement of Indian English Fiction. Mulk Raj Anand, next to with R.K. Narayan and Raja Rao has long been respected as the 'Big Three' of Indian English writing. He uses his fiction, to help lift up the untouchables, the peasants, the helots, the coolies and the other suppressed constituents of society, to human and self-consciousness in view of the abasement, apathy and desolation in which they are ruined.

Anand's alarm and sympathy for the depleted, weak and the downtrodden is present all through his fiction, especially in novels like *Untouchable*, *Coolie*, *Two Leaves and a Bud* and *Seven Summers* etc. He is a great humanist in his novels. He shows humanism as enlightenment and illumination in the wellbeing of man, true to his uppermost nature and his dignified vision. He stresses on the essential worth, dignity, and magnitude of man. Therefore, he believes and demonstrates through his novel especially *Untouchable* that a recognition of the so-called untouchables as human beings are entitled to the same rights and the opportunities as other classes of society.

Mulk Raj Anand asserts in opposition to poverty, casteism, mistreatment, religious double standards, and negative social and cultural traditions in Indian society, like child marriage, arranged marriage, the low rank of women in broad spectrum and the widow in specific and caste precincts. He also raises his voice against British rule. All over, he remains as the supporter of the underdogs. According to Mulk Raj Anand it is society, which forms the destiny of man to a great degree and against which man is in restless struggle. His trilogy, *The Village*, *Across the Black Waters* and *The Sword and the Sickle* are appropriate examples of this kind. In *The Private Life of an Indian Prince*, Anand directs more on the consciousness of the person.

Untouchable is an imaginary story set in the so-called outcastes' colony exterior of an anonymous town during the British rule. In the novel Mulk Raj Anand portrays:

> The outcastes' colony was a group of mudwalled houses that clustered together in two rows, under the shadow both of the town and the cantonment, but outside their boundaries and separate from them. There lived the scavengers, the leather-workers, the washer men, the barbers, the water carriers, the grasscutters and other outcastes from Hindu society. A brook ran near the lane, once with crystal clear water, now soiled by the dirt and filth of the public latrines situated about it, the odour of the hides and skins of dead carcasses left to dry on its banks, the dung of donkeys, sheep, 146 horses, cows and buffaloes heaped up to be made into fuel cakes.(11)

The hero of this novel is an untouchable called Bakha who is a tall strong young man. The caste system in India has become so unbending and tyrannical. Bakha lives a debauched life. His only shelter is a one-roomed mud house, which is also so dark and shabby. Anand describes Bakha's day begins as:

> Bakha thought of the congeniality of his of his home as he lay half awake in the morning of an autumn day, covered by a worn-out, greasy blanket, on a faded blue carpet which was spread on the floor in a corner of the cave like, dingy, dank, one-roomed mud house. His sister slept on a cot next to him and his father and brother snored from under a patched, ocher-coloured quilt, on a broken string bed, on the other side.(12)

Bakha is the symbolic of all the downtrodden and oppressed people in a society of Pre-Independence India. He represents the hardships and humiliation which has been the fate of untouchables like him. He is a toilet cleaner and suffers a lot because of his caste. In *Premchand's Godan: A Critical Analysis*, I.D. Sharma quotes Francis H. Stoddard's words and writes about how a novel sets a human's life story in it, he writes that "A novel is a narrative of human life under the stress of emotion. It differs from the epic in that. It is a narration of human rather than super human life, under the stress of ordinary rather than of excessive or heroic emotion"(67).

Untouchable is a sociological text that centres awareness on a number of customs, traditions, social evils etc. of Hindu Society during 1930's. At that time there was no proper system of drainage and there was foul and stinking smells far and wide. The untouchables considered as low caste people were not only underprivileged, ill-fed, ill-clothed but also sick and contaminated. Hence, Bakha's mother died because of lack of proper treatment or medication, and his father was asthmatic patient. On the other hand, the upper caste people were apathetic, wealthy, well-off, aggressive, intolerant and cruel due to their superior status or position in society. Each day Bakha had to endure similar soul-breaking torments at the hands of the towns people whose infliction him severe physical, moral and spiritual grievances while keeping him matter to hunger, humiliation, dirt and deprivation. He had to experience a kind of severe psychosomatic pain which disturbed him and restricted him from taking pleasure in the ordinary things which other Hindu community people were benefiting from. This led to a crisis of identity in Bakha. He reacted with rage, horror resentment and a desire to take revenge. E. M. Forster, a friend of Mulk Raj Anand has written the preface of *Untouchable* by which novel has perceived its aesthetic. E.M. Foster puts about Bakha in the preface:

> He has just the right mixture of insight and detachment, and the fact that he has come to fiction through philosophy has given him depth. It might have given him vagueness-that curse of the generalising mind-but his hero suffering abstraction. Bakha is real individual, lovable, thwarted, sometimes grand, sometimes weak, and thoroughly Indian.(9)

Apart from all humiliations and tortures, Bakha was not only efficient in his work but also was doing it with full dedication. As given in *Untouchable* that, "For although he did not know it, to him work was sort of intoxication which gave him a glowing health and plenty of easy sleep. So he worked on continuously, incessantly, without stopping for breadth, even though the violent exertion of his limb was making him gasp." (43)

Anand's credence in impartiality and social justice is well projected in this novel. The untouchable were expelled from all the social occasions or happenings and their association from outside or from others was quite limited and their possibility got hindered making them suffer from destitution for many decades. Nevertheless, by the end of the novel Anand proposes that it is technology, in the form of the newly introduced flush toilet that may be his redeemer by eliminating the need for a caste of toilet cleaners.

The caste system and racism equally consist of both prejudice and discrimination based in social or racial perceptions of people. Racism provides protection to the ignorant who aims to divide and destroy the social circle. Exactly like racism hampers the growth of any country so does the casteism as their ramifications are same. The orderliness of casteism blinds people as it pays no attention to the healthy social standards of justice, evenhandedness and universal fraternity. In the work called *Caste and Democratic Politics in India,* Ghanshyam Shah quotes the words of Dr. B.R. Ambedkar on this.

Dr B.R. Ambedkar says that "You cannot build anything on the foundation of caste. You cannot build a nation. You cannot build up a morality" (102).

Untouchable compels a reader to consider and foster humanitarian attitude in understanding casteism. It deals with the humanism which should be regarded as a religion for everyone. Mulk Raj Anand intensely scrutinises the distort society and narrates the tale of woe. His love for humanism makes him employ his art for the good turn of humanity. Caste and nationwide barricades have no importance for him, and he looks upon all mankind as one. The indication of contemporary social evil in the novel was extensively commended and brought him the position of India's Charles Dickens. As Dickens exposed and castigated all the evils, malpractices rampant in the legal system and in the prison of time, the exploitation, the prevalence of crime, and the evils of poverty, similarly Mulk Raj Anand's passion and compassion for humanity are boundless. In *Indian Writing in English*, Prof. K.R.S. Iyengar sums up with assumption of the novel:

> Untouchable strikes us as the picture of the place of a society, and the certain persons not easily to be forgotten; a picture that is also an indictment of the evils of a decadent and perverted orthodoxy. As a novelist addressing himself to the task of exposing certain evils, Anand has been as effective as Dickens himself. (330)

There are many issues drawn parallels between *Heart of Darkness* and *Untouchable* to bring out the plight of man caught amidst social forces beyond his control. The evaluation of both the novels states out the sense that injustice either based on caste or colour upshots only in the suffering of human being. Besides, *Heart of Darkness* is a captivating story about the racism in Africa as well as a symbol for social commentary on imperialism by Joseph Conrad. It is a literary masterpiece which embodies the essence of light contrasting with darkness. Joseph Conrad also presents the thought of human power, individual responsibility, and social justice by raising his voice against racism. Likewise, in *Untouchable* Mulk Raj Anand insists on the ideology of social justice and humanism by elevating the issue of untouchability or casteism in India. He believes in the dignity of every man without any discrimination on the basis of caste, creed or prosperity. Through his work, Mulk Raj Anand speaks against the hunger, exploitation, and the silent and intense suffering of vast number of untouchables, the destitute, the downtrodden, the beggars, the lepers, and countless oppressed ones including men, women and children.

Equally, *Heart of Darkness* and *Untouchable* believe in the possibility of achieving a better world order through the ideology of social justice and humanism. Although, both the authors come from two different nations but still they evolve same sensibility and devotion to the concerns of mankind or those who have been marginalised from a long time. Therefore, through their works, both Joseph Conrad and Mulk Raj Anand expose the silent passions that burst in the hearts of the people who are forbidden to rise up and express themselves. Both, the blacks or low caste people were supposed to have no ethical and no right to express them. But in both the novels, although belong from two dissimilar countries, writers have effectively marked out that the protagonists are moral at heart and are with integrity awaken.

In a world in which virtuousness or purity is endangered by injustice, cruelty, prejudice and hatred, goodness prevails in the form of sympathy, understanding and common sense as evident by both the novelists. In *Untouchable* Anand shows that component of humanity, compassion, sympathy and mercy which was not dead in upper class. There were some people who thought about for other people irrespective of their position in social hierarchy. Thus, he has constantly endeavoured to make his novel a medium of transmitting his ideology of humanism and social justice. His subject manifests the essential dignity of man and dignity in society. In the work named *Five Contemporary Indian Novels* Pramod Kumar Singh observes regarding Anand's vision of life, his ideology of social justice and humanism as reflected in his fiction:

> Anand is very much a man of the world, living and loving in accordance to the rhythms of his own nature. He has never been above the battle; rather, he has fought bravely against wrongs and injustices. He has composed the theme song of love and has made his voice echo in clamorous notes to arouse the conscience of humanity. (17)

Conclusion

Therefore, the comparative studies from both eastern and western perspectives have been explored in the paper to bring forefront the very painful reality that though the world has progressed immeasurably but the modern man is still in the restrains of inequality in some or the other way. Racism and casteism which are shown in both the texts are mere social constructs but bring alertness and awareness to its readers. It brings awareness and consciousness to the mind-set of people that this social evil has entangled our society and is slowly swallowing up it like a monster. Hence, these social evils can only be eradicated from world when we respect every human being equally which in turn brings social justice for everyone.

References

Achebe, Chinua. *An Image of Africa: Racism in Conrad's Heart of Darkness*. Ed. Robert Kimbrough. 3rd ed. New York: Norton Critical 1988.

Anand, Mulk Raj. *Untouchable.* New Delhi: Arnold Publishers, 1981, 11-43.

Austin, Michael J., Christina Branom, and Bryn King. "Searching for the Meaning of Social Justice." *Social Justice and Social Work: Rediscovering a Core Value of the Profession*. Ed. Michael J. Austin. University of California, Berkeley: Sage Publication, Inc., 2014, 1.

Conrad, Joseph. *Heart of Darkness*. New York: W.W. Norton and Company, Inc., 1988.

Foster, E.M. Preface. *Untouchable,* Mulk Raj Anand. New Delhi: Arnold Publishers, 1981, 9.

Iyengar, K.R. Srinivasa. *Indian Writing in English.* Bombay: Asia Publishing House, 1984, 330.

King, Bryn, and Michael J. Austin. "Social Justice from a Humanities Perspective: A Synthesis to Inform Practice." *Social Justice and Social Work: Rediscovering a Core Value of the Profession*. Ed. Michael J. Austin. University of California, Berkeley: Sage Publication, Inc., 2014, 87.

Miller, David. "The Scope of Social Justice." *Principles of Social Justice*. London, England: University of Harvard Press, 1999, 4.

MLA Handbook for Writers of Research Papers. New Delhi: East West Press, 2009.

Najder, Zdzis³aw. *Joseph Conrad: A Life*. Trans. Halina Najder. Rochester, New York: Camden House, 2007, 352.

Sarvan, C. P. *Racism and the Heart of Darkness*. Ed. Robert Kimbrough. New York: Norton Critical 1988.

Shah, Ghanshyam. *Caste and Democratic Politics in India*. Delhi: Permanent Black, 2005, 102.

Sharma, I.D. *Premchand's Godan : A Critical Analysis*. Barelly: Prakash Book Depot. 1995, 67.

Singh, Frances B. *The Colonialistic Bias of Heart of Darkness*. Ed. Robert Kimbrough. 3rd ed. New York: Norton Critical, 1988, 278.

Singh, Pramod Kumar, ed. *Five Contemporary Indian Novels.* Jaipur: Book Enclove, 2001, 17.

Chapter - 4

An Analysis of Human Wellbeing and Gender Neutrality of Mining Activities in Tribal Districts of Odisha

—*Minati Sahoo and Subrat Kumar Malik*

The paper attempts to examine the notion of gender neutrality in the mining activities in the tribal districts of Odisha. By highlighting the financial contribution of mining sector to the economy of Odisha, the paper further attempts a comparative analysis of the impact of mining on local communities in general in terms of Human Development parameters and on women in particular in terms of Gender Development parameters in the tribal and non-tribal mining districts of Odisha. It has been found that despite significant monetary contribution by mining sector to the state economy, the state has failed miserably for the improvement and development of socio-economic condition of the people in general and women in particular in tribal dominated mining district. It was found that that tribal dominated mining district have lower Human Development Index and Gender Development Index than that of their non-tribal counterparts. The prime areas in which mining operations influence women disproportionately include health, education and livelihood. Therefore, the study recommend that a comprehensive mechanism needs to be devised by government through which revenues generated by mining could be used for the development of the local communities particularly women in mining areas. It strongly emphasised that some policy initiatives must be undertaken that would enhance women's economic self-sufficiency, gender equality and wellbeing in the mining districts of Odisha.

***Key Words**: Gender, Mining, Tribal, Districts, Odisha, Development.*

Introduction

The exploitation of natural resources is traditionally argued to play a vital role in a nation's growth and development. Countries endowed with these resources are assumed to be able to transform their economies towards the path of development. Minerals constitute an important source of raw materials for most of the basic industries necessitating their exploration from earth. As long as such deposits lie dormant in the ground, they remain unproductive. For their potential to be realised, mineral deposits have to be extracted. So, mining plays an important role in the development process by converting mineral resources into a form of capital that contributes to a nation's output (Davis and Tilton, 2005). Thus, exploration of mineral resources is an essential condition for successful economic development of an economy.

Mineral resources are considered to be blessing for the economic development (Pendergast *et al.,* 2011). They undoubtedly represent the wealth of a region where they exist and open up wide vistas for the prosperity of the region. Mining is often argued to have the potential of boosting a country's economy. The sector has been the cause of extraordinary economic growth in Chilean II region as well in the country of Chile (Aroca, 2001). Discovery of large diamond deposits in the North West territories has intensified the speed and scale of development in Canadian North (Gibsom and Klinck, 2005). Similarly, copper mining in Zambia has been major contributor to the country's foreign exchange earnings (Kangwa and Lekunze, 2008). The gross value of mineral production also has positively affected the quality of life indicators such as income, housing affordability, access to communication services, education, consumption and employment (Ye, 2008; Hajkowicz *et al.,* 2011) in regional and remote Australia. In a nutshell, mining industries can generate wealth; create large-scale employment; cause infrastructure improvements; provide raw materials for most industries; contribute to world production; have sizeable world trade and foster economic growth. Therefore, mining is considered to be an important economic activity and provide a major structure upon which development of any economy gifted with rich natural resources rests (Stilwell *et al.,* 2000; Mcmohan and Remy, 2001; Brunnschweiler, 2008; Ye, 2008; Ejdemo and Soderholm, 2011). Large-scale mining development has a potential to contribute to human development and poverty reduction in the area of influence of mining activities. They can be an important economic engine for social progress (Parra and Weldegiorgis, 2015). In addition to economic growth, countries rich in minerals other than oil have experienced significant improvements in their Human Development Index (HDI) scores that are on an average better than those experienced by countries without minerals (McMahon and Moreira, 2014).

Mineral resource is one of the important natural resources of India which contributes to the national income through mineral export earnings and acts as an important input for the industrial sector of domestic economy (Sahoo *et al.,* 2014). It is also critical to country's economic and social well-being as it significantly contributes to Gross Domestic Product and overall employment (Federation of Indian Chambers of Commerce and Industry, 2013). Among the major mining states, Odisha enjoys a prominent position in India (Economic Survey of Odisha, 2014-15). The state is the leading producer of chromites, graphite, bauxite, manganese ore, iron ore, sillimanite, quartzite, pyroxenite and dolomite. In terms of mineral deposits and production, it has attained the distinction of being the largest mineral producing state in the country. Being one of the leading mineral producers of the country, contribution of Odisha to total value of production of mineral was 8 per cent. The state by contributing ₹ 27164.71 crore to value of country's mineral production claims fourth position in the country during 2012-13. Accretion to country's GDP from Mining and Quarrying sector by minerals covered under MCDR, 1988 in India was headed by Odisha having a share of 41 per cent in the same year. It is one of the richest bio-diversity regions in south-east Asia (Government of Odisha, 2007). Despite of its richness in mineral resources, it is also regarded as the homeland of the tribal having a total tribal population of about 7 million, which is 22.21 per cent of the State's total population according to 2011 Census. Tribes in Odisha form the most backward segment of its total rural population. Out of 461 types of tribes in India, Odisha has the distinction of being the homeland of 62 types of tribes, 12 types are identified as primitive tribal groups (Samal and Patra, 2015).To a great degree, minerals and tribal tracts are concentrated in the same geographic areas (Bhusan and Hazra, 2008). The state has witnessed acute regional and social disparities in development (Economic Survey of Odisha, 2014-15). Now, this raises an important question that whether mining has improved the human well being in tribal dominated mineral rich region.

Additionally, mining is an industry of extraction that necessarily brings and spreads advanced capitalist modes of economy which cause great social transformations in the area local to the mine. Consequent to these changes, new power equations come into existence, changing the gender roles amongst the people living in mining communities. Large-scale mining affects women in indigenous communities more adversely than men (Tauli-Corpuz, 1997; Bhanumathi, 2003; Bose, 2004). Mining is widely seen as tough and dirty and therefore as men's work. As mines are usually the single dominant employer in an area and employ mostly men, this combination of capitalist transformation and the introduction of a masculine form of modernity profoundly affects gender relations and family life in mining communities. Where men dominate the labour market to such a strong degree, women become forced to rely on men for their economic survival. Women are affected by mining as individuals, as workers, and as community members. They are at a substantial social and economic disadvantage to men (Sharma, 2010) and enjoy only a limited number of positive benefits from mining operations (Lahiri-dutt and Mahy, 2007). In particular, they are largely excluded from employment in mining and are seldom included in negotiations with the industry (Connell and Howitt, 1991; Kamble 2004; Gibson and Kemp, 2008). These raises important researchable questions that: Are mining activities gender biased? Whether women are disproportionately affected by mining activities? Whether women are equally benefitted from the developments that are generated from mining?

With this backdrop, an attempt has been made in the present paper to examine the human well being and gender-neutrality of mining in tribal districts of Odisha. Specifically, following are the objectives of the present study:

1. To highlight the financial contribution of mining sector to the economy of Odisha.
2. To analysis the impact of mining on human well-being in terms of human development parameters in the tribal mining districts of Odisha.
3. To examine the gender neutrality of mining activities on the basis of gender development parameters in the tribal mining districts of Odisha.

The entire paper has been divided into four sections. First section will discuss the financial contribution of mining to the economy of Odisha. Whether these financial generations have resulted in the improvement of the well being of the people in tribal mining region or not is examined in second section. The impact of mining from the gender perspective in tribal regions is discussed in the third section. And the last section concludes the present paper with some suggestions.

I. Monetary Contribution of Mining to State Exchequer

Odisha is richly endowed with large varieties of minerals which include chromite, bauxite, graphite, iron ore, manganese ore, limestone, clay, quartz and quartzite, nickel, copper, lead, coal, lead and many precious stones. Its richness in minerals can be seen in Table 4.1. Coal, Bauxite, limestone and iron ore constitute 97 per cent of the total mineral reserves in Odisha. Coal alone occupies 86.48 per cent to all minerals reserves in Odisha.

Table 4.1: Mineral reserve in Odisha (in million tons as on 2013-14)

Minerals/Ores	*Reserve*	*Per cent of mineral reserve to all minerals reserve*
Bauxite	1878.8	2.16
China clay	280.91	0.32
Chromite	176.75	0.2
Coal	75073	86.48
Dolomite	676.38	0.78
Fire clay	170.08	0.2
Graphite	8.61	0.01
Iron ore	5737.14	6.61
Lead and Zinc ore	13.48	0.02

contd

Lime stone	1768.51	2.04
Manganese ore	190.35	0.22
Heavy minerals	226	0.26
Nickel ore	219.67	0.25
Pyrophy lite	12.27	0.01
Mineral Sand	240.34	0.28
Vanadium ore	6.48	0.01
Quartz and Quartzite	134.34	0.15
Tin ore (tons)	0.02	0
Total	**86813.13**	**100**

Source: Economic Survey of Odisha 2014-15 and compiled by author.

Endowed with vast mineral deposits, Odisha occupies a prominent place in the minerals map of the country. Mining sector through its contribution to GSDP (Gross State Domestic Product), revenue from mining and export of minerals financially contribute to the state exchequer over a period of time. This contribution is utilised by the state for the socio-economic development and well being of the region in general and population in particulars. The extent of these contributions is discussed in subsequent sub-sections.

I.1 Contribution to GSDP

Table 4.2: GSDP and contribution of mining and quarrying to GSDP at current prices from 2000-01 to 2014-15 (in ₹ cr)

Year	*GSDP*	*Contribution of Mining and Quarrying to GSDP*
2000-01	484148.4	23580.8
2001-02	517037.1	25217.9
2002-03	548011.1	30348.1
2003-04	661001.4	43320.2
2004-05	777294.3	58618.6
2005-06	850964.9	71267.8
2006-07	1018394.7	86627.7
2007-08	1292744.5	122475.4
2008-09	1484907.1	159373.7
2009-10	1629464.3	155950.0
2010-11	1975299.0	218444.5
2011-12	2205892.7	260987.5
2012-13	2512204.6	268415.7
2013-14	2729799.2	298283.1
2014-15	3108102.4	321520.7

Source: Economic survey of Odisha 2014-15.

GSDP (Gross State Domestic Product) is a measure of the economic output of a state. It is the single most important tool to measure the economic growth of a state. Odisha's economy is classified as Agriculture, Industry and Services sectors as per CSO (Central Statistical Office) classification. The Agriculture Sector includes agriculture and animal husbandry, forestry and fisheries. The Industry Sector includes mining and quarrying, manufacturing, electricity, gas and water supply and construction sectors. The Service Sector includes trade, hotels and restaurants, transport, storage, communication, Finance, Insurance, Real Estate, Ownership of dwelling, Business services and Legal services, Community, Social and Personal services including public administration sectors. Mining sector has contributed significantly to GSDP of Odisha as evident from Table 4.2. During entire decade from 2000-12, mining and quarrying sector has contributed on an average of 8.7 per cent to GSDP. This shows that the economy of Odisha has been growing with a vibrantly booming mining sector (Figure 4.1).

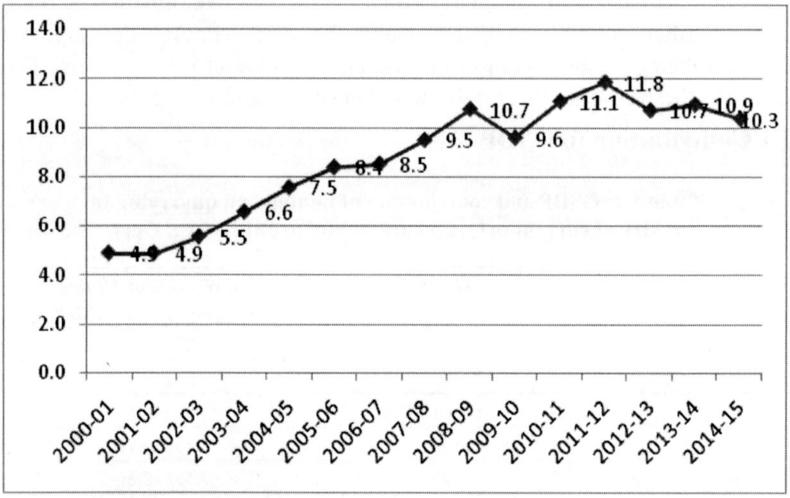

Source: compiled by author.

Figure 4.1: Percentage of contribution of mining sector to GSDP

I.2 Contribution to State Revenue

Mining Royalties and other revenues from minerals and cess on mining royalties together form revenue receipts from mining. Mining revenue has formed an important source of the total revenue of the state. Table 4.3 shows increasing trend of total revenue, Non-tax revenue and mining revenue during 2000-01 to 2009-10. Further it can be seen that mining revenue is contributing 5-7 per cent of total revenue of Odisha. Not only is this, it is also a major contributor of non-tax revenue of which it is having a share of 40-60 per cent. That is to say that half of non-tax revenue is from mining sector. Thus, it is making substantial contribution to state exchequer.

Table 4.3: Percentage of mining revenue to total revenue and non-tax revenue of Odisha from 2000-01 to 2009-10 (₹ in cr)

Year	*Mining revenue*	*Total revenue*	*Non-tax revenue*	*Mining revenue as per cent of total revenue*	*Mining revenue as per cent of non-tax revenue*
2000-01	360.41	6902.02	685.47	5.2	52.6
2001-02	376.45	7047.98	691.75	5.3	54.4
2002-03	443.53	8438.76	961.17	5.3	46.1
2003-04	550.77	9440.24	1094.55	5.8	50.3
2004-05	670.51	11850.19	1345.52	5.7	49.8
2005-06	805	14084.71	1531.9	5.7	52.5
2006-07	936.55	18032.62	2588.12	5.2	36.2
2007-08	1,126.09	21967.19	2653.58	5.1	42.4
2008-09	1,380.59	24610	3176.15	5.6	43.5
2009-10	2020.71	26430	3212.2	7.6	62.9

Source: 1. Economic survey of Odisha 2014-15.
2. Directorate of Mines 2015.

1.3 Contributions to Foreign Exchange Earnings Through Exports

The process of economic growth is a highly complex phenomenon which is influenced by numerous and varied factors; among other factors, openness to international trade is considered as one of the very important contributors to growth (Samuelson and Nordhaus, 2010). *Earning from the trade (foreign exchanges) can be a source of finance for development process*. A country rich in mineral resources by exploiting export-oriented mineral resources can dictate international market and earn huge amount of foreign exchange. Exports from Odisha composed of Metallurgical Products, Engineering, Chemical and allied Products, Mineral Product, Agriculture and Forest Products, Marine Product, Handloom and Textile Product, Handicraft Product, Electronics and Other (Computer Software and Pharmaceutical). Export performance of mineral and ores in Odisha can be judged from Table 4.4 where both total export and value of export has been consistently increasing up to 2010-11. Even the value of mineral exported is showing an upward trend though some decline has been noticed in recent some years due to fluctuation in mineral price in international market. This shows that mining sector is doing well with regard to export of minerals and also helping the state in earning foreign exchange.

Table 4.4: Total export and value of export of minerals in Odisha from 2000-01 to 2013-14.

Year	*Total Exports (in lakh tons)*	*Value of Export (₹ in crore)*
2000-01	36.63	453.8
2001-02	46	538.8
2002-03	58.7	642.2
2003-04	76.4	1186.5
2004-05	171.7	NA
2005-06	146.3	9161.2
2006-07	162	10761.2
2007-08	286.17	8333
2008-09	262.84	7814.64
2009-10	155.89	4760.43
2010-11	247.64	15894.29
2011-12	134.73	4231.79
2012-13	NA	NA
2013-14	91.51	3386.05

Source: Various issues of Economic survey of Odisha.

This section shows that Odisha enjoys comparative advantage of abundance of rich mineral resources. Its contribution to Gross State Domestic Product has been substantial. Mining revenue receipts has been steadily increasing contributing fairly to the state exchequer over last decade. The state has also emerged as a major exporter of mineral products helping the state in earning foreign exchange. This shows that mining sector has significantly contributed financially to the economy of Odisha. Now the question arises whether this monetary contribution has resulted in the development of the people in tribal mining region or not? Whether mining activities has improved the socio-economic condition of tribal? Does mining activities affect the women in proportionate manner in tribal region? Answers to these questions are analysed in the next sections.

II. Impact of Mining on Human Well-being in Tribal District of Odisha

It is inferred from above section that mining has helped the state in making its financial position strong. Whether income generated from this activity has benefitted the people? Thus, the present section will analyse the impact of mining on the people in the tribal districts of Odisha. Odisha is having thirty districts of which production of minerals takes place in eleven districts[1], hence called mining districts. Further, there are nine districts in the state that have 45 per cent or more ST population as per 2011 census. These districts are Gajapati, Koraput, Kandhamal, Malkangiri, Mayurbhanj, Nabarangpur, Rayagada, Sundargarh and Keonjhar. ST population in these districts account for two-third (i.e. 66 per cent) of the state population (Economic Survey of Odisha, 2014-15). Thus, there are five tribal districts that are mineral rich i.e. Koraput, Mayurbhanj, Rayagada, Sundargarh and Keonjhar. Now in order to assess the impact of mining on tribal well being, a comparative study of tribal and non-tribal mining district is done. This section will examine the impact on tribal population based on Human Development Index (HDI).

Human Development Index is a summary indicator of human development which brings together the twin objective of economic progress and social development. It is widely used as a measure of human development based on life expectancy, literacy level, and income level. The HDI values lies in between 0 to 1. HDI value that is more the value is towards 1 when life expectancy at birth is longer, education period is longer and the income per capita is higher. Thus, it is a measure of average achievement in key dimensions of human development: a long and healthy life, being knowledgeable and have a decent standard of living. The three dimensions of HDI are measured as follows: health attainment measured by Infant Mortality Rate (IMR); Knowledge or educational attainment as measured by a combination of adult literacy (with two-thirds weight) and 10–14 years age group literacy rate (one-third weight) and Standard of living as measured by estimated earned income (Odisha Human Development Report, 2004). The present paper has used this index to analyse the impact of mining on the people in tribal region. Table 4.5 shows human development indicators of tribal and non-tribal mining district of Odisha.

Table 4.5: Human Development indicators of tribal and non-tribal mining district in Odisha

District	*HI*	*Infant Mortality Rate*	*II*	*EI*	*HDI Value*
Non-tribal mining district					
Angul	0.481	95	0.748	0.76	0.663
Jajpur	0.333	118	0.499	0.786	0.54
Jharsuguda	0.635	71	0.757	0.773	0.722
Dhenkanal	0.468	97	0.534	0.773	0.591
Sambalpur	0.436	102	0.59	0.742	0.589
Balangir	0.468	97	0.504	0.666	0.546
Tribal mining district					
Keonjhar	0.34	117	0.547	0.704	0.53
Koraput	0.218	136	0.539	0.535	0.431
Mayurbhanj	0.782	48	0.489	0.647	0.639
Sundargarh	0.692	62	0.618	0.74	0.683
Rayagada	0.25	131	0.547	0.531	0.443

Source: 1. Economic Survey of Odisha of various years.
2. Odisha Human Development Report 2004.

Note: HI–Health Index, II–Income Index, EI–Education Index, HDI–Human Development Index.

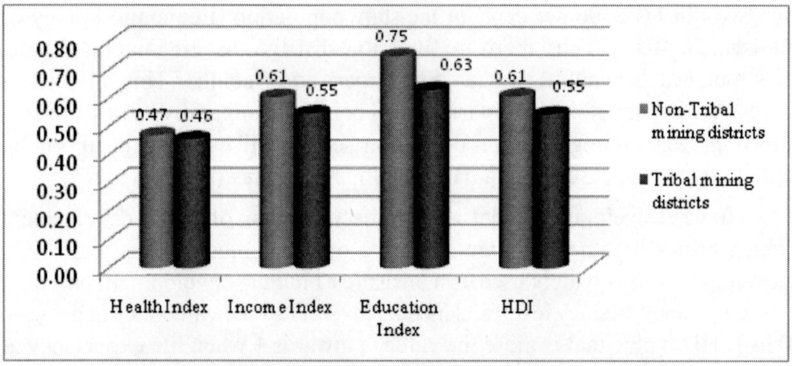

Source: Compiled by author.

Figure 4.2: Average Human Development Indicator in tribal and non-tribal mining district in Odisha

Further it can be seen from Figure 4.2 that non-tribal mining districts enjoy higher Income index and education index than tribal mining districts. That is why HDI value in these regions is higher than tribal mining districts. But the health index is more or less same in all the mining districts whether tribal or non-tribal. Mining has been most hazardous of occupation (Cho and Lee, 1978). Health hazard in mining can be occupational health hazard and environmental health hazard. Mine workers are exposed to occupational health hazard (Giuffrida *et al.*, 2001). In mining, occupation health hazards are especially associated with chemicals. Chemicals posing a physical or health hazard can enter the body via contact, ingestion and inhalation (Donoghue, 2004). In addition to the occupational health effect of mining, people who live close to mining areas may suffer the adverse effects of environment degradation in form of air and water pollution on the health. Mining regions may have a higher prevalence of certain diseases because mining alters the environment and allows disease causing pathogens and vectors to survive more freely than in other environments (Reddy, 2005).

Thus, it can be inferred from the above discussion that it is the non-tribal districts that are more economically and educationally benefited from the operation of mining activities than tribal districts but it is putting a great toll on health life of the local community of both the regions. That is why despite of enjoying high HDI index, non-tribal mining district have health index value more or less same as that of tribal mining district. This shows that while tribal districts are deprived of benefits in terms of higher income and better educational status arising out of mining projects, cost are borne in form of adverse health effect. Now, the question arises, whether these positive and negative impacts of mining proportionately affects the women community in tribal districts. Does the condition of mining women in tribal region are same as that of non-tribal region? These issues are taken up in the next section.

III. Impact of Mining on Women in Tribal Districts of Odisha

Mining affect the population in both positively and negatively. While positive impacts such as higher income, education and community development projects are important, they do not off-set the potential negatives. But did mining activities is proportionately affecting the community as a whole? So the issue now is to find out whether impact of mining is gender neutral or not. In order to assess the gender impact of mining, Gender Development Index has been used. This index adjusts the average achievement to reflect the inequalities between men and women in respect of the same dimensions as reflected in the HDI that is health attainment measured by Infant Mortality Rate (IMR); Knowledge or educational attainment as measured by a combination of adult literacy (with two-thirds weight) and 10–14 years age group literacy rate (one-third weight) and Standard of living as measured by estimated earned income. It is a direct measure of gender gap showing the female HDI as a percentage of the male HDI. The GDI shows how much women are lagging behind their male counterparts and how much women need to catch up within each dimension of human development (United Nation Development Programme, 2015). This index for tribal and non-tribal mining districts is shown in Table 4.6.

Table 4.6: Gender Development Index (GDI) of tribal and non-tribal mining district in Odisha

Non-tribal mining district	*GDI value*
Angul	0.637
Jajpur	0.386
Jharsuguda	0.687
Dhenkanal	0.531
Sambalpur	0.56
Balangir	0.518

Tribal mining district	*GDI value*
Keonjhar	0.504
Koraput	0.415
Mayurbhanj	0.621
Sundargarh	0.659
Rayagada	0.428

Source: Economic Survey of Odisha 2011-12.

As HDI, a GDI value too lies in between 0 to 1. Higher GDI value shows less gender disparity whereas a low value implies high difference between male and female with regard to HDI. Table shows that GDI value in non-tribal districts like Jharsuguda, Angul are high with 0.687 and 0.637 respectively. Similarly, even in tribal districts like Sundargarh and Majurbhanj these values are more than 0.6. Two districts where GDI value is very low are Koraput

(0.415) and Jajpur (0.386). It can be seen from Figure 4.3 that average GDI value in tribal and non-tribal mining region is not very high (0.55 for non-tribal mining region and 0.53 for tribal mining region). A comparative analysis shows that gender disparity is slightly more in tribal mining district than in non-tribal mining district as GDI in non-tribal mining districts (0.55) is more than tribal mining districts (0.52) though the difference is not very large. Since income index and education index is less in tribal dominated mining area and GDI value adjust HDI value for gender inequalities, mining disproportionately affect more the economic and education condition of women in tribal dominated mineral region. With regard to health status, men and women are equally affected by mining activities.

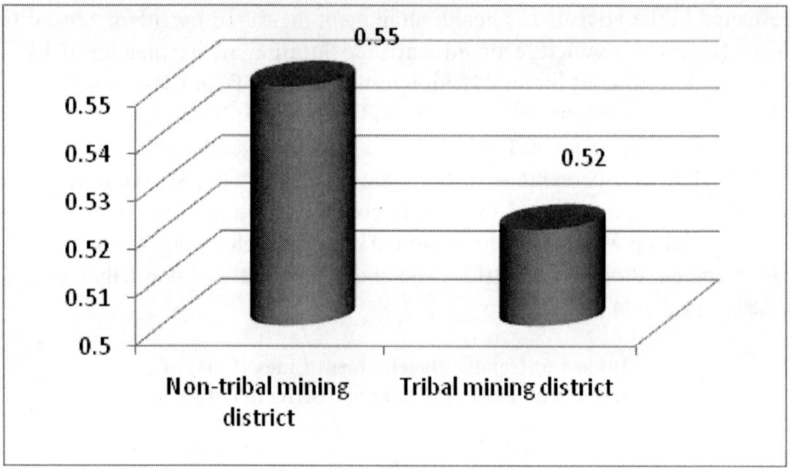

Source: compiled by author.

Figure 4.3: Average Gender Development Index in tribal and non-tribal mining district

Mining operations are often perceived as widening gender disparities within communities (Mining, Minerals and Sustainable Development, 2002). While traditional livelihood systems based on land gave women an important role in agriculture, collection of forest produce, management of livestock and related activities, the immediate offshoot of mining has been a total destruction of this role for them both from land-owning communities and agricultural labourers. There are few job opportunities for women in mining communities. Women mine workers often face discrimination, poor working conditions and unequal pay for equal work. Even the compensation and benefits are paid to men "on behalf of" their families, denying women access to mining's financial benefits and potentially increasing their economic dependence on men (Akabzaa and Darimani, 2001).

The health hazard and degeneration of health condition of women is one of the most serious impacts of mining. Hexavalent chromium is known to adversely affect women's health as it is teratogenic, causing birth defects in foetus, embryo toxic, causes still birth, reduces fertility. A study in manganese mine shows high Infant Mortality Rate and suffering of newborn from neurological problems (Das, 2013). Constant contact with dust and consuming contaminated water cause adverse impact on offspring of pregnant women in mining areas. They are exposed to various respiratory illnesses due to dust particles and become victim of skin diseases, experience malfunction of various sensory organs, which have long-term impact on reproductive health.

Further, the women are at more disadvantageous condition than their men counterparts' particularly in tribal districts. They are seriously and more profoundly affected by mining as GDI value in tribal district is lower than non-tribal region.

IV. Conclusion

It is evident from the present study that digging and selling of minerals in Odisha have strengthened the economic well being in terms of its substantial contribution towards state income. But when its trickledown effect on community is analysed on the basis of human development parameters, it is seen that non-tribal mining areas are comparatively better in terms of income and educational attainment than tribal regions. But mining affects more or less in the same degree in both the regions. That is why average HDI value in tribal mining district has lower than its non-tribal counterparts. The study while analysing the impact of mining on gender founds that women often experience the negative impacts of mining more than men. The key areas in which mining operations impact women disproportionately are economic conditions, educational and health status. Further, as gender disparity is lower in non-tribal mining area than tribal regions, tribal women are affected more due to extraction of minerals. Thus, the impacts of mining are not gender–neutral, pronounced more in tribal region than in non-tribal regions. The present study supports those works that have found mining activities to be gender biased (Sharma, 2010; Lahiry- Dutt and Mahy; Hinton, 2011).

Since women play an important role in the house and community and also have the right to equality, this problem deserves serious attention. A consideration of gender is a prerequisite for truly sustainable decisions (Goudie and Kilian, 1996). There are no laws which specifically protect the rights of women's health in mining, either as communities or as workers. A gender audit should be carried out in mining regions and should prove how sustainable mining is to women. Before sanctioning any mining projects, administrative machinery should have a long-term plan and assessment of the cost benefits of such projects from the perspectives of labour and livelihoods considering gender equity. Social impact assessments are needed to monitor and analyse impacts of the structures and functioning of the mining jobs and the communities. In particular, there is a need for a holistic, interdisciplinary examination of the interplay of work, family and community in mining regions to suggest strategies for the enhancement of human and social capital of women in the communities. Strategies emphasis on the empowerment of women by increasing their capacity to equitably participate in, control and influence the aspects of society that affect their lives should be designed. Thus, issues of women are needs to be addressed urgently and calls for gender analysis and planning which will contribute towards sustainable development and gender justice.

Notes

Angul, Keonjhar, Jharsuguda, Koraput, Jajpur, Sundergarh, Sambalpur, Bolangir, Mayurbhanj, Rayagada, Dhenkenal are the eleven mining districts in Odisha.

References

Akabzaa, T. and Darimani, A. 2001. 'Impact of mining sector investment in Ghana: A study of the tarkwa mining region', Report Prepared for South Asia Policy and Research Institute. Retrieve from http://www.saprin.org/ghana/research/gha_mining.pdf on 11/08/2016.

Aroca, P. 2001. 'Impacts and Development in Local Economies Based on Mining: The Case of the Chilean II Region' Resources policy, 27(2):119-134.

Bhanumathi, K. 2003. 'Women and Mining in India', Paper presented at the Oxfam Community Aid Abroad International Conference of Women in Mining, Melbourne.Retrievefromhttp://www.samataindia.org.in/documents/Status%20of%20Women%20Affected%20by%20Mining%20in%20India.PDFon 11/08/2016.

Bhusan, C. and Hazra, M. Z. 2008. 'Rich Lands Poor People: Is 'Sustainable Mining' Possible? State of India's environment 6th Citizens' Report, New Delhi: Centre for Science and Environment.

Bose, S. 2004. 'Positioning women within the environmental justice framework: A case for the mining sector', Gender, Technology and Development, 8(3):407-12.

Brunnschweiler, C.N. 2008. 'Cursing the blessings? Natural resource abundance, institutions, and economic growth', World Development, 36: 399-419.

Cho, K.S. and Lee, S. H. 1978, 'Occupational health hazard of mine worker', Bulletin of the WHO, 56(2):205-218.

Connell, J and Howitt, R. (eds.) 1991. 'Mining and Indigenous Peoples in Australasia'. Sydney: Sydney University Press.

Das, M. 2013. 'Impact of mining on women's health', in Mishra, P and Das A (eds.), Mining: Economic, Environmental and Social Implications (132-147), New Delhi: Abhijit Publications.

Davis, G. A. and Tilton J. E. 2005. 'The Resource Curse', Natural Resources Forum, 29: 233-242.

Directorate of Mines, 2015. 'Revenue from different minerals in Odisha', Ministry of Mines and Steel, Odisha. Retrieve from http://www. orissaminerals.gov.in/Mines/MineralRevenue.aspx? GL=revenue&PL=3 on 11/08/2016.

Donoghue, A. M. 2004. 'Occupational health hazards in mining: an overview', Occupational Medicine, 54: 283-289.

Economic Survey of Odisha, 2011-12. Planning and coordination department, Directorate of Economic and Statistic, Government of Odisha.

Economic Survey of Odisha, 2014-15. Planning and coordination department, Directorate of Economic and Statistic, Government of Odisha.

Economic Survey of Odisha of various issues, 1991-92 to 2014-15. Planning and coordination department, Directorate of Economic and Statistic, Government of Odisha.

Ejdemo, T. and Soderholm, P. 2011. 'Mining investment and regional development: A scenario-based assessment for Northern Sweden', Resources Policy, 36: 14-21.

Federation of Indian Chambers of Commerce and Industry, 2013. Development of Indian Mining Industry-The Way Forward. Mines and Metal Division. New Delhi: FICCI Retrieve from http://ficci.in/spdocument/20317/mining-industry.pdf on 11/08/2016.

Gibson, G and Kemp, D. 2008. 'Corporate engagement with Indigenous women in the minerals industry: making space for theory', In C O'Faircheallaigh and A Saleem (eds), Earth Matters: Indigenous Peoples, the Extractive Industries and Corporate Social Responsibility (104–122). Sheffield, UK: Greenleaf Publishing.

Gibson, G. and Klinck, J. 2005. 'Canada's Resilient North: The Impact of Mining on Aboriginal Communities', Pimatisiwin: A Journal of Aboriginal and Indigenous Community Health, 3(1). Retrieve from http://caid.ca/JAICH2005v3n1p115.pdf on 11/08/2016.

Giuffrida, A., Iunes, R. F. and Savedoff, W. D. 2001. 'Economic and Health Effects of Occupational Hazards in Latin America and the Caribbean', A Joint Paper of Regional Department and the Sustainable Development Department, Inter-American Development Bank Washington, D. C. Retrieve from http://services.iadb.org/wmsfiles/products/Publications/353816.pdf on 11/08/2016.

Goudie, S. and Kilian, D. 1996. 'Gender and environmental impact assessment', Agenda, 29: 43–54.

Government of Odisha. 2007. State of the Environment Report-Odisha. Centre for Environment Studies, Department of forest and environment. Retrieve from http://www.moef.nic.in/soer/state/SoE-orissa.pdf on 11/08/2016.

Hajkowicz, S.A., Heyenga, S. and Moffat, K. 2011. 'The relationship between mining and socio-economic well-being in Australia's regions', Resources Policy, 36(1): 30–38.

Hinton, J.J. 2011. 'Gender differentiated impacts and benefits of artisal mining: Engendering pathways out of poverty-A case study in Katwe Kabatooro Town council, Uganda', Thesis submitted to University of British Columbia. Retrieve from https://circle.ubc.ca/bitstream/id/.../ubc_2011_fall_hinton_jennifer.pdf on 11/08/2016.

Kamble, E R. 2004. 'A Guide to Indigenous Women's Rights under the International Convention on the Elimination of All Forms of Discrimination against Women'. Moreton-in-Marsh (UK): Forest Peoples Programme. Retrieve from http://www.forestpeoples.org/sites/fpp/files/publication/2010/10 cedawguidejan04 eng.pdf on 11/08/2016.

Kangwa, P. K. and Lekunze, R. 2008. 'An Assessment of the Economic, Social and Environmental Impacts of the Mining Industry-A Case Study of Copper Mining in Zambia', Lund University. Retrieve from http://www.lumes.lu.se/sites/lumes.lu.se/files/kaela_kangwa.pdf as on 11/08/2016.

Lahiri-Dutt, K. and Mahy, P. 2007. 'Impact of mining on women and youth in Indonesia: two mining locations in East Kalimantan'. Retrieve from https://crawford.anu.edu.au/pdf/staff/rmap/lahiridutt/CR3_KLD_Mahy_Impacts_Mining_Indonesia.pdf on 11/08/2016.

Mcmahon, G. and Moreira, S. 2014. 'The contribution of the mining sector to socioeconomic and human development', Extractive industries for development working paper, World Bank. Retrieve from https://commdev.org/userfiles/Mining%20and%20Human%20Development.pdf on 10/08/2016.

McMahon, G. and Remy, F. 2001. 'Large Mines and the Community-Socioeconomic and Environmental Effects in Latin America, Canada and Spain', Ottawa: International Development Research Centre and Washington D.C: World Bank. Retrieve from http://lib.icimod.org/record/10806/files/1606.pdf on 11/08/2016.

Mining, Minerals and Sustainable Development. 2002. 'Breaking New Ground', Report by International Institute for Environment and Development. Retrieve from http://www.iied.org/mmsd-final-report on 11/08/2016.

Odisha Human Development Report. 2004. Nabakrushna Choudhury Centre for Development Studies, Planning and Coordination Department, Government of Odisha.

Parra, C. and Weldegiorgis, F. S. 2015. 'Mining Development and opportunities for poverty reduction and human development in Latin America' Retrieve from http://papers.ssrn.com/sol3/papers.cfm?abstract_id=2699021 on 10/08/2016.

Pendergast, S. M., Clark, J. A. and Kooten, G. C.V. 2011. 'Corruption, Development and curse of Natural resources', Canadian journal of political science, 44(2): 411-437.

Reddy, S.G. 2005. 'A comparative analysis of diseases associated with mining and non-mining communities: A case study of Obusai and Asankrangwa, Ghana', Thesis submitted to University of Texas. Retrieve from http://digital.library.unt.edu/ ark /67531/metadc4839/m1/3/ on 11/08/2016.

Sahoo, A.K., Sahu, N.C, Sahoo, D. and Pradhan, B.B. (2014). 'Mineral export and economic growth in India: Evidence from VAR model analysis', Mineral Economics, 27(1):51-58.

Samal, R. and Patra, S. 2015. 'Standards of living of tribes in Kondhamal district of Odisha', EPRA Journal of Economic and Business Review, 3(2):40-46

Sharma, S. 2010. 'The impact of mining on women: lessons from the coal mining Bowen Basin of Queensland, Australia', Impact Assessment and Project Appraisal, 28(3): 201-215.

Stilwell, L.C, Minnitt, R. C. A., Monson, T. D. and Kuhn, G. 2000. 'An input-output analysis of the impact of mining on the South African economy', Resources Policy, 26:17-30.

Tauli-Corpuz, V. 1997. 'The Globalisation of Mining and its Impact and Challenges for Women', Paper presented at conference on 'Women and Mining, Baguio city, Phillippines. Retrieve from http://www.twn.my/title/mining-cn.htm on 11/08/2016

UNDP 2015.'Human Development Report'. Retrieve from http://hdr.undp.org/sites/default/files/hdr2015_technical_notes.pdf on 11/08/2016.

Ye, Q. 2008. 'Commodity booms and their impacts on the Western Australian economy: The iron ore case', Resources Policy, 33:83-101.

Chapter - 5

Gender and Globalisation: Some Policy Implications

—Saket Bihari

The understanding of globalisation would not be complete unless the issue of gender equity gets proper space in the fulcrum of development. There are reasons for this. One of the pertinent reasons is about locating the significance of 'female gender' at par with 'male' in terms of their participation in workforce. As the Indian economy is growing, the work opportunity among women appears to be vulnerable because of their marginalisation. In order to promote the status of women in the country, the issue of gender budgeting has been devised. The expectation from gender budgeting that with its effective and focused agenda, it will bring about desirable changes in the status of women stands half fulfilled because of lack of coordination between planning and implementation. A lot is needs to be done. The dominant male society has apparently praised their work outside the household boundaries but within the walls of the household, they have mostly been victimised with inhuman practices and atrocities. The need of the hour is to ensure a dignified pace for women so that they can freely express their choices in terms of job selection and realistic aspirations.

Historically, the builders and architects of modern India have always dreamt of the quest for social justice and equity in terms of women empowerment. Attempts have also been made in the past to sensitise about gender discourse and to put it into mainstream as well. But for all practical purposes, the plight of gender sensitisation has always been critical due to reinforcement and re-assertion of male as the pivot in shaping and reshaping all structural configurations in the given social set up. Even after ample shed on gender, the conceptual construct of hoi polloi has not been flushed out from the stereotypical patterns. In all known human societies, gender has been orchestrated on power matrix where physical superiority has played an instrumental role to gain an edge and advantage. The physical superiority drove all epochs of history to finally take a turn as to where men and women are to be placed. The intricate emerging hierarchies within the gender framework demand serious and logical considerations. Thus, the paper aims at locating the issue of gender in the light of globalisation process at grass root level. To perpetually participate in globalisation is to appreciate the tenants of sustainable development fruitfully which requires the equal participation of the weaker sex. With the historical narration on gender, the paper with its effective arguments shows the social segment is needed to mainstream women in equitable gender discourse.

Key Words: *Globalisation, Gender Budgeting, Equity, Development, Empowerment.*

Introduction

The understanding of globalisation would not be complete unless the issue of gender equity gets space in the fulcrum of development. There are reasons for this. One of the pertinent reasons is about locating the significance of 'female gender' at par with 'male' in terms of their participation in workforce. As the Indian economy is growing, the work opportunity among women appears to be vulnerable because of their marginalisation. In order to promote the status of women in our country, the issue of gender budgeting has been devised. The gender budgeting with its effective and focused agenda to bring about desirable changes in the status of women stands half way touched because the coterminous connection between planning out and working out have not been adjusted well. A lot is needed to be done. The dominant male society has apparently praised them but in the household they have mostly been victimised with inhuman practices and atrocities. The need of the hour is to ensure a dignified pace for women so that they can freely express their choices in terms of job selection and realistic aspirations.

Historically, all builders and architects of modern India have always dreamt of the quest for social justice and equity in terms of women empowerment. The sufficient attempts have also been put in to mainstream the gender in academic discourses, as well. But for all practical purposes, the plight in gender sensitisation has always been critical due to reinforcement and re-assertion of male as the pivot in shaping and reshaping all structural configurations in the given social set up. Even after ample shed on gender, the conceptual construct of hoi polloi has not been flushed out from the stereotypical patterns. In all known human societies, gender has been orchestrated on power matrix where physical superiority has played an instrumental role to gain an edge and advantage. The physical superiority drove all epochs of history to finally take a turn as to where men and women are to be placed. The intricate emerging hierarchies within the gender framework demand serious and logical considerations. Thus, the paper aims at locating the issue of gender in the light of globalisation process at grass root level. To perpetually participate in globalisation is to appreciate the tenants of sustainable development fruitfully which requires the equal participation of the weaker sex. With the historical narration on gender, the paper with its effective arguments shows the social segment is needed to mainstream women in equitable gender discourse.

Women and Globalisation: A Conceptual Framework

In recent years, globalisation has had a huge impact on the lives of women in developing nations. Indian women are no exception to this. Globalisation may be deployed to describe as a complex economic, political, cultural, and geographic process in which the mobility of capital, organisations, ideas, discourses, and peoples have taken a global or transnational form. The global economic institutions are seen to be privileging Western culture and political norms, and present them as models for the rest of the world, while ignoring and marginalising women's indigenous movements in developing part at the globe. Recent feminist's philosophers contend that neo-liberalism prioritises on economic growth, efficiency, and profit making over other values such as the promotion of economic justice and enhancing democracy and good governance.

Globalisation has created labour demand patterns which implicitly favour short-term, temporary employment. As a result, a short-term contracted labour migration appears to be rising with distinct gender differentiated repercussions. Migrant women are increasingly victims of trafficking, for the purpose of sexual exploitation. Due to the lack of effective mechanisms to regulate and protect the rights of labour, they move across national borders. Both legal and illegal migrants are vulnerable to human rights abuses. The impact of globalisation on democracy and governance has resulted in reduced political influence of women on the whole, especially at the level of global politics because global economic institutions are not adequately representative. At policy level, the effective impact of globalisation on women and gender relations seemingly continues to be neglected. It largely happens at the level of policy implementation. It is important to integrate gender equality dimensions in the normative, policy and operational work so as to ensure the continuing leadership of the system in promoting gender equality, development and peace within the context of globalisation where the civilisation part of our society has to grow.

In many ways globalisation has been central to the process of emerging development in India. The ruthless game of globalisation can only go at the cost of flesh and blood of ordinary people, the vulnerable are offered on its altar. People do not hesitate to use members of their own kind, so long as they faces remain invisible, in support of their own interest. For a patriarchal, capitalist, consumerist, globalise society, the lives of women and children become expandable. Moreover, globalisation has opened up broader communication lines and brought more companies as well as different worldwide organisations into India. This provides opportunities for not only working men but also women who become a larger part of the workforce. With new jobs for women, there are opportunities for higher pay, which raises self confidence and brings about independence. This has potential to promote equality between the sexes, something that Indian women have striven for. Thus, globalisation as a dynamic force has the power to uproot the traditional views towards women so they can become equal stakeholders. In sharp contrast with rural India, women in urban India have become more independent and self sufficient. The lower middle class is experiencing a shift in the way family relation works. Traditionally women stay at home taking care of domestic needs and children. Most of the urban women are setting out to earn their livelihoods. In order to cope up with advertisement enabled family needs, women have stepped out for jobs. They have gained a new momentum of efficiency in the fulcrum of household requirements.

Globalisation has made many international corporations richer. Women are suffering in globalised region because of the corporate empires. "Women work two-third of the world's working hours, produce half of the world's food, but earn only ten per cent of the world's income, and own less than one per cent of the world's property"[1]. The work available to women is almost always poorly paid, mentally and physically unhealthy, demeaning, or insecure. The impact of globalisation on women, to some extent, sounds to be adverse in the sense that they face role inconsistency while practicing life. They are forced by circumstances to work as the labour force on lower wages and they also handle household jobs which go unpaid. "The mixture of corporate capitalism and Western culture models is dissolving family and community social controls as witnessed by higher rates of family violence, rape, divorce and family breakdown"[2].

Globalisation as a comprehensive tool for development influences women in many ways. One of the ways influencing globalisation is to bring women in market economy. Market economy attempts to accumulate unlimited profit. In order to do so, capitalists tend to harness maximum human resource. In the course of harnessing labour force, they ask the workers to follow overtime norms. The overtime norm seems to be a tool for their exploitation where commodityfication of human value becomes an experience in every, now and then. When they pass through this tyranny, they face acute level of conflict in their everyday life, as role expectations are brutally natural to be addressed.

Enabling Factors of Globalisation

There are various factors which promote the process of globalisation. The cheaper, deeper and faster modes of mass communications have enabled and fuelled the pace of globalisation. Transport is much cheaper and faster. This is not only aircraft and roadways, but also ships. Very significantly, the development of containerisation in the 1950s was a major breakthrough in goods handling, and there have been continuing improvements to shipping technology since then. Many rules and regulations in business were waived off, especially rules regarding foreign ownership. Privatisation also took place, and large areas of business were now open to purchase and/or take-over.

This led to the allowed businesses in one country to buy goods and services. The movement of money from one country to another is also controlled by monopolistic market operation. This allowed businesses to move money from one country to another in a search for better business returns; if investment in one's own country looks unattractive, a business can buy businesses in another country in the larger ambit of globalisation process. Many barriers to trade have been removed. Some of this has been done by regional groupings of countries such as the EU. Most of it has been done by the WTO. This makes trade cheaper and therefore more attractive to business. Consumer tastes have changed, and consumers are more willing to try foreign products. The arrival of global satellite television, for example, has exposed consumers to global advertising. Consumers are more aware of what is available in other countries, and are keen to give it a try. There has been high growth of incomes in globalised countries, which makes large consumer markets with money to spend. Despite of India's slow economic development, Indian middle classes are doing very well and have money to spend. Although these classes are small in the context of our country, the overall populations are so huge that a small middle class adds up to many millions of consumers. Women from middle class do enjoy the equity in social resources but their participation seems to be lower in volume and content.

Moreover, five cultural flows that anchor the imagined world being promoter of globalisation are: '*ethnoscapes, mediascapes, technoscapes, financescapes* and *ideoscapes*'[3]. Ethnoscapes refers to landscapes inhibited by those human groups who live constantly on the move even if they have to settle in a single place. This space includes a variety of nomadic individuals ranging from refugees to tourists. Mediascapes are produced by the mass 'mediatic' systems and products-such as newspapers, magazines, films, among others-which disseminate information at a global level. Technoscapes are those landscapes dominated by the diffusion of both mechanical and informational technologies around the world. Financescapes, on the other hand, form the transitional texture of economic relations created by the increasing flow of capital movements. Finally, ideoscapes refer to the landscape of political ideologies and imagery often associated with a particular state or social movement, and includes the different discourses about freedom, democracy, human rights and so on. In the context of ethnoscapes, women live constantly on the move. Even if they settle in a single place, they pay their loyalty to multiple ethnic spheres. The move of male members in search of employment opportunities provided by globalisation process also influences the life course of family members particularly women. It gives rise to several innovative practices. One of them is women owning households. It forces women to take decision without the help of their male counterparts.

Mediascape as an instrument to disseminate information through magazines, and newspapers influences women empowerment. As per the latest

Census in the year 2011, the total female sex ratio in India is 940 per 1000 males. The population of India is more than 1.21 billion and out of this, women constitute nearly 50 per cent of the total population. With the growing dominance of the Internet, blog, chat, social sites etc, the use of mass media has begun and consequently, communication is rapidly evolving, changing and experimenting with itself. Internet has served as a vehicle or as a channel to convey information in a useful and easy to understand manner. This extraordinary revolution is affecting the basic structure of societies particularly the issues related to women. The rapid transformation of the boundaries between the public and the private spaces, the relationship between the new media and women's empowerment are gradually gaining grounds all around. Media is considered as an important source in helping the women empowered. It is helping as the important source and access to speak out against the oppression and marginalisation of women at the grass root level. The media is considered as the most potent and influential mean, as it has the capacity of persuading and molding opinion. The relationship of the media and the women is important because whatever image women have in our country is influenced by media. It is vital, to utilise the media for the promotion of status of women in India and divulging their roles in national development.

In the context of knowledge sphere, the issues of gender equality, equity and empowerment of women become even more significant as women have a strategic role in incubation and transfer of critical knowledge, which often forms the blue print for survival of communities to depth and minimise their risk in adverse circumstances. Women, because of their biological and social roles, are generally more rooted than men in the confines of their locality. They are therefore more aware then men of the social, economic and environmental needs of their own communities. The media is considered as the most effective and important tool in this regard as it has the power of molding public opinion. All over the world, the impact of media and new media has been witnessed in recent years, with online platforms becoming increasingly powerful mechanisms for mobilising popular support. People in India are demanding change, and they are harnessing the power of modern media to make their voices heard. Right information given by the media can empower the rural women and protect them from various forms of tyranny. The media enabled tools such as blogs; face book, social sites and internet are used for empowering the women by education, information, awareness, economic empowerment and self decision making. Thus, mediascape as an effective enabling tool of globalisation influences women immensely.

Technoscape as a diffused landscape of mechanical and information technology influences women enormously. In the recent years the public-private divide is being deeply rearticulated, for instance by the emergence of forms of public intimacy challenging the taken for granted identification between privacy and intimacy. Transformations in gender relations and the widespread uses of new technologies of communication and information are two important agents in this process. These relations can be thought as choreographies, in which women, men and digital devices play a dance where their positions and gestures depend on the positions and gestures of the other players, where contemporary digital devices and application remediate heterosexual couples relations and the production of couple intimacy is the result of the shared agency between people and devices enacted in everyday life digital practices. The inhibition-exhibition relation to gendered expression of conflicts, disquiet, vulnerabilities and empowerment provide enabling space for re-articulation of intimacy. In fact, mobile phones are becoming a player in the game of designing and defending territories. Such as men's inhibition from the domestic realm and from the accessibility and availability obligations an expectations set around mobile phone use; or women's inhibition from "annoying" their male partners with their calls and messages. The gendered way in conjunction with mobile telephony affordances and constraints, are producing the contextual norms and expectations which set the condition for privacy, or the lack of it, within current couple intimacies. In this play gender choreographies are not symmetrical; women appear to be more explicitly and tightly subjected to gendered norms, particularly related to the dynamics of inhibition-exhibition, as it is expressed in the myth of "feminine discretion". But both women and men have to deal with that tension, although from different positions and attitudes. This becomes largely acute when placed at the mechanical and information driven landscapes i.e. technoscape.

Financescape as a form of transitional texture of economic relations created by the increasing flow of capital movements influences the status of women by putting them in the workforce. In order to meet social necessities, now women are also stepping out for the jobs where market economy governs their positions. Financescape enables everyone to be the companion along with monetary flows. The migration within and outside India has been the resultant of capital flow where employment opportunity seems to be a major concern. In 1960, more women were classified as dependents, whether or not they were financially independent, and moved for family reunification purposes. Today, a higher percentage leaves for economic opportunities. Of course, not all migration is voluntary: millions are forced to move due to war, civil unrest or coercion- an issue the global community has been working to address. And even for some voluntary migrants—particularly females—conditions are not always positive. Some migrants, disempowered by poverty, or discriminated against by ethnicity or sex, may be exploited or trafficked. So finacescape may provide an impetus for the betterment of women by engaging them in gainful employment opportunities but this incentivisation may also be accompanied with all sorts of human exploitations. Finacesacpe as one of the promoters of globalisation goes with possible opportunities but to some degree of ethical crisis too.

Ideoscape as the landscape of political ideologies and imagery is associated with a particular state or social movement, and different discourses about freedom, democracy, human rights have specific implications influencing the status of women. In Indian household dimensions, women are considered as dependent entity. As a young child, she lives under the protection of her father or guardians. As a wife she lives under the protection of her husband and acts as his partner, advisor and helper. As a mother she nurtures her children and shapes their destiny. Even after implementations of effective laws and provisions to safeguard women's freedom and liberty, they are confined to restrictive conditions and stipulated that women should not meet any men outside her family without a family member present. The fathomless rural-urban divide as the enabling factor of class polarisation defines their freedom and expressions of ideas differently. The rich women get the power of distinction from the poor ones. The upper class women relatively enjoy better public space than the lower class women. The same can also be traced along Indian cultural lines. It becomes acute when the mismatch between bride-groom ages perpetrates hardships on women and resulting in their helplessness.

On most of the occasions, the labour rendered by women is not rated equal in terms of remuneration. Most often than not, domestic labour rendered by women is not efficiently counted. They are devoid of suffrage in rural areas, as they are not allowed to participate in the public domain. So their democratic rights get abrogated. If we look at the status of women in the light of Millennium Development Goals, the impression becomes more dismal. Though ideoscape as an enabling factor of globalisation attempting to bring about changes in the larger ambit of social movement, and different discourses about freedom, democracy, human rights; the effective steps are required to bring them to mainstream so that they never need piece to wipe out their tears.

Globalisation: Gender Implications

With advent of globalisation, world seems to have become an inclusive place where information is to be disseminated and integration, be achieved. It is happening in the larger fulcrum of greater trade openness which is translating into growing global economic integration and interdependence, as transnational movements of people and capital accelerate and information in the most accessible manner. Technological developments are rapidly changing the way people learn, work, and communicate. It enables people to be on move. Migration is a vivid expression of this movement. Thus, migration of people becomes an obvious reality. The movement which incorporates women becomes more vulnerable.

The new forces associated with globalisation understood as the combination of economic integration, technological diffusion, and greater access to information and have operated through markets, formal institutions, and informal institutions to lift some of the constraints to greater gender equality. Openness in trade, the diffusion of new information and communication technologies (ICTs) have translated into more jobs and stronger connections to markets for many women, increasing their access to economic opportunities. At some states and sectors, women's wages have also increased relative to those of men. Gender inequality has more costs in an integrated world. It can diminish countries' ability to compete internationally, particularly for countries with export potential in goods and services with high female employment. And given growing global awareness of women's rights, continued gender inequality can also damage a country's international standing. All these strengthen to the incentives for policy action toward gender equality around the world. Greater access to information has allowed many in developing countries to learn about life and mores in other parts of the world, including those pertaining to the role of women, possibly affecting attitudes and behaviours. A shift toward more egalitarian gender roles and norms has also been facilitated in some cases, reinforced by women's economic empowerment. But in the absence of an effective public policy, globalisation alone cannot promote gender equality. Despite significant increases in agency and in access to economic opportunities for women, the increasing tide has not lifted everybody. Those often left behind are women for whom the existing constraints are most binding. That is why pan-Indian action is required to be aimed at closing existing gender gaps in endowments, agency, and access to economic opportunities. This is necessary for our society to fully capitalise on the potential of globalisation as a force for development and greater gender equality.

Very significantly, with the help of underlying scapes women enjoy a mix taste of globalisation where social equity and justice are not necessarily in public policy. Mobile phones, the Internet, and others communication technologies, such as radio, are providing new platforms to disseminate information and increase access to services among those in remote or underserved areas and among those with lower mobility. Because women are overrepresented in these groups, they tend to benefit disproportionately from these initiatives even when the initiatives are not necessarily targeted to women. Mobile phone technology provides access to financial services, such as processing money transfers and small payments, and promotes savings. Text messaging provides women and health workers valuable information about pre- and postnatal care, nutrition, and ongoing treatments. Some health services have been combined with other tools to promote savings to pay for the cost of prenatal care and delivery. Mobile phones and the Internet also promote literacy and facilitate access to distance education, particularly higher and vocational education. Beyond access to services, mobile phones and the Internet allow women to be more connected to each other and their communities and to have a stronger social and political voice. Most of these initiatives are fairly new and have not yet been evaluated. Moving forward, it will be important to learn more about what works and what does not in each context and to continue experimenting to fully capitalise on the potential power of new technologies.

Women and Sustainable Development

Sustainable development refers to a development process which enhances peoples' capacity to create and consume wealth on a lasting basis. Learn, educate, conserve and recycle are the mantra of sustainable development. Sustainable development requires, among other things, a socio-economic, political and cultural environment which enables people to engage in and sustain the development process. The political system ought to provide stability to allow people to engage in production. Intra-ethnic conflicts, tribal wars and social tensions, as well as denial of basic human rights, constrain efforts to promote sustainable development. The social relationships between individuals and communities can either promote or constrain sustainable development. Social security is thus one of the necessary prerequisites for promoting sustainable development.

Besides social security, there is a need for economic freedom. Economic freedom in this context refers to a condition which enables people to utilise their innovative and creative capacities in the development process; protects individual economic rights to have access to productive assets, including land rights; provides a right to control one's labour in terms of decisions to engage in economic activity of one's choice; and conveys a right to control the fruits of one's labour. It also implies a right to gainful employment.

In ideal conditions, therefore, women, like men, need political stability which guarantees protection of their basic human rights, social security to be able to engage in productive activities, the right to develop and utilise their talents, fair pay for the work they perform, and the right to participate in the management of their societies as intellectuals, policy-makers, producers and consumers. Policy-makers and planners have failed to address the socially structured subordination of women to men. Unequal division of labour, legal discrimination against women and abuse of women's basic human rights have been more or less ignored by policy-makers and planners, despite the lip service paid to the elimination of sexual discrimination.

In brief, plans and policies have not been "gender responsive." That is, they have not recognised existing gender imbalances, and have not taken into account the different gender roles which men and women play. Women are therefore constrained in participating effectively in the development process because their subordinate position in society is ignored in development planning and policy making, while their concrete needs are equally ignored. This is reflected in the manner in which resources are allocated and utilised.

HDIs and Gender: Public Policy Implications

The ranking of countries on human development indices presented in Global Human Development Reports annually since 1990 has captured the imagination of policy makers, development practitioners and civil society alike. Progress on the Human Development Index (HDI) is often cited in national and international debates as a benchmark of a country's progress on key development indicators. The 2010 UNDP Global Human Development Report aimed at capturing the distributional dimensions of human development. Three dimensions of HDI i.e. income, education and health were adjusted for inequalities in attainments across people. Globally, India is ranked 119 out of 169 countries but loses 32 per cent of its value when adjusted for inequalities. Amidst growing concern over these persistent inequalities, and in light of government emphasis on inclusive growth, much needed to be done to establish equality of the values in all Indian states.

The HDI computed using the global goalposts, classifies ten states as medium human development states, while nine are low human development states. The medium human development states show an average loss of 28 per cent as a result of inequalities, while low human development states show 33 per cent loss due to inequalities on an average. This indicates that the human development outcomes alone sans inequalities measurement may mask the performance of states in a significant manner. An analysis of the impact of inequalities at a disaggregated level reveals that inequalities in the education dimension are the highest, which is in consonance with the findings of the HDR 2010. It calls for a special focus on areas and social groups that continue to face constraints in accessing education. Similarly, the inequalities are also high in the case of health. Many studies have pointed out marked differences in access to healthcare and its utilisation. In both education and health, not only is the attainment of people low, but also the extent of inequality remains high.

Legal Provisions and Gender Justice

A number of schemes have been launched by Government of India to foster women empowerment such as, *Beti Bachao Beti Padhao*, One Stop Centre Scheme, Women Helpline Scheme, Ujjawala: A Comprehensive Scheme for Prevention of Trafficking and Rescue, Rehabilitation and Re-integration of victims of Trafficking and Commercial Sexual Exploitation, Working Women Hostel, Rajiv Gandhi National Crèche Scheme for the Children of Working Mothers, *SWADHAR Greh* (A Scheme for Women in Difficult Circumstances), Revision under IGMSY in accordance with National Food Security Act, 2013 in Twelfth Plan, Support to Training and Employment Programme for Women (STEP), NARI SHAKTI PURASKAR and so on.

State Governments have also taken up steps to address the problems of women, such as LADLI Scheme, *Mukhmantri Balika* Bicycle Yojana and so on. Legal provisions have also been laid out to ensure gender equality. The principle of gender equality is enshrined in the Indian constitution in its preamble, fundamental rights, fundamental duties and directive principles. The constitution not only grants equality to women, but also empowers the state to adopt measures of positive discrimination in favour of women. Within the framework of democratic polity, our laws, development policies, plans and programmes have aimed at women's advancement in different spheres. Our country has also ratified various international conventions and human rights instruments committing to secure equal rights of women. Key among them is the ratification of the convention on elimination of all forms of discrimination against women (CEDAW) in 1993.

The Constitution of India not only grants equality to women but also empowers the state to adopt measures of positive discrimination in favour of women for neutralising the cumulative socio-economic, education and political disadvantages faced by them. Fundamental rights, among others, ensure equality before the law and equal protection of law; prohibits discrimination against any citizen on grounds of religion, race, caste, sex or place of birth, and guarantee equality of opportunity to all citizens in matters relating to employment. Articles 14, 15, 15(3), 16, 39 (c) and 42 of the constitution are of specific importance in this regard.

Constitutional Privileges available to women are as under:

1. Equality before law for women (Article 14),
2. The state not to discriminate against any citizen on grounds only of religion, race, caste, sex, place of birth or any of them (Article 15 (i)),
3. Equality of opportunity for all citizens in matters relating to employment or appointment to any office under the state (Article 16),
4. The state to make any provision in favour of women and children (Article 15 (3)),
5. To promote justice, on a basis of equal opportunity and to provide free legal aid by suitable legislation or scheme or any in any other way to ensure that opportunities for securing justice are not denied to any citizen by reason of economic or other disabilities (Article 39A),
6. The state to direct its policy towards securing for men and women equally the right to an adequate means of livelihood (Article 39(a)); and equal pay for equal work for both men and women (Article 39(d)),
7. The state to make provision for securing just and humane conditions of work and for maternity relief (Article 42),
8. The state to promote with special care and educational and economic interests of weaker sections of the people and to protect them from social injustice and all forms of exploitation (Article 46),

9. The state to raise the level of nutrition and the standard of living of its people (Article 47),
10. To promote harmony and the spirit of common brotherhood amongst all the people of India and to renounce practices derogatory to the dignity of women (Article 51(A) (e)),
11. Not less than one third (including the number of seats reserved for women belonging to the scheduled castes and scheduled tribes) of the total number of seats to be filled by direct election in every Panchayat to be reserved for women and such seats to be allotted by rotation to different constituencies in Panchayat (Articles 243 D (3)),
12. Not less than one-third of the total number of office of chairpersons in the Panchayats at each level to be reserved for women (Article 243 D(4)),
13. Not less than one-third (including the number of seats reserved for women belonging to the scheduled castes and scheduled tribes) of the total number of seats to be filled by direct election in every municipality to be reserved for women and such seats to be allotted by rotation to different constituencies in a municipality (Article 243 T (3)), and
14. Reservation of offices of chairpersons in Municipalities for the Scheduled Castes, the Scheduled Tribes and women in such manner as the legislature of a state may by law provide (Article 243 T(4)).

In the light of constitutional mandate, the state has enacted various legislative measures intended to ensure equal rights, to handle matter relating to social discrimination and various forms of violence and atrocities by providing support services especially to working women. The following classifications are available in case of women being victim of any of the crimes such as murder; robbery, cheating etc. are as under:

1. The crime identified under the Indian Penal Code (IPC):
   (a) Rape (Sec. 376IPC),
   (b) Kidnapping and abduction for different purposes (Sec. 363-373),
   (c) Homicide for Dowry, Dowry Deaths or their attempts (Sec.302/304-B IPC),
   (d) Torture, both mental and Physical (Sec. 498-A IPC),
   (e) Molestation (Sec. 354 IPC),
   (f) Sexual Harassment (Sec. 509 IPC), and
   (g) Importation of girls (up to 21 years of age).
2. The crimes identified under the special laws (SLL)

Although all laws are not gender specific, the provisions of law affecting women significantly have been reviewed periodically and amendments carried out to keep pace with the emerging requirements. Some acts which have special provisions to safeguard women and their interests are:

(i) The Employees State Insurance Act, 1948,

(ii) The Plantation Labour Act, 1951,

(iii) The Family Courts Act 1954,

(iv) The Special Marriage Act, 1954,

(v) The Hindu Marriage Act, 1955,

(vi) The Hindu Succession Act, 1956 with amendment in 2005,

(vii) Immoral Traffic (prevention) Act, 1956,

(viii) The Maternity Benefit Act, 1961 (amended in 1995),

(ix) Dowry Prohibition Act, 1961,

(x) The Medical Termination of Pregnancy Act, 1971,

(xi) The Contract Labour (Regulation and Abolition) Act 1976,

(xii) Equal Remuneration Act 1976,

(xiii) The Prohibition of Child Marriage Act, 2006,

(xiv) The Criminal Law (Amendment Act) , 1983,

(xv) The Factories (Amendment) Act, 1986,

(xvi) Indecent Representation of Women (prohibition) Act, 1986

(xvii) Commission of Sati (prevention) Act, 1987, and

(xviii) The Protection of Women from Domestic Violence Act, 2005.

Conclusion

Globalisation and gender justice need to be discussed in the light of available resources and constitutional provisions. Though laws and constitutional provisions are at work, their deplorable condition is witnessed in government reports. The economic transformation and displacement out of migration, inefficient resources to create gender specific jobs, unequal treatment of female gender, paucity of proper gender sensitisation, underpayment of female labour force, and patriarchal chauvinism are some of the major constraints to gender justice.

Globalisation as a powerful tool seems to have decreased the control of women over resources. It has led to displacement and when both men and women land up in urban slums it affects the women more due to lack of sanitation. There is increase in the violence against women in remotely located areas of India. The rhetoric of globalisation promises to remove backwardness through a worldwide exchange of information and establish a cosmopolitan culture but in actual practice since the world is based on unequal power relations these concerns are put on hold and lead to displacement and marginalisation. Hence we need a holistic approach to development and empowerment.

We need to devise an effective policy for implementation that will encourage positive outcomes for underserved population. Being gender responsive means creating an environment through site selection, staff selection, programme development, content, and material that reflects an understanding of the realities of the lives of women and girls and that addresses and responds to their strengths and challenges. We need to replicate best practices on gender governance from globe to make our country a better place to live in.

Notes

1. Kaur, H. 2010. *The impact of Globalisation on Women in India*, http://drharjothkaur.blogspot.in/2010/06/impact-of-globalisation-on-women-in.html, accessed on 30/12/2015.
2. Batra, S. 1996. *The social Strains of Globalisation in India*, New Concepts: New Delhi.
3. Appadurai, A. 1996. *Modernity at Large: Cultural Dimensions of Globalisation,* University of Minnesota Press: Minneapolis.

References

Albrow, M. 1996. *The Global Age,* Cambridge: Polity Press.

Giddens, Anthony. 1990. *The Consequence of Modernity,* Cambridge: Polity Press.

Simon, De. 2011. *The Second Sex*, New York: Vintage books.

Agrawal, P K. 2012. *India's move towards Sustainable Development,* New Delhi: M D Publications.

Nair, G S. 2008. *Revisiting Globalisation through Gender Lens,* New Delhi: Serials Publications.

Sen, A. 1990. "More than 100 million women are missing" in the New York Review, December 20.

Singh, N. 1984. *Women Problems and their Oppression*, New Delhi: APH Publishing House.

Bagchi, A. 1994. "Globalizing India: the fantasy and reality", Social Scientist 2(7&8).

George, S. 1992. *The Debt Boomerang: How Third World Debt Harms Us All*, London: Pluto Press.

Joekes, S. 1987. *Women in the World Economy*, Oxford: Oxford University Press.

Nayyar, D. 1996. *Economic Liberalisation in India*, Kolkata: Orient Longmans.

Thurow, L.C. 1996. *The Future of Capitalism,* New York: Penguine.

Chapter - 6

The Praxis of Injustice: A Glocal Investigation of Indian Culture and Its Women

—Bushra Wadood and Amina Jafri

India boasts of being one of the most ancient site of culture and civilisation where women have been recognised as goddesses and been worshipped. But in this paper, a deeper look has been taken on the issues related to women in the wake of globalisation where India has emerged as a latest booming economy in the world. This paper attempts to address those women issues which need immediate attention and action. In the last couple of years, a number of revolutionary innovations and changes have revolutionised our lives. Have these changes impacted and brought light in the lives of women as well or are they still the victims of social exclusion and been marginalised from having positive changes in their lives? This paper endeavors to focus on the ground realities of women and their social lives; how they have been perceived culturally and in what specific ways they have been portrayed in literature and media. Most importantly, the paper looks into how powerfully women have been protected and supported from Indian Legal Systems and so far what measures have been undertaken in order to bring major transformation in their lives.

Key Words: *Glocal, Melting Pot, Rainbow Ideology, Classical Patriarchy, Binary Opposition, Femicide.*

Introduction

The world is witnessing a paradigm shift due to globalisation and the national boundaries separating the nations have become "relics of a bygone era" (Ghemawat, 10). Today, it is possible for an Italian travelling in Toyota car, using Nokia cell phone, to eat Chinese foods, watch Bollywood films while sipping Coca-Cola. It is an apt example of globalisation. Toyota is a Japanese automotive company, and Nokia is a product of Finland; while Bollywood is an Indian film-industry and Coca-Cola is a US-based beverage. The convergence of cultures is an integral part of globalisation where people value and appreciate things not in its relation to its country but for its inherent quality and universal appeal. Every business policy has adapted to glocal considerations because what works in America, can miserable fail in India. Now, the international brands are manufactured, customised and marketed keeping in mind the local context. Now the world has shrunk to an extent that it has been localised and homogenised. This journey from heterogeneous to homogeneous has been pushed by the changes in world economy. In the process of globalisation, the entire world has been turned into a "melting pot" – a term which was earlier used for American society. The term "melting pot" came to be a term of common parlance when Israel Zangwill wrote a play of the same name which published in 1908. Later on, other scholars came up and suggested that referring to American culture as a melting pot would be inappropriate and should be changed. To address the plurality and diversity of culture, terms like "mosaic", "salad bowl" and "kaleidoscope" have been suggested. In 1920s, Victoria Hayward gave the term "mosaic" to describe cultural plurality of Canadian society:

> "New Canadians, representing many lands and widely separated sections of Old Europe, have contributed to the Prairie Provinces a variety in the way of Church Architecture. Cupolas and domes distinctly Eastern, almost Turkish, startle one above the tops of Manitoba maples or the bush of the river banks. These architectural figures of the landscape, apart altogether of their religious significance, are centres where, crossing the threshold on Sundays, one has the opportunity of hearing Swedish music, or the rich, deep chanting of the Russian responses; and of viewing at close hand the artistry that goes to make up the interior appointments of these churches transplanted from the East to the West…It is indeed a mosaic of vast dimensions and great breadth, essayed of the Prairie."

John Murray Gibbon was another scholar who suggested to use the term "mosaic" for referring to the multiculturalism of Americans. In his opinion which found expression in his book *Canadian Mosaic* (1938), melting pot is a misnomenclature as it gives a connotation that people who embraced American culture have lost/melted their identity, distinction and uniqueness and have forgotten their origin and ancestral roots. In the era of globalisation, the rainbow ideology has been accepted where every culture will be represented as one universal one. The rainbow ideology seeks to eradicate the differences that divide, promoting the common and similar features of discrete cultures. Globalisation has resulted in the "flattening" of the world where expansion of cities are taking place with blinding speed and the boundaries of these cities have been pushed away so much that it has blurred the lines that divides urban and rural areas. It has sprouted and given rise to mall-culture and apartment-culture as technology has made transportation and communication much easier as it was earlier. Thomas Friedman has enlisted ten such forces which has helped in the "flattening" of the world:

1. Collapse of the Berlin Wall
2. Outsourcing
3. In-sourcing
4. In-forming (Google and Search Engines)
5. Off-shoring
6. Uploading
7. Supply Chain Management
8. Workflow Software
9. Netscape (The Internet) and
10. Steroids (Personal Digital Assistants and Other Devices).

In this globalised village, the formula of success is to take on the glocalised approach. While adopting a global perspective, we cannot ignore/underestimate or avoid local market/culture/context. In this global village, it is wise to remain "culture-adopt-ready" if they want to be global player. For operating globally, it is an essential attribute to have "an astute understanding of local culture". Theodore Levitt has rightly said that "The worldwide success of a growing list of products that have become a household names is the evidence that consumers the world over, despite deep-rooted cultural differences are becoming homogenised…different cultural preferences, national tastes and standards, and business institutions are vestiges of the past. The earth is round, but for most purposes, it's sensible to treat it as flat" (Madhavan, 10). Over the last decade, India and China have emerged as global players belonging to Asia. Today, the biggest challenge is to manage diversity and understanding cultural dimensions. Not only this, a lot of other problems have also been crept in. Globalisation has also tossed up the challenge of working in a team comprising of employees diverse in culture. This diversity is not restricted to cultures only but it is very likely that people of different country, colour, caste, creed, and gender will also be hired. For facing all these challenges, Brent Rubin in his article "Guidelines for Cross-cultural Communication Effectiveness" has suggested us to become "international sojourners" who work together to "facilitate the transfer of skills, increase the likelihood of meaningful social interaction, and heighten the probability of achieving a sense of personal and professional accomplishment and growth" (quoted in Technical Communication, 45).

Now let us have a look on the condition and status of women belonging to Indian society and culture in the backdrop of globalisation. Although, there has been assimilation of cultures; racial-mix must have become acceptable and cultural-pluralism the way of the world, but gender-discrimination is still prevalent in policies, perceptions and practices. A woman has been discriminated against globally. Gender-just society seems a distant dream and accepting woman as a human being second to impossible. After their struggle to education, now women are face to face with another set of problems. Gender-discrimination and harassment at their workplace where male are in the majority has become a daily routine for thousands of women who are working for their livelihood. It is true that globalisation has transformed many things in the lives of women as well but it has also bombarded them with a whole new range of problems because of binary opposition that exists in our society. This binary opposition is brought into the focus when Saussurean Structuralist theory propounded by Ferdinand de Saussure got importance in the modern discourse and came to be regarded as a significant one. Binary opposition is a pair of opposites in which the first one is considered to have prominence over other. For example: Men/Women, Coloniser/Colonised, Day/Night, Presence/Absence and so on. It is ingrained in the minds of male that they are superior to women. This perception and attitude of dominance and authority is manifested in their behaviour, thoughts, mindset, and conscience and these beliefs of superiority are further reinforced by the traditions and customs of the society which has made the problem more complex.

There have been many instances where women are forced and pressurised to reproduce male heirs to the family and because of this insistence, their health, well-being and identity take a toll. In many societies of India, a male child is preferred over a female as they are seen as "Ghar ka Chirag" or "Kul Deepak". There have been many Indian rituals which only a male member of the family could perform like *Shradh* and *Antim sanskar.* Moreover, male child has been accepted as the one will be the heir of the family and keep alive the name of their *khandaan/kul*, whereas females are treated as belonging to the family of their husbands. If one looks for the instances of gender disparity in literature which mirrors the society, one could find many evidences that "Classical Patriarchy" exists in the society. Ismat Chughtai, Shashi Deshpande, Arundhati Roy, Manju Kapoor and many other female writers have voiced their concern in their writing for the women who have gone through these atrocious and discriminatory practices. Especially Chughtai's short fiction is replete with such instances of child marriage and 'son-stroke suffering' where a woman is harassed and tortured for not giving birth a male child or 'son' because in this case there will be no heir to carry forward the name of their family. The 'son-stroke suffering' is the outcome of being unable to bear a male child which leads the woman involved to harassment, abuse and because of this inability they live under constant threat of divorce and second marriage. In her article "Women, Islam, and the State," Deniz Kandiyoti writes that marriage is seen as the taking up the first step and entering on the threshold of motherhood. A woman after marriage enters the home of her husband as a "dispossessed individual" who can make her place in his family only after giving birth to a "male offspring".

It is endeavoured to know how culturally women have been perceived and how specifically they have been portrayed in literature and media. Ismat Chughtai (1911-1991) is a renowned Urdu writer in her short stories, there have been many instances of "classical patriarchy" in which "girls are given away in marriage at a very young age into households headed by their husband's father. There, they are subordinate not only to all the men but also to the more senior women, especially their mother-in-law" (278). Chughtai in her memoir, *Kaghazi hai Pairahan (The Paper-thin Garment)* regretfully mentions that she in her own life has seen such instances where a woman is brutalised for being unable to bear a male child, which Deniz Kandiyoti has pointed out in her article. In her autobiographical account, "Caravan Dust" ("Ghubar-e-Caravan"), Chughtai writes:

> As a child I had a very dear friend, Mangu, the daughter of our coachman. She was a little older than me and used to throw her weight around. She was married at the age of thirteen or fourteen and went away to Lucknow. When she came back with her first daughter, she was very subdued. All her playfulness had vanished and her smile had disappeared. She used to be beaten black and blue by both her mother-in-law and her husband for the crime of having given birth to a daughter. (Kumar and Sadique, 27)

The fate that Mangu meted out to is a typical example of "Classical patriarchy" and son-stroke suffering where not only the male of the household but also the female members get indulged in abusive and physical act of atrocities. In the hierarchy of patriarchal family set up, Mangu was at the base; helplessly enduring the beastly behaviour doled out to her by her own husband, the protector and the earthly God of hers. In her article "South Asian Fiction and Marital Agency of Muslim Wives," Hafiza Nilofer Khan also acknowledges this fact that marriage in Asian countries is not seen as "an association of equal individuals" but a couple is assumed to be one of the other binary oppositions where male dominates. On the issues of classical patriarchy and son-stroke suffering, Khan also concedes:

> Sometimes they are literally marked in the name of Muslim marital rites, and put through humiliation for inadequacy to produce a son. Some of these wives also have to endure physical battery, incest, extramarital affair or polygamy as their husbands try to stifle their existential conditions and efforts of self definition. (174-5)

In many societies of India, parents treat a daughter as a burden or a property whom they wish to give away at the earliest. They marry off their daughters when they are in a state of where they still have "some growing-up to do" and are not fully mature to embrace the wifely responsibility and of womanhood. A great effort was done by the social reforming societies like Arya Samaj and the Brahmo Samaj in eradicating child marriage from its roots but it continues to plague our society. Although due to the compulsion of other social reformists, later in 1927, Hindu Child Marriage Act was passed which raised the age at the time of marriage both for boys and girls but in practice nothing changed. In Sarda Act or Child Marriage Restraint Act, 14 years for girls and 18 years for boys meant compulsory for marriage. In 1948, it was amended and made 15 years of age as the eligibility for the marriage of girls. In 1978, it was again amended which made mandatory for girls to be of 18 years or above and for boys 21 years or above at the time of marriage. But unfortunately, laws and its time to time amendments have been unable to prevent parents from marrying off their minors. Commenting on the reasons of its pervasiveness in Indian society, Nagi articulates: "Some of the other reasons (of child marriage) include prevalence of social and religious customs, low status of women, poor economic conditions, inadequate educational and employment opportunities, and ineffective law enforcement machinery" (9). As far as poor economic conditions are concerned, Jarapur also corroborates this point which is revealed in his survey that "the percentage of child marriages in the case of females, is the highest in the low income group" (13).

Other than this, femicide has been a concern of many government policymakers, NGOs and private sectors who wish to bring positive changes in the social lives of Indians. Asha Vishnathan claims in her article "Femicide: The Silent Genocide Taking Place in India" that "two hundred million women/girls/infants fetuses have been killed, aborted or abandoned through deliberate acts of extermination. This is more than all the casualties of World War I and II combined. India and China are the leading countries responsible for the maximum number of deaths, eliminating more girls than the number of girls born in America. The three deadliest words in the world became *"It's a girl""*. She informs that of those who manage to survive past the fetus stage, many die before they turn six. The 2013 census shows there are 940 females for every 1000 males in India. Many NGOs have taken the initiative to help and support women by intervening but the laws are not strong enough to prevent people from doing it.

Sex-detection and sex-selection are a common practice that has engulfed entire nation. The government intervention has been inadequate and ineffective in banning this tendency. Medical Termination of Pregnancy Act of 1971 where abortion was legalised and acceptable on valid reasons has been manipulated in aborting female fetuses. Pre-Conception and Pre-Natal Diagnostic Techniques Act (PCPNDT) which came into existence in 1994, has been unsuccessful in deterring parents from sex-screening, female feticide and sex-selective abortions. The Public Health Foundation of India, a research organisation, submitted its report in 2010 on the failure of effective implementation of PCPNDT Act in India. The report concludes that this Act was unable to be implemented successfully as there was a lack of awareness about the Act in parts of India; secondly, inactive role of the Appropriate

Authorities, disregard of the law by the medical practitioners and ambiguity among some clinics that offer prenatal care services further contributed in its failure.

Rita Banerjee against all the existing skepticism and disbelief took the initiative of having "The 50 Million Missing Campaign" which started in 2006. She informs that the term "missing" used in the naming the campaign has originally been used by Noble winner economist, Dr. Amartya Sen, 1986 to draw our attention to the vast divergence in India's natural gender ratio. It is revealed in the UNICEF report of 2007 that the mortality rate for girls under five was 40 per cent higher than for boys of the same age. In this report it is evident that most of these girls died due to nutritional and medical neglect. Further India topped the list as having the highest maternal mortality rate in the world where in every five minutes; one woman dies because of pregnancy-related complications. This misogynist attitude is steeped in the very fiber of our culture.

Talking about the various ways in which people indulge in femicide, Rita Banerjee acknowledges that that this practice has ingrained in our mind. She counts its different operates mundi:

> ...female foetal abortions. An estimated 1 million female foetuses are selectively eliminated in India each year, and that number is expected to rise to 2.5 million within the next few years. Method number two is female infanticide, a practice that has a long history in India. So far there has been no national average estimated for female infanticide, largely because it is difficult to track down with there being no administrative compulsion for citizens to register births. Nevertheless, existent data gives an indication of the scale of the practice. In the state of Kerala, one of India's most progressive states, with a literacy rate of over 90 per cent, it is estimated that about 25,000 new born girls are killed every year. In other states like Bihar, where the issue of gender bias is plainly discernable, one survey reveals that mid-wives interviewed admitted to being paid to kill almost 50 per cent of the baby girls they delivered. As the number three method of elimination I listed dowry murders, also known as 'dowry deaths.' Despite the fact that a majority of dowry-related homicides of young married women in India are never even filed with the police, in the late 1990s it was estimated that at least 25,000 young married women were cold-bloodedly murdered by their husbands and in-laws in dowry extortion cases. That number has continued to rise, as the practice of dowry itself spreads to communities, like tribal groups, that traditionally never had the custom of dowry. (Banerjee)

The objectification of women body and toyification of their identity have put them in "horrendously annihilating abyss" (Banerjee). By projecting women as sex-object, Media must have glamorised the content of their programme but the consequences are far-reaching and fatal. This "historically-rooted acculturation of female homicide" makes femicide look normal and routine. Sometimes it is done in the name of family's honour, sometimes it is validated as a sacred ritual or tradition and at other times it is sanctified in the name of religion.

Conclusion

As it is a serious problem which is deeply-rooted in culture, traditions and religion, one needs to start from the grassroots. It is deemed essential for the lawmakers to protect women against their vulnerable financial state. They should be given many safeguards to survive. The problem is related to our perception and practices, so the solution should be to change the perception by highlighting the positive aspects related to having a daughter. Only governmental intervention and legal enforcement are enough. To deal with this mammoth crisis, we all at our level have to put our best possible efforts in eradicating it. NGO's, Government, Private Sector, Media, Film Industry, Theatre Artists, Teachers, Social Workers and responsible citizens have to come forward and should work together. Each one should try to tackle the problem in one's distinct way. Spreading awareness about the legal provisions, sensitising people to have gender-just society and changing the biased attitude, behaviour and mentality of perceiving a girl child are needed.

References

Banerji, Rita. "Female Genocide in India and the 50 Million Missing Campaign." *Intersections: Gender and Sexuality in Asia and the Pacific.* Issue 22, October 2009. Web. 6 Feb. 2015.

Friedman, Thomas. *The World is Flat: A Brief History of the Twenty-first Century.* Picador: New York, 2007. Print.

Ghemawat, Pankaj. "Why the World is Not Flat?" *Foreign Policy (2007):* n. pag. Web. 25 Oct. 2015.

Goodkind, Daniel (1999). "Should Prenatal Sex Selection be Restricted?: Ethical Questions and Their Implications for Research and Policy." *Population Studies* 53 (1): 49–61. Print.

Guha, Amrita. "Disappearing Daughters: Female Feticide in India." *Seneca International.* Web. 5 Feb. 2016.

http://www.seneca-international.org/2014/01/20/disappearing-daughters-female-feticide-in-india/

Implementation of the PCPNDT Act in India: Perspectives and Challenges. Public Health Foundation of India, supported by The National Human Rights, New Delhi and United Nations FPA, (2010). Web. 23 Oct. 2015.

http://www.wbhealth.gov.in/download/IMPLEMENTATION%20OF%20THE%20PCPNDT%20ACT%20IN%20INDIA.pdf

Jarapur, P.B. "Child Marriage in Malnad Area of Mysore State." *Journal of Family Welfare* 18.3 (1972): 65-71. Print.

Kandiyoti, Denzi. "Women, Islam, and the State." *Middle East Report* 173 (1991): 9-14. Print.

Khan, Hafiza Nilofar. "South Asian Fiction and Marital Agency of Muslim Wives." *Journal of International Women's Studies*, 14.3 (2013): 174-193. Web. 26 Dec. 2014. //http://vc.bridgew.edu/jiws/vol14/iss3/13//

Kraemer, Sebastian. "The Fragile Male." British Medical Journal (2000): n. pag. British Medical Journal. Web. 20 Oct. 2013.

Kumar, Sukrita Paul and Sadique, eds. *Ismat: Her Life, Her Times.* New Delhi: Katha, 2000. Print.

Levitt, Theodore. "The Globalisation of Markets." *International and Global Marketing: Concepts and Cases, 2nd Edition.* Massachusetts: McGraw Hill, 1998. Print.

Madhavan, Shobhana. *Cross-cultural Management: Concepts and Cases.* New Delhi: Oxford University Press, 2012. Print.

Nagi, B. S. *Child Marriage in India: A Study of Its Differential Patterns in Rajasthan.* New Delhi: Mittal Publications, 1993. Print.

Pfeiffer, William Sanborn and Padmaja, T.V.S. *Technical Communication: A Practical Approach, 6th ed.* New Delhi: Pearson, 2012. Print.

Rubin, D. Brent. "Guidelines for Cross-Cultural Communication Effectiveness." *Towards Internationalism, 2nd Ed.* Ed.s Louise Fiber Luce & Elise C. Smith. Heinle & Heinle Publishers, 1987.

Sen, Amartaya. "More Than a 100 Million Women are Missing.' *New York Review of Books*, Vol. 37, No. 20 . pp. 61–66 (20 December 1990), Web. 25 Jan. 2015.

http://ucatlas.ucsc.edu/gender/Sen100M.html, accessed 1 June 2009.

Vishwanathan, Asha. "Femicide: The Silent Genocide Taking Place in India." *The Alternative.* In Aug 8, 2013. Web. 15 Jan. 2016.

http://www.thealternative.in/society/femicide-the-silent-genocide-taking-place-in-india/

Chapter - 7

Transgenders and Social Justice in the Era of Globalisation

—*Poornima Jain*

Inequality is a natural and universal phenomenon. There are various forms of inequality such as social, economic, political, cultural, technological knowledge etc. Similarly, there are many basis of inequality like caste, class, region, physical fitness, education, and gender. Gender-based inequality has several implications on society and on all categories of gender. There is inequality between male and female genders, and also more significantly between male, female on the one hand and transgenders on the other. From antiquity, transgenders have remained present in every society. Nevertheless, they have remained excluded and marginalised from the larger society. They are considered as an object of pity, shame, stigma, curse, abuse, and rejection etc. Major reason for their pathetic condition is that from most developed nations like US to the developing nations like India or Bangladesh, most people lack an understanding of the meaning of transgender and have a negative attitude toward them. Consequently, trans people face a wide range of discriminating practices by the rest of the society which impedes the process of development of a nation. This poses a serious problem of social injustice embedded in the social structure. At present statistically India accounts for 4,87,803 trans population out of which 32,3120 are in rural areas and 1,64,683 residing in urban. Uttar Pradesh has total trans population of 18,734 among them 14,828 are in rural and 3,906 are living in urban areas. If divided on other lines, according to Census 2011 figures, SCs constitute 26,404, STs 639, Literates 66,249, Illiterates 71,216, total workers 38,115 and non-workers 99,350.

Globalisation has brought several transformations while changing the attitude of the government towards many unattended sections of society. Still, the conditions of TGPs worldwide are below the satisfaction level. National Transgender Discrimination Survey conducted by the National Centre for Transgender Equality and the National Gay and Lesbian Task Force (2011) found that; (1) Unemployment rate is double the population as a whole, (2) 90 per cent reported harassment on the job, (3) 47 per cent had experienced an adverse job outcome, such as being fired, not hired, or *denied a promotion, (4) 15 per cent lived on $ 10,000 per year or less, double the rate of the general population. (5) Significant housing instability: 19 per cent were homeless, 11 per cent have faced eviction and 26 per cent forced to seek temporary space in accordance to the report of NCTE and NLGBTQ Task Force 2011.*

Trans face discrimination, harassment, and violence in many areas of their lives. These conditions lead to their unemployment and to cumulative poverty. Discrimination of Trans gets intensified by other factors as caste, race, class etc. They are reported as weak, shameless, powerless, and rejected people. In this background, the paper examines the Current status of trans in Uttar Pradesh/India. Kind of abuses faced by trans in Uttar Pradesh/ India and most importantly, the kind of legal safeguards given to trans in India.

Key Words: *Globalisation, Transgenders, Social Justice, Discrimination, Exclusion.*

Introduction

Gender is one of the most pervading and given social category. It determines every aspect of our life including our name, clothes, hair length, appearance, behaviours, occupation, mobility, and so on. It is present in every document of identity, including birth certificate, ration card, voter id, pan card, passport, driving license, and so on.

It implies that, while living out one's life in a rural or an urban area, in a poor or a rich neighbourhood, nationally or globally, gender is constantly present, both in our minds and our social relations.

Gender is a social construct. Gender is assigned to each one of us based on the kind of primary sexual characteristics that we are born with. This basic idea of 'gender as assigned' is expressed through the two terms "person assigned gender female at birth (PAGFB)" and "person assigned gender male at birth (PAGMB)". Sometimes this assigned gender at birth may or may not be in the conformity of the person's idea of his/her own gender as they grow up, these persons are termed as 'transgender'.

Basics of Trans Gender Person –A person, who does not identify with the gender assigned to them at birth. TGP are known by several names in different parts of the country and world; a few are-Hijra, Kinnar, Chakka, Eunachs etc.

Transgender can be classified into three categories:

1. **Real Eunuchs or TGPs**-These are eunuchs with no trace of genitalia.
2. **Trans-woman**–A person who is assigned gender male at birth (PAGMB), but identifies with the gender female. The person may or may not have undergone sex reassignment surgery/procedures.

3. **Trans-man:** A person who is assigned gender female at birth (PAGFB), but identifies with the gender male. The person may or may not have undergone sex reassignment /surgery/procedures.

Present State of Trans in UP/India

UP has maximum proportion (12 per cent) of TGP among all states of India. Transgender people in India, named 'Hijras' generally in 'South Asia', are discriminated against in almost all walks of life. Sometimes they are seen as a figure of respect and most of the time as of hatred, fear, ridicule, and apathy. Due to multiple deprivations (socio-economic, cultural, political, moral) experienced by TGP in India or elsewhere, they have remained marginalised and excluded in all walks of life.

Population: In UP, TGP constituted 1.13 per cent of the total population of India. Out of these 73.80 per cent are from rural areas and 26.10 per cent from urban. TGP in the age group of 0-6 years formed 13.6 per cent of the total TGP population, among them 79 per cent belonged to rural and 21 per cent to urban areas.

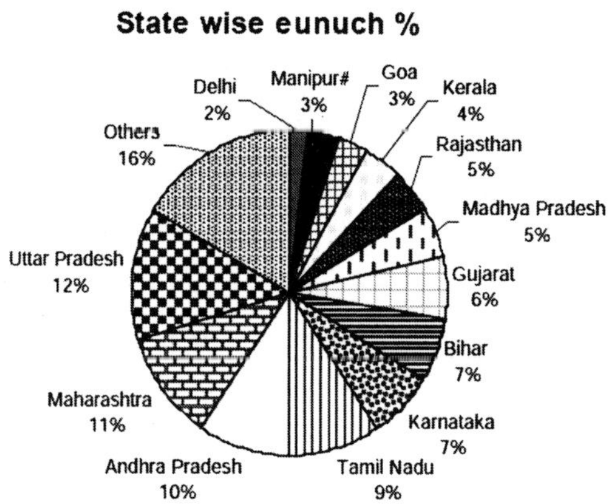

Source: Ministry of Social Justice, GOI.

SC/ST Composition: Total population of SC (TGP) in UP is 19.20 per cent out of which 85.58 per cent belonged to rural and 14.41 per cent to urban areas. Proportion of ST (TGP) is only 0.46 per cent. Majority (86.38 per cent) of them live in rural areas as opposed to (only 13.61 per cent) in urban areas.

Literacy: Literacy figures show a very frail picture as only 55.80 per cent TGP in UP are literate. Majority (67.54 per cent) of them are in rural areas as against 32.45 per cent in urban areas. These figures show a reverse picture of the rural-urban contrast in the social condition of TGP in

India. 58.8 per cent TGP are illiterate, among them 79.80 per cent belonged to rural areas and 20.19 per cent to urban. **Workers:** Only 27.72 per cent TGP are in the workforce, Majority 79.80 per cent are in rural and only 26.08 per cent are in urban areas. 54.71 per cent TGP of the total workers are the main workers.70.70 per cent of the total main workers are in rural and 29.29 per cent are in urban areas. 16.11 per cent of the total TGP workers are in the category of cultivators (96.56 per cent rural and 3.43 per cent urban). 12.03 per cent of the main workers in UP are agricultural workers (92.39 per cent rural, 7.60 per cent urban). 4.38 per cent of the total main workers are household workers (92.39 per cent in rural and 7.60 per cent in urban areas). 22.17 per cent of the total workers (main) in UP are in others category (41.73 per cent in rural and 58.26 per cent are in urban areas).

Marginal Workers (Total): 45.28 per cent of the TGP in the UP are marginal workers (77.78 per cent in rural and 22.21 per cent in urban areas). 16.14 per cent of the total marginal workers fall in the category of cultivators (94.79 per cent in rural and 5.20 per cent in urban areas). 39.57 per cent the total marginal workers are marginal agricultural workers among them an overwhelming majority (94.37 per cent) are in rural and a few (5.62 per cent) are in urban areas. Marginal household TGP in UP constitute 9.68 per cent (72.54 per cent reside in rural areas and 27.45 per cent in urban). Marginal workers in others category in UP constitute 34.59 per cent (52.33 per cent in rural and 47.66 per cent in urban areas).

Marginal Workers (0-3 months): Workers who work from 0-3 months form 79.23 per cent (76.23 per cent rural, 23.76 per cent urban) of the total marginal workers.15.76 per cent in 0-3 months category are cultivators (93.55 per cent rural and 6.44 per cent urban).30.75 per cent TGP in UP in the category of 0-3 Months marginal worker are agricultural workers (93.80 per cent in rural and 6.19 per cent in urban areas). 6.77 per cent marginal workers in 0-3 months category are household workers (73.48 per cent rural and 26.51 per cent are in urban areas.29.21 per cent TGP work in other category (almost equal proportion live in both rural and urban areas 50.96 per cent and 49.03 per cent respectively).

Marginal workers (0-6 months): In the category of 0-6 months marginal workers there are 20.76 per cent workers among TGP (83.73 per cent rural and 16.26 per cent in urban areas). Among them 3.65 per cent are cultivates (99.04 per cent rural, 0.95 per cent urban), 8.81 per cent are agricultural workers (96.38 per cent rural, 3.61 per cent urban). 2.91 per cent marginal workers in 0-6 months duration are household workers (70.37 rural and 29.62 per cent urban). Only 5.37 per cent marginal workers work in others category (59.80 per cent rural, 40.19 per cent urban). Above data show that the socio-economic condition of TGP in UP is very poor as majority (72.28 per cent) of them are non-workers (73.89 per cent the rural and 26.10 per cent the urban areas).

Data reveal that there is no exhaustive enumeration of TGP in UP/ India and on the basis of available data present state of TGP is very poor. They constitute one of the most vulnerable sections of society. Hence, need immediate action by the Government of India and counselling of the masses.

Violence/Atrocities Against Transgender

As is generally understood that TGP are untouched by the genders or TGP themselves is a myth. TGP are victims of family, police, society, STD, and TGP and their gurus. The transgender community, generally known as "Hijras" in this country, are a section of Indian citizens who are treated by society as unnatural and generally as objects of ridicule and even fear on account of superstition. Despite a pre-colonial heritage that recognised and celebrated gender diversity in temple sculptures, mythology and religious treatises, transgender people in India, today, face intolerance, stigma, discrimination and violence. Human rights violations against transgender people infuse families, educational institutions, workplaces, institutions such as law-enforcement, healthcare, media, and society at large.

Atrocities and violence against transgender people is a serious issue worldwide, but the existence of a well-recognised and defined transgender group in India makes the problem particularly visible. The violence, faced by transgenders are discrimination, lack of educational facilities, unemployment, lack of shelter, lack of medical facilities and protection from STD like HIV, care of hygiene, depression, hormone pill abuse, tobacco and alcohol abuse and problems relating to marriage, property, electoral rights, adoption. They are discriminated against in the labour market, in schools and in hospitals, and mistreated and disowned by their own families. On the streets of towns and cities around the world, they are singled out for physical attack–beaten, sexually assaulted, tortured, raped, and killed.

Transgenders' human rights are violated as they are deprived of their fundamental rights as well as also other civil rights. Transgenders have no access to bathrooms/toilets and public spaces. The lack of access to bathrooms and public spaces access is indicative of discrimination faced by them in availing basic facilities and amenities. They face similar problems in prisons, hospitals and schools. TGP get justice in terms of punitive measures, they cannot escape punishment when they are accused of committing crimes. Transgenders have very limited employment opportunities as most jobs are confined to male and female sexes. Transgenders, being a third sex, cannot even apply for most of the jobs.

The Peoples Union for Civil Liberties, Karnataka published a report on human rights violations against the transgender community in India (PUCL-K2003)[3]. It documents violence and abuse against these peoples via testimonies of many who have been directly affected, and goes on to discuss the institutional basis of all this violence. The PUCL Report reveals all too clearly the trap that transgender women often fall into in traditional societies: They become outcasts, because they have no family to harbour them, and then having no means of support - become labelled as a sex object and forced by circumstances into sex work in order to survive. Thrown away by their families, and unable to obtain proper documentation, education and employment, many kids are forced to take sex work in violent environments in order to survive.

Since prostitution is "illegal" in most traditional societies, the police become a state-supported mechanism for enforcing sex worker traditions: The police do not protect the women from abuse, but instead victimise them if they don't keep in line or if they protest the system.

Report of the Death by Burning of Chandini

On Dec. 1, 2002, Chandini, a Hijra, died of severe burns in her home in Kammanahalli, Bangalore. She had been married to Jnanaprakash, a painter, who claims that he was unaware of Chandini's sexual orientation till the day before her death; his reaction of shock and outrage as well as his threat to expose her to his parents drove her to commit suicide. But many hijras who know Chandini discount the suicide story completely and allege that Jnanaprakash, who met Chandini in a hamam, had a long-standing relationship with her (PUCL, 2002)[4]

In Sept. 2003, four kothi sex workers, Seeta, Sheela, Vimla, and Malathi (changed names) were picked up from the streets by the police and taken to Sampangi rama nagara police station in Bangalore. In the police station, they were harassed and severely beaten up, resulting in injuries on their hands, arms and feet (PUCL2004)[5] .

In different parts of India, hijras regularly face sexual assault and physical violence by police and the public. Sex work is the only option for employment, but hijras experience disproportionate amounts of violence in this domain as well. A report exploring sexual violence against hijra sex workers suggests that "the sexual nature of the violence can be understood as an apt punishment for a transgressive sexuality." HIV prevalence is between 17.5 to 41 per cent in the hijra population, which is more than fifty times higher than the general Indian adult population. Transgendered people also face discrimination and harassment in healthcare facilities. Furthermore, India has no medical guidelines for gender reassignment surgery, so many hijras resort to back alley procedures that leave them with dangerous complications.

Violence

Violence against TGP starts from the family. If they are accepted by the family, then their conditions can be improved significantly.

Family Violence: Family violence is not only physical but mental and emotional as well. It gives more than physical injury to a TGP. This is one of the most severe forms of violence against TGP because of their gender identity or expression. From the very beginning as s/he takes birth and grows up violence against transgender starts. A TGP during his childhood prefer for female clothing, make-up and attire, playing with girls rather than with boys, preferring household work culturally assigned for females, and posses a 'soft' nature like girls because of which they encountered various types of negligence, humiliation, and abusive incidents. It tarnishes the family image also. The disapproval was raised by society but ultimately also by family.[4] Transgender may be particularly vulnerable to domestic violence if they fear a partner or family member will disclose their gender identity and expose them to bias and discrimination. Other risk factors include fear they will be denied access to hormones or be forced to marry (Greenberg, 2012:198-251)[6]

Murder and Rape

UN and other human rights experts are increasingly speaking out against the murder of trans women. The Special Rapporteur on extrajudicial, summary or arbitrary executions; the Special Rapporteur on violence against women; and the European Parliament and Council of Europe have all condemned such violence (Hammarberg, 2008).[7]

Such violence may be physical (including murder, beatings, kidnappings, rape and sexual assault) or psychological (including threats, coercion and arbitrary deprivations of liberty).

Since January 2008, the Trans Murder Monitoring project has collected reports of transgenders who were killed because of their gender identity or expression. Between 1 January 2008 and 31 October 2013, there were 1,374 reported killings of trans people in 60 countries. Over 78 per cent of documented murders were in Central and South America (Balzer and Hutta, 2012).[8]

This number represents a signiûcant, sustained level of brutal violence against transgender. Over 99 per cent of the reported murders recorded by the Trans Murder Monitoring project are of trans women. Many were also brutally raped and tortured, their bodies mutilated and discarded. The vast majority of those murdered whose occupations were reported were trans sex workers.

Identity Crisis

A TGP is compelled to go through strenuous situations and struggles to be declared as a self-identified TGP in a society where it is seen as a curse. It is difficult for them to cross the boundary of male-female dichotomous gender norms and to find a healthy, safe, and peaceful space in this hetero-normative society. Thus, the conflicts relating to self-identity had diminished their human dignity and self-reliance.

Homelessness

Feminine attitudes quite often become the source of physical and psychological trauma. Most trans people were initially living with their families but after encountering various adversities, they were forced to leave home.

Some TGPs reported that they are not even being sexually safe at *gurus'* homes as they were forced to have sex with men who paid money to *guru.* Being sexually and financially abused, most of them finally left *gurus*' homes. Not all TGPs lived with guru, some rented rooms to live in isolation. They preferred to become a TGP by involving in hijragiri (traditional activities performed by the hijra). Many sold sex independently. They developed love relations with males whom they called parik. Some TGs lived together in groups resembling to a family life. Finding a safe living place is difficult to them. Most landlords did not rent rooms to TG. Most TGP's reported a 'homeless situation'.

Ageing or Death

Old age brings new and terrible threats for survival in the lives of TG. Most TG's live with frustrations and incidents of abuse and humiliations throughout their life. Ironically, death also cannot either guarantee a space, nor can it terminate the endless disgrace. According to many TG, the dead body of a TG cannot be buried normally due to multiple societal and religious resistances.

Role of the State

TGPs are excluded from familial and social life and are equally excluded from the state. In all official forms of educational institutes, various service organisations, banking sectors, citizenship forms, birth certificates, passports, and voter identification cards, sex (or gender) is shown as a rigid bivariate category. Thus, a TGP must identify as a male or a female, otherwise their fundamental citizenship rights will not be granted under any other category. In this way, the state has imposed gender on any population, including the TGP, despite the fact that gender is socially constructed.

Excluded from the Main Stream of Society

Genders of mainstream society refuse to develop social relations with the transgender. On the other hand, they prevent access of them to social institutions, resources, and services. They are dominated and abused by the members of mainstream society, are unable to exercise power or to establish citizenship rights at home or in society. Access to social, cultural, educational, legal and health services is extremely restricted from anyone with a transgender identity.

Victim of Torture, Coercion, and Cruel Treatment

Negative stereotypes that gender diversity is unnatural, immoral or pathological makes TGP's life more risky. Like other victims of gender-based violence, trans people are frequently dehumanised and blamed for their own abuse (Op.cit. p. 10).[9]

The UN Special Rapporteur on torture has reinforced concern that trans women placed within the general prison population are at risk of physical and sexual abuse. A report of the Special Rapporteur details cases of trans women being intentionally beaten on their breasts and cheekbones by prison or police guards in order to burst implants and release toxins[11]. In the absence of State protection, many trans people will not report such human rights violations. They are particularly at risk of violence and exposure to HIV.

"Many trans sex workers cannot get access to justice just because they are trans sex workers. The police in many times do not accept their complaints, ill-treat them and many times be complaints against those trans sex workers who want to be complaints. So, no justice! Courts also discriminate due to these widespread prejudices" (Discussion Paper, 2013, p. 10).[10]

Discrimination

Transgender and gender non-conforming people face injustice at every turn: in childhood homes, in school systems that promise to shelter and educate, in harsh and exclusionary workplaces, at the grocery store, the hotel front desk, in doctors' oces and emergency rooms, before judges and at the hands of landlords, police ocers, healthcare workers and other service providers. In many countries, there is no research on the ridicule, abuse and harassment trans people face. In countries where data does exist, it shows the compounding impact of discrimination and marginalisation in all aspects of trans-gender's lives. They are denied to the right to education and the right to work as well.

Transgender are particularly vulnerable to discrimination when their gender identity is visible to others, or when their previous sex details are known or easily accessible. Harassment of transgender is often targeted at their gender expression or clothes. This may include prohibiting a trans woman from having long hair or making a trans man wear a skirt. Derogatory comments may escalate to forcibly cutting a trans woman's hair, removing a trans man's binder so his chest is exposed, or stripping other clothes to reveal a trans person's body.

Trans people frequently face discrimination and rejection from their families and communities instead. This includes being excluded from their family home, prevented from attending school or forced to relinquish their children. Sometimes discrimination is perpetrated in the name of cultural or traditional values.

Right to Education

Education is essential for the development of human potential and realisation of other human rights. However, many trans children are unable to realise these rights due to stigma and discrimination. Trans and gender-variant children are particularly vulnerable at school, where teachers' and students' attitude towards them is very negative. This results in high levels of bullying, violence, truancy and exclusion from school. They often experienced loneliness and abusive treatment; rather, they were not allowed to share with classmates, extending from the classroom to the playground.

One TGP reported, when I went to school, the classmates used to criticise me. They pointed me by saying, "he is (effeminate boy). He will end up as hijra. He cannot play with us. He cannot sit with us. They used to throw me out of the class. When I went to play with the boys, they did not accept me, and even the girls also did not want to play with me. Often I found myself sitting in a corner in the class or playground. Even Teachers abuse them, influenced by predominant norms and values of society, teachers accused effeminate boys of violating school and societal 'decorum'. Some TG's claimed to have secret sexual relations with their male teachers. Eventually, they could not stay in schools, resulting in discontinuation of education which ultimately diminished future employment opportunities.

A US study found that almost half of the trans students surveyed missed a class because they felt unsafe or uncomfortable, and nearly one in six faced harassment so severe that they were forced to leave school (Greytak, 2009).[11] In 2006, the Department of Social Welfare in Tamil Nadu, India passed a landmark order protecting the rights of aravanis / hijras to attend schools and college (Harrington, 2008).[12] In 2009, Pakistan's Supreme Court held that hijras were citizens entitled to equal rights and protections under the national constitution, including financial support from the government for educational and employment opportunities, and voting and inheritance rights. (Redding, 2011).[13]

"Discrimination in education makes many trans people quit before they finish their schooling and they end up in sex work." (Op.cit., p. 10).[14]

Right to Work

Discrimination in educational institutions often prevents trans adults from finding or keeping segregated in narrow, marginalised occupations. In some regions most trans women are sex workers with limited or no rights or legal protection. (Op.cit., p. 10).[15] In some cases, many TGPs are abused verbally, physically, and sexually at workplaces for which they never received any justice. They rather lose the job because the employers do not want any mishappening on sexual ground at their workplace. Since they are denied in the job market, therefore, are forced to take up dancing, singing, and begging.

General Health Services

Trans people have the same range of general physical and mental health needs as other groups. Yet very few health surveys collect data about gender identity, severely limiting the capacity to identify health risks, protective factors or health outcomes for trans people. The cumulative impact of discrimination and relative deprivation is bound to impact negatively on trans people's health. Access of trans people to healthcare services is constrained due to marginalised social status. They are not allowed to seek healthcare at the private chambers of doctors. Healthcare professionals are often insensitive to this vulnerability. They may be ignorant of the specific health needs of trans people or lack the professional training required to meet their health needs. A large scale survey undertaken in the United Kingdom in 2007 found that 17 per cent of trans people had been refused services by a doctor or nurse because of their gender identity. Even more (29 per cent) felt that being trans adversely acted the way they were treated by healthcare professionals. (Whittle, S., *et.al* 2007)[16]

"After my friend was raped by those men because she was discovered [to be trans] she came to me...we went to the clinic to get post HIV exposure prophylaxis. The nurse told her to go home, take to her women's clothes and come back. She was already so traumatised she could not return. I believe that is why she is HIV-positive today." (GC on HIV and Law, 2012).[17]

Rapes increase the risk of acquisition of sexually transmitted infections, resulted in unwanted pregnancies, mental health issues, and suicide and have resulted in documented police- mediated negligence and abuse (Baral *et. al.* 2011).[18] identity crisis poses another problem of trans abuse within the community. In a North American study, it was found that a sample of female to male TGPs were sexually attracted to men, aiming their identity and sexuality in context of a culture of transgender empowerment (Bockting *et al,* 2009).[19]

Legal Protection

The Constitution of India prohibits discrimination on the basis of sex also (Article 15). Since gender is taken to mean only male and female, the Transgenders cannot effectively exercise or avail the benefits of constitutional rights, facilities and benefits available to the male and female genders. Due to International pressure and social injustice exercised by the society and indifferent attitude of the government, India has recently responded to this issue with a series of public forums, established by the Indian Constitution for Legal Rights and Aid, that are breaking new ground in transgender rights. During the first forum in Mumbai on November 29, 2011, transgendered people living in India spoke about rights violations, unique health needs, and experiences with violence.

It has been seen that transgenders, most of the time are denied from legal protection. UN treaty bodies have raised concerns about trans people's exclusion from anti-discrimination legislation, and about inadequate reports to combat such discrimination.

1. On 20 October 2008 at 11 A.M. the police caught the hijras near a traffic signal in the Girinagar police station and took them to the police station. The Assistant Commissioner of Police, beat one of them with his lathi, broke her bangles and made her bleed. Another hijra was forced to clean the floor of the police station. The police then charged them with false cases under Section 341 [wrongful restraint] and 384 [extortion] of the Indian Penal Code...The police asked offensive questions and taunted the crisis intervention team who went to the police station to assist: "Take of all your clothes; let me see what you've got there? Are you a man or woman?" (www.sangama.org/files/sexual-minorities.pdf)[20]

Legal Gender Recognition

In April 2014, in a landmark judgment in *National Legal Authority (NALSA)* v. *Union of India and Others,* the Supreme Court ruled that transgender people should be recognised as a 'third gender' and not only enjoy all fundamental rights, but also receive special benefits in education and jobs. Supreme Court finally recognised the rights of transgender people to vote, to get an education, or to find job.

The Ministry of Social Justice and Empowerment, Government of India is currently enacting a law for the welfare of TGP and addressing their rights. The Committee constituted by the GOI already suggested to improve their conditions. Educational opportunities to be further widened from RTE to Saakshar Bharat. Focus is to bring them in the mainstream and reintegrating them in the family. The GOI will soon discuss 'Transgender Bill' in the Parliament. The national AIDS Control Organisation (NACO) formed a National Level Committee to develop resource pool working in the field of transgender population.

Transgender People and Legal Reforms

1. **The United Nation's Perspective:** United Nation's Human Rights Commission (2012) recommends five critical measures which could at the core of free and fair legal paradigm for the empowerment of transgender people. These measures include (a) protection from transphobic violence, (b) prevention of subhuman treatment, (c) repealing of discriminatory laws, (d) prohibition of gender-based discrimination and (e) safeguarding of equal rights including right to freedom of expression, association, marriage and adoption. The UNHR report argues that in order to safeguard the rights of transgender people, we need not specifically evolve a new legal

framework but the extension of equal rights to all citizens including transgender. Thus, it is argued that "protecting LGBT people from violence and discrimination does not require the creation of a new set of LGBT-specific rights, nor does it require the establishment of new international human rights standards. For all the heat and complexity of the political debate about LGBT Equality at the United Nations, from a legal perspective the issue is straightforward. The obligations that States have to protect LGBT persons from violations of their human rights are already well established and are binding on all United Nations Member States"(Op.cit., p.12)[21].

What is necessary is the removal of the gender bias of law and a positive recognition of multiplicity and fluidity of genders.

Protection from Transphobic Crimes

Transgender people often face violence, including sexual violence. They are also random victims of hate crimes against sexual minorities. The worst form of this violence is targeted killing which is sanctioned as punishment for 'gender transgression'. "Honour" killing is also a form of violence infested upon transgender people across the world. There are also state agencies and non-state agencies who engage violently with transgender people. Without transgender people get 'equality in front of law', they cannot achieve the status of equality and non-discrimination in society. Transgender people face dire violence. Arbitrary detention of transgender people by law enforcement agencies must also be avoided. It means that that the existing legal provisions against ill-treatment, torture, violence and abuse must be equally extended to the transgender people.

Anti-discrimination Laws for TGP

Gender identity has been a ground for discrimination against transgender people. They are deprived of employment opportunities, educational opportunities, access to law and healthcare. One cannot forget that "United Nations treaty bodies have consistently held that sexual orientation and gender identity are prohibited grounds of discrimination under international law. Many states in the United States have passed laws that prohibiting discrimination against transgender people in areas such as housing, employment and education. The law needs to recognise the discriminated living conditions of transgender people and enact ameliorative legal and welfare provisions.

Sexual Rights of Transgender People: Transgender people, like any other sections of the population, have the right to adult consensual sexual activities. Importantly, they must be freed from coerced sex and also from working as bonded sex workers. Definitions of rape and sexual assault must be advanced in order to include sexual crimes committed against transgender people. Without guaranteeing freedom of expression, association, and peaceful assembly, we cannot ensure the safeguarding of the sexual rights of people with non-conforming gender identities.

Laws in Various Countries

Many European nations give the right to change gender in the birth certificate. They permit legal identity change along with the sex change. Such countries also permit marriage rights based on post-sex reassignment medical process. There is a distinction between transgender by birth and transgender by choice.

The Gender Recognition Act, 2004 in United Kingdom provides full legal recognition to transgender people. All certificates can be changed to the new adopted gender. The gender recognition certificate can also be used for annulment of marriage. A minimum period of two years after transition for the applicant to get the certificate but surgery is not legally required. Germany has a transsexual law from 1980 onwards, which allows for change of first name and gender identity determination in special cases. The change in legal gender is permitted based on a medical diagnosis of transsexual features, three years of living in the preferred gender, and the stability in preferred choice. Also, for the change in legal gender, permanent infertility and changes in outer sexual characteristics were required but removed later in 2011 revision.

Ireland does not allow for change in birth certificate. The argument goes that birth certificate is a historical document which cannot be altered. Transgender people in Ireland are not permitted to marry or enter into civil partnership based on their adopted gender. The courts later asked for a new legislation which would allow gender change in birth certificate and marriage rights in acquired gender.

Poland recognises the right to change gender without even undergoing medical reassignment. However, courts usually ask for medical evidences when it comes to many practical issues. People change their name in order to reflect gender preferences in Romania. The post-operative legal change can be made after a genital reassignment surgery. On the contrary, in Spain, legal gender/ name change in all documents could be carried out based on personal request, without any medical alterations. Hormonal treatment, except for age or health reasons, is a condition for such gender change along with diagnosis of gender dysphoria.

In the United States and Canada, the legal provisions regarding transgender vary from state to state. Because of federalism, the United States bestows the states with the right to legal rights of transgender people. Some states recognise sex reassignment but short of marriage rights. Some states allow for altering the original birth certificate to change the gender identity. In Alberta in Canada, two doctors need to certify that anatomical sex of the applicant has been changed. Australia also allows for anew birth certificate following the gender reassignment.

Legal Recognition of the Gender Status and Legal Rights of TGPs in UP/India

Until 2014, TGP never gained a heed in India. For the first time in the Census of India, 2011, they were counted as 'others' or 'third gender'.

So far none of the state governments except Tamil Nadu has made provision for changing transgender people's birth name and sex in official gazette and official identity documents either after realising their gender identity or undergoing sex transition surgeries. Notably, Tamil Nadu state government through its Transgender Welfare Board (TGWB) constituted a district level screening committee in each district to certify 'aravanis' (M t F transgender persons) after screening and provide an identity card. The content of the card include: birth (male) name, transgender (feminine gender) name, permanent address, and membership number. Card does not mention the gender identity (as transgender/aravani) of the bearer. This identity card is usually required if transgender people apply for TG-specific welfare schemes (e.g., loans for self-help groups) of TGWB, or if they go to government hospitals to obtain SRS services. While some members complained that TGWB ID card is not accepted as a valid card for identity and address proof (e.g., for opening bank accounts), some have opened bank accounts and obtained passports using this card. In recent past, Tamil Nadu state government has introduced provision for changing MtF TG people's name (from male to female name) and sex/ gender (female/'transgender') in official gazette. Besides, the government publishes sex- and name-change notice of post-operative transgender individuals whose sex change is certified by a medical doctor that included obstetrician/gynaecologist. (Arvind and Narrain 2010).[22]

However, it was not clear whether usual practise of public notification would specifically result in any adverse consequences for those individuals due to implicit/explicit disclosure of their past sex status. And, the possible benefits that transgender people might get after making changes in official gazette is yet to be tested/ clarified. In some states, post-SRS medical certificate issued by qualified SRS service providers was helpful for some transgender individuals in getting ID documents in new/self-assigned gender followed by SRS. Presently, passports are given as 'female' based on post SRS medical certificate or self-reported transgender and 'emasculation' status although there are no written guidelines from the Union government for the process of providing passport for transgender people.

Thus, male to female sex change in official documents appears to be possible only for post-operative transsexuals, leaving out pre-operative TG people (waiting to undergo SRS), TG people who are medically unfit for surgeries, and self-identified TG people unwilling to undergo SRS–all of whom might want to change their gender in the official identity documents. Furthermore, lack of uniformity in the way gender/sex ('transgender' 'woman') is mentioned in the post-operative (SRS) medical certificates and lack of uniform procedures in the name and gender change in identity documents means many trans people could not be able to have identity documents that have their desired name or 11 District screening committee functions under the Chairmanship of District Collector and members included Deputy Director of Medical and Rural Health Services, District Social Welfare Officer, a clinical psychologist, a psychiatrist, and a transgender community representative. The committee assesses psychological (Transgenderism) status and emasculation status (that is, whether or not the person has undergone emasculation or sex change operation). In particular, role of the community representative is to assess whether the person belongs to the transgender community (irrespective of self-identify of the person). In June 2011, the United Nations Human Rights Council expressed grave concern at acts of violence and discrimination, in all regions of the world, committed against individuals because of their sexual orientation and gender identity. It requested the office of the United Nations High Commissioner for Human Rights (OHCHR) to prepare a study documenting discriminatory laws and practices and acts of violence. The study was tasked with specifying how international human rights law can be used to end such human rights violations. The resulting report concluded a pattern of human rights violations emerges that demands a response.

Indian Constitutional Framework and the Naz Decision

India has a well-established framework of fundamental rights embedded in the Constitution. With the recent Naz decision (see below) there is a new precedent to discern transgender rights being recognised by the Constitution. The four important provisions from the point of LGBT rights are:

Article14. The State shall not deny to any person equality before the law or the equal protection of the laws within the territory of India. Article 15. The State shall not discriminate against any citizen on grounds only of religion, race, caste, sex, place of birth or any of them. Article 19. All citizens shall have the right: (a) to freedom of speech and expression; (b) to assemble peaceably and without arms; (c) to form associations or unions; (d) to move freely throughout the territory of India; (e) to reside and settle in any part of the territory of India; and (g) to practise any profession, or to carry on any occupation, trade or business. Article 21. No person shall be deprived of his life or personal liberty except according to procedure established by law. In terms of criminal law, until the decision of the Delhi High Court in *Naz Foundation* vs. *NCT Delhi* in 2009, all non-penovaginal sexual relationships among consensual adults were a criminal offence under Section 377 of the

Indian Penal Code meriting a maximum punishment of life imprisonment. The said provision violated Article 17 and Article 2(1) of the ICCPR.

The importance of the Naz decision was that it gave a new interpretation to the existing framework of Constitutional Rights. These four provisions included above are the heart of the Fundamental Rights Chapter. Prior to the Naz decision, it was never seen fit to apply these provisions to LGBT persons. What the Naz decision did was to apply the understanding of Constitutional rights to a minority which had never been deemed worthy of rights protection or judicial consideration. As the Delhi High Court observed, invoking Jawaharlal Nehru: 'If there is one constitutional tenet that can be said to be underlying theme of the Indian Constitution, it is that of 'inclusiveness'. This Court believes that Indian Constitution reflects this value deeply ingrained in Indian society, nurtured over several generations. The inclusiveness that Indian society traditionally displayed, literally in every aspect of life, is manifest in recognising a role in society for everyone. Those perceived by the majority as "deviants" or "different" are not on that score excluded or ostracised'.

Taking the Naz decision forward: *National Legal Services Authority v. Union of India:* The National Legal Services Authority has been proactive in addressing the concerns of the transgender community by initiating judicial sensitisation programmes about the issues facing the transgender community in various states. In Karnataka, the State Legal Services Authority, then headed by Justice Manjula Chellur had organised workshops on the issues of transgender people and the law in Belgaum, Gulbarga, Shimoga and Bangalore. This initiative was part of a larger national programme spearheaded by the National Legal Services Authority (NALSA) to bring this issue in the judicial mainstream. Justice Altamas Kabir, who then headed NALSA has publicly stated that he has proposed an amendment to a bill that is being discussed around extending adoption rights to various religious groups on the lines of the Special Marriage Act, to also include provisions that will enable transgender persons to legally adopt.

NALSA has taken this concern forward by now filing a public interest litigation (PIL) specifically related to entitlements for transgender people. The NALSA petition states that Article 21 of the Constitution provided fundamental right to life and personal liberty that could not be denied to transgender people. It further stated: "Right to life includes right to live with human dignity and transgender are entitled to bare necessities in life such as food, nutrition, clothes, shelter, medical facilities, right to education and to adopt children, and marry. Every citizen has the right to decide their sex orientation and to espouse and determine their identity including transsexual, transgender, transvestites and they are entitled to be considered as third and equal sex. The Citizenship Act of India uses the expression person without reference to sex. Transgender, being citizens of India, ought to be entitled to vote and to contest elections as they are natural persons. Many hospitals and other institutions do not admit them in women's ward because women do not feel comfortable or free in their presence and in men's ward they face sexual abuse. Provision of separate wards in all hospitals and other institutions is necessary. Various manifestations of deprivation are the consequence of the practice of recognising only two sexes-or-genders for various facilities, amenities and privileges; that is, male and female. There is an urgent need for recognising the third gender that is transgender. Treating a transgender as a legal non-entity was a violation of Articles 14, 15 and 16 of the Constitution and it was arbitrary and discriminatory, NALSA noted and sought a direction to the Centre and States to recognise them as a third category for the purpose of conferring various benefits."

In relation to NALSA's petition, the Supreme Court in its order dated October 1, 2012, has observed: "This petition has been filed by National Legal Services Authority to recognise and grant Transgender a legal status as a third gender and to recognise their rights under Articles 14, 15,16 and 21 of the Constitution of India. Petitioner also seeks direction to the Union of India and State Governments to grant equal protection and rights to Transgender as available to males and females of this country. The question involved is of considerable public importance which calls for an authoritative pronouncement which will have far reaching consequence to Transgender community." (Discussion Paper, 2013)[23]

Legal Gains for the Transgender Community in India

The binary division of aspects of life leaves no space for the TGPs in the division between male and female. The society and the law, is negative towards acknowledging them as part of it (Abhyankar, 2012).[24] The traditional dichotomous gender paradigm is oppressive (Burdge, 2007).[25] While the struggle at the level of the Courts continues, some important advances have been made in transgender rights without much fanfare in some ways amounting to a silent revolution. In India, one's gender and sex is fixed at birth and is used in all subsequent legal transactions. Thus, binary classification of gender into male and female that does not recognise a third gender category, as the Peoples' Union for Civil Liberties (PUCL) Report on 'Human Rights Violations against the Transgender Community' argues, turns the transgender status of hijras into that of a legal non-entity. The PUCL report recommends that "Civil rights under law such as the right to get a passport, ration card, make a will, inherit property and adopt children must be available to all regardless of change in gender/sex identities." (PUCL-K 2003)[26]

Furthermore, India does not recognise sex changes on identity cards, which makes it impossible for an intersex person or hijra to choose a legal female identity in most states. Lack of legal recognition has important consequences in getting government ration (food-price subsidy) shop card, passport, and bank account.

The UNDP Report (2010) 'Hijras/Transgender in India: HIV, Human Rights and Social Exclusion'[24] recommends: "Develop action steps toward taking a position on legal recognition of gender identity of Hijras/TG need to be taken in consultation with Hijras/TG and other key stakeholders. Getting legal recognition and avoiding ambiguities in the current procedures that issue identity documents to Hijras/TG are required as they are connected to basic civil rights such as access to health and public service, right to vote, right to contest elections, right to education, inheritance rights, and marriage and child adoption."(Chakrapani, 2010)[27]

Elections: For the purposes of securing an Election ID card, persons can use the category called 'Other'. Also, when it comes to contesting elections as women, it must be noted that openly transgender persons have contested elections as women in India. The Madhya Pradesh High Court in a ruling in Kamala Jaan's case ruled that hijras are not women and are not entitled to contest elections within the category of seats reserved for women. However, in 2009, Veena S contested elections for the Bangalore Municipality.Veena herself was not the first transgender person to contest local elections with at least eleven transgender persons before Veena taking the electoral plunge and winning the elections.

ID Documents: The recognition of transgender people is seen in new identity documents such as the Unique Identification Number with the gender category including male, female and transgender (though, access to this still has been limited)[27]. It is estimated that over 19,000 transgender people across the country have been issued Aadhaar Cards that recognise them as a third gender (Sethi, 2012)[28].

During months of hearings, the election commission heard written and oral testimony (or "representations") from "various individuals and interest groups", according to TOI. Election commissioner Qureshi explained, "When the representation came, we readily agreed. Why should a section of the population be left out? The decision will help in mainstreaming a section of the population. I am sure even government would like to do the same". (TOI Nov 13, 2009) [29]

Property: In the opinion of the MP High Court, a hijra woman was allowed to receive property from her Guru because the court accepted that the community cannot transfer property to anyone outside of the community. In this ruling the court explicitly acknowledges the existence of a distinct 'eunuch' class with its own customs and rituals that must be respected (AIR1990 MP 334)[30].

Legal Gains for TGP Community at the State Level

The States of Karnataka and Tamil Nadu over the past few years have implemented the most progressive policies for transgender and gender-variant people in India. These states serve as promising examples of what can be realised in the rest of India.

Karnataka

Legal classification as 'backward' community: The government is now grappling with the question of what systems to set in place to help identify communities marginalised on the basis of their gender identity. The impetus for these benefits in the state were a direct result of a number of developments in the state, the most important of these being the C.S. Dwarakanath Backward Classes Commission Report of 2010, which emerged through a series of testimonials before the Commission in the same year. The Commission recommended that the transgender community be included in the category of more backward communities (2-B) that would then entitle them to government benefits. The Commission recommended to the Government of Karnataka to include the sexual minorities called Hijras, Kothis, Jogappa, Female to Male [transgender people], Mangalamukhis, and Transgenders in the Category II (B) of the Backward Classes List. The basis for this decision was their finding that none of the persons from these communities who they had spoken to got government jobs either in Government Departments or in the non-government agencies (Dwarkanath, 2010)[31].

Economic Justice: Intensive efforts of local queer rights groups have resulted in a Government Order that secures benefits for 'gender minorities' – a term that encompasses a range of gender identities including kothi, hijra, female to male transsexuals, mangalamukhis, and jogappas. The Karnataka Government has recently enacted orders that provide for socio-economic benefits for these people[33]. The Karnataka High Court recently appointed C. Anu, a transgender person, to an administrative job in the Group D category (Chakrapani, 2012)[32].

Identification: Government officials have acknowledged the lack of identity documents as one of the main reasons for the limited efficacy of existing schemes for transgender people. In its 2012-2013 Budget, the Karnataka Government has instituted an initiative entitled Lingathwara Alpasankhyathara Yojana (Gender Minorities Programme) proposing to implement trainings, loans and subsidies through NGOs working in the area (because transgender people may not have permanent addresses and may have issues with. Currently the state government is in consultation with sexuality rights groups and psychiatrists in NIMHANS to evolve methods of identifying persons who will be eligible for state benefits.

Civil Society: Bangalore University has announced reservation for transgender persons in its postgraduate courses. In addition, the National Institute of Neurosciences and Mental Health (NIMHANS), in collaboration with NGOs, is establishing mechanisms to identify transgender people who will be eligible for medical entitlements under the Karnataka government order.

Conclusion

Realising the right to development for trans people, like other marginalised groups, is about core development issues such as gender justice, poverty reduction, mitigating negative health and HIV consequences, the protection and exercise of human rights and combating gender-based violence. It requires trans people's inclusion in society on an equal basis with others.

It is impossible to be included within a community and society if one's very existence is denied. Yet such exclusion is routinely experienced by trans people when there are only two, binary sex options (male or female).

All human beings are born free and equal in dignity and ought to be entitled to enjoyment of human rights without discrimination on the basis of sexual orientation or gender identity. Everyone is entitled to equality before the law and equal protection of the law without any such discrimination. Transgenders are also part of society and have equal, rights as are available to other persons. The discrimination based on their class and gender makes the transgender community one of the most disempowered and deprived groups in Indian society. In view of the constitutional guarantee, the transgender community is entitled to basic rights i.e. Right to Personal Liberty, dignity, Freedom of expression, Right to Education and Empowerment, Right against violence, Discrimination and exploitation and Right to work. Moreover, every person must have the right to decide his/her gender expression and identity, including transsexuals, transgenders, hijras and should have right to freely express their gender identity and be considered as a third sex.

In 2003, the Hon'ble High Court of Madhya Pradesh upheld the order of an Election Tribunal which nullified the election of a Hijra, Kamala Jaan, to the post of Mayor of Katni, on the ground that it was a seat reserved for women and that Kamla Jaan, being a 'male' was not entitled to contest the seat. It is submitted that all the citizens of India have a right to vote and to contest elections. But in the electoral rolls only two categories of the sex are mentioned–male and female. This is unfair to the third sex of India as they are deprived of their statutory right to vote and contest elections.

Transgender persons must be properly documented in census. There is need for statutory reservation in education, elections and employment both in the public and private sectors. They need to be empowered and uplifted by facilities for higher education and vocational training to upgrade their earnings and status in society so as to promote their acceptability in society.

Since transgenders are prone to health risks and setbacks, they need to be provided proper medical facilities, including health insurance and clinics, where free or subsidised treatment should be made available.

The different manifestations of discrimination and deprivation are a consequence of the practice of recognising and providing only for the male and/or the female sex. This gets reflected in prescribed forms for applying for various privileges, facilities or amenities, as these do not reflect that a person may belong to a gender, other than male or female.

Therefore, it would be worth Suggesting that treating TGP as 'Third Gender' is again discriminating them, rather, TGP MtF should be counted and treated as female and FtM as male. They should not be discriminated on any ground, a social approval to this is a precondition for giving social justice to TGPs.

Notes

- Data on Transgender persons is based on the Census Report 2011, GOI.
- The National Centre for Transgender Equality is the nation's leading social justice advocacy organisation winning life-saving change for transgender people. NCTE was founded in 2003 by transgender activists who recognised the urgent need for policy change to advance transgender equality in Washington, D.C.
- October of 1973 in New York City, the National Gay Task Force was started, then transforming to the National Gay and Lesbian Task Force now known as National LGBTQ Task Force.

References

1. Census of India, 2011, GOI.
2. Jaime, M. et al. (2011). Injustice at Every Turn: A Report of the National Transgender Discrimination Survey. National Centre for Transgender Equality and National Gay and Lesbian Task Force, Washington:
3. PUCL-K, (2003). Human Rights Violations against the Transgender Community: A PUCL Report.
4. www.sangama.org/files/sexual-minorities.pdf
5. Op.cit. p. 7.
6. Greenberg, K. (2012). 'Still Hidden in the Closet: Trans Women and Domestic Violence', Berkeley Journal of Gender, Law and Justice, 27 (1) pp. 198-251.
7. Hammarberg, T. (2008). Hate Crimes: The Ugly Face of Racism, Anti-Semitism, Anti-Gypsyism, Islamophobia and Homophobia, Strasbourg: Council of Europe, Strasbourg.
8. Balzer, C. and Hutta, J. (2012). Transrespect versus Transphobia WorldWide, TGEU, pp. 22 and 68.
9. Op.cit. p. 10.
10. Discussion Paper (2013). Transgnder Health and Human Rights, UNDP.

11. Greytak, E. *et al.* (2009). Harsh Realities: The Experiences of Transgender Youth in Our Nation's Schools. GLSEN. New York.
12. Harrington, M. (2008). "The Rationing of Rights" in Tehelka Magazine, 5 (15).
13. Redding, J. (2011). From 'She-Males' to 'Unix': Transgender Rights in Pakistan and the Criminal Law Origins of a Constitutional Case, Global Commission on HIV and the Law (2012) p. 53.
14. Op.cit. p. 12.
15. Op.cit. p.10.
16. Whittle, S., et.al. (2007). Engendered Penalties: Transgender and Transsexual People's Experiences of Inequality and Discrimination, Press for Change, London. p. 16.
17. Global Commission on HIV and the Law (2012), p. 51.
18. Baral, S. Beyrer, C. and Poteat, T (2011). Human Rights, The Law, and HIV among Trans Gender People. In Third Meeting of the Technical Advisory Group of the Global Commission on HIV and Law.
19. Bockting et al (2009). Gay and Bisexual Identity Development among Female to Male Trans Sexuals in North America: Emergence of a Trans gender Sexuality. Archives of Sexual Behaviour, 38(5), 688-701.
20. www.sangama.org/files/sexual-minorities.pdf
21. Born Free and Equal: Sexual Orientation and Gender Identity in International Human Rights Law, New York and Geneva.
22. Arvind and Narrain, S (2010). "CJ Reference: Human Rights, Sexual Orientation and Gender Identity Background paper for the 15th Annual Meeting of the Asia Pacific Forum of National Human Rights Institutions.
23. Op.cit. p. 12.
24. Abhyankar, G N (2012). Legal Rights of Eunachs- Indian and International Perception. Available at SSRN 243007.
25. Burdge. (2007). Bending Gender, Ending Gender: Theoretical Foundations for Social Work Practice with the Transgender Community, Social Work, Vol. 52, No. 3 (July 2007).
26. Peoples' Union for Civil Liberties, Karnataka (PUCL-K), (September 2003); Human Rights Violations Against the Transgender Community; pp. 7-11.
27. Chakrapani, V. (2010). Hijras/Transgender Women in India: HIV, Human Rights and Social Exclusion. UNDP (India).
28. Sethi, A. (2012). Getting Aadhaar Card Big Challenge for Transgenders, Deccan Herald.
29. TOI Nov.13, 2009.
30. *Illyas and Others* v. *Badshah, alias Kamla.* AIR 1990MP 334. https://indiankanoon.org/doc/490695/
31. Dwarakanath, C.S. (2010). Backward Classes Commission Report.
32. Chakrapani and Narrain (2012). Legal Recognition of Gender Identity of Transgender People in India: Current Situation and Potential Options, UNDP (India).

Unit - II

Socio-economic Aspects of Globalisation

Chapter - 8

Smart City and the New Indian Middle Class

—***Pratick Mallick***

Smart city is the newest term in the politics of Indian urbanisation oriented to ameliorate the environmental conditions of human beings and to ensure their survival. Smart city projects target the reduction of carbon footprint in the uses of different modern contrivances. Every-year Conference of Parties *(CoP) summits held and take pledges to reduce the environmental pollution across the world on an egalitarian basis. Obviously, some provisions of privileges for the third world countries are made in terms of providing extra period for implementations of the decisions of those summits. However, the paper intends to demonstrate how such damage control mechanisms generate two separate challenges to domestic politics in India as a developing society. First, such preferences given to the developing and backward countries are sometimes criticised by thinkers of* state theories *and* post-neo-colonialist *in the age of globalisation by unbridled use of the communicative devices like computer, mobile phones, air conditioners etc. emitting Green House Gases. These gadgets have been the basic consumables to the Indian middle class, which is no more* only *representation of middle class but the* new *version of the Indian middle class. Due to continuous progress in the Tertiary sector of the economy and commercialisation of education, the New Indian Middle Class (NIMC) is continuously assuming numerical preponderance and psychological stronghold so much so that they have become almost both consumers as well as producers in the present globalised Indian market. Secondly, as already indicated, with an innate psychological intent for better life-styles and systemic alienation generated due to over indulgence in mechanical works, this class is indulging in the* politics of forgetting. *Subsequently, causing a steady transformation in the subaltern politics in India which includes the transformation in the nature of leadership as well as the policies being formulated remained highly NIMC centric.*

Key Words: *New Indian Middle Class, Smart City, Environment, Policy, Market.*

Introduction

This is the age of smart cities that follows the principles associated with the concept, amenities, deficiencies, and challenges of the smart cities. Before smart cities, there emerged the popularity of smart phones, which, if deeply analysed, does not have much discrepancy in principles with smart cities. I think I should begin with the smart phones because it will help one to develop the ideas step by step; smart phones are found nowadays in the hands of the most of the young people even much below the age of being eligible for earning both physically as well as educationally. Smart phones are also found being used by almost all others who belong to the lower rungs of the societal hierarchy, like housemaids, drivers, rickshaw-pullers, even the owners of small tea stalls. Psychologically, using smart phones prepares them being somewhat accustomed to a better life-style, that is, an inner feeling of getting rid of their traditional lives of constant wants and complaints.

Similarly, this is the age of smart cities. The Government of India in recent past has launched a policy of making 100 Indian cities smart. The government is taking initiatives in making them smart in all respects. Therefore, we should first try to understand what this so-called smartness is! In the parlance of postmodernism, the binary is smart and unsmart. These two terms are based on the extent of *scientism*; in other words, at the time when the secondary sector of the economy became the most dependable vein of the national economy, the purpose of science became limited to manufacturing of the equipments for the sake of manufacturing the daily consumables. Therefore, that era was concerned with building up machines for manufacturing the daily merchandises to be sold in market. At that time, therefore, attention could not be made towards the consequences of such mechanisation. By consequences, pollution got produced out of the emission of the Green House Gases (GHGs) like Chlorofluorocarbon (CFC) etc. In other words, the factory-based economy had the responsibility to provide the market with various consumables; as a result, it could not find chances to pay attention elsewhere, particularly, to pollution. Therefore, pollution has so far aggravated the situation of health, hygiene, physical appearance of various natural and artificial elements at stake. To get rid of such crisis, almost all countries of the world come forward to build up a common platform of making pledges of reducing pollution. Terminologically speaking, pollution can be reduced by reducing the carbon footprints. So, from the viewpoint of environmental degradation, newer technologies should be acceptable. But, it is not that pollution does not take place at all. Even many of these technologies are death-monger, even carcinogenic.

Science of Pollution

In due course it is necessary to denote what carbon footprints means; carbon footprints roughly means the existence of carbon (C) in any form—be that in gaseous forms like that in Carbon Di-Oxide (CO_2), Carbon Monoxide (CO) etc. or in liquid forms like the soluble state of CO_2 etc. In this regard, we should keep in mind the question as to the effects of C. Why C is so much concerned about? Let me explain very briefly the chemical particulars of C.

Carbon is most used in rural areas in the form of *Active Charcoal* as the rural people prefer using wooden fuel; the reasons are manifold. It ranges from their *generational tradition* to *poverty* to *under/no development*. Whatever the reasons, the ultimate result is that the environment gets polluted out of the smoke which contains mostly CO. Related to this, another area of Chemistry is important to reflect upon. That is the *Properties of Gases* or *the Laws of Gases*. There is a famous law—*Charles' Law*—according to which, the volume of a gas of a certain mass at 0°C temperature will increase or decrease with the increase or decrease (as the case may be) in the temperature of the environment. According to this, 1° C increase in temperature will cause $1/273^{rd}$ volume of a gas in a given environment. Therefore, it can be said that in an environment full of pollution, it is natural for the temperature to increase as a consequence of which, the gas is supposed to spread across a larger scope of environment. In other words, the emission of C leads to increase in temperature; and, that temperature increase leads to expansion in the volume of the gas concerned. Therefore, it will hinder the normal movement of fresh air with sufficient volume of Oxygen (O_2). As it is an innate characteristic of C is to promote heat, so in such case, the temperature will continue to be high always.

Evolution from Old to New Economy

The word 'smart' is used mainly to denote *efficient uses of polluting elements*. As already indicated, a carbon footprint reflects the Green House Gases produced out of human activities, generally expressed in equivalence with Carbon Dioxide (CO_2). It may be in various manners. The most sought-after way to it is the swapping of old machines instead of lessening production. In fact, in this age of globalisation, assembling of accessorial parts of an entire machine is on vogue. Obviously, this leads to reduction in the emission of carbon as the production gets decentralised. But, on the other hand, environment being *open* across the world, it does not matter whether a colossal volume of pollution is shared across a large volume of area in a de-constructed manner. Therefore, the best policy to target reduction of the carbon footprint is the *replacement of old machines at the behest of the new kind of modern ones*. Obviously, so much so far, this is all about on the part of the investors who are sometimes to be *protected* by the government in the Keynesian manner, in which state assumes the role of a physician. Then, we should look into the use of consumable machines by the individuals. In this regard, it is essential to consider the theories of *determinism* as well as *neo-determinism*. By *determinism*, it is meant that nature determines the behaviour of human beings. Thomas Malthus was a scientific determinist who emphasised both influences of different environments as well as the limitations that the earth put upon the social process of development (Husain, 2004: 274). Even Carl Ritter has also opined that the physical environment determines the course of human development (*ibid*). He was further justified by Charles Darwin in his

Origin of Species (1859). However, in the wake of innovations, they are supposed to enjoy such contrivances as are necessary to be triumphant over the nature. For instance, we now use at random the air-conditioner and refrigerators in order to keep ourselves and food items respectively cool and fresh even when stale. Contrary to *determinism*, this is termed as *neo-determinism* in which human beings behave in the way they want instead of what and how nature provides. Griffith Taylor, an Australian geographer, who coined the term *stop-and-go-determinism* elaborated the concept of *neo-determinism*. He said that in short term, it is the choice of people as to what they would do to environment but in the long-term the nature is to win over human beings forcing human beings to make a compromise (*ibid*: 287). But, this *neo-determinism* generates GHGs amplifying the causes of global warming in a broader dimension so much so that the effects of over-uses of such machines are identified as the instruments of ice-melt even in the polar region, on the high and inaccessible altitude of the Himalayas, superfluous increase in the height of sea-level, thereby, promoting the causes of the worldwide flood; the serious crisis is not to end with that only. Such floodwater once evaporates, there will remain hardly any origin of water in existence for future uses. That means, the world *may* thenceforth face a permanent drought. Therefore, keeping these in view, it is necessary that carbon footprints should be used very economically in a cost-effective manner so that it does cause (1) no further by-products of carbon out of indiscriminate use of technology, (2) deliberate reduction of carbon emission, (3) deliberate increase in the deposition of O_2. *Sociologically* and in terms of Economics, it can be assured that the ability to afford neo-determinism as such is within well reach of the new Indian middle class who like to lead lives in sophisticated manners, by investing into a better life-style as distinguished from the traditional habit of improvisation almost in everything in terms of the daily lives. It is even said nowadays that this class consists of the people the credibility of the economy can rely upon.

Smart Cities *vis-à-vis* the Developed and the Developing

The concept of smart cities is the highest stage of *online development*. In other words, the journey starts with e-governance and reaches the highest level in terms of *smart cities*. We are already aware of what e-governance is. But, it should be classified in terms of distinct extent of development by merging with the ideas of *cybernetics* which in greater degree of intensity and effects should surface out in the garb of modified forms of *demand polity* and *command polity* as developed by Rudolph and Rudolph (1987). The positive feedback stage of e-governance can be termed as *demand e-governance polity*, in which the citizens need to be aware of governmental policies, actions and welfare activities as well as utility policies. Till then, e-governance functions as a source of public information and, the citizens use it at their will. But, in due course, when all the public dealings are done only online, it becomes a compulsion for all the citizens. It can be termed as the *e-governance polity by default* or, interchangeably as, *command e-governance polity* in which the government agencies are found to determine the mode of interactions between the citizens and governments only in terms of internet. This leads to *compulsory usage of computers and internet.* As a result, the consumption of handy and portable communication devices like smart phones, tab and laptops, dongles and pen-drives find luck in huge purchases on a mass scale. Simultaneously, such devices emit radiation in a no-negligible manner. The *World Health Organisation* (WHO) has revealed the radiation levels of smart phones whose usage is going to be absolute in near future in India. WHO declared that such radiation is *possibly carcinogenic* (Aamoth, 2011). Smart phones emit *radio frequency* that is absorbed by human body. Recently, Indian Railways decided to launch an App for the passengers to purchase rail tickets instead of standing in queues at the ticket counter; obviously, such decision has so many merits like waiving wastage of time for the passengers who can buy tickets on the way itself, nipping in bud the tendency of some passengers not to buy tickets on pretext of long queues at the ticket counter as well as reduction of necessity for manual employees in the Railways. Still, it cannot shrug off the issues of radiation of smart phones due to the possibility of mass use of them only for purchasing rail tickets.

In this regard, we should be sensitive to the use of particular terms. There are **two terms** we should be well aware of—*developed* and *developing*—in reckoning the logistics of the discourses between smart *citisation* (not, *urbanisation*) and its host, the new middle class, who subscribes to the technology-based upliftment. Here, the term *citisation* has been used instead of *urbanisation* because the former is a degree of development of what is already urban. In other words, when the rural turns into a town/city, it is *urbanisation*. But, if a city itself shrugs off the snags of secondary sector approaches and takes on hyper-technology as a mode of transformation, then it should be termed *citisation*, not *urbanisation*. However, back to the main polemic, let me, however, first attempt the term *developing*. It implies an *extent of betterment over the rural or the agrarian.* But, on the other hand, the *developed* means betterment in output at par with the *process of producing the invisibles*. In other words, while the *developing* implies not being detached from the basic economic structure, the *developed*, on the other hand, justifies nothing but the *Structural Adjustment Policy* (SAP). Therefore, the term—*developing*—could be used when there was growth in the secondary sector of the economy whereas the term—*developed*—must entangle a measure by which damages out of the primary and secondary sector(s) of the economy can be controlled by the Tertiary economic growth. *Smart cities* require meticulous institutionalisation of the green economy with the intents of not compromising the human needs to be satisfied in reality. It should be coupled with the *economical* uses of resources by the people who require a proper acculturation of environmental preservation through their daily activities.

Environmental Protections and the World Forum

Since the first decade of the last century, there have been so many concerns to fight against environmental pollution. Even it has become a major chapter in the practice of International Law. In 1972, the *United Nations Conference on Human Environment* was organised in order to ultimately result into the *Stockholm Declaration* of fundamental protection of environmental principles for the sake of the mankind (Singh, 2003: 559). In 1987, there appeared the *Montreal Protocol* as a part of the legal protection of the Ozone layer (*ibid:* 560-2); in 1992, there was organised the *United Nations Conference on Environment and Development* (UNCED or the Earth Summit) in Rio de Janeiro in Brazil (*ibid:* 562-4). These apart, there have been several conventions related to the conservation of environment like *Convention on Biodiversity* (1992), *Convention on Climate Change* (1992), Forest Principles as a part of the *United Nations Food and Agricultural Organisation* (FAO) and later UNCED. Every year, there is held the *Conference of Parties* (CoP) to address the issues related to environmental preservation. The most striking in these all is the phaseout options of cutting the carbon footprints. The phaseout is of two types; one is based on the polluting agents like CFC etc., and the second type is done in terms of development of the countries—developed (or, the first world) and developing (or, the third world). If it is critically analysed, it must not be tough to perceive that the second type of phase-out is not an independent variable. It rather depends on the first type in the sense that the first world is always expected to manage the polluting agents much more efficiently than the third world. As efficiency is also related to time, the third world cannot be expected to emulate the first world in reaching the target in a very short span of time; the basic reason is the fund constraints of the third world because, first, there is huge pressure of population; secondly, the society is full of different chronic problems along with low level of mass education and awareness; thirdly, such countries are basically poor traditionally being colonies of the first world and currently being vulnerable to neo-colonial exploitation as Immanuel Wallerstein has evinced at in his *World System Theory* (2004).

Now, the question is, in accordance with what Wallerstein tried to establish, as to what the phase-out options actually imply in simple parlance! In fact, this is, obviously, a pattern of structural adjustments made towards meeting up the necessities for the third world societies. In other words, they require to be heard by the forum of the first world, thereby, intending to deserve some preferential treatments. We are already well aware of what neo-colonialism meant even few years back during the cold war. It was also termed as the economic imperialism. That might have been the best example for justifying the rationales raised by Wallerstein; but when it is concerned with environmental degradation and preservation, it can be said that it has heralded the first world a new series of options to manipulate the third world countries. On the pretext of cutting down the carbon footprints characterised not to go by the geo-political borders, it paves the way for first world interference with the internal matters of the third world. This can be termed as *neo-post-colonialism*. Therefore, it is the opinion of some Kantian thinkers of *statism* or state theories that such development in the equation between the first and third world(s) is basically a kind of violation of the principles of the United Nations Charter itself, that almost all the countries have given their concurrence to. Again, when challenged with the other side of the same coin that since this is a world platform and the members subscribe to the unanimous decisions and policies, it is never expected that any of them would object to the implementation of those policies. Besides, as such conventions depend on the decision of individual state whether or to be member thereof, it does not seem to be violative, in principle, of sovereignty of the states. But, the question is: if a country does not become a member or signatory or ratifier of such documents, and is considered to be a potential violator of peace of the world, can it not be refrained beforehand? The answer is: yes; this is clearly mentioned in the UN Charter that even if not being a member of the United Nations, it is required to behave in such a manner that would not be the cause of disruption of world peace and security at large.

Smart Cities vis-à-vis New Indian Middle Class

Now, if asked as to how middle class in India is related in the affairs of smart city, it should be considered that there are behavioural interlinks between the two. The idea, definition, and behaviour of the new Indian middle class have undergone a change over the past when the Indian economy was a closed one. In other words, Indian middle class is now new; *new* in the sense that people belonging to this class have become *netizens* and this relation with internet now starts even before the school leaving stage. Truly speaking, nowadays so many young school-going teenagers are very often found to be boast of possession of more than one android mobiles and i-pads or tabs. They go out to play in the afternoon, not in the grounds very few of which still exist due to rapid urbanisation, but to cybercafé to play online. What a paradigmatic change in the mode of playing, indeed! Even they play football online instead of that in person in proximity with nature. The cybercafés are nothing but a room where so many computers are located in a pattern with glass protection from the outside dust. Therefore, the radiation that all the computers continuously emit gets stalled inside the room itself, to be gradually inhaled by those young teenagers to the utter damage of their hygiene. The parents nowadays are much different from their erstwhile counterparts in the sense that with a very meager number of children, the former who are in general absorbed in the Tertiary sector economic behaviour of competition seem to be ascriptive of the same kind of orientations upon their children in case of education. As a result, the parents hegemonise the ideas of playing in the ground as wasting time that could have been instead invested in their education. Besides, each city is now on the process of continuous enlargement to accommodate the demands for development. Consequently, vacant spaces hither and thither are also seldom sights now. And, sky-high buildings–both for residential as well as commercial and office purpose(s) in this Tertiary sector economic phase–stand erect, putting games and sports at stake. The active section of the society in this economic culture is none but the new Indian middle class. Therefore, not only the evicted or socio-economically marginalised, but also the next generation of the new Indian middle class itself get very badly affected in imbibing such artificial culture that go against the natural grain of human beings. Further, this class gets their young wards oriented to a high extent of individualism so much so that they need not be communitarian by nature because the innate philosophy of communitarianism being the social aspect of cooperation and prosperity together, as if justifying the *variable-sum game*, now gets eclipsed as also replaced greatly with the help of modern technology available in smart city.

Another indicator of the continuous increase in the contestations between development and improvement versus degeneration is the recent mis-happenings in terms of MMS scandals found in newspapers often nowadays. Even the increase in the number of railway run-over of youths with mobiles on ears is on rampage now. All these indicate that the young group of India is too highly attached to the newer technologies to. Simultaneously, this further points out that their families have that purchase capacity to afford such new technological gadgets at the behest of their demands. This makes them branded with a new class that wants to enjoy modernity at the sacrifice of money. Alternatively speaking, this is a class that does *not* want to reach the status of very high responsibilities; they want only such a life-style that seems to be better than that needs efforts to *live.* In that case, they really do not bother about deposition for the ill-days. As a result, money gets into circulation in a constant manner, thus, keeping up the liquidity of currency in market. Over last thirty years the Indian market has transformed into that of an enthusiastic pro-capitalist state with the neo-liberal ideology replacing the erstwhile pro-capitalist state system with the socialist ideology (See, Kohli, 2010: 13-4). Given the LPG (Liberalisation Privatisation Globalisation) Policy launched by the then Government of India under the Prime Ministership of P. V. Narasimha Rao and Finance Ministership of Dr Manmohan Singh, Indian market became open for foreign investments; in this regard, one point should be noted that privatisation rather than liberalisation was not made the main target, as a consequence of which the public sector units (PSUs) were not indiscriminately privatised indeed although the policy prescription consisted of tariff reduction, liberal foreign investment laws, and cutting back on public investments (*ibid:* 14). As a result, the Indian middle class got the chance of garnering itself in a new manner, becoming producers as well as consumers at the same time. Therefore, today's *100 smart cities* project of the Government of India is symptomatic to the continuation of the interests of the new Indian middle class.

This apart, the predominance of the first world culture is instrumental in manufacturing the orientation of *politics of forgetting* in reality. There is a controversy concerning the happening of the politics of forgetting. While a school of thought led by Leela Fernandes (2004) is ready to indicate to the alliance between state and middle class in terms of policy-making by which the poor become the scapegoats, another school of thought hesitates accepting so, and rakes up the doubt that if so, then how the change in consumption practices of the poor can be explained! In terms of the paradigm as explained by Fernandes seems to be somewhat identical with what Pranab Bardhan had been keen to highlight by means of his doctrine of *Dominant Proprietary Coalition* (for this term, see Bardhan, 1984: Chapters 6-7). The state-capital alliance for growth is leading to bypassing inequalities in terms of urban-rural divide, class division and regional conflicts (Kohli *op cit.*). In this regard, land acquisition is a major type of making *policies* of forgetting. Obviously, liberalisation has prompted in few States in the last few decades that land of the poor is to be acquired for the sake of establishing industries. India witnessed consequently the fuming of new social movements getting deliberately politicised into such a dimension that, India witnessed, paved the way for the dethronement of even the decade-long regime.

In this regard, state governments in India now need to cultivate the issues related to the establishment of the smart cities. The common people should be consulted on the part of governments. In this regard, the present Government of West Bengal has taken various commendable initiatives. It has also planned that the views of the residents of the proposed smart cities in West Bengal would be taken into consideration to develop it as a smart city in near future. Salt lake is that kind of example in this regard (Chakraborti, 2015). Thus, popular participation is greatly ensured with democratic involvements of the residents in West Bengal by the present regime led by Smt. Mamata Banerjee as the Honourable Chief Minister of this province.

Incidentally, it is alleged by some political anthropologists that middle class identity is concerned with *spatial purification* that wants to cleanse spaces of the poor and working classes, as if thus *forgetting* the subordinated or downtrodden social groups such as squatters and street vendors (Fernandes, 2004: 2416). Here, again, it is necessary to point out the initiatives of the governments to rehabilitate the so-called *forgotten.* With regard to the street vendors, several state governments have laws, which are detrimental to the street vendors. The Government of West Bengal during the regime of the Left Front had become infamous across India for the *Operation Sunshine* that took place the nights of November 16-17, 1996, when more than a hundred thousand street vendors were forcibly evicted from the streets. Even in 1997, the then Kolkata Municipal Corporation Act was amended; it was the Bill No. 33 of 1997 that later became Section 371 of the KMC Act, including 'any basket, receptacle or goods on pavement, street, park or garden for display or sale' (Sub-Section 1). There it was mentioned as newly inserted that any hawker contravening or abetting in contravening Sub-Section 1, shall be punished with rigorous imprisonment for a term not extending up to three months or fined ₹ 250 (For the brief overview of the entire Hawker episode in 1996-97, see Bhowmik, 2006). But, the new regime that came to power in 2011 took special measures for the street vendors in their first tenure (2011-16) itself. This is a commendable step towards providing livelihood opportunity to everybody—organised or unorganised. This is the basic pledge of democracy to provide support on the part of the government. Incidentally, the process of eviction of the illegal squatters needs policy implementation with perfection; in Old Delhi, when the slum dwellers were evicted and given official certificates of displacements, the evicted people became legal claimants in the category of the *displaced persons* (Chatterjee, 2013: 68). Now, it is much smoother to gauge the idea of politics of forgetting in brief. There are so many examples all over India such as Leela Fernandes has highlighted the situations in Mumbai of 1990s. In this regard, it is necessary to remember the language of Professor Partha Chatterjee who vehemently criticised the way the refugees and squatters were given shelters along the rail-lines towards Budge Budge in South Calcutta during the period of monolithic Congress rule in West Bengal through a process of *political negotiation* (Chatterjee, 2013: 13-4). These people were gradually politicised for the rulers after Congress that he described lividly in his famous book—*The Politics of the Governed: Reflections on Popular Politics in Most of the World* (2004) in terms of the anomalies in the application of rule of law there.

Environment, Development and Consociational Democracy

So far as the politics of forgetting is concerned, there is also a symbiosis between tribal population and development. Smitu Kothari (1993) alleges that almost 200 tribes comprising approximately one-third of India's population are displaced and half of them due to development. Massive urbanisation and industrialisation have been able to displace them (Nandy, 2007: 121). This has even put into oblivion the traditional vocations of some other communities (*ibid*). In due course of the discussion of environment-induced development and consequences thereof, in some regions the original environmental conditions have prompted demands for mega-dams, diversion or monopolisation of water resources, deforestation for the sake of better industrialisation of agriculture. As a result, when those demands are fulfilled, the sociological consequences are found to be unwanted because the process to the effect of that demand-fulfilment as such led to evictions from the original habitat and mandatory immigration to towns and cities in search of square meals as happened to Farakka Barriage many decades ago when it was built up. The build-up of this Barriage led to emigration from Southwest fringes of Bangladesh to India, from Bihar and West Bengal to other fringes of India (Swain, 1996, Report 41; Nandy *op cit.*: 122). This has been analysed by Ashok Swain (1996) as an *environmental trap*. Therefore, the response to demands ultimately fails to fructify provided the planning fails to be made meticulously. So far as politics is concerned, this kind of happenings provides the society with some leadership, not with first-hand experiences but from the educated and financially capable sections of the society, that is, the middle class. The interests of a large part of this class are directly related to the newly emerging economic actors in the current scenario of globalisation. The surge for professional qualifications is thus justified in terms of getting jobs in the Tertiary sector, and maintaining that for a considerable period of time. So, there should be raised a question if the politics of forgetting is basically the forgetting of those who are vulnerable to the development with hardly any chance of recovery from their present status of social security. In other words, it may be argued that this might be such a type of capitalisation of the society that the new entrants into the new Indian middle class do not become hindrances to the class identity itself and ultimately do not help but keeping itself detached from the upper stratum of the new middle class. Therefore, primarily, it is a question whether there is an identity of the class itself, which is basically approximated by the rich middle class people; and secondly, if the new entrants are unable to cope with the former as a social solidarity. This second question would be valid provided it can be justified that those who were subalterns at one point of time, particularly, in terms of earning and expense are now becoming members of the new Indian middle class. They try to emulate the richer middle class people at least by investing much into their daily life-styles as compared to their erstwhile cost-effective orientations to expense. Therefore, the concept of pauperisation stands a big challenge of discourse in the face of the new Indian middle class that ultimately consociationates the fragmented community orientations together.

Another major area of development is the issues of crimes that take place in newer forms with the help of newer technologies in this age of Smart Cities. So, it is vehemently necessary to link this with the security and reactions of the new Indian middle class. Normally, this class wants to live undisturbed, that is, free from any kind of unwanted infestations at the hands of the miscreants. Smart cities depend on various modern technologies that help in detection of major crimes. To be very true, a majority of the miscreants nowadays being accustomed to hyper-technological gadgets fail to get detached from these at the time of committing the crimes; it has been rather found out that the miscreants commit crimes deliberately by using the modern gadgets. Therefore, from the viewpoints of policing, uses of these modern gadgets have facilitated the detectives with easy detection of the criminals.

Conclusion

The world is becoming busier each passing day. The people are getting attuned with continuous interactions with the world only by means of the technologies. This has also the economic aspect of prosperity in all respects—individual, national as well as international. So, by no means is it possible to shed the ideas of using technologies. Therefore, the best way-out is using the smart technologies that provide huge facilities at one skin-touch. These technologies are better than the previous ones so far as pollution is concerned; these technologies also abilities to save time, save us from insecurities. Obviously, such technologies need to be within the common reach. The Indian middle class nowadays are market-friendly. To be more specific, people belonging to this class are good earners. At least, they have good purchase capacities. So, it is expected that they can assure betterment of the environment by using such technologies, which will reduce emission of GHG(s) in actions. One thing, in this regard, we should not forget that in this regard, is that smart technologies do pollute the environment less as compared to the traditional technologies but it is not that the smart technologies do not pollute at all. In fact, slow and gradual personal involvement with such technologies may act upon the health and hygiene of those who can afford such technology, that is, the new Indian middle class. In addition, by means of such smart technologies, state also can reach people more directly, that will be able to generate more accountability to the people. In this age of globalisation, state has to compete with the private investors. So, form that point of view, the new Indian middle class stands as a bridge between the public services and private entrepreneurship. On the other hand, socio-politically and socio-economically speaking as well, there are also some transformations in politics by which the so-called subalterns are now getting chances to join the middle class. Nevertheless, it is also true that to be environmentally befitting to the needs of sustainable development for the present age as well as the next generations, beautification of public areas is required, which is a basic part of the orientations of smart cities. In fact, it must be remembered by the common people that there is no conflict between environmental de-pollution and beautification. And, the new Indian middle class with a large coverage of the population should assume the effects of the potentials of economical uses of natural resources in order to avoid various collateral hazards of environmental pollution.

Since it is related to environment, there should not be any conflict among all classes particularly on the point of environmental degradation and preservation. And, the new Indian middle class having the potentials of becoming the largest portion of the total Indian population is supposed to take the leadership in ensuring efficient management of natural resources through the smart city projects for the sake of betterment of the entire society at large in all respects of preservation and prosperity.

References

Aamoth, Doug. 2011. 'Smartphone Radiation: The 10 Highest and 10 Lowest Emitters', *Techland Time,* June 01; [techland.time.com/2011/06/01/smartphone-radiation-the-10-highest-and-10-lowest-emitters/].

Bardhan, Pranab. 1984. Expanded edition of Indian impression 1998. *The Political Economy of Development in India* (Paperback). New Delhi: Oxford University Press.

Bhowmik, Sharit. K. 2006. 'Social Security for street vendors', *Seminar*, 568 [www.india-seminar.com/2006/568/568_sharit_k_bhowmik.htm].

Chakraborti, Suman. 2015. 'Departments join hands for smart cities in West Bengal', *Times of India* [online], October 19.

Chatterjee, Partha. 2004. *The Politics of the Governed: Reflections on Popular Politics in Most of the World.* New York: Columbia University Press.

————. 2013. *Lineages of Political Society: Studies in Postcolonial Democracy* (Paperback). Ranikhet: Permanent Black.

Fernandes, Leela. 2004. 'The Politics of Forgetting: Class Politics, State Power and the Restructuring of Urban Space in India', *Urban Studies*. 41 (12): 2415-30.

Husain, Majid. 2004; Reprint 2008. *Evolution of Geographical Thought*. Jaipur: Rawat Publications.

Kohli, Atul. 2010; Fifth impression 2014. *Democracy and Development in India: From Socialism to Pro-Business* (Paperback). New Delhi: Oxford University Press.

Kothari, Smitu. 1993. *Theorising Culture, Nature and Democracy in India*. Delhi: Lokayan.

Nandy, Ashis. 2007. *The Romance of the State: And the Fate of Dissent in the Tropics* (Paperback). New Delhi: Oxford University Press.

Rudolph, Lloyd I. and Rudolph, Susanne H. 1987. *In Pursuit of Lakshmi: The Political Economy of the Indian State.* Chicago: University of Chicago Press, and Delhi: Orient Longman.

Samal, Kishore C., 2007. *Poverty, Social Capital and Natural Resource Management*. Jaipur: Rawat Publications.

Sen, Amartya. 2000; Fifteenth impression 2011. *Development as Freedom* (Paperback). New Delhi: Oxford University Press.

Singh, Gurdip. 2003. *International Law.* New Delhi: Macmillan India Ltd.

Swain, Ashok. 1996. *The Environmental Trap: The Ganges Diversion, Bangladeshi Migration and Conflicts in India*, Report 41. Uppsala: Department of Peace and Conflict Research, Uppsala University.

Stiglitz, Joseph. 2007. *Making Globalisation Work*. London: Penguin Books.

Varma, Pavan K. 2007; Reprint 2014. *The Great Indian Middle Class*. Gurgaon: Penguin Books.

Wallerstein. Immanuel. 2004. 'World-systems Analysis', in George Modelski (ed.), 'World System History', in *Encyclopedia of Life Support Systems* (EOLSS), Developed under the auspices of the UNESCO, EOLSS Publishers, Oxford, UK.

Chapter - 9

Globalisation and Withering of Handloom Industry: A Study of Weavers of Varanasi District of Uttar Pradesh

—*Arvinder A. Ansari*

Handloom is not only the means of livelihood for weaving community but is also a cultural tradition defining a way of life for Indian weavers that caters to the need of a diverse cultural ethos ranging from exquisite fabrics to popular items of mass production for daily use. The traditional 'Banarasi' weave has attained supremacy in weaving customs of India and is characteristically recognised for its auxiliary amplification, the accompanying weft, captivating over the accustomed weave for its finest fabrics like silk and the unbeatable designs that continue to be the part of learning skills from generation to generation. The best skilled Banarasi saree weavers in Varanasi are primarily Muslims belonging to Ansari Community, which use to be prosperous community prior to introduction of New Textile Policy 1985. During 1990s, the liberal policy of government on imports and the emergence of competition among imported and domestic products has led to competition in the sector, as a result, handloom sector lagged behind. Handloom sector based and dependent upon manual work whereas power loom involves machine work, which makes it cost efficient and cheaper, thereby leading to displacement of handlooms from the market. Due to globalisation, the power loom has taken the place of handlooms, subsequently; the art has come to an edge of extinction. Hence, bringing severe repercussions which include poverty and unemployment amongst most of the handloom weaving households. Moreover, as a consequence of globalisation, it gradually has been displaced from the country. Today, thousands of looms have been abandoned as inexpensive Chinese silk fabrics cascade Indian markets, throwing numerous weavers who used to make the iconic Banarasi silk saree, out of work. Weaving has been one of the most ancient occupations of the country and has been providing the employment to more than half of the population, after agriculture. For most of the families in the country, handloom weaving has been the source of livelihood and an art, which they have been preserving for generations. The concern of the government should be the protection and preservation of Banarasi Saree, which is not merely a piece of cloth, but also an ancient art and a way of living. It is in this light that the paper analyses the impact of trade liberalisation on the economic and social life of the weavers of Varanasi district.

Key Words: *Globalisation, Banarasi Saree, Handloom, Weavers, Employment, Poverty.*

Introduction

Globalisation is a much discussed and debated topic for the last couple of decades. It is complex and multidimensional. In a simple understanding it refers to the flow of information, material, knowledge, capital and technology. Through the improved communication and accessibility to advanced technology, people of the world have come closer; making the global shrink. It has further bridged the gap of social, economic and cultural diversity making it a homogenous entity and at the same time instead of assimilation of local culture into the global one, accepting and accommodating the two, resulting in a hybrid culture and a heterogeneous world.

Globalisation means different things to different people. For some it is a process of structural adjustment increasingly emerging as a kind of irreversible process that challenges the importance of the authority and welfare functions of the state. For others like David Held, globalisation leads to development of 'transnational networks and relations across all areas of human activity, goods, capital, people, knowledge, communication and weapons as well as crime, pollutants, fashions and beliefs rapidly move across territorial boundaries'. Globalisation has marked not only patterns of international exchange but also marked patterns of hierarchy, power and unevenness. Thus, it becomes important to evaluate its pros and cons, to analyse its benefits to human society with the inequality, unemployment and growing poverty that has been the product of it. With this background, the following paper has made an attempt to analyse the impact of globalisation on the handloom industry of Eastern Uttar Pradesh.

India has been acknowledged for the art of the weaving all across the world. Indian muslin (silk) has been a world-renowned textile. The ancient silk route from China to Central Asia passes through India. Through their world class weaving products, weavers provided an identity to India. A village without a weaver was considered to be a myth in the Indian scenario where millions of looms across the country were producing the traditional beauty of a precious heritage called Indian handloom. It was not only the means of livelihood for weaving community but also a cultural tradition and a way of life for Indian weavers.

At present, Indian handloom caters to the livelihood need of millions of people across the country. In India, nearly 27.83 lakh handloom households are engaged in weaving and allied activities, out of which 87 per cent are located in rural areas and remaining 13 per cent in urban areas (Handloom Census, 2009-10). While in Uttar Pradesh alone there are total 5,86,463 handloom workers engaged in weaving activity and handloom is still acknowledged as second employment spawning sector after agriculture. (*Ibid*, p. 65)

Post liberalisation the crisis in the life of weavers has deepened, the weavers who used to provide a distinctive individuality to the country in ancient and medieval times are now facing existential crisis. They are frequently conferred with their own identity for getting a socially meaningful life in modern India. Vasanthi Raman, Jayati Ghosh, PVCHR reports and others have also highlighted that the process of liberalisation led by globalisation has created crisis amongst handloom weavers.

Three new elements were introduced in India with New Economic Policy (NEP), i.e., liberalisation privatisation and globalisation (LPG). Globalisation is the process of increasing integration of Indian economy with the world economy through the reduction in import duties and export restrictions, promotion of the foreign investment and permission for the flow of foreign technology and skills (Y. Gurappa Naidu, 2006). The processes that were introduced with NEP aimed at higher rate of per capita income, full employment, self-reliance, reduction of inequalities and poverty. The correlation between globalisation and poverty can been traced through the dynamic argument which sees free trade reducing poverty as free trade leads to growth and growth reduces poverty (M. Tariq Majeed, 2012). However, seen in the Indian context this does not hold true. As the Dependency theorist argue, the developing countries like India has limited access to the markets of the developed countries thus making a narrow export base. Globalisation thus, does not lead to absolute convergence and eradication of poverty (ibid, p480). Further as Kurian suggests, the people who are resource less, uneducated and those who make their livelihood through traditional production activities do not benefit from globalisation, rather those who can play the game, does.

Globalisation has been experienced both as a positive and negative phenomena, in the different sectors of economy. It is believed that structural adjustment policy (SAP) of India in 1990's; especially liberalisation of economy and its openness and connectedness with the global economy has been immensely affected many sectors of Indian economy and the handloom sector is no exception.

India's progression towards trade liberalisation has resulted in high economic growth rates, increases in exports and imports and positive growth rates in certain sectors. But this growth has been jobless growth, bringing with it increasing inequality and a deceleration in the decline of poverty rates. Only a small proportion of India's manufacturing industries have performed well: traditional sectors of mass employment, such as textiles and leather, have seen declining growth rates, job losses and decreasing incomes. Millions of poor workers in traditional sectors of employment are facing increased hardship and poverty as a result of liberalisation policies and a lack of adequate protection and support. The handloom sector plays a very important role in the country's economy. This manufacturing sector is one of the hardest hit by the Indian economic reforms policies.

In this paper more specifically an attempt has been made to understand the impact of globalisation on the traditional occupation of handloom weavers in Eastern Uttar Pradesh after the implementation of NEP of India. The paper is part of empirical study carried out in Varanasi and Azamgarh district. Four hundred and twenty households have been chosen through purposive sampling for the study of handloom weavers from the field that include 300 rural areas, 120 urban households. This was followed by a series of in-depth interviews that covered men and women who are directly or indirectly part of this industry. The representation of those weaving Banarasi Saree and other who are weaving general materials has also been taken into account.

In secondary sources, the analysis of the all three Handloom Census Data has been used. Various government and non-governmental organisations reports have been referred as basis of information, like that of planning commission, Ministry of Textile and Department of Handloom, Handloom Department of Uttar Pradesh. Concerned journals, periodicals, books and newspaper reports also form the part of secondary sources.

Context

The decade of 1990s was significant in terms of policy changes. It changed the environment for functioning of the small industries, like that of handloom in India. As M H Balasubrahmanya (2004) mentions in his article, 'Small Industry and Globalisation Implications: Performance and Prospects', the policies emphasised the beginning of the end of the protective measures for small industries and promotion of competitiveness in terms of technology, finance and marketing.

The initiation and expansion of globalisation and Indian textile industry turned up simultaneously in the 1990s. The Indian textile industry, in expectancy of the economic liberalisation of Indian economy was predominantly an unorganised industry. Furthermore, this policy had also anticipated the infusion of the huge unorganised and decentralised Indian textile sector under the organised textile industry.

During 1990s, the economic liberalisation of Indian economy got further on to astonishing growth of the handloom industry. However, as a consequence of globalisation, it gradually has been displaced from the country.

Today, thousands of looms have been abandoned as inexpensive Chinese silk fabrics cascade Indian markets, throwing numerous weavers who used to make the iconic Banarasi silk saree, out of work. Furthermore, globalisation of Indian textile industry has seen an intangible advance in the total industrial production factor of this industry, which presently rose at 14 per cent. The most momentous step among them was prologue of "The National Textile Policy 2000". This policy conceptualised to premeditate on the divergent issues like intensified global contention in the post, 2005 trade formulation under WTO, enormous import ambit of reasonable textiles from other Asian neighbours, magnificent production cost concerning other Asian rivals, implementation of bombastic manufacturing technology, destitute supply chain management and massive freight cost and immense unorganised and decentralised sector.

The new textile policy which, promised liberalisation phase also marked the onset of the current crisis in the handloom industry in Eastern UP in the early 1990; since 1995, the impact of crisis became visible and acquired full-blown proportions since 2003.

National Textile Policy

The noticeable shift in policy concerning textiles took place with the New Textile Policy (NTP) of 1985 which in turn was incorporated in a paradigm shifts in the development perspective. The shift was the result of state controlled import substitution to that of export-oriented growth with the new liberalised market economy playing a considerable role. The prominence was primarily on modernisation, effectiveness, productivity and market competition in quick disparity to the earlier policy force on employment generation, equality and social justice. This shift was complimentary to the power-loom and mill sector. It marked a departure from the previous policies not only in terms of objective and emphasis but also in understanding the very nature of the textile industry. Regardless of the marked shifts from past policy, the NTP of 1985 also accentuated the noteworthy role of handlooms by providing assurances to safeguard their distinct character as also to facilitate handloom weavers to apprehend their full potential and ensure higher earnings for them (GOI, 1985:4).

The handloom (Reservation of Articles for Production) Act, 1985 was a foremost initiative for protecting the handloom from the power-loom and mill sector, which was taken up by preserving 22 articles in the handloom sectors for special production in the handloom sector. Besides the assurance made by government in the textile policy that this act "shall be strictly enforced and machinery for doing so shall be suitably strengthened" (GOI, 1990). However, the act was barely executed. Instead, the act was thrown down the gauntlet in court by powerful mill and power-loom lobbies. The policy not only favoured the mills and the power loom in ways of withdrawing of all restrictions but also financial, technological assistance was provided to them to occupy the market quickly. One of the immediate causes of the crisis was that the prices of yarn were highly fluctuating, despite the promotion of the export of yarn and cotton under the NTP of 1985 (GOI, 1990). The violation of the Hank Yarn Obligation by the spinning mills, the crisis and closure of the cooperative spinning mills, trade liberalisation encouraging exports of yarn and dyes have compounded the problems of the weavers by paving the way for an acute yarn crisis. The review of three censuses of handloom weavers conducted in 1987-88, 1995-96 and 2009-10 the fact that emerges is the shifting of an independent artisan to that of the dependent one.

A study by Arti Kaul revealed that not a single handloom weaver knew about schemes of 'production reservation' and it has only stayed on paper for last many decades. Though the initiatives were in the direction of protecting handlooms, but the implementation stalled. Thus, the shift introduced by NTP from small labour intensive handloom industry to capital and technology intensive large mills and power loom got further amplify in the years that followed.

The overall performance of any small industry in the Indian context is done on the basis of its absolute growth in units, employment, production and exports. The following sections analyse the impact of NTP that came along globalisation on the handloom sector.

Implications of Policy Changes

The new textile policy, which promised liberation for the textile industry failed to accomplish it. Instead the vigor and dynamism that it had anticipated remained unrealised even after decades. The handloom industry faced a number of challenges which this paper attempts to highlight through the study of handloom industry in Eastern UP.

Marketing

Marketing is a vivacious factor for the survival and growth of the handloom industry. The development of marketing facilities for the handloom products constitutes an essential part of the plan for all round development of the industry. At the production level, the government should spend huge resources to the handloom industry. Without developing marketing facilities, would necessitate protection of the industry for a long time to come at the cost of public exchequer of labour to their units.

Problem of Cheap Imports

Although our handloom products have gone global, other countries have also got the opportunity for free trade in India. In the era of globalisation, where India faces flood of import of textiles from both China and US, the regional specialisation of handlooms is a critical factor that provides a well-defined product identity, something sought after at great cost and effort by the modern consumer industry (Uzarmma, 2003). The availability of Chinese fabric crepe, in the market and other products at a cost lesser than the weaver's cost has added to the woes of the weavers. Thus, weaving has not remained a benefiting occupation because the production cost of handloom weaving is more than that of the mill's product. These are a few of the many factors, which have kept the weaving sector lagging behind.

There has been a sharp rise in exports of silk yarn with adverse and destructive consequences for both the accessibility and the prices of silk yarn. The only left option for the handloom weavers, faced as they are with a series of onslaughts on their lives and livelihoods, is to further squeeze their wage levels as a strategy of survival. However, the wages were already below subsistence levels and there were hardly any options left.

Declining Demand

Handloom sector is less adaptable to the changing fashions and consumer preferences. No change has been made to make handloom production more innovative and creative due to lack of experience and exposure. In the case of both urban and rural areas of Varanasi, the weavers are still producing traditional fabrics like saree, dhoti, *gamchha*, etc., and the core aspect in the wake of this predicament is that weavers do not have any type of inspiration or information about today's consumer's preferences.

The weavers are not able to capture the mood of fashion. Despite the fact that efforts are being made and it has been observed that *grihasthas* have started making use of WhatsApp and internet for business purposes. The studies conducted have documented that weavers have reported that the demand of the handlooms products have declined, one important reason is that weavers from rural area have no means and access to modern fashion world and are not aware of consumer choices. Most of the weavers continue producing banarsi saree in traditional style. Globalisation has made them misfit and liberalisation has made silk yarn expensive, the weavers are losing their space to power looms.

The Impact of Chinese Silk

After the 1990s, competition from Surat affected the Banarasi saree industry in every possible way, with regard to design, material and even prices. The new synthetic fabric that was familiarised was decidedly cheaper and there was a large-scale replication of Banarasi saree designs. But the demand for pure silk among the upper classes helped the Banarasi saree industry survive this onslaught. However, since 1998, Chinese silk (crepe) started offering a stiff competition to Banarasi silk. Besides, there has been a change in the tastes of the clientele with a preference for embroidered silk (crepe). There was also a rise in the prices of Chinese silk yarn accompanied by a reduction in the excise duty on finished goods. The weavers have expressed their concern on promoting power looms through various schemes and exporting of Chinese fabric, the weavers have been heavily impacted by the Chinese silk. 37 per cent of respondents believe that the competition with handloom has increased due to the introduction of Chinese silk. While 63 per cent of the respondents believe that the duplicate sarees made up of Chinese silk have also posed challenge to indigenous pure silk sarees woven on handlooms. The weavers and artisans came together in a forum called the Bunkar and Dastkar Adhikar Manch (BDAM) at a convention in Banaras on September 21, 2005 to discuss their plight and demanded to exclude textiles from the WTO. (Bose, 2007).

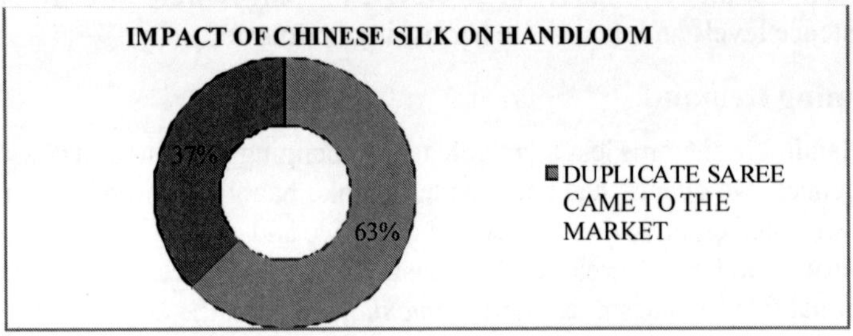

Graph 9.1: Impact of Chinese silk.

The share of handloom in total clothing and handloom weavers in Uttar Pradesh declined by one-fifth in the first census from 1987-88 to 2009-10. The production of the handloom sector has not decreased but the share of the powerloom sector has increased over the years in the total production that has led to such disparity. This also means that the processes of liberalisation, privatisation and globalisation, in fact, benefited the cloth sector at large. These processes have helped the power loom sector in the form of more availability of machines and a newer technology as well as in the form of better access to world market which has fuelled the growth of this industry.

Fluctuating Supply of Yarn

Yarn is the basic raw material for the handloom sector and is being supplied by the spinning mills and composite textile mills in the form of 'hank yarn'. The New Economic Policy of 1991 further deteriorated and intensified the inconsistencies set in wave by the New Textile Policy of 1985. The neo-liberal system, led to an increase in the consumption of blended fabrics due to the Multi-Fibre Agreement. Between 2000-01 and 2004-05, Chinese silk fabrics imported to India grew by a steep rise. An unbelievable rise was observed in the export of yarn between 1987-88 and 1991 along with the sheer rise in the prices of yarn principally of the low counts used by weavers. In fact, the policy should have been reverse cheaper Chinese yarn and more expensive Chinese fabric were required if the interests of both the weavers and the Banarasi silk industry are to be protected. The weaver industry protested and demanded to increase the import tariffs on Chinese silk fabric and also bringing an anti-dumping case against Chinese silk fabric. However, the WTO negotiations-NAMA- (Non Agricultural Market Access) proposed to liberalise manufacturing and industrial trade; and developed countries would seek elimination of import tariff in certain sectors like textiles, footwear and leather. This would make it difficult for the government to increase tariffs (Francis and Lenin, 2003). The industry depends on the raw materials and it is found that the average consumption of silk per loom per annum is as low as10 kg still weavers of Varanasi are facing difficulties in purchasing raw materials as they are not getting the desired materials because either it is out of market or is available at exorbitant prices. The constant increase in the prices of raw materials and problem of difficulty in identifying the genuine raw materials also raise (Pandey, 1981). So non-availability of the raw material is creating the crisis for the handloom sector. Sometimes weavers are also forced to live without work which creates situation of unemployment for the weaving community. There is also evidence that in 1998 the government controlled China's yarn which became the cause of weaver's suffering. Hank yarn is tax free and receives subsidy, and this is used by the mills its availability is also a serious issue because it is controlled by the mills.

Sometimes the price of yarn becomes very high at the time of purchase. The product of the handloom depends also upon the cost of the yarn which is decided by the traders. According to some of the respondents, sometimes they have to sell their products at low prices. It is also evident that the weavers are not educated enough so as to think and take appropriate decisions according to the market trends. Earlier, there were handloom corporations and cooperative societies which used to purchase the local weavers' prepared goods at fair prices but since their closure the middlemen or local traders are playing a dominating role in the marketing. Fluctuating costs of raw materials do not hamper those who are working on *bani* (dependent weaver). Perhaps, that is a reason why handloom weavers have been shifting from independent weaving to dependent weaving.

Competition with Powerloom

With the preface of power looms in the sector of textile industry, the threat to handlooms has incredibly increased. The census data of 2009-10 shows a decline in handloom weaving industry. A decline over 15 per cent in the number of household and non-household units engaged in handloom-related activities has been recorded all over the country. Although there has been a slight change in the number of workers, but the number of looms have declined by almost eight per cent. Therefore, there has been a higher absorption of both worker and looms in the units in 1995-96 compared to 1987-88. Whereas in 1987-88 there was an average of 2.25 workers and 1.26 looms in the unit, in 1995-96 the corresponding figure were 2.58 and 1.37, respectively. According to our research survey, the threat is highest among the 87 per cent of the rural population who have been using handlooms for weaving purposes. While for 11 per cent the population, threat is moderate and for 2 per cent there is no threat. Whereas, the urban weaver population feels 100 per cent threaten to be taken over by power looms. The coming of powerlooms has affected the urban area the most. Other most important reason for the decline of handloom is that the competition from the powerloom have the advantage of a more productive technique, regardless of the smaller units among them have in the past qualified for support from the government in the form of reservation of areas of production and lower rates of taxation. The government's absence of seriousness regarding the handloom sector is reflected in the area where intentions have to be backed by concrete budgetary allocations. In 1997-98, the handloom was allocated 27.5 per cent of the total textile budget, whereas in 2006-07 this allocation nosedived to a mere 7.9 per cent. Between these years, the allocation of the handloom sector has been consistently declining (K. Srinivasulu, 2010).

Competition with Powerloom is the major concern in promotion of handloom products. This competition in all respects has enlarged after introduction of powerloom sector that replaced the handlooms and took plentiful settlements in the name of handloom industry in relation to consumption of yarn, production of reserved item.

Shift from Handloom to Powerloom

The expansion of powerloom industry meticulously affected the handloom sector. The handloom sector is antagonising troubles due to competition from power looms. For example, a handloom weaver, it takes six to seven days to weave a pure silk sari that costs around ₹ 4000. In comparison to this, on a Powerloom four such sari are manufactured in one day in Varanasi, art-silk and synthetic sari produced on Powerloom easily pass as a pure silk and such sari, is accessible at around half the price.

Another most crucial factor that was discovered during this research was that the amount of handlooms that have been replaced by the powerlooms. According to the population Census, the number of persons engaged in weaving and spinning in the handloom sector recorded a negative growth rate of 2.6 per cent per annum during the period 1981-1991, whereas according to the two rounds of the handloom census the rate of decline has been 2.9 per cent per annum between 1987-88 and 1995-96. In our data survey, in the rural areas, 182 of the sample population agree with the replacement while 118 of the responses disagree. While in urban areas, according to 82 of the responses, handlooms have been replaced by powerlooms while, according to 38 of the responses handlooms have not yet been replaced by powerlooms.

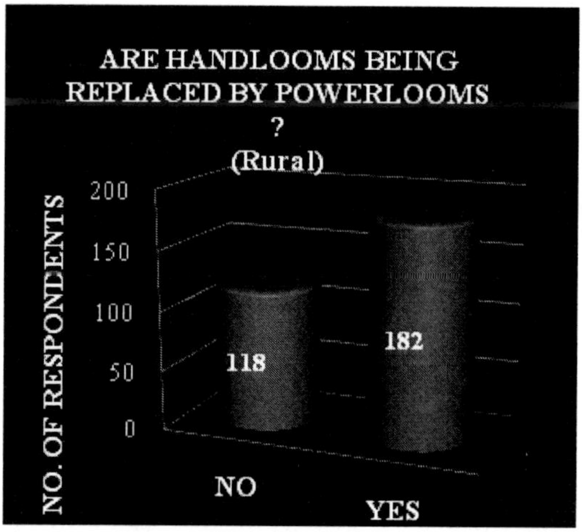

Rural

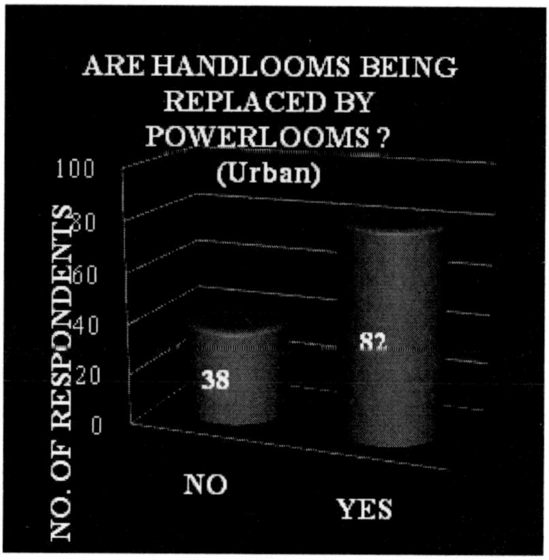

Urban

Graph 9.2: Number of Handlooms Replaced by Power-looms.

One obvious consequence of the explosion of powerlooms was the decline in the handloom production. Even official figures show that the share of handlooms in decentralised sector production fell from close to 40 per cent in 1980-81 to 20 per cent in 1992. And further, despite an officially recorded increase of handloom sector in decentralised sector output still remained at 20 per cent in 1999-2000 (Chandrasekhar and Ghosh, 2001).

Impact on Employment

The number of handloom weavers and allied workers as per the Second census of handloom of India (1995-96) and third Handloom Census of India (2009-10) has decreased.

Table 9.1: Decrease in the Number of Handloom Weavers and Allied Workers

Sr. No	*Census*	*Number of handloom weavers and allied workers in Lakh*
1	1995-96	65.50
2	2009-10	43.31

Source: Yojana, May, 2011.

The handloom sector is considered as the second employment generation sector after agriculture but between the second and third Handloom Census about 22.19 lakh handloom weavers and allied workers has left this occupation.

In developing countries like India where unemployment is a big issue, people like handloom weavers who are skilled workers are leaving this occupation and shifting to unskilled sectors most of the time as most of the handloom weavers belong to the lower strata of the society and do not possess mainly skills. On one hand where the government is busy making efforts to reduce the unemployment situation through schemes like MGNREGA (Mahatma Gandhi National Rural Employment Gurantee Act) where unskilled person get employment guarantee of a hundred days, on the other it has not been able to arrest the decline in handloom weaving,which are forcing people to leave skilled jobs and shift to other livelihood earning works.

This poses a serious problem as large number of the skilled labour force are forced to shift occupation and are rendered unemployed.The idea with which Indian economy moved towards liberalisation was to lessen the gap that existed among people in terms of income and quality of life. A contrasting result emerged instead, as was seen in Varanasi. It is clear that various schemes and policies have emerged as initiatives by the government but it lacks in implication. This gap between the policy and practice has to be build through engagement in the process of building policy rather than implementing the top-down policy model. An effective policy can be build only through praxis as policy based on theory that is divorced from practice has material consequences for the affected communities, here, handloom weavers. The infrastructural constraints faced by the handloom industry, such as power, water, transport, communication are a prerequisite for efficient working of any economic activity. Inadequate economic, technical and social infrastructure is the major factor that affects the competitiveness of any small industry. Thus, different policies need to be formulated taking the context into consideration.

Low Wages and Unemployment

There have been evidences that the wages of the weavers in Varanasi and other districts of the Eastern Uttar Pradesh have not increased since the last decade. Even the PVCHR (People's Vigilance Committee on Human Rights), which works in associations with the Asian Human Rights Commission in the region, in their report stated that Varanasi handloom weaver's wages have been reduced about half. This fact is very disturbing for weaver's community as the costs of living has increased in terms of food, housing, education and health facilities due to many factors, which some claims are results of the LPG (Liberalisation, Privatisation and Globalisation) but the wages have not increased in same proportion. Rather the wages of the weavers have decreased during this time as the factors contributing to unemployment have been rampant in this sector and the advent of better technology in the power-loom has added to the woes of handloom workers in many ways. Two pronged woes in form of lower wages and increased costs of living have devastated many a weavers in the region. This has compelled many of them to commit suicide rather than continuously living in chronic poverty. But again this phenomenon is not just a result of bad policies but some local and individual factors have also affected it.

PVHCR has reported, for example the length of saree which was weaved in this region earlier was around five meter which is now 6 meters due to some changes in fashion and demand and the wage has decreased to half. Thus labor for weaving a saree has increased and the wage has decreased. This has led to estrangement from work for many weavers as it is impossible to maintain a family in such conditions and they are compelled to leave the occupation.

Economic problems due to meager earnings have not allowed them to be able to look after health and they suffer from disease like tuberculosis and asthma etc. Health problems are also responsible for low production of the handloom, which has accentuated all other problem in weaver's community in Eastern Uttar Pradesh and particularly Varanasi. After liberalisation, new technology was introduced in power looms, which has the capacity to weave about 50 to 80 sarees in a day and reduce the cost of production of power loom. But the handloom weavers who are already suffering from poverty and other abjections of life cannot compete with new technology, as the cost of production is higher in the handloom sector, thus handloom weavers are lagging behind the power looms in the market. Thus low production and consequent low wages in handloom sector has again compelled them to quit the occupation.

It is evident from the data that technology does not create unemployment directly but it eventually leads to low costs or wages in case of weaving, which affects any sector negatively. The income of handloom weavers has declined to such an extent that they cannot even meet their basic needs. On average, a weaver earns just ₹ 60 to ₹ 70 a day, and even this is not certain. Due to livelihood crisis and related indebtedness, many weavers in recent times have committed suicide and they are also compelled to sell their blood in order to be able to meet the needs of their family. Cases of selling of small children have also been reported occasionally in local media, which have also highlighted the serious crisis that pervades the daily life of most weavers. (Vasanthi Raman, 2013).

Low cost of weaving is directly associated with the development of power-loom, it has not only created the low cost for weavers but also created the situation of unemployment in area. Handloom weaver's sons want to weave on power-loom in their locality but even in power-looms there is no job. A rough estimate shows that single power-loom replace around 9 to 10 handloom weavers. In this situation of unemployment, weavers are ready to work on low wage. So the unrest and hopelessness have emerged among the handloom weavers inVaranasi, even those who are weaving with power-loom also sold their power looms and try to migrate as labourer to gulf countries. Power-loom is also copying the design and the cost of power loom products is low in the market.

Migration of Weavers

Weavers have now started migrating to various cities on the country. Some of them have become salesmen and are doing the job of the middlemen. Many of them have migrated to Surat,Bhiwandi and Bangalore, are using their skills in mills, weaving the way they used to weave and are getting better opportunities. Because of globalisation, child labour and women problems have come out in the open as the government is re-checking its policy. The notion of the women empowerment and *school chalo abhiyan* is also a creation of globalisation.

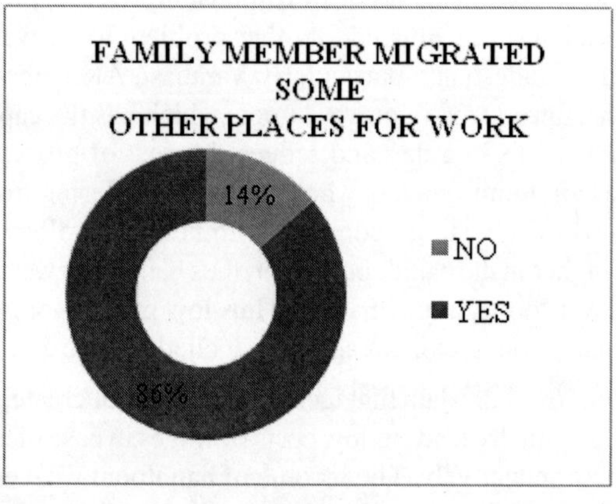

Rural

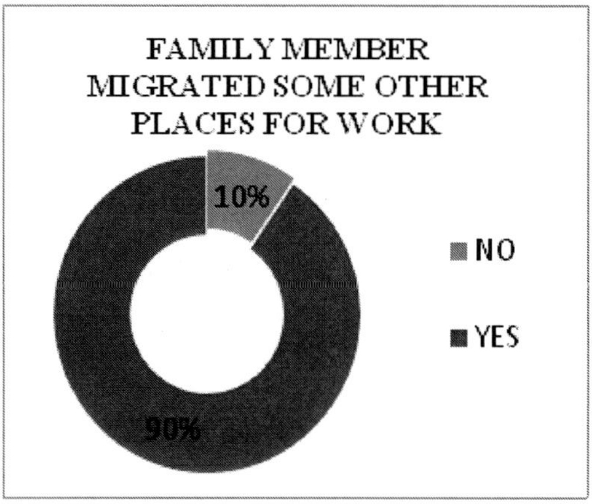

Urban

Graph 9.3: Migrations.

According to our field research,weavers are migrating from Mubarakpur and Varanasi because of the push factors, 86 per cent of respondents in rural cluster reported to have their family member migrated to some other places for work, while 14 per cent reported not to have their family member migrated to some other places for work. On the other hand, in urban cluster, 90 per cent respondents reported to have their family member migrated to some other places for work, while, 10 per cent respondents reported not to have their family member migrated to some other places for work. Handloom weavers do not want to migrate from their own place but it is forced migration. In Marxian perspective, if we analyze this forced migration it is basically class struggle, because poor weavers are unable to compete with machine made products and the capitalists. It is capitalist or petty bourgeoisie who create an environment where handloom weavers are forced to surrender in front of mills and power-looms.

Respondents of Varanasi told that the weavers are migrating to weaving centers such as Bhiwandi, Bangalore and Surat. It is because of their familiar occupation, which they prefer. Reasons of migration of weavers to other weaving locations are various, 53 per cent of them responded that no profit from handloom was the reason for their migration to other profession. 12 per cent described inflation in the market to be the main reason. Thirty per cent described bad economic conditions to be the reason for their migration. Five per cent of the respondents wanted to work in abroad.

The downward occupational mobility is taking place among handloom weavers. When these weavers are leaving their traditional occupation and choosing other occupations and shifting to rickshaw plying, to work as labourer at construction site etc, others are living in the abject poverty as weavers are not easily able to adapt to other occupation, it is both emotional and economic setback to them, some of them have taken selling vegetables or earning their livelihood as street hawkers.

Exploitation of Weavers

B. P. Pandey (1981) pointed out that most of the times weavers work with the master weavers and take loan from them time to time and in this process a time comes when the wage earners become bonded labourers of the Master Weavers. He pointed out that the weavers have to take loans for social and religious rituals, illness and payment of loan etc. which becomes the cause of their misery and they fall in a vicious circle. The weavers do not take the loans from the banks owing to certain reasons such as lack of influential persons to approach, bribery and ignorance about the banking procedure. These things compel them to take money from the master weavers and in such a manner they find themselves caught in the vicious circle and to come out of this circle becomes impossible for the poor weavers.

Family

Weaving, being a household occupation, the structure of weaver's family is joint in nature. However, low wage in handloom weaving, poverty and sometimes lack of enough space in household leads to change in the family structure. But the ethos of togetherness of the family has been carried out. Weaver communalities consisting predominately of Ansari prefer to live in joint family, but due to financial crisis, they are not able to live with their brothers. This emerges as social and emotional crises, as one of the respondents also pointed out that they are living in a phase of *qayamat* (doomsday) where everybody is busy. In group discussions weavers expressed that economic crises has also impacted ethos of togetherness, they are forced to live in separate household to divide the economic burden the members of handloom weavers family are not able to generate enough profit to help their family and maintain this at large. The erosion of traditional social organisation of family under market forces has made the impact of crises cumulative.

Health Conditions of Weavers

The other major problem is the health, for the weaver's family in Varanasi. In the due process of handloom work, weavers suffer from asthma, bronchitis, tuberculosis, arthritis, eye problems etc., due to the exposure to yarn dust. Living conditions of the weavers in urban areas of Varanasi is very poor. The nature of houses in Madanpura, Philikothi area of Varanasi looks like slum where there is not enough sunlight and fresh air inside the house. This poor living condition of weaver's family get them trapped in acute health problem.

Most of the respondents reported that at least one or two members of their family are suffering from some of these diseases. The preventive health care system in our country is poor especially in rural areas; even poor people do not get the facility of free healthcare. The family also suffers because of the poor health condition of the head/working hands of the household. Though there is provision of free health insurance, but in practice situation is different. The distribution of the insurance is one thing but the success of the scheme is another. The step motherly attitude of doctors to these patients is further discouraging.

It is also believed that economic crisis have led several weavers addicted to alcohol and drugs due to their struggle with poor economic condition. Addiction to drugs and alcohol has increased the violence in families, beating and abusing to their wives and children are now common problems in these families.

It is also one of the major causes of the breakdown of joint family, which also make negative impact on the family environment and children. Neglect of ageing parents, living separately from their sons and still continue weaving for their livelihood was also observed, this is other harsh reality of old handloom weavers in Varanasi and adjoining areas. Financial crises are more acutely felt during the festival and marriages, it forces weavers to take loan from *grihastha* and finally weavers get into the trap of exploitation where weavers have to work on very low wages till repayment of the loan. These are various Non-governmental organisation and media reports, which show that the incidence of suicide is also found among the handloom weavers.

Children of Weaving Families

Children commonly enter the handloom weaving industry between the ages of six to twelve and continue to work in that occupation for their entire life. Parents argue that when they are not capable of getting the jobs after getting education then what is the relevance of education. There is a misconception among handloom weavers that they think due to their community identity they will not get job in other sectors. Even today we can see many handloom weavers' children in the age group of 5-8 are not enrolled to school. It is also noted during the fieldwork that dropout rate is quite higher among these children. Handloom weaving is a part of family life thus children are one of the supports for the poor parents in making and throwing shuttle. The engagement of the children is proportionately higher in Mau district than Varanasi. The education level of weavers' children gets affected due to this reason. The poor weavers want them to engage in their traditional occupation. The engagement of children in this sector also indicates the problems of their sector. According to report of PVCHR, children are the worst sufferers as they are pushed to penurious conditions but weavers consider it as getting them involved in their own tradition. Children help in creating the design pattern and also operate the shuttle (*dharkipherna)*, which speeds up production process.

The overall crisis in this sector affected children in several ways. Sometimes it appears as malnutrition in acute poverty, some families have food problem, etc. The other implication can be seen among children and youths as delinquent behaviour. This situation in the family increases the delinquent behaviour among the youths.

Work participation of children is much higher than the figures, since it is household unit, work contribution of children is taken for granted as carry bundles of sarees from looms to kharkhana, making bundles of sarees, distributing and collecting *nari* (bobbin) from different households, all these allied activities are performed by small male children.

Poverty is very high so even though weavers want their children to go to school, very few government schools are there and in private school fees is very high. Therefore, people send their children to the Madrasa because that is the only option available to them. Though, they are aware that Madrasas are more suitable for religious education rather than formal education. No modernisation of madrasa has taken place and school chaloabhiyan of some NGO's has made lives of these weavers more difficult, they are in dilemma, they fail to understand how suddenly their children have become child labourers in their own homes.

Conclusion

Overall, the performance of handloom industry shows that the handloom industry faced a number of challenges in the era pertaining to globalisation and liberalisation.Globalisation has reduced weavers to labourers rather than ensuring them a sustainable livelihood through weaving. The problem is when the globalisation process (which involves with it, 'development' and 'modernisation') views handlooms as technology. This is in contrast to the earlier view that sees weavers and their weaving as 'natural'. When handloom is considered as technology, the weaver too becomes an inevitable part of that technology. The weaver's function in relation to the loom and the loom's function in producing textiles become very visible. The two must function together in order to produce handloom material. Thus, 'the attempt to 'modernise' handloom weaving therefore highlights the problems of process and ideology in relation to mainstream globalisation...When technophiles suggest that hand loom weavers could benefit from 'new' technologies, they are stumped when asked how. They can only point to e-commerce as a form of salvation'.

Globalisation, further, has increased economic and social interactions between countries but social divisions are widening and while the proportion of people living in dire poverty has fallen in recent years, the absolute number has risen with the increase world population. It is generally assumed that the initial years, the poor are faced with difficulties however in the long run, globalisation benefits them all. However, this did not hold true in the context of India. Globalisation, in the Indian context has been uneven as resources, economic, social and natural, are distributed unevenly. The already rich minority has appropriated it. Contemporary development, in India, thus is deeply asymmetric as inequalities are widening and increasing.

In the handloom sector, a number of players are involved, such as traders, exporters, importers, Sattiwala (middleman), Master weavers (Grihastha) and handloom weavers. Who has benefited by liberalisation? Handloom products have gone global and their production has also increased but the number of handloom weavers and handlooms has only declined. So it is clear that handloom weavers have not benefitted in the least. The other thing that most of the respondents stated was that earlier they were weaving independently but now they had become dependent weavers. So, globalisation has directly benefitted the other people involved in this business while its demerits have seeped in into the lives of weavers, especially the handloom weavers.

The next major challenge for handloom producers is to match their mode of production to the existing market system that globalisation has created. Market is not a reliable source of livelihood for weavers as it is dependent on passing fashion, design, technology, credit and operates on mass production line making the weaver into labour, like factory machines that produces cloth. The customers too, in the globalised market, are far away and no longer part of the weavers' social and cultural environment. The processes of modernity and globalisation driven by the interests of multinational corporations are alienating the weavers from their markets and also from their consumer community, by de-linking them from trader feedback and interpersonal exchanges between producer and consumer.

The trajectory of the present crisis has to be viewed at various levels, since the present crisis has differentially affected all sections of the industry. The ordinary weavers, both self-employed ones and the poor *bunker* working for wages have been the hardest hit, especially the handloom weavers. The wages for different tasks in the saree industry have also decreased thus halving the incomes of the weavers. The closing down of thousands of handlooms and the accompanying pauperisation of lacks of weavers has one extremely significant implication and that is the de-skilling of a vast population. Thus, even if the industry revives, the skilled weavers are no longer available, since they have been dispersed and dispossessed.

Further problem occurs from neo-colonialist development models that regard the prevailing forms of globalisation as liberating. For them, a sustainable livelihood for weavers could be a possibility with better incomes disregarding the quality of life and further perpetuating the idea that weavers need to be 'developed'; seeing development as synonymous with modernisation. The idea of modernisation is itself situated within the neo-liberal framework and 'can easily become a tool of displacement and disempowerment in the name of upward mobility, where 'upward' and 'mobility' are part of a linear notion of progress embedded in a colonial hierarchy and logic'.

The weavers at the handloom did try to cope with the increasing competition. However, the handlooms lacked designs and thus could not keep pace with the demand and variety, which the customers from all over the world required. The units produced by the handloom industry in a day are far less than that of a product produced by the machine in a mill or a powerloom. Thus, as the Indian economy opened its doors, the handlooms faced increased competition and suffered in terms of growth, employment, output and export.

The present handloom crisis is part of a larger paradigm change with implications for the society as a whole. Banaras, an ancient pre-industrial urban centre, an artisanal city, is now steadily giving way to malls. The very identity of the city was inextricably linked to the Banarasi saree industry. Handloom can survive only in two conditions, first if government provides proper incentive or marketing support for the handloom and second, if the demand of handloom product increases among the masses. In the era of globalisation where existence of market is notion of country, the potential of handloom can be saved. We can say that the specialty of handloom becomes important, what is unique in handloom that will make handloom different.

Our observation is that the demands of weavers are totally self-less and are purely dedicated to their profession of weaving. All of them demand better conditions to continue their work. They have a true interest in earning but by hard work. This might be the reason they even tend to migrate in the search of work. In this case the present government can look upon the condition of this whole population who genuinely wants to work hard and earn.

The weavers of Eastern Uttar Pradesh have lost the shine of their life and products in the last two decades. Though we may not find a direct exploiter but the conditions have become such that their quality of life has degraded and they have become poorer. The weavers try to assert their agency within global spaces through their own decisions regarding what processes and negotiations are needed in order for them to maintain their livelihoods. If the present government could provide some prospects it can save the dying ancient profession of the country. After all, it is not only the death of the Banarasi saree, but also the death of an eminent prosperous culture that has been renowned worldwide for centuries.

The structures formed and continue to develop in order to respond to unexpected variations in the globalisation process are deeply hegemonic and imperialist in nature.Tremendous changes in recent decades promise greater freedom and access to resources, yet those who are left in global capitalism trap, become increasingly marginal and poor.

References

- Bismillah, Abdul.1987. Jheeni Jheeni Beeni Chadaria, New Delhi: Rajkamal Prakashan.1987.
- Bose, TarunKanti. 2007. 'Globalisation Pushes Varanasi Weavers to Hunger and Death'. Action Aid PVCHR and Asian Human Rights Commission.
- Bardhan Pranab. 2007. Poverty and Inequality in China and India: Elusive Link with Globalisation. Economic and Political Weekly.
- Chandrasekhar, C.P. and Jayati Ghosh (2001). In Defence of Handlooms, Business Line, Tuesday, 2 October.
- Dogra, Bharat. Struggle of Handloom Weavers to Save Livelihood and Skills. New Delhi : Social Change Paper, 2010.
- Francis, Bijo and Lenin Raghuvanshi "Handloom has become live grave for weavers": Effect of WB-IMF-WTO on weavers and marginalised communities', Unpublished report: People's Vigilance Committee on Human Rights: 2003.
- Jena, Pradeep Kumar. 2010. 'Indian Handicrafts in Globalisation Times:An Analysis of Global-Local Dynamics'. Interdisciplinary Description of Complex Systems 8(2), 119-137.
- Jain, L C. 1985. '1985 Textile Policy End of Handloom Industry'. Economic and Political Weekly.
- K. Srinivasulu, 2010. Textile Policy and Handloom Sector, Serial Pulications, New Delhi.
- Mamidipudi, Annapurna and Gajjala, Radhika. 2008. 'Juxtaposing Handloom Weaving and Modernity: Building Theory through Praxis'. Taylor & Francis, Ltd. on behalf of Oxfam GB. Development in Practice, Vol. 18, No. 2 (Apr., 2008), pp. 235-244.
- Majeed, M. Tariq. 2012. 'Poverty Consequences of Globalisation in OIC Countries: A Comparative Analysis'. Pakistan Institute of Development Economics, Islamabad. Papers and Proceedings PARTS I and II The 28th Annual General Meeting and Conference of the Pakistan Society ofDevelopment Economists Islamabad, November 13-15, 2012 (Winter 2012), pp. 479-492.
- Naidu, Y. Gurappa. 2006. 'Globalisation and Its Impact on Indian Society'. Indian Political Science Association. The Indian Journal of Political Science, Vol. 67, No. 1. pp. 65-76.
- Pandey, Gyanendra. "The Bigoted Julaha" Economic and Political Weekly, Vol. 18, No. 5: January 29,1983 pp. PE19-PE28.
- Pandey, Manager. Bhakti Andolan Aur Soor Das Ka Kabya. New Delhi: Bani Prakashan. 1997.
- Pandey, Anand, B.P. Banaras Brocades: Structure and Functioning.Varansi: Publication, Gandhian Institute of Studies.1981.
- Raman,Vasanthi. The warf and the Weft: and Gender Identity among Banaras Weavers. New Delhi : Routeledge Publication. 2010.

- Raman, Vasanthi. Entangled Yarns: Banaras Weavers and Social Crisis, New Delhi : IIAS. 2013.
- Sharma, Mridula, Sharma, Harsh and Naqvi, Talmeez F. 2005. 'Survival of Aligarh Lock Manufacturing Industry'. Economic and Political Weekly. Vol. 40, No. 39.
- Subrahmanya, M. H. Bala. 2004. 'Small Industry and Globalisation: Implications, Performance and Prospects' Economic and Political Weekly. Vol. 39, No. 18. pp. 1826-1834.
- Tarkowska Elzbieta and Grzego³owska-Klarkowska Helena. 2003. 'Globalisation and Poverty Some Comments and Queries on the Margin of the Globalisation Discourse in Poland'. PolskieTowarzystwoSocjologiczne (Polish Sociological Association). pp. 321-331.
- Uzarmma. "Rethinking handloom", Seminar 523-March,2003, pp. 17-22.
- Reports Handloom Census of India (2009-10) NCAER.
- Handloom Census of India, (1987-88) NCAER.
- Joint Census of Handlooms and Powerlooms, 1995-96 (JCHP). 2004. New Delhi: National Council of Applied Economic Research (NCAER).
- Annual Report (2003-04), Ministry of Textile, Government of India.
- Ninth Report of Standing Committee Report on Labour (2005-06), Ministry of Textile, Government of India.
- Report on Handloom, accessed from http://planning.up.nic.in on 27/04/2014.
- Government of India (GOI). 1985. Statement on Textile Policy, 1985. Ministry of Supply and Textiles, Department of Textiles.
- People Vigilance Committee on Human Right, report on handloom weavers Varanasi: (as accessed from www.pvchr.com)
- Uzarmma (2003). "Rethinking Handloom", Seminar, No. 523, March.

Web Sources

- Reddy, Narsimha (2011). Handloom Weavers as a Vote Bank, as accessed from http://tsr.net.co/2011/05/handloom-weavers-as-a-vote-bank/1104 on 29/11/2013.
- www.indiastat.com Dated 14.05.2014.
- http://www.socialsciences.in/article/1985-textile-policy-and-handloom-industry-policy-promises-and-performance.

Chapter - 10

Globalisation and Economic Growth: Implications on Employment and Poverty in India

—*Surendra Meher and Ruchi Bhalla*

Globalisation generally refers to social and economic integration among different countries in the world. It also implies the movement of capital, technology, people, and culture across countries. As a process it was initiated in India during early 1990s and was accompanied by other measures like liberalisation and privatisation. Number of policy measures was undertaken in post-globalisation period. One of the important implications of globalisation has been that economic growth accelerated at a faster rate especially after mid 1990s. A new kind of information revolution with increased density of market took place with the advent of globalisation. However, in most of the developing countries including India, a large section of population could not avail the desired benefit of such changes. There seems to be declining employment growth after 1990 with increased employment causalisation. Most of the workforce took shelter in the informal sector. The impoverisation of small and marginal farmers continued and we did not witness a significant decline in the poverty of the masses. In other words, the aspect of human development especially for the vulnerable sections of the society remained more or less untouched. With the background, the paper seeks to examine the different aspects of globalisation and economic growth and its implications on changes in employment pattern and poverty of the masses. The paper uses secondary data such as National Sample Survey Organisation, Statistical extracts, Census of India, National Accounts Statistics and other available documents to come to the conclusion.

Key Words: *Globalisation, Liberalisation, Privatisation, Growth, Employment, Poverty.*

Globalisation, usually interpreted as cross-border movement of goods and services through economic interdependence. It is also a process of movement of people, culture, capital, knowledge and ideas across the national boundaries. It is, however, not a new phenomenon. Mercantilist writers such as Adam Smith, J.W. Horroks, Alexander Gray and Eric Roll emphasised that during fifteenth century, states were being made powerful by accumulating gold and silver through trade and commerce. Countries such as Britain, France were made stronger by accumulating wealth through such means. One would however agree that the form of globalisation involving trade and commerce across the world have changed and taken a new shape when most of the developing countries embraced it since late 1980s. Economic liberalisation and privatisation was initiated as part of the process of globalisation. A comprehensive structural adjustment programme involving cut in public expenditure specially subsidy, introduction of flexible labour market, liberalisation of external sector were also being followed. Gross trade, foreign direct investment (FDI), capital flows and technology transfers have risen across the world. It has greatly facilitated the process of integration through declining transport costs and the advent of Information and Communication Technologies (Bhalla, 2008). Globalisation is, however, not simply confined to trade, investment and financial inflow, but also extends to flow of services, technology, information and ideas across national boundaries (Nayyar, 2006). The process, thus led to accelerate growth rate of participating countries and benefits to consumers by availing new varieties of goods and services at cheaper cost.

Nevertheless, Scholars were quite sceptical about the adverse impact of globalisation. Stiglitz (2002) in his 'Discontent of Globalisation' argues that poor countries did not get the benefits of globalisation as their national economies are regulated by international institutions, which is evident by low level of development in Sub-Saharan Africa. Nayyar (2006) concluded that incidence of poverty increased in most countries of Latin America, the Caribbean and Sub-Saharan Africa during the 1980s and the 1990s, though the Asian countries managed to experience a decline in the incidence of poverty during this period. It therefore seems that industrialised developed nations have gained the most in the process of globalisation. It is pointed out that inequality in terms of wages and incomes has registered an increase almost everywhere in the world which has been associated with an increasing casualisation of the workforce. Employment opportunities in the organised sector have stagnated so that labour absorption was possible largely in the informal sector.

Adverse impacts of globalisation have also been noted specially on social sector, human development and employment. Chandrasekhar and Ghosh (2007) in the context of China and Indian economy revealed that the strategy of development is delivering relatively high growth without commensurate increases in employment, especially in the organised sector; and the bulk of new employment is in lower productivity activities under uncertain and often oppressive conditions. While regular employment had been declining as a share of total usual status employment for some time now (except for urban women workers), wage employment had continued to grow in share because employment on casual contracts had been on the increase. Kannan and Ravindran (2009) found that the jobless growth in the organised sector in India has profound implications on the distribution of surplus between capital and labour. Shyam Sundar (2010) found that tensions arising out of the measures, policies and strategies of employers and the government have resulted in increase in the incidence of labour management conflicts. Further, employers have also been aggressive in initiating lockouts in the post-reform period. According to Roy (1997), poverty still continued to exist in most rural part of the country, therefore, both national and international policies could be used to stimulate growth and reduce poverty especially in developing countries. Mahendradev (2000) in the context of South Asian countries pointed out that much effort is needed to reach the stage of more productive employment and higher labour incomes. The development strategy should be such as to raise investment in physical and human capital and help develop institutions and governance and reduce inequalities. It is in this context that many scholars have tried to study the impact of globalisation on growth and employment, poverty and inequality. An important consequence is that it has brought into focus the central issue of growth and development—namely, to what extent is the process of industrial revolution and diversification of labour force into non-agricultural sectors in developing countries like India has been accelerated or hampered by the new wave of liberalisation of trade and increased FDI.

The present paper examines the growth and employment scenario in India during the period of globalisation. It analyses the incidence of poverty as per the data revealed by the National Sample Survey Organisation. The first section deals with the conceptual and theoretical aspects of globalisation. The second section examines the growth and employment trends in India. Third section examines the incidence of poverty in India and final section presents concluding remarks.

Conceptual and Theoretical Aspect of 'Free Trade and Globalisation'

Globalisation has been defined by scholars in different ways. It has been agreed that globalisation is a gradual integration of countries or economies through unrestricted movement of goods, services and capital. It also involves movement of knowledge, ideas, technology, culture and many others. According to Nayyar (2006), globalisation is used in a positive sense to describe a process of integration into the world economy. It is used in a normative sense to prescribe a strategy of development based on rapid integration with the world economy. (Bhalla, 2008) defined globalisation as gradual integration of economies through free movement of goods, services and capital. The term 'globalisation' is used widely, but often in different senses. Used in a broader sense, one may include under the ambit of globalisation, the adoption of supra-national standards in economic arrangements in a country (Balakrishnan, 2010).

A narrower definition of globalisation is a process of unification of world economic order through reduction of barriers such as tariffs, export fees and import quota (Wikipedia).

There have been considerable discussions and writings among economic historians regarding the beginning of the process of globalisation. To Gunder Frank, 'there was a single global world economy with a worldwide division of labour and multilateral trade from 1500 onward' (Frank, 1998). Bentley (1999) argues that even before 1500, 'trade networks reached almost all regions of Eurasia and sub-Saharan Africa and large volumes of commerce encouraged specialisation of agricultural and industrial production'. It has been agreed that the history of globalisation dates back to 1492 when Christopher Columbus stumbles on the Americas in search of spices and 1498 when Vasco da Gama makes an end-run around Africa and snatches monopoly rents away from the Arab and Venetian spice traders.

Adam Smith, being a mercantilist writer, also believes 1500 AD as an important landmark of world history as far as global trade and commerce is concerned. In his 'Wealth of Nation' (1776), he profoundly gave specific importance to international trade and viewed trade as important vehicle to economic growth. He explained international trade expands the scope of division of labour and market, and division of labour directly impact on economic growth. Heberler (1950) pointed out trade as engine of economic growth as it can lead to full utilisation of otherwise domestic resources. Heckscher and Ohlin Model also suggested that countries are different based on abundance of factors especially capital and labour (Feenstra, 2004). The labour abundant countries would benefit by specialising labour intensive commodities and the capital abundant countries would benefit by specialising capital intensive commodities, both countries would thus benefit, if fair and free trade is allowed. Romar (1986) and Lucas (1988) also provided a convincing and rigorous basis for the positive relationship between international trade and long run economic growth and development. The theory postulates that lowering trade barriers will speed up the rate of economic growth and development by allowing developing nations to absorb technology developed in advanced countries at a faster rate than with a lower degree of openness. It also leads to rapid introduction of new products and services. Nevertheless scholars such as Singer and Prebisch argued that the countries particularly those of third world who keep exporting primary articles experiences a secular deterioration in terms of trade (Toye and Toye, 2003). It has been argued that the less developed countries produces agricultural goods which have lower income elasticity of demand and the rich countries produces manufactured goods having greater income elasticity of demand, as a result when trade expands, the developed countries gain much through improvement in terms of trade. Therefore, according to the explanations given by Singer and Prebisch, the present global economic order may not bring much benefit to the less developed countries, in turn, there is possibilities of widening of economic inequality across countries over time.

The process of globalisation with free and fair trade, have however, created a new wave for the developing countries. The new upcoming of sectors such as information and communication technology, and inflow of foreign direct investment, capital and technology have deepened the process of globalisation. For the developing economies, the growth of these sectors proved to be a boom to their economies. Globalisation gained momentum after 1980s when most of the countries began to integrate with each other. This was the time when the economies were facing low growth rates with high unemployment. Globalisation and closer integration of economies have had significant impacts on the economies of both developed and developing countries.

Globalisation has bought about a change in the employment situation through trade liberalisation, through encouraging exports and imports vis-à-vis increasing incentives for invention and innovation. To Heckscher and Ohlin, free trade between economies would enable to effectively utilise their abundant factor either in the form of labour or capital. The increased exports would then help in generating employment directly or indirectly through new investment. This new investment would create more opportunities and would lead to demand led growth. This would create jobs and would absorb abundant labour. At the other corner of academia, the process of globalisation have a negative impact on employment growth, which are being measured by declining employment elasticity in the post-globalisation phase Papola (2012), Sharma (2006). Further an increase in exports would generate more direct and indirect employment through demand led growth while increase in imports may displace protected industries and led their eventual closure. (Dasgupta and Singh, 2007).

Impact of Globalisation on Growth and Employment in India

Indian economy is now in an era of globalisation and liberalisation. This was witnessed in late 1980s and more formally in early 1990s. This has been indicated by the measures taken on trade policies and several other structural adjustment programmes. For instance export and import duties have been reduced as a part of policy measures to facilitate trade and exchange. The export sector is given special importance in order to promote exports. Exchange rate devaluation was undertaken so as to facilitate export and curtail import to further improve trade balance. Foreign direct investments as well as foreign institutional investment were also encouraged. Globalisation has helped Indian economy to integrate with world economies in the form of open trade, flow of new and innovative technology and encouragement to more investment. As a result of these initiatives, Indian economy experienced a sharp rise in growth.

Growth of Gross Domestic Product by various sectors in Indian economy has been depicted in Table 10.1. It has been seen that during early fifties, growth rate of GDP was merely two to three per cent. The GDP growth did not pick up even during sixties and seventies in their early years. However, during the period of 1990s impact of globalisation started to be seen in the form of high growth in GDP and across sectors of Indian economy. Growth rate of the economy reached a peak of eight per cent during 1999-00 and 8.9 per cent in 2010-11. The fruits of globalisation are however seen more in service sectors such as Financing, Insurance, real estate and business services and in the areas of trade, hotels and restaurants. The reform packages thus helped the economy to grow at its maximum. In the case of agriculture sector, however, there were variations in growth. The contribution of agriculture to the Gross Domestic Product declined significantly though population depending on agriculture did not decline in that rate. Data revealed by economic survey 2014-15 suggests that contribution of agriculture, forestry and fishing, mining and quarrying was 53.7 per cent in 1951 declined to 16.4 per cent in 2011-12.

Table 10.1: Growth of GDP at Factor Cost by Industry of Origin (2004-05 Prices)

Year	*Agriculture, forestry and fishing, mining and quarrying*	*Manufacturing, construction, electricity, gas and water supply*	*Trade, hotels, transport and communication*	*Financing, Insurance, real estate and business services*	*Community, social and personal services*	*Gross value added at factor cost*
1951-52	1.9	4.6	2.6	2.3	3	2.3
1952-53	3.1	-0.4	3.3	4.2	2.1	2.8
1961-62	0.3	6.9	6.5	4.3	4.7	3.1
1962-63	-1.4	6.2	5.9	3.4	7.1	2.1
1971-72	-1.7	2.5	2.3	5.2	4.5	1
1972-73	-4.4	3.4	2.2	3.9	3.3	-0.3
1981-82	5.2	7.4	6.1	8.1	2.1	5.6
1982-83	0.6	0.2	5.5	9.5	7.7	2.9
1991-92	-1.4	-0.1	2.3	10.8	2.6	1.4
1992-93	6	3.6	5.6	5.4	6	5.4
1995-96	0	12	13.4	8.1	7.3	7.3
1996-97	8.9	7.2	8.1	6.2	8.1	8
1997-98	-1.3	3.3	7.5	11.7	8.3	4.3
1998-99	5.9	4.3	7.7	7.8	9.7	6.7
1999-00	2.8	6.2	11.4	13	12	8
2001-02	5.5	2.7	8.6	6.2	4	5.4
2002-03	-4.9	7.1	8.3	7.2	3.8	3.9
2003-04	8.2	7.9	11.2	5.3	5.3	8
2010-11	8.3	7.6	12.2	10	4.2	8.9
2011-12	4.4	8.5	4.3	11.3	4.9	6.7

Source: Economic Survey (2014-15), Government of India.

It thus appears that growth in GDP after globalisation has been more likely due to the growth in service sectors. It has been estimated that during 2011-12, nearly 60 per cent of the GDP was accounted for by the service sector alone. On the other hand, contribution of agricultural sector has declined and that for manufacturing sector is almost stagnant. Since agriculture and industry happens to be the sectors that absorb employment, the income and living conditions of population depending on agriculture specially the small and marginal farmers has been deteriorated. In other words, interpersonal inequality in per capita income for population in different sectors of the economy has widened after globalisation.

Trends of Employment Growth

It is evident that globalisation has lifted Indian economy by putting at a high growth path. It has introduced new varieties of goods and services for consumers at a reasonable price. With the mechanism of foreign investment and flow of capital across borders, it facilitated learning through exchange of ideas and technology. However, it remains to be seen to what extent it has benefitted the poorer and to unemployed in the country. Economic theories mentioned above and prediction of globalisation suggests that globalisation tend to improve employment condition in Indian economy, through proper utilisation of its abundant labour resources. With the opening of the world economies to integrate themselves with each other created the opportunities of new and productive jobs. There appears to be a mixed result. Table 10.2 below reveals (as estimated by Behera, 2012) that from 1993-94 to 1999-00, 24.18 million jobs were added and highest recorded from 1999-00 to 2004-05.

Table 10.2: Number of Workforce (in Million) and their Growth

Year	*Rural*			*Urban*			*All*
	Male	*Female*	*Total*	*Male*	*Female*	*Total*	*India*
1993-94	187.66	104.29	291.95	65.1	17.4	82.5	374.45
1999-00	198.81	105.91	304.72	75.64	18.27	93.91	398.63
2004-05	218.85	123.96	342.81	90.42	24.62	115.04	457.85
2009-10	231.9	104.5	336.4	99.8	22.2	122	458.4
Compound annual growth rate (%)							
1993-94 to 1999-00	0.97	0.26	0.72	2.53	0.82	2.18	1.05
1999-00 to 2004-05	1.94	3.2	2.38	3.63	6.15	4.14	2.81
2004-05 to 2009-10	1.17	-3.36	-0.38	1.99	-2.05	1.18	0.02

Source: Behera (2012).

where 59.22 million jobs were added. However, in the subsequent NSS periods, net job addition is only 0.55 million. Consequently, employment growth was highest during the period 1999-00 to 2004-05 i.e. it grew at the rate of

2.81 per cent and only 0.02 per cent from the period 2004-05 to 2009-10 at the all India level. This period experienced a negative growth in employment for both rural female and urban female category.

During the period 1999-00 to 2004-05, urban female category have recorded significant growth in employment followed by urban male 3.63 per cent and rural female 3.22 per cent. It thus seems that large chunk of employment has been created in urban areas in this period. The decline in employment during the period 2004-05 to 2009-10 has been attributed to decline in Workforce Participation Rate and that increase in employment has been taken place in the construction sector after the period of economic reform (Behera, 2012).

Globalisation has, no doubt, created jobs, but jobs so created required adequate skills and employability among the labour force. The backdrop of globalisation made large number of people unemployed as they were unskilled. The number of unemployed in India rose from 3.98 million in 1973-74 to 9.15 by 1999-00 and further to 11.21 million by 2004-05 (Bhalla, 2008). The reason behind this could be that the process of globalisation replaced million of workers with new technology. Globalisation has compelled employers to become efficient to sustain in the age of competition. As a result, cost reduction techniques were being followed by the employers leading to use of more capital and labour saving technology. (Shyamsundar, 2010) revealed that the rather frequent incidence of strikes (more than a dozen since mid-1990s), increasing work stoppage incidence in public sector, lockouts by larger establishments and the 'agitational connect' are the issues that emanated from reforms and re-structuring processes.

Table 10.3: Unemployment Rate Based on Usual Status and Daily Status (in Percentage)

NSS Rounds	*Rural Male*		*Rural Female*		*Urban Male*		*Urban Female*	
	Usual Status	*Daily Status*	*Usual Status*	*Daily Status*	*Usual Status*	*Daily Status*	*Usual Status*	*Daily Status*
50th (1993-94)	2	5.6	1.3	5.6	5.4	6.7	8.3	10.4
66th (2009-10)	1.9	6.4	2.4	8	3	5.1	7	9.1
68th (2011-12)	2.1	5.5	2.9	6.2	3.2	4.9	6.6	8

Source: NSSO 68th Round January 2014.

Table 10.3 makes it clear that globalisation did not make a significant impact as far as reduction in employment is concerned. Unemployment rate in different NSS period has been noted based on both usual status and daily status basis. It might be seen that unemployment rate in case of usual status is higher than daily status. From NSS round 50th to 66th i.e. from 1993-94 to 2009-10, there appears to be a higher unemployment rate in rural areas based on daily status. In the latest period, however, there appears to be a decline in the rate of unemployment which could be attributed to several employment generation programmes such as MNREGA. However, unemployment rate is still higher in the latest NSS period i.e. during 2011-12. It may therefore be asserted that globalisation and neoliberal economic policies could not make significant dent as far as reduction of unemployment is concerned.

Economic survey 2014-15 noted that annual compound growth of employment during 1999-00 to 2004-05 was 2.8 per cent which declined to 0.5 per cent during the period 2004-05 to 2011-12. It is further noted that during period 2009-10 to 2011-12, 13.9 million workforce were added which did not keep pace with the increase in labour force i.e. 14.9 million during same phase.

Quality of Employment

Though there seems to be some increase in employment specially from the period 2004-05 to 2009-10, it remains to be seen to what extent the quality of employment has increased. The quality of employment could be judged whether a person is engaged in regular category or in self-employed or as a casual worker. Regular employment ensures job social security with some degree of satisfaction in work. On the other hand, causal employment does not ensure any kind of social security. Further, in case of self-employment, one has to see the income generating capacity, more a person is trained and skilled more is the income earning capacity. Table 10.4 reveals percentage distribution of workers by type of employment.

Table 10.4: Percentage Distribution of Workers by Type of Employment

	Rural Males			*Rural Females*		
NSS Rounds	*Self Employed*	*Regular wage/Salaried employees*	*Casual Labour*	*Self Employed*	*Regular wage/Salaried employees*	*Casual Labour*
50th (1993-94)	56.7	8.7	34.6	51.3	3.4	45.3
66th (2009-10)	53	8.7	38.3	50.3	5.5	44.2
68th (2011-12)	54.1	10.2	35.7	53.5	7.6	38.9
	Urban Males			*Urban Females*		
50th (1993-94)	41.1	42.7	16.2	37.2	35.5	27.3
66th (2009-10)	40.9	42	17.1	35.4	44.4	20.2
68th (2011-12)	41.6	43.6	14.9	36.8	48.7	14.6

Source: same as Table 10.3.

It could be seen that as on 2009-10, more than 90 per cent workers constituted self employed and casual workers in rural areas. Out of them, more than 50 per cent workers were self employed. During 68th round i.e. in

2011-12, there appears to be some rise in the proportion of regular workers. The scenario is almost same for rural female as well, but proportion of regular female workers is somewhat less than male workers. In urban area, however, more than 40 per cent workers happened to be regular workers and the proportion of casual labour is less than rural areas. During the latest NSS round, the percentage of self employed has increased in both rural as well as urban areas. It may be asserted that percentage of self employed workers have increased due to the scope arises out of the integration of the economies. As the generation of open trade and increased in exports were facilitated the casual labours saw the remunerative effect of it. Nevertheless, skill and employability of Indian labour force is quite low and it may not be expected that self-employment so created in the advent of globalisation would be so remunerative. A study by Jha (2009) reveals that only 5.06 per cent are vocationally trained in total labour force in India compared to 98.8 per cent in Korea Republic, 75.33 in Germany, 78.11 per cent in Canada.

In Indian economy, the size of unorganised sector is far more than that of organised sector. This number is very large and it is being projected that this number may be increasing overtime. This projection has been clearly brought out by the National Commission for Enterprises in the Unorganised Sector (NCEUS). Unorganised sector has been explained by the ILO as all the workers in the informal sector (minus a small fraction who are entitled to social security benefits) plus those workers in the organised sector who do not enjoy any social security benefits. NCEUS estimated that the unorganised workers constituted 92.4 per cent of all workers during 2004-05. During the period 1999-00 to 2004-0, 60.7 million new jobs were created. Out of these, 52.3 million jobs were created in the informal/unorganised sector, and 8.5 million jobs were created in the organised sector, which are informal in nature (Bhalla, 2008). It has further been brought out that the growth rate of real wages has decelerated during 1999-00 to 2004-05 and real earnings of workers and wages of casual labour have increased at a much slower rate than during 1993-94 to 1999-00. Himanshu (2007) also concluded that the real wages decelerated for all workers significantly during 1999-00 to 2004-05 compared to the period 1993-94 and 1999-00. The decline in wage rate was found for both rural and urban areas and in both agriculture and non-agriculture, male and female and at all level of education. Therefore, the ultimate result is that despite very high growth of employment, the entire increase in workforce has joined the already large army of unorganised workers with unsatisfactory conditions of work, decline in real wage and lack of any social security.

It is thus seen that though there has been a perceptible change in employment, its quality has been deteriorated. The share of informal sector in employment has been increasing and their position on the aspects of health and education has been declining over time. Therefore, though globalisation created a pleasant environment but the fruits of this were not enjoyed by a major section of the society. Although employment rate has increased and it is a sign of positive development but the quality of employment was very disappointing for a major proportion of workers. Not only this, the conditions of work seem to have deteriorated in terms of lack of social security and other amenities at work place. This is due to the technology that required skilled labours and productive labourers. The income levels of most of the informal workers are rather low—the casual labourers and self-employed have very low incomes. No wonder, the incidence of poverty among informal workers is significantly higher than among formal workers. International labour organisation has been playing an important role in setting standards for the quality and working condition of workers. After the rapid deterioration in the position of informal sector workers it has set itself the challenge to achieve decent work for all by promoting "opportunities for women and men to obtain decent and productive work, in conditions of freedom, equity, and security and human dignity" (ILO, 1999).

Incidence of Poverty

The available data on the incidence of poverty suggests that poverty rates in India and across states have been reduced after the phase of globalisation. An estimate of poverty head count ratio reveals that poverty ratio for the country as a whole declined from 46.5 per cent in 1983 to 39 per cent in 1987-88 and further to 28.7 per cent in 2004-05 (Himanshu, 2007). According to Bhalla's findings, globalisation has resulted higher growth which in turn has resulted in poverty reduction, in his analysis, the incidence of poverty as well as number of poor has declined perceptibly in the entire post-reform period from 1993-94 to 2004-05. It has also been asserted that rapid poverty reduction took place prior to globalisation i.e. from 1983 to 1993-94 due to unprecedented growth of agriculture. The available data also indicate that the incidence of poverty is higher in rural areas compared to urban areas. Bhagwati (2001) argued that growth is desired because it would reduce poverty. According to him, growth reduces poverty because of three reasons (a) it creates jobs that 'pull up' the poor into gainful employment by providing more economic opportunity (b) it generates revenues which help to build more schools and health facilities and (c) it creates incentives that enable poor to access these facilities and also for the advancement of progressive social agendas.

Table 10.5 makes it clear that poverty ratio has declined from the period 2004-05 to 2011-12. At the all India level, rural poverty and urban poverty ratio stood at 25.7 per cent and 13.7 per cent respectively during 2011-12. States such as Himachal Pradesh, Kerala and Punjab poverty both at rural and urban areas remains at single digit level. Considerable reduction in poverty has been noted in states such as Andhra Pradesh, Tamil Nadu, Uttarakhand and Rajasthan. Nevertheless, high poverty ratio still persists at some Eastern and North-Eastern states such as Arunachal Pradesh, Bihar, Assam, Odisha,

Jharkhand and Chhatishgarh. This is a big cause of concern. Therefore, it is essential that the process of economic reforms must take care of the cause of poor in those states.

Table 10.5: State-wise Incidence of Poverty by Rural and Urban Status

States/UT	*2004-05*			*2009-10*			*2011-12*		
	Rural	*Urban*	*Total*	*Rural*	*Urban*	*Total*	*Rural*	*Urban*	*Total*
Andhra Pradesh	32.3	23.4	29.6	22.8	17.7	21.1	11	5.8	9.2
Arunachal Pradesh	33.6	23.5	31.4	26.2	24.9	25.9	38.9	20.3	34.7
Assam	36.4	21.8	34.4	39.9	26.1	37.9	33.9	20.5	32
Bihar	55.7	43.7	54.4	55.3	39.4	53.5	34.1	31.2	33.7
Chhatisgarh	55.1	28.4	49.4	56.1	23.8	48.7	44.6	24.8	39.9
Delhi	15.6	12.9	13	7.7	14.4	14.2	12.9	9.8	9.9
Gujarat	39.1	20.1	31.6	26.7	17.9	23	21.5	10.1	16.6
Haryana	24.8	22.4	24.1	18.6	23	20	11.6	10.3	11.2
Himachal Pradesh	25	4.6	22.9	9.1	12.6	9.5	8.5	4.3	8.1
Jammu and Kashmir	14.1	10.4	13.1	8.1	12.8	9.4	11.5	7.2	10.4
Jharkhand	51.6	23.8	45.3	41.6	31.1	39.1	40.8	24.8	37
Karnataka	37.5	25.9	33.3	26.1	19.6	23.6	24.5	15.3	20.9
Kerala	20.2	18.4	19.6	12	12.1	12	9.1	5	7.1
Madhya Pradesh	53.6	35.1	48.6	42	22.9	36.7	35.7	21	31.7
Maharashtra	47.9	25.6	38.2	29.5	18.3	24.5	24.2	9.1	17.4
Odisha	60.8	37.6	57.2	39.2	25.9	37	35.7	17.3	32.6
Punjab	22.1	18.7	20.9	14.6	18.1	15.9	7.7	9.2	8.3
Rajasthan	35.8	29.7	34.4	26.4	19.9	24.8	16.1	10.7	14.7
Tamil Nadu	37.5	19.7	29.4	21.2	12.8	17.1	15.8	6.5	11.3
Uttar Pradesh	42.7	34.1	40.9	39.4	31.7	37.7	30.4	26	29.4
Uttarakhand	35.1	26.2	32.7	14.9	25.2	18	11.6	10.5	11.3
West Bengal	38.2	24.4	34.2	28.8	22	26.7	22.5	14.7	20
All India	**42**	**25.5**	**37.2**	**33.8**	**20.9**	**29.8**	**25.7**	**13.7**	**21.9**

Source: Directorate of Economics and Statistics, Government of India (2014).

Bhalla (2008) further noted that the number of poor in India continued to be very large; there are as many as 315 million poor people in the country in 2004-05, compared with 324 million in 1983. Out of these as many as 232 million, that is nearly 76 per cent, lived in villages. It has further been noted casual labourers had the highest incidence of poverty and the regular workers the lowest. And, the incidence of poverty among self-employed was lower than among casual labour but higher than among the regular workers.

Table 10.6: Poverty Ratio by Employment Status 1993-94 and 2004-05

Work status	*Rural persons*		*Urban Persons*	
	1993-94	*2004-05*	*1993-94*	*2004-05*
Self-employed	27.76	16.41	31.52	24.17
Regular employed	16.87	9.58	16.03	11.65
Casual workers	49.44	31.52	55.63	45.31
All Workers	34.72	20.83	29.66	22.21

Source: Bhalla (2008).

It has been further noted that in rural areas, the incidence of poverty is less compared to urban areas specially among self-employed category. It has been remarked that most of the self-employed in agriculture in rural areas are land owning farmers and they are generally better off than workers engaged in low productivity manufacturing in rural areas. Most of workers belonging to agriculture including small and marginal farmers, industrial workers, and workers in construction sector belong to informal sector. It is estimated that more that 92 per cent of total workers constituted informal workers and one would expect that majority of the poor constituted informal workers. It thus appears from the above analysis that the process of globalisation, has no doubt picked up economic growth with service sector playing a major role. On the other hand, agriculture and industry that absorb workers could not perform better which is clear from their declining or stagnant contribution to Gross Domestic Product. The process of globalisation has made workers to shelter in informal sector. Though poverty ratio has declined, there continued to be large number of population still below poverty line.

Conclusion

Globalisation is a process of gradual integration of countries or economies through unrestricted movement of goods, services and capital which also involves movement of knowledge, ideas, technology and culture. The process of globalisation has been an age old process. As the economic theories postulate, globalisation and free trade would bring about a significant change for developing countries on the aspects of growth and employment. It would enable them to utilise their abundant factor such as labour and increased flow of trade would help for generating employment through new investments. With the upcoming of sectors and revolutions in information technology, the process has deepened and created a new wave for the developing countries. In early 1990s several measures were undertaken to initiate the process of globalisation in India on the front of trade policies and structural adjustment programmes. For instance, export and import duties have been reduced as a part of policy measures to facilitate trade and exchange. The export sector is given special importance in order to promote exports. Exchange rate devaluation was undertaken so as to facilitate export and curtail import to further improve trade balance. Foreign direct investments as well as foreign institutional investment were also encouraged. Globalisation has helped Indian economy to integrate with world economies in the form of open trade, flow of new and innovative technology and encouragement to more investment. As a result of these initiatives Indian economy experienced a sharp rise in growth from a very low level prior to the phase of globalisation. Consumers find it beneficial through new varieties of goods and services.

The impact of globalisation is also seen in the front of employment and poverty. The period from 1999-00 to 2004-05 seen as a boom for employment growth, but thereafter it declined significantly. Some scholars found reduction in employment elasticity with respect to output (Papola, 2012; Behera, 2012; Sharma, 2007). It has been established that the process of globalisation replaced million of workers with new technology. Globalisation has compelled employers to become efficient in order to sustain in the age of competition. As a result, cost reduction techniques were being followed by the employers leading to use of more capital and labour saving technology. People with adequate skills and training found themselves absorbed in lucrative service sector. Globalisation has further made a clear cut divide between organised and unorganised sector. Most of the workers took shelter in the informal sector due to structural adjustment programmes initiated and employers found it suitable to use technology to make them competitive resulted in displacement of workers. Poverty ratio also appears to decline during post-globalisation. But in absolute terms millions of population are still in the abject of poverty. Workers in informal sector and other casual workers are found to be more vulnerable than workers in formal sector.

Therefore, it is high time to include the poor and informal workers in the process of globalisation. An integrated policy is required to create adequate employment opportunities to take the advantage of globalisation. Employment generation schemes specially 'gainful self employment' and wage employment programme with due emphasis on rural asset building must be continued. Skill development, training for the unemployed is essential to find gainful employment. Further, a host of social security schemes need to be continued with holistic manner for the poor and informal workers.

References

Bhalla, G.S. 2008. 'Globalisation and Employment Trends in India', *The Indian Journal of Labour Economics,* 51(1): 1-23.

Balakrishnana, P. 2010. *Economic Growth in India: History and Prospect*, New Delhi: Oxford University Press.

Behera, Deepak Kumar. 2012. 'Economic Growth and Employment Trrends in India, 1983-2010: What does the Latest Employment Data Reveal?', *Indian Journal of Labour Economics*, 55 (2): 265-279.

Bentley, J. H. 1999. 'Asia in World History', *Education About Asia* 4(1):5-9.

Chandrasekhar, C. P. and Ghosh, J. 2007. 'Recent employment trends in India and China: An unfortunate convergence?' *Social Scientist*, 35:19–46.

Dasgupta, S, Singh, A. 2007. 'Manufacturing, Services and Premature Deindustrialisation in Developing Countries: A Kaldorian Analysis in Mavrotas', in George and Shorrocks, Anthony (ed.), *Advancing Development: Core Themes in Global Economics* (436-456) Palgrave MacMillan in association with the United Nations University World Institute for Development Economics Research (WIDER).

Ezell, S, Atinson, S. 2014. *The Indian Economy at a Crossroads* (Available at: http: //www2.itif.org/2014-indian-economy-at-crossroads.pdf)

Economic Survey. 2015. Ministry of Finance, Department of Economic Affairs, Economic Division, Government of India.

Feenstra, Robert C. 2004. 'The Heckscher–Ohlin Model' in *Advanced International Trade: Theory and Evidence*, Princeton University Press.

Frank, A. G. 1998. *Reorient: Global Economy in the Asian Age*. Berkeley, C A: University of California Press.

Goldar, B.N. 2014. 'Globalisation, Growth and Employment in the Organised Sector of the Indian Economy'. *Working Paper WP 06/2014,* Institute for Human Development ISBN: 978-81-88315-44-4.

Himanshu, 2007. 'Recent trends in Poverty and Inequality: Some Preliminary Results', *Economic and Political Weekly*, 42(6) 497-508.

ILO, 2009. 'Towards an Employment Strategy for India' (Available at: http: //www.ilo.org).

ILO, 1999. Decent Work. International Labour Organisation.Geneva.

M. McCartney. 2009. *Political Economy, Growth and Liberalisation in India, 1991-2008.* Routledge.

Jha, Praveen. 2009, 'The Well Being of Labour in Contemporary Indian Economy: What's Active Labour Market got to do with it?' *Employment Sector, Employment Working Paper* No.39, ILO.

Kannan, K.P, and G. Raveendran. 2009. 'Growth Sans Employment: A Quarter Century of Jobless Growth in India's Organised Manufacturing' *Economic and Political Weekly*, 44(10): 80-91.

Kevin, H. O' Rourke and Jeffrey G. Williamson. 2002. 'When did Globalisation Begin?' *European Review of Economic History*, 6(1): 23-50.

Mahendra, Dev. 2000. 'Economic Liberalisation and Employment in South Asia: II', *Economic and Political Weekly*, 35(3): 135-146.

NCEUS, 2007. 'Report on Conditions of Work and Promotion of Livelihoods in the Unorganised Sector.' *Ministry of Small Scale Industries. Government of India,* New Delhi.

NSSO, 2006. 'Employment and Unemployment Situation in India 2004-05.' Report No. 515(61/10/1), *Ministry of Statistics and Programme Implementation Government of India*, New Delhi.

NSSO, 2014. 'Employment and Unemployment Situation in India July 2011-June 2012', Report No. 554(68/10/1), *Ministry of Statistics & Programme Implementation, Government of India*, New Delhi.

Nayyar, Deepak. 2006. 'Globalisation, History and Development: a Tale of two Centuries', *Cambridge Journal of Economics*, 30(1): 137-159.

Papola, T S. 2012. 'Employment Growth in the Post Reform Period', *Keynote Paper on the theme 'Employment in the Post-Reform India'*, 54th Annual Conference of the Indian Society of Labour Economics, 20-22 December, 2012, Varanasi.

Stiglitz, Joseph E. 2002. *Globalisation and Its Discontents.* New York: Norton and Company.

Shyam Sundar, K.R. 2010. 'Emerging Trends in Employment Relations in India' *Indian Journal of Industrial Relations*, 45(4): 585-595.

Sharma, Alakh N. 2006. 'Flexibility, Employment and Labour Market Reforms in India,' *Economic and Political Weekly*, 41(21): 2078-2085.

Roy, Sumit. 1997. 'Globalisation, Structural Change and Poverty: Some Conceptual and Policy Issues,' *Economic and Political Weekly*, 32(33/34): 2117-2135.

Toye, John and Richard Toye. 2003. 'The Origins and Interpretation of the Prebisch-Singer Thesis', *History of Political Economy*, 35(3): 437-467.

Chapter - 11

Globalisation and Education: Exploring Dimensions of Equity, Equality and Excellence

—*Tapan R. Mohanty*

At the turn of the twenty-first century, globalisation has emerged as the most pervasive process of social transformation. After industrial revolution and colonialism it is the globalisation that has brought a significant transformation into social and economic facets of the globe. Globalisation with its emphasis on economic integration and principle of free trade has not only altered the instruments and mechanisms of cultural exchange but has also significantly affected the delivery mechanism as well as value of social goods like education. In this paper an attempt has been made to provide a critical analysis of the impact of globalisation on education particularly of primary education. While doing so, the paper makes generalisations by critically analysing all levels of education to derive a comprehensive understanding. In fact, the study intends to highlight the fact that under the aegis of globalisation there has been increase in the number of private English medium schools which are trying to fulfill the educational demands of an aspiring middle class on increased commercialisation intent. On the other hand, the government schools suffer from low infrastructural facilities and poor quality of teaching due to negligence and lack of adequate funding. The article is divided into five subsections in the form of an introductory description of globalisation, role of state in the educational provisioning, marketisation of education and the balance between equity, equality and excellence. The paper concludes by underlining that despite the mushrooming growth of private schools and occasional islands of excellence, the quality of education in government primary schools is poor and is creating strong hurdle for poor, deprived and marginalised students to create a better future for them using educational tools as a means of socio-economic transformation.

Key Words: *Globalisation, Primary Education, Privatisation, Educational equity, Pedagogic Transformation.*

August Comte envisaged sociology as the study of social statics and dynamics and it is the study of social dynamics that has taken the form of sociology of social change. This discipline underlines the invariability of change, its directions and dimensions or in other words, the structure, function and process of change. It also takes into account of the processes of diversity of traditions and virtuosity of performances. Tradition, transformation and transition constitute the essence of social change. According to sociologist, social change can be a product of orthogenetic or exogenetic forces. Besides, there are numerous factors viz. demographic, ecological, biological; cultural those can bring substantive alternation in existing profile of the society. In terms of degree and pervasiveness these factors and processes vary from each other as far as their impact on society is concerned. But some of these processes are macro processes those have lasting and extensive influences over a huge population and larger territory. Industrialisation, urbanisation, modernisation, colonisation and globalisation are categorised under the macro processes of social change. After industrial revolution and colonialism it is the globalisation that has brought a significant transformation to social and economic facets of the globe.

Globalisation with its emphasis on economic integration and principle of free trade has made it imperative to have international collaboration and transnational interaction at least in economic and cultural exchange. But in the process it has transcended designed territories and defined limits. As a result its cultural calibrations are much more obvious and apparent than its perceived economic effect. One of such examples is the pervasiveness of market economics and its apparent impact on a seemingly different field i.e. education. In this paper an attempt has been made to provide a kaleidoscopic analysis of the impact of globalisation in education particularly in primary education though a perceptible stream of generalisation about all levels of education is discernible. In fact, the paper perceives the entire gamut of education from its intrinsic and expressive perspective rather than its extrinsic and instrumental dimension, hence the emphasis on its holistic feature.

The article is divided into few subsections for clarity of thought and expression besides making it comprehensive, succinct and organised. However, the issues dealt in the essay are arguably complicated and therefore, efforts are made to make it more illustrative rather than exhaustive. Similarly, premium is placed on substantive issues rather than theoretical and methodological paradigms. The first section is introductory which tries in brief to acquaint the reader with the issue at hand while the second section deals with conceptual and definitional terrain.

The third one provides a small theoretical introduction while the fourth one is substantive and is based on various arguments and counter-arguments. For a better conceptual and pragmatic perspective a comparative analysis of role of the state is provided to contrast it that of the market. In a way the attempt can described as an effort to make use of comparative method espoused by Max Weber.[1] Final section of the article contains my concluding observations though ideally I will prefer the readers to derive their own inferences.

Globalisation: A Thematic Portrayal

Globalisation is no longer discussed either as a process of trade liberalisation or an innocuous design to integrate the world. Rather globalisation is conceived as process of social transformation, of mitigating the time and space, of intermixing people, policies and practices. The 1990s have seen a boom in writing about globalisation. According to Waters (1995:1), it is the concept of 90s, 'a key idea which we understand the transition of human society into the third millennium' (*Ibid*)[2]. He further adds that it refers to a social process in which 'the constraints of geography and cultural arrangements recede and in which people become increasingly aware that they are receding' (Waters, 1995:3). Globalisation is best understood as expressing fundamental aspects of time-space distantiation.

'Globalisation concerns the intersection of presence and absence, the interlacing of social events and social relations "at a distance" with local contextualities' (Giddens, 1991:21[3]). David Harvey (1989:240) too refers to the fact that globalisation describes our changing experience of time and space or 'time-space compression'[4]. In this context globalisation can both be explained and experienced through three 'I's namely; Information, Ideas and Images can be sustained through another 'I' i.e. Institutionalisation. Information dissolves meaning and the social into a sort of nebulous state leading not at all to a surfeit of innovation but to the very contrary to total entropy (Baudillard, 1981: 100)[5]. For Baudrillard, then the new communication technologies have promoted a global culture of instant but meaningful communication, in which time and space horizons have collapsed. He argues that this new social order based on the dominances of signs rather than material production-the 'metallurgic' society has become a 'semiurgic society' (185). 'In this society the boundary between images and reality implodes, so that the latter becomes meaningless. There is no longer any space in which we can ground ourselves and our understanding of the world and *claim it to be isolated and insular (italics added).* He reiterates that 'history has vanished into a hyperspace where it has lost all meaning' (Baudrillard, 1988:36)[6].

Taking global-local dichotomy and dynamics Giddens feel that globalisation is the intensification of worldwide social relationships which link distant places in such a way that local happenings are shaped by events occurring many miles away and vice-versa (1990:64).[7] The impact of globalisation has been loud and decisive particularly in cultural sphere, it is not merely the shrinking of space that has altered our conception of distance but it is the invasion and penetration of self that is more palpable and pervasive. In fact, it is increasingly being realised that 'McDonaldisation' (Ritzer, 1996) and 'Coca-colonisation' is a form of neo-colonisation of non-Western world by feitishized Western goods carrying with them hugely invasive connotations of West's success and affluence. The increasing global reliability on these products as well as a pervading sense of conspicuous consumption of occidental life style has made this process is extremely difficult to arrest.

Considered in these parameters we can perceive the impact of globalisation of education and the nature and dimension of educational policy put forwarded under the behest of globalisation as well as its perceived and real impact on primary education. Commercialisation of education and privatisation of educational institutions is nothing new and was always on cards but the way it has got the momentum and massiveness clearly underlines the effect of globalisation. Privatisation of education, accreditation of courses, exorbitant pricing and stratification of educational programmes can be categorised as the ill effects of globalisation.

Education and Development

Defined as the 'manifestation of divine perfection already in man' (Vivekanada, 2001: 506)[8], education has been in the forefront of contemporary discourse. The study of education is the study of knowledge and the specific branch that deals with it is known as 'epistemology'. Generally speaking the quest for knowledge is inherent in man and largely is a product of his consciousness. But formal education is understood, as the 'internalisation of values and indoctrination of professional training' is essentially a cultural product. But such an all-inclusive definition is bound to create ripples and invite multiple reactions. No wonder that we have divergent views regarding the nature, scope and perspective of education, its form and content, directions and dimensions. However, formal education system largely explained through institutionalised curriculum, pedagogy and training and structured layers of formalised hierarchy is a product of fairly recent times. Theoretically this can be explained from three important but mutually exclusive viewpoints namely, functionalist, Marxist and modernist.

Sociologically speaking functionalist view of education is traced in the writings of French sociologist Emile Durkheim and his followers' viz. Talcott Parsons, Kingsly Davis, Wilber E. Moore addressed education as a process of socialisation meant to train the young. It further emphasises the fact that education facilitates the process of division of labour by allocating specialised roles to specific individuals and groups, based on their aptitude and merit. Though one can find the root of this approach in the writings of early Greek thinkers like Plato, Aristotle and libertarians like John Locke, J.S. Mill, Mathew Arnold etc., it has achieved its full expression in the hands of sociologists. While Marxists follow an altogether different argument claiming education as an instrument of 'class domination' and 'exploitation'. Marx and Engels perceived education as a means of subjugation and method to incapacitate the working class spirit of revolution. Philosophers like Louise Althusser consider education as a part of 'Ideological State Apparatus' used to instill and inculcate particular values promoted and prescribed by the State. This view is further articulated by leading left intellectuals viz. Antonio Gramsci, Niccos Polantzas, Ralph Millband, Herbert Marcuse etc., and empirically verified by Samuel Bowels and Herbert Ginties in USA and A. H. Halsy in UK. Radical like Evan Illich has prescribed 'de-schooling' of society while Paul Freiero has talked of 'conscientisation' of education and Left leaning sociologist C. Wright Mills had perceived 'meritocratic' American education system as a conspiracy of privileged against the social underdogs.

The Modernist approach to education is almost similar to that of capitalist and has incorporated certain concerns and ideals of the left. It protects the interest of the rich while providing minor concessions to the poor in terms of 'positive discrimination', merit and means scholarship, provision of teaching-learning materials etc. Commercialisation of education and marketisation of institutions of learning, making education a viable money-spinning 'industry' is an offshoot of modernisation of education. Transportation of education from 'ivory towers' to 'intelligent tool box' via satellite besides transferring data from class room to clients situated in 'home' and transporting degrees across the national frontiers is a result of 'globalisation of education'. This has been possible mainly through the revolutionary changes in information technology and knowledge revolution.

Education encompasses schooling of both children and adults, in specially designated educational institutions, training associated with economic enterprises and informal education of children and adults in the home and in the community. Over their lifetime people learn more from informal sources than from formal, but in this perspective emphasis is given to formal education not only due to the availability of data, but also due to the fact that informal education is generally complementary to and to some extent dependent on the formal education system. Education empowers poor by attacking ignorance, building skills, and by changing the outdated attitudes and values (UNESCO-PROAP, 1998)[9]. In the human capital framework, by imparting skills, education enhances the productivity of the people in the labour and thereby enhances their earnings, taking the poor over the poverty line. In the wider human development framework, it enhances the very quality of life-much more of the poor than the rich (Sen, 1997)[10].

However, the effectiveness of this powerful tool of socio-economic development largely depends upon its spread and utilisation. Access, retention and quality are three major stumbling blocks in allowing education to achieve its goal. In almost all developing countries apart from lack of access and quality provisions, extension of education has also suffered from the lack of social opportunities. The presence of acute social hierarchy, gender discrimination and group dynamics has affected the progress of education at societal level.

But more than these there are significant number of children and groups who remain outside the reach of education due to socio-economic disabilities. Education cannot fulfill its mission and society cannot reap benefits unless and until the educational needs of these disadvantaged groups are properly addressed. This task is easier said than done. It requires dedication, innovation and patience besides huge resources.

The point that needs to be emphasised here is the interlinkage between education and globalisation. Our earlier description has provided with enough inputs to understand and realise globalisation and a definitional comprehension of education but they do not suffice a conceptual clarification of meaningful relationship between the two. Education and globalisation are both processes of social change and have influenced our life-world and worldviews besides enormously influencing our attitudes and aptitudes. But when we look at the impact of globalisation on education the focus get shifted from a generalised explanation of interconnectivity to a more specific and precise realm of analysis. In this context it becomes mandatory to inquire what is the substantive and structural transformation brought about by globalisation in education system and to make it more precise one needs to focus on a particular stratum of education i.e. primary, secondary and higher. This also includes changes in the site and context of education as well as changes in the educational equations manifested in terms of definite and perceptible normative standardisation of behavioural patterns exhibited by various players.

The site of education here of course, refers to the place where teaching-learning activities takes place i.e. class rooms, laboratory and library. Usually educational activities have been restricted to definite clusters of physical space and an institutional pattern of difference and discrimination have been built around them over a period of time. In ancient India students were let to the personal care of the teachers and used to spend a considerable period of time in the hermitages. In the serene surroundings of forests teaching was more of a transcendental process of integration of real with ethereal. In sylvan surroundings, silhouetted seminary and somber silence an effort was made to achieve synergy with the ecosystem.

Twenty-first century is often described as the era of 'knowledge revolution' and the supremacy of knowledge over other materials products is critically acclaimed. It seems that everybody has accepted if grudgingly the idea of French sociologist Bourdieu who felt 'knowledge is the power and is a form of capital'. Discussing the problem of underdevelopment and causes of poverty among nations the World Bank felt that "poor countries and poor people– differ from rich one's not only because they have less capital but also because they have less knowledge" (World Development Report-1999-2000)[11]. The infrastructures of newly evolving global order are ideas, images, information and imagination and all these are controlled by knowledge. Knowledge encompasses wisdom, critical reasoning and reflexivity. The infotech revolution has made the world smaller and we are fast becoming global citizens via satellite networking. The new term 'netizen' is replacing citizen and all are grouped as members of a "global village". Professionalisation of 'knowledge centres' and marketisation of education is kernel of the process of knowledge distribution, its production and reproduction. Commodification of knowledge and commercialisation of education has ensured the identity of education as a 'consumable' product. This feature will be separately and systematically dealt in the ensuing deliberation.

Education, Market and Principles of Discrimination

Marketisation of education will have a cascading effect on society particularly in exacerbating the social chasm, i.e. layers of stratification and inequities among various segments of population. This is more so in case of technological innovation and modernisation of infrastructure. Following facts can substantiate social discrimination and consequent exclusion. By the beginning of the 1990s, most people in sub-Saharan Africa were poorer than they had been thirty years before. Of the population about 500 million, nearly 300 million are living in absolute poverty (Leys, 1996)[12]. In developing countries as a whole, nearly 800 million people do not get enough food, and about 500 million are chronically malnourished and more importantly almost one-third of the population of developing countries–about 1.3 billon lives below poverty line. The infant mortality rate, at around 350 per 1000 live births, is about nine times higher than in the advanced industrial countries (UNDP, 1995).[13]

At least 80 per cent of the World's population still lacks access to the most basic communication technologies, and nearly 50 countries have less than one telephone line per 100 people. There are more telephone lines in Manhattan than there are in the whole of sub-Saharan Africa. While the United States has 35 computers per 100 people, even rapidly developing South Korea has only nine, while for Ghana the figure is as low as 0.11 (Leys, 1996). Although the number of internet users has expanded dramatically in recent years, its use is still largely confined to Western Europe and the United States. This will wreak havoc by funneling the undercurrents class tensions and sense of relative deprivation. In the end it will open the flood chaos, anarchy and destruction of social fabric.

In the presence such vicious and pervasive socio-structural inequality education becomes an instrument of domination and tool for cognitive colonisation. It has been found that modern state has relied upon education to propagate a common system of values, a shared sense of national identity, and a uniform conception of good citizen to bring about the cultural and political homogenisation of its members. It catches its citizen young, seeks to shape them in a standard moral and cultural mould, and ensures that their values, wants, preferences and expectations of the state are broadly similar and do not cross the officially permissible range of diversity. The more a state is able to achieve this objective by controlling education the less it needs to rely on coercion and violence. It is therefore, hardly surprising that in every modern state education is compulsory, free, closely watched and monitored by the state, and particularly attentive to the integration of minority and immigrant communities.

Indeed Public provision of education has traditionally been considered necessary to the promotion or protection of a number of commonly held equity and efficiency objectives. The following arguments typically underpin the case; first the benefits of education accrue not only to its direct recipients, but also to society at large; the presence of such 'externalities' encourage smaller expenditures on education, in the absence of state provision, that would be beyond the means of many poor families, even when their children were able to and diligent enough to gain access. Third, since, education helps to determine future individual incomes, market allocation would strengthen existing inequalities, by giving privileged access and higher future incomes to richer groups (Colclough, 1991: 196-213)[14]. We can find numerous constitutional provisions in India to provide education for citizens. But this was much before the onslaught of 90s, which made the role of state and their influence vastly different. In fact, the sate is no longer in control of their affairs the sepctre of globalisation looms large over them and globalisation is a different form of colonisation.

Education in India

The poor shape of education has led to a lot of consternation both among the public and the policy makers and efforts were made to improve educational standards. From 1950s India has made significant effort in improving the educational system particularly at primary level. But during the early 80s India had realised its difficulties and the result of their filtration with the programme of adult education. Later significant inroads were made towards revolutionising the system of primary education.

The question of primary education cannot be discussed without explaining the parameters of improving primary education. Broadly, these parameters can be defined as access, retention and quality. Access refers to the availability of the opportunity of education to the children of school going age and within approachable distance. Retention refers to the capability of the system in retaining the enrolled children in the school till they complete the course. Similarly, quality refers to the provision of education that improves the learning quality and achievement levels of the students. In other words, access refers to enrollment; retention to the practice of reducing wastage and stagnation in the school system and quality means the improvement in the standard of practice, enactment, transaction and preaching of learning material. Systematically, all these mean radical pedagogic transformation.

In all these levels across the board and perceptive changes have introduced in India to bring some sort of dynamism into the system. India has a problem regarding access. The geographical and topographical peculiarities have ensured the failure of education in reaching among all the communities notably tribes and aboriginal residing in deep forests and inaccessible hinterlands. Further, the social and economic disparities arising out of faulty developmental designs had stopped the effects of trickledown theory resulting in creation of large sections of underprivileged and deprived communities. In recent years India has introduced many a projects and programmes both independently and with the help of donor agencies and countries to retrieve the situation. District Primary Education Project, Nutritional Support Scheme to Primary Schools, Bihar Education Project, Lok Jumbish are some of the centrally and externally assisted schemes to improve the educational map of India (Mohanty: 1998)[15].

India has made rapid strides in primary education over the years in general and since 90s in particular as far as the improvement in access is concerned. There has been substantive improvement in number of schools, in number of teachers and the percentage of budget share. But not enough attention is given to retention and quality. Retention continues to be a major problem at primary level and many students just dropout from their school in midst of a session. Studies by Varghese and Govinda, Sujatha, Nayar in India and Brooke and UNESCO have found significant variation in enrollment and retention suggesting the presence of wide spread dropout. Unfortunately we do not have sufficient and substantial data on dropout to prove it conclusively as State and Central governmental educational officers are quite apprehensive in providing adequate and appropriate data on dropout (experiences from field).

However, before delving into the dynamics of quality of education, it would be pertinent and helpful if an observation can be made into the question of private education. In recent times a lot of noises have been made over private education particularly at the primary level. Whatever the reason and consequences of it may be but one cannot deny its existence. In India private education have come a long way and more often than not are define class and status at the sphere of education. In a study on the private education in India James Tooly had made a comparison of this system across the world. In his research he has looked at "Objectivo" in Brazil and Delhi Public School in India as two examples of private education system and has lauded their role in providing quality education besides offering social services (Tooley: 2000).

Quality is very important aspect of education and is more so in case of primary education. And it is most neglected aspect in the whole gamut of education. In recent times efforts are on to the improve the quality of education and expert committees have been set up all over the developing countries to improve the school quality as well as quality of teaching. New pedagogies are being tried out and curriculum development schemes are on progress. Context based learning and learning through experience as well as alternative learning practices are being promoted to bring a positive and holistic change in educational system at primary level. Similarly, teacher training is given importance to equip the teacher in transacting the learning process properly and perfectly. This is expected to boost learning achievements. It is believed that with these concrete steps and with the increased accountability and commitment of the administrators, parents, teachers and practitioners of education we will soon see better results.

Invented by management Guru Peter Drucker and lapped up by the policy-makers of the world 'privatisation' has been a fashionable concept in contemporary discourse of informed citizenry. Described as transfer of state ventures to the hands of private entrepreneurs at an agreeable cost and de-regulation of trade coupled with withdrawal of state monopoly in public enterprises, this has fast entering into hitherto sacred space of education. Under the aegis of this powerful process private parties have come forward to provide education i.e. quality education to interested consumers with a price tag not to be monitored by the state. This is a fairly new trend but has been greatly pulverised by another significant process known as 'professionalisation'. These twin processes operating in tandem have stormed the academic bastion. As result we are witnessing the growth and development of a leviathan called 'global education industry' to burrow a term from Professor James Tooly[16]. But the moot question is can we expect the private sector to come to the rescue of dilapidated and moribund academic structure without significant scope for profit. It would be childish to expect 'philanthropy' from hard-boiled businessmen to invest in education without substantial return.

Then it is fair to know which section or segment of education will receive the royal patronage and wisdom of private sector. This requires a rational explanation and sustained interrogation as there has been a virtual mushrooming of private primary and higher educational institutions. As far primary education is concerned the situation is truly gloomy. The quality of primary education is absolutely abysmal, studies by various agencies and individuals at various point of time have the wide educational gap exists in primary education system in the country. There are regional disparities, class differentiation, and differences in terms of medium, means and social relations. But the most important is the public-private debate where the state run schools comes into direct competition from the private run institutions. The study by World Bank, PROBE and others have shown beyond reasonable points of doubt about the lack of quality education in government schools and more so in case of disadvantaged sections and disadvantaged localities.

Notes

1. See Max Weber, Methodology of Social Sciences. Ed. by Edward A. Shils and Henry A. Finch, New York: Free Press (1949).
2. Malcom Waters, Globalisation. New York: Sage (1995). p. 3.
3. Anthony Giddens, The Consequence of Modernity. Cambridge: Polity Press (1991).
4. Harvey David, The Condition of Postmodernity. Cambridge: Blackwell (1989).
5. J. Baudrillard, Simulacra and Simulation. Michigan: University of Michigan Press (1981).
6. J. Baudrillard, Selected Writings (ed. Mark Poster). California: Stanford University Press (1988).
7. A. Gidden, The Consequence of Modernity. California: Stanford University Press (1990).
8. Vivekanand, The Complete Works of Swami Vivekanand (ed. Swami Adiswarananda) Calcutta: Ramkrishnana Mission.
9. See Report of the Jomtien Conference on Education for All, UNESCO: PROAP, Bangkok.
10. A. Sen, Choice, Welfare and Measurement. Harvard: Harvard University Press (1997).
11. World Development Report. Washington: World Bank, 2000.
12. C. Lays, (1996). The Rise and Fall of Development Theory. Oxford: Oxford University Press.
13. UNDP (1995). Human Development Report, New York: UNDP.
14. C. Colclough (1991), "Who should learn to pay?" An Assessment of Neo-Liberal Approaches to Education policy, In C. Coclough and J. Manson (eds) **State or Market: Neo-Liberalism and the Development Policy Debate**. Oxford: Clarendon Press. pp.196-213.
15. T. R. Mohanty, (1998). 'Primary Education in India: Present Trends and Prospects', **Curriculum and Teaching**, Vol.13, No. 2.
16. James Tooley (1999), The Global Education Industry. London: IEA/IFC.

References

Amin, S. (1976). **Unequal Development**. New York: Monthly Review Press.

Apter, D. (1965). **The Politics of Modernisation**. Chicago: Chicago University Press.

————(1987). **Rethinking Development**. London: Sage Publications.

Ayar, R. V. (1996). 'Educational policy, planning and globalisation', **International Journal of Educational Development**. 16 (4), pp. 347-354.

Boudon, R. (1974). **Education, Opportunity, and Social Inequality: Changing Prospects in Western Society.** London: Wiley.

Bourdieu, P. and J.C. **Reproduction in Education, Society and** Passeron (1977) **Culture**. London: Sage Publications.

Baudrillard, J (1988). Selected Writings, ed. Mark Poster, Cambridge: Polity Press.

————(1998). "The End of the Millennium or the Countdown", **Theory, Culture and Society** 15, no.1:1-9.

Bell, D. (1973). **The Coming of Post-Industrial Society**. New York: Basic Books.

Beynon, J. (2000). **Globalisation: The Reader**. London: Athlene Press.

Biersteker, T. J. (1978). **Distortion or Development?** Cambridge, MA: MIT Press.

Bowles, S. and H. Gintis (1976). **Schooling in Capitalist America: Educational Reform and the Contradictions of Economic Life**. New York: Basic Books.

Brock-Utne, B. (ed.) [1995]. **States or Markets? Neo-liberalism in the educational policies of sub-Saharan Africa**. Rapport. No.1, Oslo: Institute for Educational Research.

C. Chase-Dunn (1985). **Transnational Corporations and Underdevelopment.** New York: Prager.

Castles, S. (2000). "Development, Social Transformation and Globalisation", **Working Paper Centre for Asian Pacific Transformation Studies,** Wollongong: University of Wollongong. Also available online at: http://www.uow.edu/research/cetres/capstrans/pubs/publications.html (12 May 2000)

Colclough, C. (1991). "Who should learn to pay?" An Assessment of Neo-Liberal Approaches to Education policy, In C. Coclough and J. Manson (eds) **State or Market: Neo-Liberalism and the Development Policy Debate**. Oxford: Clarendon Press. pp.196-213.

Commission on Global. **Our Global Neighborhood**. The Report of the Governance (1995) Commission on Global Governance, New York: Oxford University Press.

Dube, S. C. (1994). **Tradition and Development**. Delhi: Vikas Publishing House.

Dumont, L. (1977). **From Mandeville to Marx: The Genesis and Triumph of Economic Sociology**. Chicago, IL: University of Chicago Press.

Evans, P. B., D. Rueschemeyer **State versus Markets in the World System.**

and E. H. Stephans (1985). London: Sage Publications.

Frank, A.G. (1969). **Capitalism and Underdevelopment in Latin America: Historical Studies.** Rev. Ed. New York: Monthly Review Press.

Freiero, P. (1972). **Pedagogy of the Oppressed.** New York: Herder and Herder.

Friedman, M. (1955). 'The role of government in education', in R. A. Sols (ed) **Economics and the Public Interest**. New Brunswick, NJ: Rutgers University Press.

Fuller, B. (1986). 'Raising School Quality in developing countries'. **World Bank Discussion Paper**: 2. The World Bank, Washington, D.C.

Gandhi, K. (1999). **Education: Challenges of the Twenty-first Century-The Global Context**, New Delhi: Vikas Publishing House.

Ghai, D. (1993). 'Structural adjustment, globalisation and social democracy', In **Market Forces and World Development**, eds. R. Prendergast and F. Stewart, London: Macmillan.

Govinda, R. & Varghese, **The Quality of Basic Education Services in** N.V. (1991). **India: A Case Study of Primary Schooling Madhya Pradesh**. Independent Study, New Delhi: National Institute of Educational Planning and Administration.

Green, Andy (1997). **Education, Globalisation and the Nation-state**, London: Macmillan.

Hallak, J. (1998). **Education and Globalisation**. Paris: UNESCO (IIEP Contributions No. 26).

Harbeson, J. W. (1993). Civil Society and Democratisation in Africa: Some Preliminary notes from the field', **Africa Voices,** 2,3, Fall/Winter.

Harvey, D. (1989). **The Condition of Postmodernity: An Enquiry into the Origins of Cultural Change**, Cambridge: Blackwell.

Held, D. et al. (1999). **Global Transformations: Politics, Economics and Culture**, Cambridge: Polity Press.

Hindess, B. (1987). **Freedom, Equality and the Market: Arguments on Social Policy**. London: Tavistock Publications.

Holton, R. J. (1998). **Globalisation and the Nation-State**, New York: St. Martin Press.

Illich, I. **Deschooling Society**, Harmondsworth: Penguin Books.

Johannes, B. (1990). 'Market and State in Advanced Capitalist Societies', in A. Martinelli and N. J. Smelser, (eds.) **Economy and Society: Overviews in Economic Sociology**. New Delhi: Sage Publications.

Keily and Marfleet. **The Rise and Fall of Development Theory**.

Leys, C. (1996). Oxford: Oxford University Press.

Madison, G.B. (1998). **The Political Economy of Civil Society and Human Rights**. London: Routledge.

Mattleart, A. (1983). **Transnationals and the Third World: the Struggle for Culture**. South Hadley, MA: Bergin and Garvey.

Marginson, S. (1997). **Markets in Education**, Sydney: Allen and Unwin.

Mills, C. W. **The Sociological Imagination.** New York: Oxford University Press.

Mohanty, T. R. (1996). **Culture, Development and Society**, Unpublished dissertation submitted to Jawaharlal Nehru University, New Delhi.

———(1998). 'Primary Education in India: Present Trends and Prospects', **Curriculum and Teaching**, Vol. 13, No. 2.

———(1999). 'The Future of Higher Education: A Student's Vision', Book Review, **Journal of Educational Planning and Administration**, Vol. xiv, No.1, pp. 103-105.

———(2000). 'Global Education Industry: Lessons from Private Education in Developing Countries', Book Review, **Journal of Educational Planning and Administration,** Vol. xiv, no.1, pp. 213-17.

———(2002). 'State, Market and Globalisation: Social Dimensions of Economic Principles, **Aligarh Law Journal,** AMU (forthcoming).

———(2003). 'Education and Urbanisation: Mapping the Margin', **Education and Society**, (Forthcoming).

Nayar, D. (ed.) [2002]. **Governing Globalisation: Issues and Institutions**, Oxford: Oxford University Press.

Portes, A. (1997). "Neoliberalism and Sociology of Development: Emerging Trends and Unanticipated Facts", **Population and Development Review** 23: 229-59.

Poster, M. (1990). **The Mode of Information: Poststructuralism and Social Context,** Cambridge: Polity Press.

Ritzer, G. (1996). Mac Donaldisation, London: Sage.

Robertson, R. (1992). Globalisation. London: Sage.

Schultz, T. W. (1961). 'Investment in Human Capital', **American Economic Review**, 51:1-17.

Scott, P. (ed) (1998). **The Globalisation of Higher Education**, Buckingham: Oxford University Press.

Singh, K. and D. Ikeda (1998). **Humanity at the Cross-Roads: An Inter-Cultural Dialogue**, New Delhi: Oxford University Press.

Smith, D. and J. Borocz. **A New World Order? Global Transformations** [eds](1995). **in the Late Twentieth Century**, Praegar: London.

Stewart, F. (1994). 'Education and adjustment: the lessons of the 1980s. In **Market Forces and World Development,** eds. R. Prendergast and F. Stewart, London: Macmillan.

———(1995). 'The social impacts of globalisation and marketisation. **In People: From Impoverishment to Empowerment**, eds. U. Kirdar and L. Silk, New York: New York University Press.

'Globalisation and Education', **International Journal of Educational Development**, 16 (4), pp. 327-334.

Stiglitz, J. (1998) 'Towards a New Paradigm of Development: Strategies, Policies and Processes', ***Ninth Raul Prebish Lecture***, Geneva.

———(2002). **Globalisation and Its Discontents**, New York: W. W. Norton and Company.

Streeck, W. and 'Community, Market, State and Associations?

P.C. Scmitter (1985). The Prospective Contributions of Interest Governance to Social Order', **European Sociological Review**, 1:119-38.

Sujatha, K. (2000). **Education of Indian Scheduled Tribes: A Study of Community Schools in the District of Visakhapattanam, A.P.**, UNESCO, Paris: International Institute of Educational Planning.

Sujatha, K. (2000). **Education Among Tribals.** EFA Study. New Delhi: National Institute of Educational Planning and Administration.

The Hindustan Times (2001) Indian News Paper (Bhopal), 29th December.

Todaro, M. (1981). **Economic Development in the Third World**, 2nd ed. New York: Longman.

Tooley, J. (2000). **Global Education Industry: Lessons from Private Education in Developing Countries**, New York: IFC.

UN (United Nations) [1999] Vulnerability and Poverty in a Global Economy, (**Report of the Committee for Development Policy**), New York: UN.

UNDP [United Nations. **Human Development Report**, New York: Development Programme] (1992) UNDP.

———(1994). **Human Development Report**, New York: UNDP

———(1997). **Human Development Report**, New York: UNDP.

———(1999). 'Globalisation with a Human Face', Background Papers, Vol. 1, pp.109-22. **Human Development Report**. New York: Oxford University Press.

————(1999) **Diversity and Disparities in Human Development: Key Challenges for India**, UN, New Delhi: Oxford University Press.

UNESCO (United Nations **World Education Report**, Oxford: UNESCO.

Educational, Scientific and Cultural Organisation), [1993]

————(1996). 'Learning: the Treasure within', **World Education Report**, Paris: UNESCO.

Varghese, N.V. (1996). "District Primary Education Programme: The Logic and Logistics", **Journal of Educational Planning and Administration.** Vol. 5.

Vivekananda, S. (2001). **Selections from the Complete Works of Swami Vivekananda**, Kolkata: Adwait Ashram.

Waters, M. (1995) **Globalisation**. London: Routledge.

Watkins, K. (2001). 'Does globalisation Make the World More Unequal?' **NBER Working Paper**, No.8228.

World Bank (1990) **Primary Education a World Bank Policy Paper**, Washington, DC: World Bank.

————(1994). **Higher Education: The Lessons of Experience**, Washington D.C.: The World Bank.

————(1995). **Priorities and Strategies for Education: A World Bank Review**, The World Bank: Washington, D.C.

————(1999). Knowledge for Development: **World Development Report**, 1998-99.

————(2000). Entering the 21st Century, **World Development Report** 1999/2000. New York: Oxford University Press.

————(2000). Higher Education in Developing Countries: Peril and Promise. (**Report of the Task Force on Higher Education and Society**).

————(2001). **World Development Report-2000/20**01: Attacking Poverty, New York: Oxford University Press.

————(2002) **Globalisation, Growth and Poverty: Building an Inclusive World Economy**. The World Bank Group, New York: Oxford University Press.

Chapter - 12

Globalisation and Town Identity

—Haresh Narayan Pandey

The research paper attempts to study the formation of cultural identity in the wake of globalisation in a multi-castes and multi-religious town Shamli *situated in Muzaffarnagar District of Uttar Pradesh by the use of techniques of data collection like observation, focus group discussion and interview schedule. The objectives of the paper is to understand formation of cultural identity in the town Shamli by delineating into the details like which aspect of globalisation- media or market is the most influential, what kind of new hybrid structures have emerged, and to record the kind of new social and cultural celebrations have started in Shamli in the contemporary times. To derive a comprehensive picture, blend of positivist, phenomenological and social anthropological category in an integrated fashion has been used for developing discussion around concept of various local, regional and national identities vis-à-vis globalisation. It is well understood that the process of Globalisation stems from technological revolution in communication and production processes, and viewed as homogenising and hybridising in nature, operating in the socio-cultural life of people. It also symbolised global circulation of dominant western socio-cultural products and practices resulting into spreading cultural imperialism of the west. The process led to the formation of a new social and cultural identity pattern in community or group which was comparatively far more complex in nature and conflicting with the local identity. As a result, people in the community or group feel lost their true identity and find themselves in some kind of identity conflict. As a result, people in town has experienced disintegration of collectivities, rise of individuality, tensions and conflict between the old and the new generations; emergence of manyfold new socio-cultural celebrations, and rise of several hybrid structures in the areas of food, cloths, films, etc.*

Key Words: *Homogenisation, Hybridisation, Imperialism, Culture, Identity.*

Introduction

The present chapter is an attempt to study identity formation of a multi-caste and multi-religious town i.e. Shamli, Muzaffarnagar district, Uttar Pradesh in the light of globalisation. The process of globalisation has been dealt mainly in its homogenisation, heterogenisation, Coco-Colanisation and McDonaldisation natures relating to infusion of consumer culture and identity.The chapter has been divided into three sections for addressing its main objectives- To study the identity formation of Shamli by focusing broadly on the social-cultural life of people in the family, neighbourhood and community; which aspect of globalisation- media or market is the most influential in this process; which new social and cultural celebrations have started in the town; and what are the hybrid structures formed during the identity formation of Shamli in the wake of globalisation. The first section of the paper, deals with homogenising and hybridising nature of globalisation, their relation to consumer culture and cultural identity, and method of research. The second section, emphasises on the town, its structure, and some problems. And the last, focuses on the changing identity of Shamli in relation to the process of globalisation and conclusion.

Globalisation and Cultural Identity

The process of globalisation starts with revolution in communication technology and its broader use by people leads to quick circulation of financial capitals, messages, symbols, cultural product, etc. at global level. It brings proliferation and diversification of technologies, and a search for new markets consequently seen as an enlargement of the scope of electronic media through use of telephone, television, fax, email, Internet and migration of people. It finally infuses homogenisation of consumer products and market process in the realm of commodity, cultural symbols, styles and behavioural pattern of people. The homogenising nature of globalisation puts pressure on traditional notion of sovereignty and autonomy of culture that elevates sense of cultural identity and distinctiveness.[1] This homogenisation process has been European in nature in general and American in particular, that is widely witnessing in Coco-Colanisation and McDonaldisation. McDonaldisation has tremendous power to generate a set of values and products, which has a competitive advantage over others and also has a capacity to reproduce itself more easily than others model of consumption. It continues to make inroads to the global market place mainly through efforts of multinational corporations (MNCs)/ transnational corporations (TNCs). The McDonaldisation has been a metonym of forces of late modern capitalist globalisation spreading uniformity, efficiency, calculability and control across the world.[2] The homogenisation has been proliferating consumer culture that spreads cultural imperialism by obliteration of cultural differences and cultural plurality. It leads to generation of sense of alertness and consciousness of identity among various cultural communities across the world. The process of globalisation has a disruptive influence upon local cultural practices as it converts traditional objects of arts and aesthetics, custom and ritual use into marketable commodities. It has not only disrupted the cultural autonomy but also destabilised the life of people by creating a networks of competition, price, war and exploitative class. In such condition people from local cultural community and group feel loss of their cultural identity.

Tomlinson (1991) has tried to analyse successfully cultural imperialism by using categories of nation-state, media, modernisation and capitalism. Modernisation and media together generates cultural imperialism by proliferating cultural hegemony are considered more important for the study.[3] The effect of cultural imperialism has not been noticed only on individual culture but also on the world cultures in a global historical development, which is reformulated through ongoing process of modernisation. Giddens (1990) views globalisation as direct consequences of late modernisation. The global cultural hegemony is precipitated, recognised and seen directed through a particular modern way of life that reduces the idea of modernity to the capitalist society and producing homogenisation. This homogenisation corresponds to cultural imperialism that produces the sameness, which has been seen as a threat to the diversity and richness of culture in the global era. This sameness constantly destroys the rich diversity of culture that is produced by the cultural capacity of adoption to the physical environment, local condition, etc. And transnational corporations (TNCs) have become the major players for such cultural homogenisation and spread of cultural imperialism. The moderniation produces cultural synchronisation and poses threat to the cultural autonomy and cultural practices, which are necessary for actual survival of any cultural community. It generates deeper question about cultural identity and requires attention to the historical process of cultural change and modernity. Tomlinson has viewed media imperialism as another way of implanting cultural imperialism. In the case of media imperialism, media has been placed at the centre of the majority of the cultural practices. And when media is placed at the centre of relationship and cultural process then it turns the colour of cultural domination into media domination. In the contemporary world, revolution in information and communication technology (ICT) has made various print and visual media, and their uses very powerful and dominant in the majority of the socio-cultural activities including leisure activities, employment, opinion building and helping things becoming transparent, etc.. He claims that the importance of virtual identity occurring through interface of media and culture in which media has transformed the sense of public and private life by making access to almost all aspects of life. The meaning of various items and making them accessible to all irrespective of gender, age, strata and region are also changing rapidly. Here, Tomlinson has given the example of the American TV series Dollas, which had become not only the byword for cultural imperialism but also acquired central question of tension in the international communities in 1980s. The multi-national corporations (MNCs) play the most significant part in development of modern global capitalism and they help media for fitting into the world of capitalism by providing all ideological support for its promotion, protection and extension. And media plays a helping role in corporate marketing by manipulating audiences and making them good consumers of capitalist production by infusing sense of brand loyalties and commodity satisfaction in various consumers across the world. The cultural imperialism spreads distinctive and dominant culture of multinationals and producing homogenised global culture. The cultural imperialism has been serving capitalist system by producing good life to consumer and lures all kinds of powerful people across the world. The cultural imperialism is having a tendency of producing cultural convergence through syncretism and homogenisation and TNCs/MNCs act as the principal agents for such convergence. They do it by developing global investment, marketing strategies and transnational advertisings that create cultural acceptance of various cultural products for their target markets.

The emergence of hybridising nature of globalisation has been based on the blend of global with local. This blend is framed on the basis of requirement of global to the local and vice-versa. It gives rise to a hybrid structure, which is new and different in content and form from the earlier one. The globalisation and its trend create tension due to assertion of identity and culture at local level in various ways. The idea of global versus local, international versus national, and universal versus particular have been promoted and understood as creating hybridity on the same line. It is not only seen and perceived as the process of dynamic source of progress and change, but also as the source of tension and contradiction because the second part of duality is noted as reaction against the first. Robertson (1995) does not view global and local separately as global lies beyond the local or global excludes local or as locals are having full of properties existing over and beyond the global system. He says that these local units may be constructed in terms of their process and action without denial of global dynamics in the world as whole. In a comprehensive model global does not counter posed to local rather local is necessary included within the global. Robertson's idea of globalisation in general sense, involves both linking of localities and also invention of localities. The idea of such globalisation has been closely related to responses of various categories of individual, regional, societal, ethnic, gender and consumers seen in the form of tailoring and advertising goods and services on the basis of global and local market. Robertson claims that it leads to construction of differentiated consumer tradition, which is exemplified clearly in tourist industry. He has used the idea globalisation to clarify the major problematic of global-local polar relationship where the idea of local is framed mainly as a form of opposition or resistance to the global or to the homogenising trend of globalisation. He believes that both global and local exist as two aspects of the same process of globalisation.[4]

Pieterse (1995) has described happening of hybridisation in several structural sense like nation-state formation, global-local dynamics, market and commodity price, supranational and subnational regionalism, political economy, and organisation space, which are another way of raising reconstruction of issues of some form of identities. The increasing structural form of globalisation provides hybridisation by increase in available mode of various international, transnational, non-governmental, micro-regional, macro-regional, and municipal-local levels organisation, which ultimately crisscrossed by functional, professional, informal and communicational uses. The networks of organisation, function and ideology have created informal space inhabited by diaspora, migrant, refugees, exiles, etc. of various socio-cultural identities across the world. He has argued that the hegemony of the West has been started very recently that is from industrialisation period but the Europe until fourteenth century has also been the recipient of cultural influence from the orient. For the purpose of elaborating such idea he has cited various phenomenon happening around the world such as-Thai boxing by Moroccan girl in Amsterdam, Asian rap in London, Irish bagels, Chinese tacos, Mardi Grass Indians in the United States, Peter Brook directing Mahabharata, and Ariane Manouchkine staging a Shakespeare play in Japanese Kabuki style for a Paris audience in the Theater Soleil. He further pronounces by saying that these are not resulted by cultural uniformity standardisation, cultural notion of synchronisation but it has overlooked the counter-current impact of the non-West.[5] For him the non-West has played major role in hybridisation process but has been less recognised. He claims that hybridisation in cultural area refers to mixing of the different cultural categories, forms, beliefs of Asian, African, European, and American culture in origin and producing a global culture through global mélange. This mélange is taking place in various areas of culture such as food, music, play, drama, dress and dressing pattern, arts, painting etc. and producing a different hybrid category and forms, and this stage is known as hybridity. These hybrid forms, in one angle, appear to be exotic and from other angle, reflect trans-cultural class affinities. The culture, its elements, and objects, which have been existing prior to hybridisation is viewed as territorial culture. It stems to emerge from localise learning process and having endogenous, orthogenetic, authentic, inward looking and community-based characteristic for identity. These properties and characters are transformed into different trans-local, exogenous, heterogeneous, outward looking, network and strangers after hybridisation. The cultural form and cultural relation also get changed and transformed from separateness and concrete/discreet to hybrid, mixed and fluid in nature. And due to crisscrossing of cultures, cultural forms get transformed in appearance and identity, that is well understood with the example of cyborg. If one accepts the culture as hybrid identity then globalisation means hybridisation of hybrid cultures. This culture focuses on the new trans-local cultural expression that is interdependent in nature, and it requires new cooperation, which evokes new cultural imaginary after the hybridising form of globalisation.

Friedman (1995) refers to cultural hybridisation as an image of mixing of pure and original strains to produce new form. This image and identity are understood with basic view of culture and race where people practice a specific way of life in terms of a notion of common substance. The identity practice of an individual and group is not what he or she is labeled but it is about the identification of an existential world, the attribution of meaning to the world, object, person and relation. This identity practice is rooted in the way of immediate experience, which is structured in a definite social context, and is called identity space. Friedman claims that this identity space in the process of globalisation is derived from the identity space of modernity. The essentialism of substance and meaning of culture are generated by such space together. The production of local difference in global relation is not considered as globalisation of culture or meaning but it is proved as global relation in the production and consumption by giving a global control over local consumption through product of differentiation. He has given some example of production of various African cloths in the European countries to clarify it. He claims that identification is an ongoing practice and the concept of culture upon which the notion of globalisation is based and is the product of identity space of modernity. He considers globalisation as a product of parameters of modernity and the way in which modern nature of subjects identify the world.[6]

Globalisation and Consumer Culture

The process of globalisation has been spreading consumer culture and turning society into a consumer society, mainly by diffusion of consumer desire and wish for getting a specific way of style of life. Bauman (2001) describes consumer society as a socially constructed society, which is a way of life and the only way of life available to all. In this society consumption is self-propelling and has its own purpose. All living creatures have to consume to stay alive i.e. for biological existence. But human beings consume more than the necessity of their sheer survival, and they do it in accordance with their elaborate social standards of decency, propriety and good life. The social standard differs with time and in the past, human beings had fixed number of needs, which had to be satisfied in order to survive. Thus, for human beings, the survival of both biological and social was the purpose of consumption and once it was met there was no point of consuming more. The falling below and climbing above of such standard was considered a fault. Bauman claims that distinctive mark of consumer society and consumerist culture has not been primarily to elevate a fast rising volume of consumption but it is an emancipation of consumption from its past instrumentality of limits of needs. It proliferates in terms of norms and new plasticity of needs, which make consumption free from functional bond and absolving it from needs of only justification of pleasurability. The idea of consumption in consumer society has its own purpose and has been self-propelling in nature. The consumer society is measured its progress by ever rising demand and proclaims the impossibility of gratification. He says that consumer society and consumption are not about satisfying needs but desire and wish. Desire is volatile and ephemeral evasive, capricious and essentially non-referential phenomenon. It is narcissistic in nature and is bound to stay insatiable so it is always having its survival at stake. It makes the consumer- the consuming desire of consumer. The desire makes consumer ready to go for shopping even when he is in constraints also. He tries to trace the history of consumerism with story of breaking down solid and inflexible obstacles i.e. need, which puts a limitation to the free flow of fantasy to the more fluid and expandable form of desire. He says that desire has brought consumer addition to its present state but is not able to keep pace and has outlined its usefulness. So the turn of desire has come to an end. The more powerful and versatile stimulant is needed to match consumer demand with the rising volume of consumer offer. He has suggested wish a much needed replacement for it.[7]

The cultural identity, in contemporary time, can be understood with the idea of taste, life style, habits and consumption. The acts of purchase, ownership, display and consumption of certain commodities have been for both breaking old and expressing new identity. Bourdieu (2010) talks of how one social group distinguishes oneself from other group through act of consumption, aiming for forming and maintaining its identity. He claims that habit has both generative principle of objectively classifiable judgment and the system of classification of these practices. Habit is the relationship between the two capacities- the capacity to produce classifiable practices and works, and the capacity to differentiate and appreciate these practices and products. It represents a social world i.e. the space of life style. This relationship has been established between characteristic of economic and social condition and the distinctive features associated with the corresponding position in the universe of life style. He makes it more clear with the idea of class distinction on the basis of elaboration of economic capital and cultural capital. Bourdieu sketches out that in the French society certain profession like a teacher in comparison to other enjoys high status because he commands high level of cultural capital while he receives low payment or low economic capital than other profession. Life style is related to choice of products and desire for goods and is not the consequence of income. But it has been the result of a way of life, which is distinctively precipitated through the process of socialisation in the habitus. It is to say that distinct life style and social distinction has not been the function of income but primarily result of different socialisation. The social identity is defined and asserted through difference, which is inevitably inscribed within the disposition of habitus. It can be better understood with the example of taste of consumption of 'sweet pulse' by the Gujarati community, which distinguishes them from other community in their choice and desire for such food and life style in India. The taste and life style have been reflected in human body in terms of its gesture, posture and shape, etc. It is considered the result of economic, social and cultural products. Bourdieu ideas of habitus, life style and consumption have provided a platform for analysing different dynamics of identity relating with family, socialisation, class and caste, etc.[8]

Consumer culture has been seen a unique culture of consumption by giving a meaningful practice to the everyday life. It is a dominant mode of cultural production developed in course of modernity along with rise of capitalism in the West. Slater (1997) claims consumer culture has been bound up with the central values, practice and institution such as choice, market relation and individualism of the Western modernity. The prime moving force of consumer culture is consumption, which has been a social-cultural process. The consumption idea of consumer culture is dominated by the consumption of commodities in which cultural reproduction is exercised through free personnel choice in the private sphere of everyday life. The consumer culture is not only a way of consumption but also certainly a dominant way of ideology and scope. With the help of its ideology consumer culture has capacity of structuring and subsuming all other ways to a great extent. This ideology has been the part of Western agenda, and asserting its own difference from rest of the world, which is modern, progressive, free, rational, civilised, affluent, and possessing the universal values. Consumer culture has been the result of advance Western business, western market, western way of life and the universalising the western modernity. It has been the part of making modern world, which is experienced by a special actor who has been free, rational and not governed by tradition. The consumer culture can be equated with mass culture. In the democratic society the desire and taste of masses, who are newly empowered by money and democratic rights are reduced to consumption. It grows along with modernity and spreading its universal attributes such as freedom, choice, individuality, etc. and helping also the growth of culture of capitalism. Thus, consumer culture is called as the culture of capitalism. In capitalist society, profit is not achieved through regulation of consumption, suppression of decadent culture, traditional codes and laws but by the promotion of the consumption of commodities, goods, services, and experiences have been produced in market for consumers. The consumer's consumption is structured by distribution of material and cultural resources (money and taste) in the market relations and mediated by market relation that is why it is also called a culture of market society. The product of consumer culture has not been outcome of tailoring needs of individuals or one groups or communities rather than produced by impersonal and general relations of market exchange. This consumer culture appears to be universal in values and scope as it provides a land of freedom to all to become the consumer.[9]

Sklair (1991) has chosen to analyse consumer culture with an ideology of global consumerism in the global era. He has suggested three-economic, political and cultural practices spreading by globalisation process in the Third World. Each sphere is typically characterised by a representative institution, cohesive structure of organised and patterned practices, which can only be properly understood in terms of their transnational effect. The primary agent of economic institutional practice is the transnational corporation (TNC). The chief agent in the political sphere is the transnational capitalist class (TCC). The institution of cultural ideology of consumerism is expressed through transnational mass media that is considered principal agent of spreading cultural ideological sphere. Each of these primary agents typically produces the result of its practices like TNC produces commodities and services necessary to manufacture and sell them. TCC produces the political environment within which the product of one country can be successfully marketed in another. The cultural ideology of consumerism produces the values and attitudes that create and sustain the need for the product.[10] He sketches out global ideology of consumerism to analyse the activities and impacts of transnational corporations, which are supposed to be the wheels of the process of globalisation. The culture-ideology of consumerism produces values and attitudes that create empirical distinctions and spreading consumer culture. TNCs get involved in host country politics, and the culture-ideology of consumerism is largely promulgated through the transnational corporations by involving mass media and advertisement. Members of the transnational capitalist class often work directly for transnational corporations (TNCs), and their practices and life style has been a major exemplar for the spread of consumerism. The economic transnational practices are those economic practices that transcend national boundaries. These practices may be entirely contained within the borders of a single country but their effects are transnational in nature. The transnational corporation enters into a group where sellers, intermediaries and buyers are parts of the same global organisation. He has used the idea of transnational capitalist class as a social category that is comprised of entrepreneurial elite, managers, professional, politicians, etc. The transnational capitalist class can be viewed as involving in political struggle between capital and labour, and domestic and transnational political organisation. And TNCs interfere in the host country politics and aim to downgrade certain domestic practices by making comparison with new and more glamorous transnational practices and to create a comprador mentality. A comprador mentality is the attitude that the best practices are invariably connected with the global capitalist system. It is an ideological struggle between those who believe that TNCs will inevitably damage the Third World development prospects in the long run, and against those who believe that there will be no development prospects without TNCs. The transnational political practices penetrate and connect domestic practices by incorporating and mobilising them in the interests of the global capitalist system. In order to facilitate it the TCC promotes a comprador mentality throughout society by making various needed linkages. The mass media performs many functions for global capitalism by speeding up the circulation of material goods through advertising, which reduces the time between production and consumption. It systematically blurs of the lines between information and entertainment, by aiming promotional practices of products. It has created ideology of consumerism that helps in transforming and utilising public mass media to create into opportunities to sell ideas, values and products by spreading consumerism across the world.

Research Method

The researcher, as a part of his doctoral work, has conducted an empirical study of identity formation vis-à-vis globalisation by taking a town-Shamli, Muzaffarnagar district, Uttar Pradesh (UP), as a unit of analysis. The study would be pertinent to understand the theoretical backdrop discussed in the first part of the piece. The process of identity formation involves pre-global and post-global social-cultural formation in the town. For the purpose of the study both primary and secondary data are used. To generate primary data interview schedule, focused group discussion and observation research techniques are mainly used. The structured and open ended nature of interview schedule is prepared and used for the study. It provides enough space and freedom to the respondents to express their views and opinion about concerned questions, which help to generate authentic and reliable first-hand information from the field. For generation of primary data sample of 200 families/ households from Shamli town have been selected using the stratified and purposive sampling. The observation technique has been used at various occasions of socio-cultural celebrations like birthday, marriage anniversary, carrying *kanvariya*, organising and doing *kirtan, jagaran,* etc. The focused group discussion with family male members and young boys are also conducted. In the interview various socially, culturally and politically influential people, priest from all Hindu, Muslim, Sikh and Christian community and local leaders, business men, both old and young male members and boys from young generation, and students and their peer groups are also included as respondents from the town. The interview schedules have incorporated specific research questions covering concepts of globalisation, culture, identity, market and media process, and rural and urban nexus. To this end, radio, cell phone, Internet, television (TV), dress pattern, food habits, leisure activities like cinema, films, music, family, occupation, gender relation, family and marriage, migration and mobility, and new socio-cultural festivals and celebration are given special emphasis. The limitation of the study has been that it could not generate empirical data from groups like young girls and women from the town. It is because the socio-cultural condition of Shamli did not allow the researcher to include them as respondents.

It is a study of cultural identity formation of the town in the era of globalisation. The process of globalisation, its relation with local culture and its responses are analysed for understanding changing town's identity at two levels. At the first level, positivistic, phenomenological and social anthropological approach are used for the study of culture, and at the second level, the study of the impact of revolution in ICT and its broader use by masses as a new separate category has become obligatory to use because it has revolutionised various institutions and interaction patterns of people in the world in general and in India in particular. The impact of technological revolution in the system of information and communication technology (ICT) and its wider use by masses has widely influenced the socio-cultural institutions and their related interaction patterns because it has revolutionised various institutions of finance, banking, trade, style of life, leisure activities, etc.. The positivism is more scientific but providing less comprehensive reality of people. The more sensitive and reflexive, etic and emic category has been used, which is offered by phenomenological and social anthropological category respectively for people and their various socio-cultural practices in life. The research and analysis of culture need both conceptual and substantive dimensions at all-local, regional and national levels as they are considered the building blocks of Indian culture. The cultural and social boundedness of locality and region have been evident in various studies of castes, families, kinship, and rural communities that reflect the changing and transforming nature of Indian contemporary reality. The present study has used the blend of above mentioned both levels of approaches – positivist, phenomenological, social anthropological, and new ICT category at one level and at other the blend of local, regional, national and global cultural categories for understanding the changing socio-cultural practice and identity of the town vis-à-vis globalisation.[12]

The Town-Shamli- Shamli has been named after the name of Lord Krishna. According to a famous story, as people say, Lord Krishna while going to Kurukshetra for Mahabharata War from Hastinapur opted this route and took night halt in this town. The name of town was kept on his name as Shyam Wali earlier and then changed to Shyam Nagari and in the last it became Shyamli over a period of time. But now it is popularly called Shamli. The town Shamli is located around sixty kilometers away from Saharanpur Mandal and approximately hundred kilometers away from the national capital New Delhi. It is directly connected to various cities like Panipat, Baghpat, Meerut, Saharanpur, Haridwar, Dehradoon, etc. of different states of Uttar Pradesh (UP), Haryana, Uttarakhand (UK) and Punjab. The weather of Shamli is similar to surrounding districts of Saharanpur and Muzaffarnagar and it is a *tahsheel* of the district Muzaffarnagar and situated around thirty seven kilometers in the west of the district headquarter. Shamli is the second most populated town after district Muzaffarnagar, UP. The total population of the town was 70,478 in 1991, it became 89,861 in 2001 census but now in 2011 census it reached to 12,74,815 and out of which male constitutes around fifty four per cent and female forty six per cent. The main reason for this meteoric rise of population in the town has been migration of the rural population to the town areas in search of good schools and colleges for education of children, employment, business, trade and other livelihood opportunities. Shamli has been elevated to a district from town in September 2011 named as Prabuddha Nagar first and in July renamed as Shamli on the huge public demand. It is both multi-castes and multi-religious town and the various Hindu, Jain, Sikh, Christian, and Muslim religious communities are largely found here.

Shamli is known as *dharm-nagari* evident with the presence of various old and prestigious temples. There are around two hundred temples situated in its different areas and the main temples are Guljari, Hanumanteela, Barkhediwala Mandir, Makuwala Mandir, Satiwala Mandir, Atthiwala Devi Mandir, Dasiwala Mandir, Kuttiwala Mandir, etc. In addition to that there are various temples for Jain community; *gurudwaras* (Temple of Sikh community), churchs and mosques are also located in the town for Sikhs, Christians and Muslims respectively. The biggest *gurudwara* in town is Punjabi Colony *Gurudwara*. Around forty seven mosques are noted for Muslims and the main mosques/*masjids* are Jama Masjid, Kureshiyan Masjid, Gariwali Masjid, Kalandarshah Masjid, Timarshah Masjid, and Hakimjiwali Masjid. People of Jain and Sikh communities also visit Hindu temples happilyin the town. There is only one *madarasa*, which caters the need of Islamic studies of Muslims in Shamli. The main localities/*mohallas* in the town are- Punjabi Colony, Kaka Nagar, Dayanad Nagar, Charan Singh Colony, Teacher's Colony, Khedi, Vikas Nagar, Majara, Saraswati Vihar, Jain Mohalla, Brahman Mohalla, C.V. Colony, Hanuman Tilla, Timsa, Nopua, Railpar, Bankahadi Mohall, Madihar, and Badiyal. The residential area in the town has also been developed on the basis of community and its occupation. Like Punjabi and Jain communities are engaged in trade and business and they have developed their own residential areas in the town. Punjabis are residing in both old and new Punjabi Colonies, Jains are in Jain Colony and Muslims in their own *muhallas* in the town. Teachers in the town stay mostly in one area that is called Teacher's Colony. Muslims in the town are mostly engaged in the business and trade, repairing and maintenance activities, automobiles, wooden and iron work, running shops. The new colony, teacher's colony, etc. are *muhallas* where high grade officials like *tahsildar*, police station officer, inspectors, sub-divisional magistrate (SDM), retired police officials, college principals, retired vice-chancellor, Shamli Nagar Palika's chairman and its members, teachers of post graduate college, member of legislative assembly (MLA) and industry's manager reside.

Shops of both kinds of retailer and whole shops are found in the Shamli and catering to needs of not only of the town but also of many other small towns such as Jhinjhnana, Burana, Bhilwal, etc. and eighty surrounding villages.

The town has mixed character of both commercial and residential area, which has made it congested as there is no particular place for parking, loading, unloading and reloading of the vehicles. Several shopkeepers and commercial institutions have encroached upon the side spaces of roads, which have made roads narrow and cause obstacles in smooth flow of traffic, transportation, and trade and business. The Government of Uttar Pradesh has constructed one City Committee/*Mandi-Samiti* located on Bhaiswal Road, which has registered eighty seven whole-sale shops equipped with modern facilities. The development of several commercial shops on both sides of the roads renders the possibility of commercial development on it. The industrialisation of town provides good opportunity for employment, trade and business. The main industries of town are sugar, *khandsari* (materials made by juice of sugarcane), wooden spoon, rim and axel *(Dhure)*, *buggi* (Male Buffalo Cart), Ice-cream's stick, paper industry, artificial garments, and steel and aluminum utensils. The town has a big sugar mill known as Sir Shadilal Sugar Mill that has the capacity of 1200 employees working in it. *Buggi*, and rim and axel (*Dhure*) industry has a total of forty three industrial units registered with 129 employees. The Shamli Distaliray Chemical Works, Niketa Paper Private Ltd., Sikka Paper Mills and J. S. Jain Industry are the prominent small industries situated in the town. Several medium and small scale industries are found in the town with 339 and 799 number of employees working in these industries. These industries are of steel and iron casting, electrical repairing and servicing, plastic goods, rubber textile, steel furniture, cement, hosiery, readymade garments, paper printing/tube, cotton power loom, oil and oil cake, rim and axel, *ayurvedic* medicine and various leather items. The development of industry has not happened in an organised way on the road sides of the town. The development of such industries is found mainly on Shamli- Muzaffarnagar Road, Shamli-Karina Road and Shamli- Delhi Road. The reasons for the development of these industries on road sides are not only availability of raw materials but also of chance of trading of produced materials. The development of *kutir-udyog* (Small Scale Industry) related to black smith, iron smith, etc. are unfolding on two-Shamli-Delhi Road and Shamli-Karina Roads mainly in the town.

There are seventy six educational institutions in the town, out of which two are Post Graduate Colleges, three Inter Colleges, six High Schools, seven Junior High Schools, fifty Primary Schools and eight Montessori Schools. Health is considered an important need of community facility and one general hospital of total sixty beds and one lady hospital, one Homeopathic hospital, one aurvedic dispensary and one Family and Child Health Centre, forty private clinics, twenty nursing homes, one animal hospital, and one artificial fertilisation centre for animals are located at various parts in the town. Recreation facility is essential for the mental and physical development of the people. Several playgrounds, cinema halls, clubs and community centres are also located in the town for fulfilling such needs. There are presently six parks namely Rotary Park, Bachcha Park, Jain Milan Park, Agrawal Park, Tanki Colony Park and Pragati Market Park, seven cinema halls, two community centres for the social-cultural activities, five *dharamshalas,* fifteen clubs for catering the need of amusement and two libraries but not of good standard are situated in the different parts of the town. These facilities are considered insufficient for the current populations of the town. According to data obtained from Shamli Nagar Palika, two Over Head Tanks of different capacity-one producing 100,000 gallons water and other 500,000 gallons water, fourteen tube wells/*nalkoops* of producing 9,60,000 liters water per hour are observed in the town. There are 9,565 home connections and 325 public connections registered for water supply in Shamli. The standard of water supply has been 180 liters per individual per day. An inappropriate arrangement of sewage system is noticed in Shamli due to which it faces acute problem of water logging. The supply of electricity to Shamli is carried out through electricity grid and a total 10,509 electric connections out of which maximum 6900 connections are mainly residential in nature. There are four sub-stations and each of which has the capacity of eleven Kilowatts. Currently two Telegraph Offices, one Head Post Office and six small post offices, several international subscriber dialing (ISD), subscribers telephone dialing (STD), public call offices (PCOs) and one fire-brigade office are found in the town. According to Jila Sevayojana Karyalaya Muzaffarnagar, eleven Nationalised Banks, two Sahakari Banks and one Bhumi Vikas Bank are working and providing banking facility to people in the town and surrounding areas. There are many *dharamshalas* and marriage hall of both private and public nature are found in the town, which are used by public for marriage, religious preaching / *pravachan*, family function, socio-cultural gathering, etc. These *dharmashalas* are used by all Hindu, Jain, Punjabi, Muslim and Christian communities. Considering the needs of all communities into account Shamli Municipality has constructed several community centers located at the different parts of the town.

There are three kinds of roads-State road or *Prantiya Marg* or *Raj Marg*, *Pramukh Marg* or main road and local road found in the town. *Prantiya Marg* is situated in mid of the town and various industrial units are located on its sides, and several branches of both *Pramukh Marg* and local road are connected to it. And many branches of *Pramukh Marg* and local road are connected to largely Panipat-Khatiyama and Meerut-Karnal roads, which fall in the first category. The second category of road is known as *Pramukh Marg*/main road connects Shamli to various towns such as Jhinjhnana, Burana, Bhilwal and Malheri of the local area. And the width of these roads varies from 60 feet to 120 feet at several places. The industrial encroachment on these roads produces hindrance to smooth traffic and transportation in the town also. All the roads of Shamli Nagar Palika (Shamli Municipality) come under the category of local road. The main local roads are M. K. S. Road, Railway Road, Naya Bazaar Road, Vaisya College Road, Hospital Road, Milla Road, Diwanpur Road, Bhaiswal Road, and Majara Road. There are many roundabouts (*Chaurahas*) found in the town, which connect these roads and these are Subhash Chouk, Bada Bazar Chouk, Gandhi Chouk, Hanuman Road Chouraha, Fountain Chouk, Sabjipura Chouk, Vijay Chouk, Ajanta Chouk, Karaina Road Chouk, Azad Chouk, Buran Road Chouk, Ayodhya Chouk and Barasandi Chouk. Apart from these *chourahas* there are two very busy *tirahas (*Three side roads emerging from one point on road)—M. S. K. Road Tiraha and Mill Raod Tiraha are functional in the town. There are six bus stands found in the town including Roadways Bus Stand, which are situated in the congested localities of the town. The Roadways Bus Stand receives 234 buses daily and provides facilities of communication and transportation to all sides passengers. Roadways Bus Stand connects Shamli directly to Delhi, Baraut, Saharanpur, Muzaffarnagar, Karaina, Panipat, Haridwar, Dehradoon and others cities in the country. There are no formal /planned Taxi and Truck Stand in the town but both truck and taxi services are available in Shamli at two places – Shamli Police Station and Chaman Tanki on the main roads only. Trucks are parked on the road side and only two Truck Stands on Railway Road and New Mandi Bhaiswal Road are noticed in the town. Around 900 trucks are registered under the current existing Truck Union in Shamli, which are used for transportation of various local items of sugar, *khandsari*, vegetables, industry products, etc. from the town to the different states like Punjab, Haryana, Delhi, Uttarakhand, etc. in the country.[11]

Globalisation and Changing Identity of the Town

The study shows that the town-Shamli has been experiencing high degree of rural-urban nexus that is required for fulfilling people various needs, is also essential for understanding social-cultural changing identity of the field. Singh (1999) claims that the country-town nexus has been an important category to understand conflict and contradiction emerging with social interaction, and has become central concern for expressing social reality.[13] Sharma (1999) refers to structural-cultural change, and specific local condition for analysing change and transformation occurring in country-town nexus in Indian society. He has also pointed out other important categories emerging from such nexus that includes money lenders, artisans, shopkeepers, workers, priests, teachers, revenue officials, bank officers, etc.. These categories influence planning, programmes, and structure corresponding to impress upon people's life tremendously in both villages and town leading to changes in structure, structure-function and local condition that have made hierarchy of country-town unavoidable.[14] The country-town nexus with emergence of various socio-economic categories and their relation with interaction and social reality in Indian society has been analysed mainly with the process of modernisation.

And the process of globalisation, as late modernisation (Giddens, 1990), along with above mentioned categories helps in emerging and combining several new categories such as Internet cafe, mobile, ATM, malls, brands and their items in the areas of clothes and foods, entertainment, etc. are not only changing institutional set up but also having changed interaction process and pattern, social reality and identity observed in the field.

The process of globalisation with its homogenising nature has put profound impact on cultural transformation and changing habits, tastes, behaviour, life style, values, etc. has influenced the content and form of cultural categories at all local, regional and national culture, that has made people alert and conscious about their cultural identity (Tomlinson, 1991; Piterse, 1995; Hall, 2003 and Singh, 2012).The collectivities in terms of family, community, neighbourhood and socio-cultural practices are main constituents of town's cultural identity and residing in joint family and following neighbourhood and community values and practices has been highly desired and respected, observed in Shamli. The spread of global consumer culture and market process (Sklair, 1991 and Slater, 1997) lead to breaking down of collectivities like joint family, neighbourhood and community practices in the town. The breaking down of joint family nowadays happens very early, unlike before, just after marriage of sons observed in every caste and community in the town. It is not for the desire of land, property etc. but in the aspiring for opting a new life style directed towards more entertainment and enjoyment and less for delivering responsibility and accountability towards members of family, neighbourhood and community. This enjoyment and entertainment in town's life can be achieved easily in nuclear family separately but not in joint family because it imposes more restrictions in life. In the influence of rise of nuclearity of family, generation gap and individuality the old generation people in the town feel that the young generations do not pay respect to them as they did. Like the new generation boys-girls are engaged in activities such as sharing *charpai* (Cot) with their elders, taking their wives for films and shopping, speaking openly to girls on roads, etc., which are not permitted and adored by the old generations in the town. All these activities of the new generation boys-girls are observed spreading shamelessness/*ashleelta,* vulgarity and eroding cultural life rapidly in the town in light of globalisation. The spread of consumer culture generates a clash between the old town's culture and life style, which is collective, endogenous, closed and inward looking, and community oriented; and the new global cultural life style, that is claimed to be individualistic, open, hedonistic, exogenous, and outward looking as a part of consumer culture (Friedman, 1995 and Pieterse, 1995),) resulting in changing identity of the town. The globalisation has been evident not only involving in the processes of erosion of community and neighbourhood life but also creating new kinds of virtual community and virtual localities (Singh, 2012 and Appadurai, 1997) that are more important for the youths and their activities in Shamli. These virtual communities and virtual localities are like actual community and neighbourhood, and may contribute to fulfill their various new wishes and needs on the one hand and on the other and help in flaring up crisis of cultural identity. The community and neighbourhood life have been experiencing alarming situation in the influence of globalisation because the youths indulge in committing anomic and dangerous act like suicide or its attempts. And when the elders try to suggest and control them then they do not accept and revolt, which really make them fearful in families in the town and area. Instead of making a channel between two generations, on the contrary, *Khap Panchayat* of *Jat* community (A prestigious body of *Jat* caste comprised of local influential and powerful community members) has passed a resolution banning use of the western dresses like jeans, top, T-shirt, carrying mobile, etc. in public by *Jat* girls in the area. They view it mainly as community concern for maintaining their cultural identity and pride (Rashtrira Sahara, 2011).[15] It is not only *Jat* community but Muslim community in the town also does not allow its young girls wearing these mentioned Western-American dresses in public. The spread of consumer culture not only flouts traditional values and practices of local culture but also providing new opportunities and life chances to the people observed in the field. It happens mainly with bringing local culture in global relation by less local and more global control. In such influence the youths observed migrating from the town to various cities of India for acquiring modern/global education, occupation and opportunity that bring them directly in contact with other cultural practices, values and life styles, predominantly led by the process of globalisation. It not only helps in replacing the traditional value, cultural practice and life style by providing alluring alternatives to the new generations but they also make indigenous items and things down in terms of both desire and respect noted in the town and area. These migrants from the town have been helping local youths by generating a new kind of subculture (Brake, 1985) especially when they return from migrant cities to Shamli, become referent to the local youths, which raise consciousness and commitment in the indigenous old generation to their local culture and identity.[16]

The process of hybridisation and formation of hybrid structures are observed in the field mainly in the areas of socio-cultural celebrations, and consumerable items such as food, dress, clothes, films, songs and dance. The various socio-cultural celebrations and changing town's identity are observed occurring mainly at two levels in the field. Firstly, the socio-cultural celebrations, which have been canonical in nature existing before globalisation in the practice of people in Indian society at national level in general and at the local and regional level at particular are also experiencing change in their spread and celebration in the Hindu society. It includes important socio-cultural celebrations like *Holi*, *Dipawali*, *Dashahara*, *Karvachauth*, *Bhaiyaduz*, *Kanvariya*, *Kirnat* and *Jagaran* for all caste and community of the Hindus; *Mahabir Jayanti* and *Guru's* Jayanti (Birthday of Mahabir and Guru for Jains and Sikhs respectively), *Lohdi* for Sikhs; and *Eid*, *Bakarid*, and *Muhharram* for Muslims. The Ravidas *Jayanti* and Ambedkar *Jayanti* (Birthday of Ravidas and Ambedkar) are only celebrated by only Hindu Dalit community separately in Shamli, which were not celebrated by them earlier. It provides a separate identity to the Dalit community in both the town and area (Ram, 2008), is considered the result of long struggle and movement of the Dalits in India and use of global mass media has helped them in raising and spreading consciousness and awareness for them tremendously.[17] The celebrations of Hindu festivals like *Holi*, *Karvachauth* and *Bhaiyaduz* were earlier limited only to some families of upper castes and were like referent group celebrations for lower caste families, who were not celebrating them in the town. But now they started celebrating because of globalisation, that has succeeded not only in breaking the bond of auspiciousness of a child birth in family for *Holi* celebration only, was practiced in the town, but also spreading desire and awareness about these mentioned celebrations. And now all Hindu castes, Jain and Sikh in the town celebrate many Hindus festivals together and engaged in sharing more and more common identity and keeping cultural milieu of the town and area intact that started occurring approximately three-four decades before only. Secondly, socio-cultural celebrations mainly marriage anniversary, valentine day and birth day, which are European/American in nature of origin as popularly known, new to the town and area are celebrated by families of all castes and communities. Both marriage anniversary and valentine day are expected to be celebrated only by couples- Married couple in the case of marriage anniversary and unmarried friends and lovers, basically young boys and girls (Commonly called boy-friend and girl-friend- which are objectionable terms to the people in the town and area) in the town. Both marriage anniversary and valentine day are not celebrated openly and couples celebrate them secretly. Young boys and girls celebrate birth-day and valentine-day secretly mainly with friends in the surrounding mentioned towns and the ICT like cell phone and Internet help them in giving/taking information for fixing meeting, venue, etc.. But some college principals, teachers, community leaders and guardians are aware of such meetings and celebrations, and sometimes these young boys and girls are caught by them red handedly, that created tension in the town and area. And usually, such tension and clash acquire caste, community and religious colour in the town and area, as it is not viewed as good and consider as a threat to the cultural identity. The birthday celebration of children is also done at home, does not mean only lighting candle and cutting cake with relatives, friends and family members and receiving gifts from them, as it occurs in the Western-American life. But along with this in many Hindus, Jains and Sikhs families perform worship/*puja*/*katha*/*yangya*, taking blessing/*ashirvad* from elders, going to temple and *gurudwara* for doing *darshan*, *puja* and *dan* (Visiting temple for worshipping, donating food, money, cloths, etc. to the deserving poor). And in some of the Muslim families, sometimes, they also offer food to poor as *dan* in mosque on this occasion. It is distinctively celebrated in accordance to their cultural beliefs and practices as a blend of influence of market, media and religious-cultural practices of all Hindu, Jain, Sikh and Muslim communities producing hybridity observed in the town. Both homogenisation and hybridisation aspects (Tomlinson, 1991; Friedman, 1995; Robertson, 1995; Singh, 2012) of globalisation process have been observed operating in such celebrations. The homogenisation process mainly by attracting, enticing and inducing desire for celebrating them in all castes and communities and hybridisation in putting various local identity practices into the global cultural packages are observed in celebration of these festivals. The globalisation process, with its homogenising nature has also contributing in dissolution of cultural differences and making various local and regional socio-cultural celebrations extinct such as *Ramlila, Raslila, Dhola*, etc. witness in the field, which are the cause of worries as these celebrations were the source of creativity, earning and identity of various cultural groups and communities in the town. Now, people take less interest in celebration of Raslila and Ramlila as they take interest in watching serials and films in TV. Both *Ramlila* and *Raslia* are more than a week long celebrations of life activities of Lord Ram and Lord Krishna and *Dhola* is occasional and seasonal singing of songs by some old expert people in the town and area. They provide messages against ill and evil social-cultural practices in the town and area.

Media in comparison to market is the most important and influential wheel of globalisation as considered by the people, which plays unforgettable role in identity formation in the town. Two global media apparatuses-TV and mobile are significant in this process observed in the field.[18] The contemporary TV programmes like-serials, films, advertisements, reality shows, etc. are focusing more on showing illicit relationships, pre and extra-marital relationships, body parts, vulgar and dirty kind of dresses, songs, dialogues, close relations of young generations of various sorts, etc., which the old generation people from all castes and communities do not like and they consider these programmes dangerous and harmful to their children, cultural values, norms and identity in the town. These programmes not only spread the American-Western lifestyles, values, beliefs, cultural practices, etc. but also replace indigenous programmes from the market rapidly, which used to transmit indigenous cultural values, beliefs, practices, and style of life among people. These western cultural items and programmes are such alluring and powerful that they even influence construction and transmission of various local-regional programmes, films, serials, songs, etc. of *Hariyanavi*, *Punjabi* and Hindi languages. They are mainly prepared by mixing and remixing of global, national, regional and local contents and forms of these cultural items and products, and produce different sorts of hybridity in songs, dialogues, films, dresses, etc. observed in the town. The mass media has the capacity of bringing capitalist market influence in homes successfully with its programmes in general and advertisement programme in particular, that is considered as poetry of capitalism (Paterson, 2005).[19] The role of market in identity formation is also noticed powerful and crucial as people from all castes and communities in the town feel that mass media helps in providing information, creating and sustaining need and desire for consumption of various cultural products that can be fulfilled by the market only resulting in the spread of cultural consumerism (Sklair, 1991) and changing identity.

The process of McDonaldisation (Ritzer, 2010) does not show much influence on identity formation of people directly and not a single outlet for global food items like pizza, burger, chowmine, coffee, etc. is found in the town. But these items like burger, chowmine, etc. are prepared with the use of indigenous ingredients producing hybridity and sold in several local shops in the town. The people from all castes and communities in the field do not show keen desire to go out for having food as it is considered very unhygienic, unhealthy and un-prestigious. But the process of McDonaldisation has influenced upon the migrant youths of all castes and communities as they get opportunities of tasting these new food items in the migrant cities.[20] The process of Coca-Colonisation in contrast to McDonaldisation shows high impact in identity formation of people in the town and area. The different sorts of soft drinks like Pepsi, Coca-cola, Sprite, Mazza, Fruiti, Fanta, Mirinda, Limka and Thumsup are found everywhere and offered in the hospitality of relatives, guests, friends and common people on various occasions and also in daily usual life in the town with pride and respect. The process of hybridisation has been observed in the main areas of food items, dresses, songs, and films in Shamli. For example, use of sugarcane juice with eating burger and noodles, using soft drink with eating *bhujia*, *dam-aallo* (Both are local made food items like onion, potato, etc.), etc. using local oil, vegetables and spices in preparation of noodle, chowmine, etc., and wearing *kurta* on jeans, sport shoes on *salwar-kurta*, wearing ear rings, *topi* on head on jeans and T-shirts, wearing *lungi* and T-shirt, etc. The hybridisation process is also seen operating in the area of films, songs, dialogues, etc. noticed in the dominant Hindi cinema in general and also in local-regional *Hariyanavi* and *Punjabi* films in particular. The old generation people do not like much to see such new Hindi and English films as they think they cannot be been watched in family together with daughter, sons, daughter-in-law, etc. as the actors and actresses in films are dressed very dirty/*bhadda*, their dialogues, songs, acts, etc. spread *ashleelata*/dirtiness, vulgarity, and nakedness/*nangapa*. For example some of new songs verbatims are like *'choli kepeecheykyahai'*; *'chhamma-chhammabaje re teripayjania'*; *'bidi jalailejiagar se piya, jigar me badiaaghai'*; *'Billo rani kaho to apanijan de du'*; *'hothrasileterehothrasile'*; *'babujijaradhirechalo.... Bijalikhadi-Bijalikhadi'*; *'Pappu cannot dance sala'*; *'mahi re.....magdanasibaku-chaurhai'*; *'hat ja tau pichheke.... nachan de mainujibharke'*; *'jo nai – naikudiokonajarlagatehai......unkochhotiumar me hi chashme lag jatehai'*;

'pahala peg yarondeshikatha...... dusara peg angrejikatha', etc. ('What is there under the bodice; your anklets/ lower leg's ornaments of girl/lady speak chhamma-chhamma..; 'lit bidi/ local leafy cigarette by heat of your bosom........ there are much fire in it..'; 'if you ask for, I can give you my life Billo rani ......', 'your lips are juicy..'; ' gentleman walk slowly.....Bijali is standing here...'; 'Pappu cannot dance sala....'; 'destiny demands other things.....than you desire..', 'uncle go back let me dance fully..........', 'people who looks at girls....... forced to use spectacles in early age because their eyes get damaged while watching girls/them ....' 'let me drink first English wine then .... I will have the local/*deshi* wine later', etc.). They are spreading vulgarity, dirtiness and polluting mentality of all generation people in general and young generation in particular. These films songs are influenced by global cultural package in all their lyrics, music and style of singing and acting for generating pleasure seeking desire among people and spreading consumer culture rapidly among all castes and community in the field. The tendency of watching films and TV programmes in old generation in the town has also been increased many folds. But, unlike youth, old generation people are appreciative and inclined to watch religious programmes such as *Ramayan, Mahabharat, Krishna,* religious song *(Bhakti Geet*), knowledge spreading programmes, news, discovery etc. in TV. They also view that globalisation is good and suggest young generation to watch them because they proliferate indigenous socio-cultural values, norms and practices in the town and adjacent area. The hybridisation shows reinforcement of localisation for expressing identity issues and can be explained easily with popular phrase 'think globally and act locally' (Robertson, 1995). The local identity of Shamli has been changing to global because of locally produced items like rim and axel (*Dhure*) by local small scale industries are now exported to the global market of various European, American, African and Asian countries, as informed by owners of these small industries. The observation in the field force to suggest that one can easily see opposite of R. Robertson's famous phrase 'think globally act locally' i.e. more easy to understand identity formation of town in global era.. The opposite 'think locally and act globally' of above phrase 'think globally act locally' may helpful to explain identity of the local town Shamli in better manner-since think locally is related to the thinking of producing at local level and act globally inspire to export these local made products, that help in understanding some locally produce acquiring a global identity and raising the identity of the local town to the global.

Conclusion

Both homogenising, hybridising, Coco-Colanisation and McDonaldisation perspectives of globalisation have directly influenced the identity of all castes and communities by impressing upon collectivity of family, neighbourhood, community and generation gap, which have been important constituent parts of our cultural identity in the town. And role of media has been more pertinent than market in such changing identity formation by providing not only in new cultural celebrations and practices such as birth day, valentine day and marriage anniversary for all castes and communities but also has been influencing indigenous socio-cultural practices and making several socio-cultural celebrations found in all caste and communities less desirable and respected, becoming extinct in the town and area. The process of hybridisation is widely spreaded occurring in the areas of food, clothes, films, songs, dialogues, etc. in all caste and communities in Shamli shows the importance of localisation in the cultural life of the people. And youths from the town are indulged in various anomic activities such as celebration of birth day and valentine day, which are not appreciated by the elders in the town and area. And when they want to check youths then various unpleasant cases of suicide, its attempt, clash and conflict of family, group, caste and religious community are observed. It is suggested here that the launching of new channel that can represent people from all caste and community, isurgently needed, which will help in dealing with these problems emerging in the town and area in the wake of globalisation.

Notes

1. Prof. Y. Singh in his book, *Culture Change in India: Identity and Globalisation,* critically evaluates culture, its process and identity formation in Indian society, in the wake of globalisation. It examines use of ICT, migration of people and increasing inter cultural interaction of local, regional and national levels. It deals with the rise of popular culture and changing the forms and style of entertainment, value, behaviour, style of life and identity.
2. G. Ritzer in his book, *McDonaldisation: The Reader,* views McDonaldisation as the most dominating force of globalisation that help in changing the life style, culture and identity of people across the world in the global era.
3. J. Tomlinson in his book, *Cultural Imperialism: A Critical Introduction,* traces homogenisation with the development of cultural imperialism through the process of modernisation in historical frame and influencing all cultures across the world. It spreads the sameness by obliterating cultural differences and producing consciousness about cultural identity. In the process, media plays important role by influencing both private and public life tremendously.
4. Roland Robertson in the chapter, 'Glocalisation: Time-Space and Homogeneity–Heterogeneity' has discussed hybridisation and production of hybrid structure, after a blend of global and local and vice-versa, but not viewing both global and local as opposite and reactionary. They are seen as two sides of the same coin. The process of globalisation is searching and linking of localities.
5. Jan Nederveen Pieterse in the chapter, 'Globalisation as Hybridisation' has analysed globalisation as hybridising process in the various structures of state, polity, economy, organisation, and space operating through structuring and restructuring of one or other issues of identity at micro- macro, regional, national and transnational levels. The various cultural areas of food, cloths, music, play, dress, etc. are evidently seen producing hybrid structures after global mélange

that is with process of hybridisation, operating against the western cultural homogenisation.

6. Jonathan Friedman in the chapter, 'Global System, Globalisation and the Parameters of Modernity' relates globalisation with modernisation for producing hybridisation in the cultural areas. He has claimed that hybridisation occurs with mixing of originals in the social-cultural space that is a space of modernity, produced after the process of modernisation. The identity of individuals and groups has been framed on the basis of meaning and experience acquired in such context.
7. Z. Bauman has described that the consumer culture and its spread that turns society into a consumer society, with use of ideas of need, desire and wish in his article- 'Consuming Life'. The idea of consumption in this society is viewed as self-propelling and consumers consume products in accordance to satisfy their social standard mainly.
8. P. Bourdieu in his book, *Distinction: A Social Critique of the Judgment of Taste,* has analysed how the idea of taste, life style, habits and consumption are important in the formation and maintenance of cultural identity in the French society. The life style and habit of individuals together develop the different choices of individuals, that is result of socialisation in the habitus/family. The individual's economic and cultural capital also play important and decisive role in such culture and identity.
9. D. Slater in his book, *Consumer Culture and Modernity,* has evaluated the production and reproduction of consumer culture during the course of modernity in the capitalist society. The consumer culture is culture of capitalism or culture of market society. The modern universal values such as rationality, freedom, choice, market relations, etc. help in spreading it and changing the meaning of everyday life.
10. Leslie Sklair in his book, *Sociology of the Global System,* claims that globalisation has been proliferating cultural ideology of consumerism in the Third World. And its economic, political and cultural sphere have been characterised by their institution, structure and practices, separately, having transnational effects. The role of transnational corporations, transnational capitalist class and media are also considered very important into it.
11. Various documents such as Uttar Pradesh District Gazetteers: Muzaffarnagar, Department of District Gazetteers, Government of Uttar Pradesh, Uttar Pradesh,1980, Primary Census Abstract, Census of India, Directorate Census Operation, Uttar Pradesh, 2001, Vol. III, Shamli Mahayojana Praroop-2021 Muzaffarnagar, Jila-Udyog Kendra, Muzaffarnagar,1996 and Google Site have been used for knowing the location, population, infrastructural development, its different institutions, communities settlement, traffic, trade, transportation, small scale industries, and problem and prospect of the town-Shamli, Muzaffarnagar, UP.
12. Prof. Y. Singh in his book, *Culture Change in India: Identity and Globalisation,* critically evaluates culture, its process and identity formation in Indian society, in the wake of globalisation by mentioning the above mentioned categories.
13. Prof Y. Singh in the chapter, 'Country Town Nexus: Social Transformation in Contemporary Indian Society' tried to show country-town nexus across Indian

society through various indicators of castes, kinship, marriage, *jajmani* system, etc., used in several studies conducted by various scholars across India.

14. Prof. K. L. Sharma in the chapter, 'Country-Town Nexus in India: A Macro View' has discussed country-town nexus on the basis of dynamic relationship of internal structure, social stratification, macro structure forces of science and technology, government policy, migration, education, etc. in Indian society.
15. The Western Uttar Pradesh has been *Jat* community dominated area. It is a closed cultural area where practice of honour killing is on rise and *Khap Panchayat* plays a dominant role into it. It, usually, appears in the regional and national news. *Jat Khap Panchayat* passed a resolution banning girls to wear jeans, t-shirt, top, etc. and carrying mobile in public appeared in a national newspaper *Rashtrira Sahara*, January, 2011.
16. Michael Brake in his book, *Comparative Youth Culture: The Sociology of Youth Culture and Youth Subculture in America, Britain and Canada,* has explored youth culture and subculture referring to a particular way of life, values, behaviour, etc. against the dominant culture, by using ideology, class, culture, identity, social reality, education, occupation etc. of the youth, in the plural western society.
17. Prof. Nandu Ram in the chapter, 'Dalits Movements in India: A Perspective from Below' has analysed Dalit in contemporary India with social discrimination and discontent along with their assertion and movements from a wide range of timeframe from latter part of the nineteenth century to the present day. Dalit is recently an identity coined term and demonstrates pride, self-respect of untouchables and scheduled castes on the one hand and, and on the other, it exemplifies the ill treatment given to them by others in Indian society. The pride and self-respect of Dalit is rooted in their socio-economic and political achievements, who are untouchables subjected to untouchability, discrimination, exploitation and subordination.
18. Arjun Appadurai in his book, *Modernity at Large: Cultural Dimensions of Globalisation,* claims that media, migration and its interconnectedness provide the basis of imagination as constitutive feature of modern subject. The media in general and electronic media in particular provides an environment in which modern and global appear to be the flip sides of the same coin. The combined effect of electronic media (TV, films, computer, telephone) and migration produces the public sphere that defines core link of modern, global and social-cultural change.
19. M. Paterson in his book, *Consumption and Everyday Life,* has analysed everyday life in a capitalist society with the help of concept of consumption and its many faces by focusing on various terms such as choice, experience, consumption as every day act, commodification, nature, space of consumption, etc.. He portrays media advertisement as poetry of capitalism. It develops consumer culture and media, play utmost important role into it. In the theorisation of consumption and consumer culture the various relations of nature and environment, consumer and producer, brands, advertising, shopping and identity, etc. are interesting and important.
20. G. Ritzer in his book, *McDonaldisation: The Reader,* views McDonaldisation as the most dominating force of globalisation that changes life style, culture and

identity of people across the world in the global era. He refers it as the most influential development in the contemporary society. It is a process by which the fast food restaurants chains are coming up and dominating across the world. It is not like iron cage but beyond it and also prompts majority of the socio-cultural life beyond its origin.

References

Appadurai, Arjun. 1997. *Modernity at Large: Cultural Dimensions of Globalisation.* Delhi: Oxford University Press.

Bauman, Zygmunt. 2001. 'Consuming Life', *The Journal of Consumer Culture.* 1 (1): 9-29.

Bourdieu, Pierre. 2010. *Distinction: A Social Critique of Judgment of Taste.* London: Routledge.

Brake, Mike. 1985. *Comparative Youth Culture: The Sociology of Youth Culture and Youth Subculture in America, Britain and Canada.* London: Routledge.

Friedman, Jonathan. 1995. 'Global System, Globalisation and the Parameters of Modernity', in Mike Featherstone et al. (eds.), *Global Modernities* (69-90). London: Sage Publications.

George, Ritzer. 2010. *McDonaldisation: The Reader*. New Delhi: Pine Forge Press.

Giddens, Anthony.1990. *The Consequences of Modernity*. Cambridge: Polity Press.

Hall et al. 2003 (eds). *Modernity and Its Futures*. Cambridge: Polity Press.

Jila-Udyog Kendra. 1996. Muzaffarnagar. UP.

Paterson, Mark. 2005. *Consumption and Everyday Life.* London. Routledge.

Pieterse, Jan Nederveen. 1995. 'Globalisation as Hybridisation' in Mike Featherstone et al. (eds.), *Global Modernities* (45-68). London: Sage Publications.

Primary Census Abstract. 2001. *Census of India.* Vol. III. UP: Directorate Census Operation.

Ram, Nandu. 2011. 'Dalit Movements in India: A Perspective from Below' in Nandu Ram (ed.), *Dalits in Contemporary India: Discrimination and Discontent* (37-68). New Delhi: Sidhdhant Publications.

Rashtrira Sahara, January. 2011.

Robertson, Roland.1995. 'Glocalisation:Time-Space and Homogeneity – Heterogeneity' in Mike Featherstone et al. (eds.), *Global Modernities* (25-44). London: Sage Publications.

Shamli Mahayojana Praroop-2021. 2001. Muzaffarnagar: Muzaffarnagar Vikas Pradhikaran. UP.

Sharma, K. L. 1999. 'Country-Town Nexus in India: A Macro View' in Sharma and Gupta (eds.), *Country-Town Nexus: Studies in Social Transformation in Contemporary India* (43-60). New Delhi: Rawat Publications.

Singh, Yogendra. 1999. 'Country Town Nexus: Social Transformation in Contemporary Indian Society' in Sharma and Gupta (eds.), *Country-Town Nexus: Studies in Social Transformation in Contemporary India* (1-10). New Delhi: Rawat Publications.

Singh, Yogendra. 2012. *Culture Change in India: Identity and Globalisation.* New Delhi: Rawat Publications.

Sklair, L. 1991. *Sociology of the Global System.* New York: Harvest/Whratsheaf.

Slater, D.1997. *Consumer Culture and Modernity*. Cambridge: Polity Press.

Tomlinson, J. 1991. *Cultural Imperialism: A Critical Introduction.* London: Pinter Publishers.

Uttar Pradesh District Gazetteers. 1980. Government of Uttar Pradesh. Muzaffarnagar: Department of District Gazetteers. Uttar Pradesh.

Unit - III

Globalisation, Environment and Sustainable Development

Chapter - 13

Globalisation, Climate Change and the Dynamics of Sustainable Development

—*Nandkishor More and Shashi Kumar*

Even before the call of sustainable development much highlighted by Gro-Harlem Brundtland in Our Common Future, *the land mark report submitted under the aegis of United Nations Conference on Environment and Development (UNCED) popularly known as Earth Summit, the process of globalisation of world economies and use of natural resources was already in place. The division of world into two major 'Blocks' representing Developed and Developing nations have introduced new dimensions of alignment: one with technology centric and the other conservation based but technology deficient. It thus appeared as if on the existence of former, the genesis of the later is dependent. However, those who contemplated the issues of sustainable development brought attention towards the most pertinent questions, development for whom? by whom? and how? The interesting dimension to the duo of Globalisation and Sustainable Development added another feather with the emerging threats of Climate Change directly affecting the society and indirectly to the forces which govern it. Thus, new dimension of Climate change as one of the most important global environmental challenges emerged with deep seated implication for food production, water supply, health, energy etc. Moreover, the heat of Climate Change has already started producing results having very real consequences on people's lives. Because of increase in surface temperature, melting of snow and rise in sea levels is rampant resulting into several climate related eventualities like flooding, droughts, cyclone etc. occurring in many parts of the world eventually affecting the socio-economic life of people. Rethinking of global development model, based on principles of scientific sustainability is an absolute necessity at present and the scientists are by and large convinced now that human beings have caused much harm to mother Earth by letting global warming over the last 60 years or so. The IPCC's Fifth Assessment Report (AR5) suggests that without additional efforts to reduce GHG emissions beyond those in place today, the global surface temperature towards the end of the twenty-first century will increase by 4.8°C, and sea levels could rise as much as 0.8 meters, compared to pre-industrial levels. Significantly, the adverse impact of climate change has hindered in accomplishing the task of protection and promotion of human rights of common masses. In this context, sustainable development has direct bearing on the concerns of human rights. Moreover, the environmental degradation and problem of climate change has given a new dimension to sustainable development by making it more complex and intriguing issue.*

***Key Words:** Globalisation, Global Warming, Climate Change, Sustainable Development, Social Justice.*

Introduction

In 1983, the U.N. General Assembly created the World Commission on Environment and Development, an independent committee of twenty-two members, headed by Gro Harlem Brundtland, the Prime Minister of Norway. Designed to examine global environment and development to the year 2000 and beyond, the commission was constituted to reassess critical problems, to formulate realistic proposals for solving them, and to raise the level of understanding and commitment to the issues of environment and development. Rather than presenting a gloom and doom report about the destruction of natural resources, the Commission brought important report *Our Common Future* in 1987, that offers an agenda advocating the growth of economies based on policies that do not harm, and can even enhance, the environment. The commission recognises that the time has come for a marriage of economy and ecology, in order to ensure the growth of human progress through development without bankrupting the resources of future generations. This was however an arduous task for anyone regarding the object the chairman remarked. "A Global Agenda for Change" was what the world commission on environment and development was asked to formulate. It was an urgent call of United Nations General Assembly.

Sustainable Development: Conceptualisation

The concept of Sustainable Development seems to be "a seductively simple concept" (Birinie and Boyle, 1992), but it becomes complex and controversial notion when its applicability is made in the context of determining the indictors of sustainable development in relation to developed and developing countries. (M. Redclift, 1982; Kuik and Verbruggen, 1991) Originally, the term Sustainable Development primarily used in the report of Brundtland Commission (*Our Common Future*, 1987). The Commission draws upon several notions in its definition of sustainable development which is the most frequently cited definition of the concept to date. A key element in the definition of Sustainable Development is the unity of environment and development. The Brundtland Commission argues against the assertions of the 1972 Stockholm Conference on the Human Environment and provides an alternative perspective on sustainable development, unique from that of the 1980 World

Conservation Strategy of the International Union for the Conservation of Nature. The Brundtland Commission pushed for the idea that while the "environment" was previously perceived as a sphere separate from human emotion or action, and while "development" was a term habitually used to describe political goals or economic progress, it is more comprehensive to understand the two terms in relation to each other (We can better understand the environment in relation to development and we can better understand development in relation to the environment, because they cannot and should not be distinguished as separate entities). Brundtland argues: "...the "environment" is where we live; and "development" is what we all do in attempting to improve our lot within that abode. The two are inseparable."

The Brundtland Commission insists upon the environment being something beyond physicality, going beyond that traditional school of thought to include social and political atmospheres and circumstances. It also emphasise that development is not just about how poor countries can ameliorate their situation, but what the entire world, including developed countries, can do to ameliorate our common problems.

Sustainable development is the kind of development that meets the needs of the present without compromising the ability of future generations to meet their own needs. The two key concepts of sustainable development are: (1) the concept of "needs" in particular the essential needs of the world's poorest people, to which they should be given overriding priority; and (2) the idea of limitations which is imposed by the state of technology and social organisation on the environment's ability to meet both present and future needs.

Most agree that the central idea of the Brundtland Commission's definition of "sustainable development" is that of intergenerational equity. In sum, the "needs" are basic and essential, economic growth will facilitate their fulfilment, and equity is encouraged by citizen participation. Thus, another characteristic that really sets this definition apart from others is the element of humanity that the Brundtland Commission integrates.

The definition gave light to new perspectives on the sustainability of an ever-changing planet with an ever-changing population. Brundtland Commission (Our Common Future) The document was the culmination of a "900 day" international-exercise which catalogued, analysed, and synthesised written submissions and expert testimony from "senior government representatives, scientists and experts, research institutes, industrialists, representatives of non-governmental organisations, and the general public" held at public hearings throughout the world.

Its mandate was to: "[1] re-examine the critical issues of environment and development and to formulate innovative, concrete, and realistic action proposals to deal with them; [2] strengthen international cooperation on environment and development and assess and propose new forms of cooperation that can break out of existing patterns and influence policies and events in the direction of needed change; and [3] raise the level of understanding and commitment to action on the part of individuals, voluntary organisations, businesses, institutes, and governments". (Our Common Future, 1987) "The Commission focused its attention on the areas of population, food security, the loss of species and genetic resources, energy, industry, and human settlements - realising that all of these are connected and cannot be treated in isolation one from another" (*Ibid* : 27). The Brundtland Commission Report recognised that human resource development in the form of poverty reduction, gender equity, and wealth redistribution was crucial to formulating strategies for environmental conservation, and it also recognised that environmental-limits to economic growth in industrialised and industrialising societies existed. As such, the Report offered "the analysis, the broad remedies, and the recommendations for a sustainable course of development" within such societies. (*Ibid* : 16)

However, the Report was unable to identify the mode(s) of production that are responsible for degradation of the environment, and in the absence of analysing the principles governing market-led economic growth, the Report postulated that such growth could be reformed and expanded; this lack of analysis resulted in an obfuscated-introduction of the term sustainable development.

The report deals with sustainable development and the change of politics needed for achieving it. The definition of this term in the report is quite well known and often cited elsewhere too:

"Sustainable development is development that meets the needs of the present without compromising the ability of future generations to meet their own needs". It contains two key concepts:

- the concept of "needs", in particular the essential needs of the world's poor, to which overriding priority should be given; and
- the idea of limitations imposed by the state of technology and social organisation on the environment's ability to meet present and future needs."

Sustainable Development and Human Rights have close relation. Dominic McGoldrick argues that Sustainable Development and Human Rights are integrated conceptions. According to him, the protection and promotion of human rights values as enshrined in International Human Rights law is the core of integrated structure of Sustainable Development. (McGoldrick, 1996) The Principle 1 of the UN Conference on Environment and Development's Rio Declaration states that "human beings are the centre of concern for sustainable development" and that "are entitled to a healthy and productive life in harmony with nature." [See the Stockholm Declaration (1972),

Principle.1]. The environmental protection is also important component of Sustainable Development. A World Charter for Nature was adopted in 1982, Principle 4 of the Rio Declaration states that "in order to achieve Sustainable Development environmental protection shall constitute an integral part of the development process and cannot be considered in isolation from it."[1] Economic development is also concern with Sustainable Development. The World Trade Organisation also plays a key role in focusing on the trade-related aspect for having sustainable development. Importantly, the UN Secretary General's *Agenda for Development* formulated in 1995 has a "five dimension of development": peace as the condition, the economy as engine of growth, the environment as the basis for sustainability, justice as a pillar of society, and democracy as good governance.

At the international levels, under the aegis of United Nation the Sustainable Development Goals (SDG) has been recently formulated 25th September 2015 which is also known as Post-2015 SDG, replacing the Millennium Development Goal (MDG) which was set in 2000 and got ended in 2015. The Post-2015 SDG adopted by UN Member States has contains seventeen sustainable development goals that would guide global development efforts on poverty eradication, food security, environmental sustainability and the rule of law to be achieved till 2030.[2] The SDG officially known as *Transforming our World: The 2030 Agenda for Sustainable Development*, considered as successor to the Millennium Development Goals. The resolution is broader intergovernmental agreement among nations of the world to ameliorate the problems of the world being faced by the peoples at present time. Largely, it includes ending poverty and hunger, improving health and education, making cities more sustainable, combating climate change, and protecting oceans and forests.

The environmental problem like climate change is understood as problem of consumption rather than production patterns. Therefore, judicious consumption pattern rather than a production-based vision for environmentally sustainable economic development is need of the hour for the protection of environment and for prevention from the adverse impact of climate change. (Prasad *et al.,* 2009; Sanwal, 2008). In economic term, Sustainable development means maintenance of inter-generational well-being, that is, the total well-being of the individuals in future generation does affect decline in compare to present generations (Stavins, R.N, *et al.* 2003). In other words, sustainability understood as non-declining intergenerational well-beings over time (Arrow *et al.,* 2012).

Globalisation and Sustainable Development

Globalisation is both a result and a force of modernisation and capital expansion. It entails the integration of all economic activity (local, national and regional) into a 'global' market place, and transcending geo-political borders and is not subject to regulation by nation states.

Globalisation is derived by neo-liberal economic measures that based on principles of 'economic freedom' and 'consumer choice'. These measures include liberation of trade and finance, deregulation and privatisation which have been nailed down over the past more than three decades by the Washington Consensus, the unprecedented rise of corporate power, the formation of WTO and burgeoning bilateral and regional free trade and investment agreements.

It has been argued that many of the world's people live in what may be described as a corporatist society with soft pretensions to democracy. Globalisation affects them in tangible and intangible ways. The neo-liberalist forces that tend to shape and frame globalisation in terms of markets and opportunities for growth result in power slipping away from citizens to corporate elites. In examining this argument, John Ralston Saul suggests that globalisation refers to the rise of economic ideologies embodied by the corporate sector, and to the erosion of grassroots democracy. In fact, he argues that the corporatist movement started in the nineteenth century as an alternative to democracy (Saul, 2005). Crossley and Watson argues that it is the executive directors of these powerful banks [i.e. International Monetary Fund and World Bank] and transnational corporations (TNCs) that can direct, or at the least influence, the policies of individual countries and national economies by integrating them into regional or global economies, and by making it increasingly impossible for them to regulate and control their own affairs (Michael, C and Watson, K, 2003; Satterthwaite *et al.,* 2007).

It was assumed that globalisation would bring economic growth in developing countries, but instead of this, the economies of developing countries have become even more depended on forces of international market mainly controlled by corporate powers houses of the world. Consequently, it led to economic stagnation, increased unemployment, income poverty, economic vulnerability and environmental destruction in several developing countries (Guttal, 2007; U B Singh *et al.,* 2014).

Globalisation a process with many facets. Globalisation of capital market leads to greater international capital flows which increase the vulnerability of emerging markets into crises. Makin says that globalisation supports growth in developing countries. However, during bad times, globalisation also increases human sufferings (Wall Street Journal, 1999).

Globalisation is a dynamic process driving the integration of national markets into world market. WTO promotes free international trade in goods and services around the world. Large regional trading alliance treaties of the countries like ASEAN, NAFTA, European Union, APEC have also been founded to encourage cross-broader trade flows by eliminating import quotas, tariffs and export restriction (Markin, 2000).

Impact of Climate Change

Climate change is one of the most important global environmental challenges, with implications on food production, water supply, health, energy, etc. Addressing climate change requires a good scientific understanding as well as coordinated action at national and global level. It is argued that as the developed countries have contributed much in green house gas emission, hence the responsibility for restriction on green house gas emissions largely lies with the industrialised world, though the developing countries are also likely to be the source of an increasing proportion of emission level in present era and in future. The projected climate change under various scenarios is likely to have implications on food production, water supply, coastal settlements, forest ecosystems, health, energy security etc. The adaptive capacity of communities likely to be impacted by climate change is low in developing countries. The efforts made by the UNFCCC and the Kyoto Protocol provision are clearly inadequate to address the climate change challenge but are important. The most effective way to address climate change is to adopt a sustainable development pathway by shifting to environmentally sustainable technologies and promotion of energy efficiency, renewable energy, forest conservation, reforestation, water conservation, etc. The issue of highest importance to developing countries is reducing the vulnerability of their natural and socio-economic systems to the projected climate change. India and other developing countries will face the challenge of promoting mitigation and adaption strategies, bearing the cost of such an effort, and its implications for economic development (R Loske,1996).

The global carbon cycle involves interaction among the atmosphere, oceans, soils and vegetation and fossil fuel deposits. The ocean contain 39,000 giga tonnes of carbon (GtC), fossil fuel deposits about 16,000 GtC, and the atmosphere about 760 GtC and fossil fuel combustion, about 270 GtC. Of this, 180 GtC has ended up in the atmosphere, while 110 GtC has been absorbed by growing vegetation and the remainder by the oceans. It is the increasing concentration of atmospheric CO_2 that is the cause for concern about global climate change.

The combustion of fossil fuels and other human activities are the primary reasons for increased concentrations of CO_2 and other greenhouse gases. Between 1990 and 1999, an estimated 6.3 GtC/year was released due to the combustion of fossil fuels, and another 1.6 GtC/year was released due to the burning of forest vegetation. This was offset by the absorption of 2.3 GtC/year each by growing vegetation and the oceans. This left a balance of 3.3 GtC/year in atmosphere[3]. Controlling the release of greenhouse gases from fossil fuel combustion, land-use change and the burning of vegetation are therefore obvious opportunities for reducing greenhouse gas emissions. Reducing greenhouse gas emissions can lessen the projected rate and magnitude of warning and sea level rise. The greater the reduction in emissions and the earlier they are introduced, the smaller and slower the projected warming and the rise in sea levels. Future climate change is thus determined by historic, current and future emissions. Of the six aforementioned GHGs, CO_2 accounted for 63 per cent, methane 24 per cent, nitrous oxide 10 per cent and the other gases the remaining 3 per cent of the carbon equivalent emissions in 2000. Thus, in addition to CO_2, global mitigation efforts need to focus on the two largest and rapidly increasing GHGs.

India is a large developing country with nearly 700 million rural population directly depending on climate–sensitive sectors (agriculture, forests and fisheries) and natural resources (such as water, biodiversity, mangroves, coastal zones, grasslands) for their subsistence and livelihoods. Further, the adaptive capacity of dry land farmers, forest dwellers, fisher folk, and nomadic shepherds is very low (Ravindra Nath and Sathaye, 2002). Climate change is likely to impact all the National Communications Report of India to the UNFCCC (GoI, 2004, 2005, 2006, 2007, 2008, 2009).

South Asia is most vulnerable to climate change. The region faces daunting climate related development challenges. The impacts of climate change in the form of higher temperature, more variable precipitation and more extreme weather events are already felt in South Asia. The region is already marked by climate variability and a higher incidence of natural disasters. The region has also a long and densely populated coast line with low lying island that are vulnerable to sea level rise. Urbanisation poses an additional challenge in the region. Women, poor and indigenous people are most vulnerable to climate risk.

Among the 32 states and Union Territories in the country, 22 are multi-disaster prone. About 40 million hectares of land in the country has been identified as flood prone and on an average 18.6 million hectare of land is flooded annually. About 57 per cent of area of the country is vulnerable to seismic activity. About 18 per cent of country's total area is drought prone, approximately 50 million people are annually affected by droughts and about 68 per cent of total sown area of the country is drought prone. India has a long coastline of 8040 km. which is exposed to tropical cyclones arising in the Bay of Bengal, the Arabian Sea and Indian Ocean. The Indian Ocean is one of the six major cyclonic prone regions of the globe The Coromandal coastline is more cyclones prone, with 80 per cent of the total cyclones generated in this regions. Risk to the existing housing stock in various states and union-territories had been estimated by Expert Group set up by the Ministry of Urban Affairs and Employment, Government of India. About 3.9 million houses are susceptible to earthquakes of very high intensity, about 20 million houses are susceptible to damage due to winds and about 9.3 million houses are susceptible to damage due to floods. Besides the risk of earthquakes, cyclones and floods are liable to very high damage and destruction of vulnerable houses under heavy rains. Some 49 per cent of the total housing stock is liable to very high damage from natural hazards, while about one per cent of the total housing stock gets destroyed every year. It is to be noted that in earthquake, 80 per cent of the casualities are due to collapsing buildings. Brick and stone buildings without proper support are liable to collapse. Non-engineered building continue to be built in the areas prone to natural disasters. Unemployment, poverty backwardness, migration from rural areas and increasing price of land and construction, million of people are occupying disaster prone areas. Thus, about six per cent increase in disaster affected population has been reported. The changing topography due to environmental degradation has also increased the vulnerability in the country. In 1988, 11.2 per cent of total land areas was flood prone, but in 1998 floods inundated 37 per cent geographical area. Three major disasters that India have experienced in the recent past are the super cyclone in Orissa (1999), earthquake in Gujarat (2001) and Tsunami (2004) in Tamil Nadu, Pondicherry, Andaman Nicobar Island and parts of other southern states. Frequent disasters lead to erosion of development gains restricted options threatened by hazards.

The continent of Asia is particularly vulnerable to disaster strikes. Between the years 1991 to 2000 Asia has accounted for 83 per cent of the population affected by disasters globally. Within Asia, 24 per cent of deaths due to disasters occurred in India, on account of its size of population and vulnerability. Floods and high winds account for 60 per cent of all disasters in India. Many parts of the Indian sub-continent are susceptible to different types of disasters owing to the unique topography and climatic characteristics. About 54 per cent of the sub-continent's landmass is vulnerable to earthquake while about 4 crores hectares is vulnerable to periodic floods. The country has suffered four major earthquakes in the span of last 50 years along with a series of moderate intensity earthquakes that have occurred at regular intervals. Since 1988, six earthquakes have struck different parts of the country. Tsunami in India killed 10749 persons while $1068 million loss or damage to properties was reported.

Short-term and long-term changes in climatic variables such as temperature and perception may pose hazards to urban system. Changes in the climatic variables are likely to impact future patterns of spatial growth and development in cities and act as a stressor in addition to existing pressures. The populations most venerable to climate change are those living in slums and informal settlements that often lack access to basic services and infrastructure (IDS, 2007). Apart from the risk to coastal populations from sea level rise, cyclones, storm surges and other associated impacts, a high proportion of urban settlements in the low and middle-income countries are one sites that are at risk from flooding or landslides. The key primary and secondary order impacts on cities are due to short-term and long-term changes in climatic variables have been stressed elsewhere too (Kuik, O and Verbruggen, H, 1991).

Urbanisation vis-à-vis Globalisation

Growing urbanisation is possing serious environmental challenges in India in terms of changing land use pattern, increasing carbon emission, solid wastes generation and disposal, air and water pollution and poor sanitation amenities. A large segment of urban population in India resides in slums, squatters and informal settlements. These settlements are often located in low laying areas prone to direct and indirect risks due to various forms of environmental degradation including changes in the climate and lack of basic urban services (Satterthwaite *et al.,* 2007). It is to be noted that out of 35 cities in India having population over a million, 18 are in coastal states. Major challenge for cities in the face of rapid population growth is to maintaining sustainability within the social, economic and environmental dimension. Urban systems are at risk to different kinds of hazards. Several factors contribute to the urban risk profile (Tony Markin, 2000).

The implementation plan of the parties to the 2002 World Summit on Sustainable Development has 81 references to "at all levels" in just 50 pages. This could be read as either an acknowledgement that many problems have causes and solutions that span multiple levels or as an admission of ignorance or willingness to address particular levels and cross level interactions (Arrow *et al.,* 2012). Either way, understanding cross scale interactions in the human-environment system is seen as increasingly important. Further there is a long history of disappointments in policy, management, and assessment arising from the failure to take into proper account the scale and cross-scale dynamics in human-environment systems: collapsing fisheries, trans-boundary pollution problems, vulnerability to repeated extreme events like floods and droughts, and the inability to address human-induced disease outbreaks (Millennium Ecosystem Assessment, 2005).

Climate change and possible response strategies have high scientific and policy relevance but are also associated with major controversies. The time frame of a century or more involved in any analysis of climate change, as well as, the complexity of natural and socio-economic systems and their interactions–all shrouded by deep uncertainties–pose major scientific and policy challenges. There needs to be a shared understanding of these challenges in order to come to grips with the possible magnitude and nature of climate change and to craft response strategies. This all makes climate change perhaps one of the most challenging issues to be addressed by interdisciplinary research and by policy measures to date. How will human drivers ranging from the realm of demographics, economics, and technology to social behaviour and institutions shape future emissions of greenhouse gases (GHGs)? Are there ways of "bending down" the curve of ever increasing radiative forcing? What will be the consequences of radiative forcing change on global, regional, as well as local climates both in terms of changes in magnitude (e.g., warming, precipitation) as well as in nature (most prominently variability and possibilities of extreme events)? What will be the impacts on natural and human systems of a changing climate? Finally, what are the feasibilities, costs, and benefits (in terms of avoided impacts) of response strategies? There are sufficient scientific and policy reasons to justify interest in climate change and to devote a full Special Issue to this topic. However, interest in itself needs to be complemented by new analytical and methodological perspectives. The work by Grubler *et al.* provides key findings that are also of wider interest beyond the climate change universe. For instance, the paper highlights the importance of the persistence of urban clusters in industrialised countries (as well as Latin America) combined with a vast potential for megacity (Africa) and urban corridor (Asia) growth in developing countries. The paper suggests that developments in Asia will be particularly dramatic over the next five decades considering the economic growth with an unprecedented scale of emerging urban agglomerations in terms of population and economic activities that could surpass many-fold the currently most dense urban corridors, such as Boswash in the USA or Shinkansen in Japan. Grubler *et al.* emphasise the need for new infrastructure "backbones" along urban clusters rather than networks of "island" cities, particularly in the Asian urbanisation "hotspots" of Bengal and the Chinese coast (Satterthwaite *et al.* 2007; ADB, 2009; IDS, 2006; WB, 2009).

Conclusion

To conclude it is reiterated that South Asia is the most vulnerable to climate change. The region faces daunting climate related development challenges. The impacts of climate change in the form of higher temperature, more variable precipitation and more extreme weather events are already felt in South Asia. The region is already marked by climate variability and a higher incidence of natural disasters. The region has also a long and densely populated coast line with low lying island that are vulnerable to sea level rise. Urbanisation poses an additional challenge in the region. Women, poor and indigenous people are most vulnerable to climate risk. Though Agenda for Sustainable Development, which includes a set of 17 Sustainable Development Goals (SDGs) and 169 targets to end poverty, fight inequality and injustice, and tackle climate change by 2030 though it is target for 15 yrs to all the nations of the world (UN-SDG, 2015; CEE, MoEFCC, 2015). In many ways it is a challenge to complete the force of globalisation and to achieve the goals of sustainable development.

Notes

1. UN General Assembly Res. 37/7, See D. McGoldrick, "From the New International Economic Order to the Agenda for Development", in BIICL, Essays on Privatisation (1996).
2. See https://sustainabledevelopment.un.org, UN Res. A/RES/70/1.

References

1. Arrow et al. (2012), "Sustainability and the Measurement of Wealth", Environment and Development Economics, 17 (3): 317-53.
2. Burtless, Gary *et al.* (1998), Globalphobia: Confronting fears about open Trade, Brooking Institution, Washington DC.
3. *Crisis in Asia: Spawns Millions of Newly Poor,* Wall Street Journal, April 6, 1999.
4. Crossley, Michael and Keith Watson (2003), Comparative and International Research in Education: Globalisation, Context and Differences (New York: London: Routledge).
5. Dominic McGoldrick (1996), Sustainable Development and Human Rights: An Integrated Conception', The Int'l and Comparative Law Quarterly, Vol. 45, No. 4, Oct, pp. 796-818.
6. Government of India, (2004), Initial National Communications to the United Framework Convention on Climate Change, Ministry of Environmental and Forests, Government of India.
7. John Ralston Saul (2005), The Collapse of Globalisation and the Reinvention of the World.
8. Kuik, O and Verbruggen, H, (1991), In Search of Indicators of Sustainable Development, Springer, Netherlands.
9. M. Redclift (1989), Sustainable Development: Exploring the Contradictions, Routledge.
10. Mukul Sanwal, Sustainable Development Perspective of Climate Change, Vol.43, No.15, 12 April, 2008, Economic and Political Weekly.
11. *Our Common Future*, (1987), Oxford University Press.
12. P.W. Birinie and A.E. Boyle (1992), International Law and the Environment, Oxford Univ. Press.
13. Ravindranath, N. H. and Sathaye, J. (2002), Climate Change and Developing Countries, Kluwer Academic Publishers, Dordrecht, Netherlands.
14. See https://sustainabledevelopment.un.org , UN Res. A/RES/70/1.
15. Shalmali, Guttal (2007), Globalisation', *Development in Practice* Vol. 17, No. 4-5, August, pp. 523-531.
16. Stavins, R.N, A.F Wagner and G Wagnerl (2003), "Interpreting Sustainability in Economic Terms: Dynamic Efficiency Plus Intergerational Equity," Economic's Letters, 79: 339-43]
17. Tony Markin (2000), Globalisation : Context and Controversies. *Agenda*. Vol. 7 No. 7, pp. 293-302.

    UN General Assembly Res. 37/7; See D. Mc Goldrick, "From the New International Economic Order to the Agenda for Development", in BIICL, Essays on Privatisation (1996).
18. ADB (2009), Rethinking Transport and Climate Change, Asian Development Bank, Manila.
19. Alhuwalia, I.J (2006), India Urban Infrastructure Report, Ministry of Urban Development, Government of India, New Delhi.

20. Ahmad, S. and Choi, M.J (2010), Urban India and Climate Change: Mitigation Strategies towards Inclusive Growth, Theoretical and Empirical Research in Urban Management 6 (15).
21. Bebb, J and Kersey, J. (2003), Potential impact of climate change on waste management (R&D Technical Report). Environment Agency. Entec UK limited, UK.
22. Berggren, K., Svensson, G. and Viklander, M (2008), Urban drainage and climate change : a problematic approach? MISTRA Newsletter 1, Sweden.
23. CSE (2011), Policy Paper on Septage Management in India. Centre for Science and Environment and Forest, New Delhi.
24. Government of India (2004), India's Initial National Communication to the United Nations Framework Convention on Climate Change, Ministry of Environment and Forest, New Delhi.
25. Government of India (2006), National Urban Transport Policy, New Delhi: Ministry of Urban Development, Government of India.
26. Government of India (2007), India: Addressing Energy Security Climate Change, Ministry of Environment and Forest, Government of India.
27. Government of India (2008), National Action Plan on Climate Change, Ministry of Environment and Forest, Government of India, New Delhi.
28. Government of India, (2004), Initial National Communications to the United Framework Convention on Climate Change, Ministry of Environment and Forest, Government of India.
29. Government of India, (2004), Initial National Communications to the United Framework Convention on Climate Change, Ministry of Environmen and Forest, Government of India.
30. Government of India, (2007), Report of the steering committee on urban development for the Eleventh Five Year Plan (2007-20120). Planning Commission, Government of India.
31. Government of India, (2008), Report of The Working group on Disaster Management for the Eleventh Five–Year Plan.
32. Government of India, (2009), Ministry of Housing and Urban Poverty Alleviation. Rajiv Awas Yojana. Guidelines for Slum Free City Planning Peer Experience And Reflective Learning (PEARL), printed by National Institute of Urban Affairs.
33. Government of India, National Action Plan on Climate Change (2008), Prime Minister's Council on Climate Change.
34. Government of India, National Action Plan on Climate Change (2008), Prime Minister's Council on Climate Change.
35. Gupta, V. (2005), Climate Change and Domestic Mitigation Efforts, Economic and Political Weekly, March.
36. ICC (2011), Background Note, 2nd India International Water Summit, December, 15-16, 2011, Indian Chamber of Commerce, New Delhi.
37. ICLEI, (2007), City of Keene, New Hampshire Climate Adaption Action Plan Summary Report.
38. IDS, (2007), Building Climate Change resilient cities, Focus Issue 2.6 Institute of Development Studies, Sussex.

39. Intergovernmental Panel on Climate Change (IPCC) (2007), Climate Change 2007: The Physical Science Basis. Contribution of Working Group I to the Fourth Assessment Report of the Intergovernmental Panel on Climate Change (Solomon, S., D. Qin, M. Manning, Z Chen, M. Marquis, K.B. Averyt, M. Tingor and H.L Miller (eds). Cambridge University Press, Cambridge, United Kingdom and New York, NY, USA.
40. Khatri, K.B. and Vairavamorthy, K. (2007), Challenges for urban water supply and sanitation in the developing countries, UNESCO IHE, Institute for water. Education discussion draft paper, Deift. Netherlands.
41. Loske, R. (1996), Scope of the Report: Setting the Stage Climate Change and Sustainable Development, Third Assessment Report, Group III, PCC.
42. Mathur, O.P., (2009), Slum–Free cities. National Urban Poverty Reduction Strategy 2010-2020, Ministry of Housing and Urban Poverty Alleviation Government of India, New Delhi.
43. Pangare, et al. (2006), "Spring of Life: India's water Resources", Academic Foundation, New Delhi.
44. Prasad, N., Ranghieri, F., Shah, F., Trhanis, Z., Kessler, E., and Sinha, R., (2009), Climate resilient cities a Primer on reducing vulnerabilities to disaster. The World Bank, Washington DC.
45. Sathaye, J. et al. (2006), Climate change, Sustainable Development and India: Global and National Concerns, Current Science, Vol. 90, No.3, February 10.
46. Satterthwaite, D, Huq, S., Pelling, M., Reid, H. and Lankao, P.R., (2007), Adapting to climate change in urban areas: the possibilities and constraints in low-and middle income nations. London: Human settlements discussion paper series, International Institute for Environment and Development (IIED), London.
47. Singh, M. (2010), Making India slum free: a ray of hope. SHELTER. Vol.12, No.1, HUDCO (Housing and Urban Development Corporation Ltd.) New Delhi.
48. Singh U.B. et al. (2014), Challenges of Urban Management in 21st Century Indian, Global Research Publications, New Delhi.
49. Sridhar, K.S and Surender Kumar (2013), India's Urban Environment, Economic and Political Weekly, Feb.9.
50. Sridhar, Kala Seetharam and Om Prakashan Mathur (2009), Costs and Challenges of Local Urban Services: Evidence from India's Cities (New Delhi: Oxford University Press).
51. USAID. (2010), A Rapid Assessment of Septage Management in Asia: Policies and Practices in India, Indonesia, Malaysia, Philippines, Srilanka, Thailand and Vietnam. USAID.
52. World Bank (1999), What a waste: Solid Waste Management in Asia, Washington DC.
53. World Bank (2006), India's Water Economy: Bracing for a Turbulent Future, Oxford University Press, New Delhi.
54. World Bank (2006), India Water and Sanitation: Bridging the Gap between Infrastructure and Services Washington DC, World Bank.
55. World Bank, (2008), Benchmarking Urban Water Utilities in India, World Bank, New Delhi.
56. WSP (2010), Benchmarking for Performance Improvement in Urban Utilities, World Bank, New Delhi.
57. Sustainable Development Goals: A Reference, CEE, MoEF, New Delhi, India.

Chapter - 14

Climate Change and Environmental Degradation: A Concern for Sustainable Development in India

—*Abhishek Pandey*

Environmental Degradation and Climate change is one of the most pressing challenges facing humankind today. Science about climate change is quite convinced that its impacts are being felt across the globe with increasing temperatures, changing weather patterns, increasing frequency of extreme events, melting glaciers and rising sea levels. Almost all the countries are feeling the heat, though to a varying extents. As a fastest developing country, India's challenge is to meet its development aspirations in a carbon-constrained world. The challenges before developing country like India become more strenuous due to financial constraints and lack of expertise for adaptation and mitigation technology and therefore much more exposed to bear the brunt of climate change. Climate change is expected to boast far reaching implications for India due to its high dependence on natural resources and also the potential to violate constitutionally guaranteed rights to life and livelihood of the people. The efforts made by the UNFCCC and the Kyoto Protocol provisions are clearly inadequate to address the climate change challenges. The Supreme Court of India has issued principle guidelines in the past in some landmark cases that appears as a ray of hope to protect the potential violation of rights of people due to climate change. The highest issue of importance to developing countries are to reduce the vulnerability of their natural and socio-economic systems to the projected climate change. The wide ranging potential impacts of climate change on sustainable development and vice versa, suggest that the linkages between these two aspects need to be analysed critically in a developing country like India to realise the goal of sustained economic development. The paper concludes by underlining that the most effective way to address climate change is to adopt a sustainable development pathway by shifting to environmentally sustainable technologies and promotion of energy efficiency, renewable energy, forest conservation, reforestation, water conservation strategies etc.

Key Words: *Sustainable Development, Biological Diversity, Climate Change, Ecological Meltdown, Mitigation, Adaptation, Environmental Degradation.*

Introduction

Climate change is one of the complex problems facing mankind today. The overriding complexity of the problem is attributed to its deeper global ramifications on a vast range of issues impacting the very survival of life on Earth. Understanding such a complex issue with vast and varied dimensions and implications, assumes greater significance for all stakeholders, especially for our policy makers. There are varieties of perceptions regarding the exact size and consequences of climate change. Yet, it is no secret that risks emanating from climate change are indeed profound, which call for urgent mitigation. There is now strong evidence that climate change is a reality.[1] Today, it has been scientifically established that significant global warming is occurring. Warming of the climate system is unequivocal, as is now evident from observations of increases in global average air and ocean temperatures, widespread melting of snow and ice and rising global average sea level.[2] There is no denying the fact that the problem exists and it is assuming alarming proportions, each passing day. Therefore, there is an imperative need to take urgent and strong measures in the interest of calibrating an appropriate response to meet the emerging challenges of climate change. Climate change is not an isolated issue. It has several aspects and inter-linkages namely, science and technology, economy and trade, diplomacy and politics - that makes it not just another issue in this complicated world of proliferating issues, but the mother of all issues. Climate change, however, is different from other problems facing humanity and it compels us to think differently at many levels. It obliges us to think about what it means to live as part of an ecologically interdependent human community. In the face of much diversity that characterises human society, climate change provides a potent reminder of one thing that we share in common - the planet Earth.[3] All nations and all people share the same atmosphere. And, we only have one. Addressing the climate chaos by all the countries both individually and collectively will be critical to the human well-being and prosperity of the present as well as the future generations.

Understanding Climate Change

Climate change is the biggest threat that mankind is facing today. The climate change is a change in the statistical distribution of weather patterns and changes over millions of years. It may be referred to a change in average weather conditions or change in the time variation of weather around long-term weather conditions. It is caused naturally by some geological process augmented by the human beings through their activities causing the process of global warming to hasten and thereby creating alarming situation globally. Most experts agree that the impact of global warming has been in a worrisome measure, as evident from the melting of glaciers. Coastal storms and cyclones are also increasing in frequency and intensity. Although climate change is a product of unsustainable consumption of non-renewable forms of energy, the harmful impact of climate change will be felt more by those nations with limited resources and coping capacity. Since the Industrial Revolution, man-made activities had added significant quantities of Greenhouse Gases (GHGs).[4] Climate change is a global negative externality primarily caused by the building up of GHG emission in the atmosphere. The incremental impact of a tonne of GHGs on climate change is independent of where in the world it is emitted. These emissions impose a cost on both the present and future generations, which are not fully recouped from the emitters of these emissions. This formed the starting point for a globally co-ordinated policy action and the need for the international climate change negotiating regime. ***UNFCCC***, set up in 1992, although global in space, differentiates the commitments and responsibilities of parties on the basis historical responsibilities, economic structures, and on the basis of principle of 'equity' and ***CBDR*** which is at the core of the climate change debate. The largest share of historical and current global emissions of GHGs has originated in developed countries. Scientists attribute the global problem of climate change not to the current of GHG emission but to the stock of historical GHG emission. Most of the countries, particularly the industrialised countries, having large current emissions are also the largest historic emitters and the principle contributors to climate change. The convention therefore lays down legally binding commitments for the developed countries, taking into account their historical responsibilities and also squarely puts the responsibilities on developed countries for providing financial resources, including for the transfer of technology, needed by the developing countries. The convention also acknowledges that climate change actions taken by developing countries are contingent on the resources made available to them.[5]

Understanding Sustainable Development

The concept of sustainable development was largely developed by the World Commission on Environment and Development, more commonly known as the Brundlandt Commission in 1987. The main objectives of Sustainable Development are reviving growth, changing the quality of growth, meeting essential needs for jobs, food, energy, water and sanitation, conserving and enhancing the resource base, reorienting technology and managing risk and merging environment and economics in decision making. Sustainable development is development that provides economic, social and environmental benefits in the long-term, having regard to the needs of living and future generations. Thus, the main objective is the satisfaction of human needs and aspirations. According to the commission's document ***"OUR COMMON FUTURE"***, Sustainable Development is defines as ***"It is a dynamic process***

designed to meet today's needs without compromising the ability of future generations to meet their own needs".[6] Thus, Sustainable Development is a process of change in which resource use; economic policies, technical development and population growth are in harmony and enhance current and future potential for human progress. In fact, the development of economy and environment must be integrated to make the development sustainable.

Strategies for Sustainable Development

- Greater attention to the problems of the poor.
- Local input in planning and managing resources development.
- Proper Resource Planning to internalise all the external costs.
- Wiser management by improving resource availability by reducing wasteful uses.
- Remove inequality.
- Decrease the use of resource capital by emphasising durable goods, recycling and reuse of materials.

Priority Areas for Achieving Sustainable Development

- Slowing down population growth for addressing all the other priority areas.
- Reduce Poverty, Inequality and Third world Debt which includes improving health, longevity and literacy.
- Making Agriculture Sustainable which includes reducing soil erosion and decreasing the use of harmful agricultural practices.
- Reforestation and afforestation of wastelands, protection of other living resources.
- Controlling Green House Gases and Ozone Depletion.
- Curbing the loss of biodiversity and land degradation.
- Improving the efficiency of water use and protecting water quality
- Reducing air pollution and water pollution.
- Improving production processes, waste treatment and recycling processes.

Climate Change and Environmental Degradation: Problem and the Controversy

The Kyoto reduction, by itself, is inadequate to achieve a stabilisation of climate change by 2100. A continual and larger reduction, similar to that stipulated in the Kyoto Protocol for the 2008–2012 period, will be needed in the future in order to begin to stabilise long-term greenhouse gas emissions. Even if stabilisation of greenhouse gases is achieved, global warming will still continue for several decades and sea levels will continue to rise for several centuries. IPCC studies make it abundantly clear, however, that industrialised countries alone cannot achieve this reduction. Even if their emissions were reduced to zero in the near future, the current trends of growing emissions from developing countries alone could force the atmospheric concentration to exceed stabilisation levels of 550 ppm.[7] The participation of all countries, including the developing countries such as India, is essential for a successful worldwide effort to arrest the growth of greenhouse gas emissions. What is the best method to justly and equitably distribute the burden of stabilising climate change among the countries? This issue lies at the heart of much of the ongoing negotiations under the auspices of the UNFCCC. India, the fifth largest emitter of greenhouse gases from fossil fuel in the 1990s, has suggested that the 'right' to pollute the atmosphere be apportioned to all countries on the basis of their population. Using this gauge, China and India, the only countries with populations in excess of a billion each, could legitimately emit greenhouse gases to a greater extent, than other countries with lesser population, for some decades. But, as their greenhouse gas emissions today are less than this proposed allocation, they could 'sell' some of the 'rights' to the industrialised countries. Countries usually propose burden-sharing formulae that favour their economies, and other countries have suggested schemes based on inherited and future emissions, a country's contribution to temperature change, GDP, and land area and other resource endowments. In the global climate change debate, the issue of largest importance to developing countries is reducing the vulnerability of their natural and socio-economic systems to projected climate change. Their concerns include increasing food security, reducing freshwater scarcity, protecting the livelihoods of forest dwellers, dry land farmers and coastal settlements and reducing health risks. Though there is a visible shift in the global discussions towards adaptation at the Climate Convention-related meetings, the focus continues to be on mitigation of greenhouse gas emissions. Adaptation can complement mitigation as a cost-effective strategy to reduce climate change risks. The impact of climate change is projected to have different effects within and between countries. Developing countries have to carefully evaluate the need for, and the roles of global and national institutions in promoting both mitigation and adaptation programmes. Mitigation and adaptation actions can, if appropriately designed, advance sustainable development and equity both within and across countries and between generations.[8] The pervasiveness of inertia and the possibility of irreversibility in the consequences of the interactions among climate, ecological and socio-economic systems are major reasons why anticipatory adaptation and mitigation actions are beneficial. Thus, the inertia and uncertainty imply that targets and timetables must be fixed for avoiding dangerous levels of interference in the climate system. A number of opportunities to exercise adaptation and mitigation options may be lost if action is delayed.

Global Climate Change: Effects

Global climate change has already been observable effects on the environment. Glaciers have shrunk, ice on rivers and lakes is breaking up earlier, plant and animal ranges have shifted and trees are flowering sooner. Scientists have high confidence that global temperatures will continue to rise for decades to come, largely due to greenhouse gases produced by human activities. The Intergovernmental Panel on Climate Change (IPCC) forecasts a temperature rise of 2.5 to 10 degrees Fahrenheit over the next century. According to IPCC, the extent of of climate change effects on individual regions will vary over time and with the ability of different societal and environmental systems to mitigate or adapt to change. The IPCC predicts that increases in the global mean temperature of less than 1.8 to 5.5 degrees Farenheit above 1990 levels will produce beneficial impacts in some regions and harmful ones in others. Below are some of the regional impacts of global climate changes forecast by IPCC:[9]

- *North America:* Decreasing snowpack in the western mountains, 5 to 20 per cent increase in yields of rain-fed agriculture in some regions.
- *Latin America:* Gradual replacement of tropical forest by savannah in eastern Amazonia, risk of significant biodiversity loss through species extinction in main tropical areas.
- *Europe:* Increased risk of inland flash floods, glacial retreat in mountainous areas, reduced snow cover and winter tourism.
- *Africa:* By 2020, between 75 and 200 million people are projected to be exposed to increased water stress, yields from rain-fed agriculture could be reduced by upto 50 per cent in some regions by 2020.
- *Asia:* Freshwater availability projected to decrease in Central, South, East and Southeast Asia by the 2050, coastal areas will be at risk due to increased flooding, death rates from disease associated with floods and droughts expected to rise in some regions.

India's Concern and Climate Change

India is a large developing country and most of her population directly depends on climate-sensitive sectors (agriculture, forests and fisheries) and natural resources (such as water, biodiversity, mangroves, coastal zones, grasslands) for their subsistence and livelihoods. Further, the adaptive capacity of dry land farmers, forest dwellers, fisher folk and nomadic shepherds is very low. Climate change is likely to impact all the natural ecosystems as well as socio-economic systems of India. Some of the projected impacts of climate change in India are as follows:[10]

Water resources: The hydrological cycle is likely to be altered and the severity of droughts and intensity of floods in various parts of India is likely to increase.

Agriculture: Simulations using dynamic crop models indicate a decrease in yield of crops as temperature increases in different parts of India. However, this is offset by an increase in CO_2 at moderate rise in temperature and at higher warming; negative impact on crop productivity is projected due to reduced crop durations.

Impact on health: Changes in climate may alter the distribution of important vector species (for example, malarial mosquitoes) and may increase the spread of such diseases in new areas.

Impact on forest: Climate impact assessments using BIOME-3 model and climate projections for the year 2085 show 77 per cent and 68 per cent of the forested grids in India are likely to experience shift in forest types under A2 and B2 scenario, respectively. Indications show a shift towards wetter forest types in the north-eastern region and drier forest types in the northwestern region in the absence of human influence. Increasing atmospheric CO_2 concentration and climate warming could also result in a doubling of net primary productivity under the A2 scenario and nearly 70 per cent increase under the B2 scenario.

Desertification: Climate change leading to warming and water stress could further exacerbate land degradation, leading to desertification. The United Nations Convention to Combat Desertification (UNCCD) aims to address the problem of land degradation, which is linked to climate change.

Coastal zone: Sea level rise is projected to displace populations in coastal zones, increase flooding in low-lying coastal areas, loss of crop yields from inundation and salinisation.

India's Response to Climate Change Challenges

The impact of Climate Change is so far-reaching that no country can now afford to sit on the side-lines. India, with 17 per cent of the world's population, contributes only 4 per cent of the total global greenhouse gas emissions against 30 per cent approx. of the US and 25 per cent of the EU countries. In terms of per capita GHG emissions, India is further lower (about 23 per cent of the global average) as compared with the per capita emission of US and in EU. The divergence in the status becomes starkly obvious when seen against the backdrop of the fact that around 55 per cent of India's population still does not have access to commercial energy. It has been India's stand not to agree to any commitments related to reducing greenhouse gas emissions. India stands for equity in global negotiations on climate change. India believes that since developed countries are more responsible for the problem, owing to their historical as well as current emissions, they must deliver on their commitments to stabilise and reduce their emissions of GHGs. In order to meet the demands of rising standards of living and providing access to commercial energy to those lacking it, the total emission of greenhouse gases is bound to increase in India and also in other developing countries.[11]

Climate Change and Sustainable Development in the Indian Context

India is committed to a path of sustainable development. Though India's per capita emissions are lowest in the world, we have recently adopted a National Action Plan on Climate Change. As a responsible nation, we are mindful of our obligations. Our efforts, of course, would be greatly enhanced with global support, especially in terms of financial flows and technology access. India has been pressing at the UN Framework Convention on Climate Change and other international conferences for collaborative development of clean technologies and immediate transfer of existing technologies which are environment friendly. India has also been trying to impress upon developed countries to transfer environmentally sound and cleaner energy technologies into the limited public domain for use by developing countries for early adoption, diffusion and deployment accompanied with transfer of financial resources. India had also called for early operationalisation of the Adaptation Fund and Special Climate Change Fund under the United Nations Framework Convention on Climate Change for addressing Climate Change issues in the developing countries. India is a partner to the new Asia Pacific Partnership on Clean Development and Climate which consists of key developed and developing countries— Australia, China, Japan, South Korea and the USA besides India. It focuses on development, diffusion and transfer of clean and more efficient technologies and is consistent with the principles of the UNFCCC and complements the efforts under the UNFCCC and will not replace the Kyoto Protocol. In the past two decades, the key environmental challenges in India have been sharper. *THE STATE OF THE ENVIRONMENT REPORT* by MoEF clubs the issues under five key challenges faced by India.[12]

1. Climate Change,
2. Food Security,
3. Water Security,
4. Energy Security,
5. Managing Urbanisation.

Climate change is disturbing the natural ecosystems and is expected to have substantial adverse effects in India mainly on agriculture, water storage in the Himalayan glaciers which are the source of major rivers and groundwater recharge, sea-level rise and threats to along coastline and habitations. Climate change will also cause increased frequency of extreme events such as floods and droughts. This in turn will impact India's food security problems and water security. As per the *Second National Communication*, submitted by India to the UNFCCC, it is projected that the annual mean surface air temperature rise by the end of the century ranges from 3.5 °C to 4.3 °C, whereas the sea level along the Indian coast has been rising at the rate of about 1.3 mm/year on an average. These climate change projections are likely to impact human health, agriculture, water resources, natural ecosystems and biodiversity. Concerned of the threats imposed by climate change and pressure on natural resources, sustainability and environment are increasingly taking centre stage in the Indian policy domain. India has been part of 94 multilateral environmental agreements. India has also voluntarily agreed to reduce its emission intensity of its GDP by 20-25 per cent over 2005 levels by 2020 and emissions from the agriculture sector would not form part of the assessment of its emission intensity. Indian economy is already moving along a lower carbon and sustainable path in terms declining carbon intensity of its GDP which is expected to fall further through low carbon strategies. It is estimated that India's per capita emission in 2031 will be lower than the global per capita emission in 2005. Together with the national efforts in different sectors, India also recognises that rural areas are equally prone to stress and pressure from natural resource exploitation. In this context, schemes for rural development and livelihood programmes are very relevant. A majority of the works under the MGNREGS are linked to land, soil and water. There are also programmes for non-timber forest produce-based livelihood, promotion of organic and low-chemical agriculture, and increase of soil health and fertility to sustain agriculture-based livelihoods. These schemes help mobilise and develop capacities of community institutions to utilise natural resources in a sustainable manner and their potential can be further developed. Along with efforts to incorporate sustainability in the rural development process, India is increasingly making efforts to integrate the three pillars of sustainable development into its national policy space. In fact, environment protection is enshrined in our Constitution (Articles 48A and 51 A[g]). Various policy measures are being implemented across the domains of forestry, pollution control, water management, Green Rating for Integrated Habitat Assessment, Coastal Zone Regulation Zone, Eco-Labelling, etc. Over a period of time, a stable organisational structure has been developed for environment protection. The Twelfth Plan with a prominent focus on sustainability makes provisions and provides for many more opportunities like this. Over the years, arguments in favour of looking beyond the conventional measure of GDP and taking into account the environmental damage caused by production of goods and services received attention. An expert group under ***Prof. Sir Partha Dasgupta*** has been set up to develop a framework for '***Green National Accounts***'. In fact, the ***Central Statistics Office*** has been publishing comprehensive environment statistics since 1997. The process of putting in place a system for natural resource accounting was initiated by ***MOSPI*** (Ministry of Statistics and Programme Implementation).[13]

India's Climate Friendly Measures and Sustainable Development

Despite the fact that India's contributions to greenhouse gas emissions are very small, the Government of India has taken many measures to improve the situation in this regard. The Ministry of Environment and Forests is the nodal agency for climate change issues in India. India has initiated several climate-friendly measures, particularly in the area of renewable energy. It has one of the most active renewable energy programmes besides having perhaps, the only dedicated Ministry for non-conventional energy sources in the world. India had adopted the National Environment Policy 2006 which provides for several measures and policy initiatives, to create awareness about climate change and help capacity building for taking adaptation measures. A major afforestation programme covering 6 mn hectares has been launched under the XIth Plan for this purpose. On 30th June 2008 India unveiled its National Action Plan on Climate Change (NAPCC) with a view to lay down the priorities and future actions of the government for addressing climate change and updating India's national programme relevant to addressing climate change. The National Action Plan identifies measures that promote our development objectives while also yielding co-benefits for addressing climate change effectively. Eight national missions (solar mission, energy efficiency, sustainable habitat, water, Himalayan ecosystem, green India, Eco-green agriculture and knowledge) have been specifically outlined to simultaneously advance India's development and climate change related objectives of adaptation and GHG mitigation. However, we have not set any quantitative goals towards emission reduction. Experts suggest working out quantitative goals and specific institutional mechanisms and regulations in respect of all eight missions, besides evolving certain feasible and verifiable indicators for each mission for their impact assessment. Besides, the Indian Government has initiated "Green India" programme which envisages undertaking massive afforestation of degraded forests land in the country. Financial resources to be mobilised include funds available under "Compensatory Afforestation Fund Management and Planning Authority (CAMPA)", mobilising funds from the market, developing partner associations, and income from tree felling at ecologically appropriate intervals.

Twelfth Five Year Plan on Sustainable Development and Climate Change[14]

The Twelfth Plan strategy suggests that there are significant co-benefits for climate action with inclusive and sustainable growth. India as a large responsible player with very low income has also to ensure that these efforts are matched by equitable and fair burden sharing among countries, taking into account the historical responsibilities for emissions. These issues are being discussed in the UNFCCC. India's approach to a low-carbon growth strategy explicitly recognises that policies have to be inclusive and differentiated across sectors according to national priorities, so as to lower the transaction costs of implementing the policy and conform to a nationally fair burden-sharing mechanism. An expert group on Low Carbon Strategies appointed by the Planning Commission has outlined the lower carbon strategies for the following major potential carbon mitigation sectors:

1. *Power-* On the supply side, adopt super-critical technologies in coal-based thermal power plants; use gas in combined heat and power systems; invest in renewable technologies. On the demand side, to accelerate adoption of super-efficient electrical appliances through market and regulatory mechanisms, enhance efficiency of agricultural pump sets and industrial equipment's with better technology; acceleration of power sector reforms.
2. *Transport-* To increase the share of rail in overall freight transport; to improve the efficiency of rail freight transport; improving the share and efficiency of public transport system; completion of dedicated rail corridor.
3. *Industry-* Adopting best available technology of Greenfield Plants in the iron - steel and cement sectors; modernise and adopt green technology at an accelerated place.
4. *Buildings-* Evolve and institutionalise green building codes at all levels of government.
5. *Forestry-* Green India Mission to regenerate at least 4 million ha of degraded forest; increase density of forest cover on 2 million ha of moderately dense forest; and overall increase the density of forest and tree cover on 10 million ha of forest, waste and community lands.

IPCC Assessment Report[15]

The Intergovernmental Panel on Climate Change reviews and assesses the most recent scientific, technical and socio-economic information produced worldwide relevant to climate change. The IPCC in its recent report published in 2014 has observed that there has been an increasing trend in the anthropogenic emissions of greenhouse gases since the advent of the industrial revolution. The period 1983-2012 is likely to have been the warmest thirty year period of the last 1400 years. Two major findings of the report are-

1. Contribution (Per cent) by different countries to cumulative global CO_2: USA(21.2), EU(18.4), CHINA(10.7), RUSSIA(7.4), BRAZIL (4.4), JAPAN(3.3), INDIA(2.8), CANADA(2.2).
2. Sectoral Emissions (Per cent) to Global Green House Gases: Electricity and Heat production (25), Agriculture, Forestry and Other land use (24), Industry (21), Other Energy (9.6) and Buildings (6.4).

Status and Progress of National Action Plan on Climate Change[16]

(i) *National Solar Mission*- Financial outlay allocated under 12th Plan is rupees 8795 crores. During 2014-14, additional 522 MW generation capacity by grid connected solar power projects.

(ii) *National Mission on Sustainable Habitat*-Total fund for implementing the programme was allocated equal to rupees 950 crores. Notable progress achieved under this mission includes-energy conservation building code 2007 made mandatory for new as well as old buildings, green building norms made mandatory for the CPWD since 2009.

(iii) *National Water Mission*- Financial outlay allocated under 12th Plan is rupees 196 crores.

(iv) *National Mission for Sustaining the Himalayan Ecosystem*- Financial outlay allocated under 12th Plan is rupees 1500 crores.

(v) *National Mission for Greener India*- Total fund for implementing the programme was allocated equal to rupees 1300 crores.

(vi) *National Mission on Sustainable Agriculture*-Financial outlay allocated under 12th Plan is rupees 1300 crores.

(vii) *National Mission on Strategic Knowledge for Climate Change*- Total fund for implementing the programme was allocated equal to rupees 2500 crores. However, the expenditure to undertake the activities under the scheme will be met out of the budget allocation of the existing scheme of the Department of Science and Technology.

Conclusion

Climate change is the defining issue of our times. It is perhaps, the greatest challenge to sustainable development. It should be addressed by all countries with a shared perspective, free from narrow and myopic considerations. The developed countries need to look beyond their narrow self-interests and work jointly with the developing countries to evolve cooperative and collaborative strategies on the issue of climate change, which is of immense relevance for the future of mankind. Climate change needs to be accounted as one of the potential risk factors affecting the outcome of any development programme and here comes the need for sustainable development. Fostering sustainable development requires the effective management of naturally human and physical capital. Global level generosity in promoting and protecting democracy, exchange of technology, maintaining stability of prices in various economies, judicious use of all environmental material throughout to enhance human development and sustainable development can be achieved only if the environment is conserved and improved. India is conscious of the challenges of climate change and has implemented several major programmes to address the climate variability concerns. However, the efforts so far in the direction of meeting the challenges of climate change have been sporadic and incoherent. We urgently need a new economic paradigm, which is global, inclusive, cooperative, environmentally sensitive and above all scientific. According to Jeffrey Sachs, a perceptive commentator, "The world's current ecological, demographic and economic trajectory is unsustainable, meaning that if we continue with "business as usual" we will hit social and ecological crises with calamitous results". Sustainable development based on addressing the needs of the poor and optimal harnessing of scarce resources of water, air, energy, land, and biodiversity will have to be sustained through more cooperative endeavours. Then alone, we could make some headway in saving our lone planet from the brink of climate disasters.

References

1. Dasgupta, Chandrashekhar, 'Shifts on Climate Change', The Telegraph, Calcutta, 2 September, 2008.
2 Dutt, Gautam and Gaioli, Fabiina, 'Coping with Climate Change', Economic and Political Weekly, 20 Oct., 2007.
3. Shivay ,Y.S. and Rahal, Anshu, 'Effect of Global Warming on Crop Productivity', Kurukshetra, July 2008.
4. Morton, Oliver, 'Megachange: The World in 2050', The Economist, London, 2012.
5. *Ibid.*
6. Dutt, Gautam and Gaioli, Fabiina, 'Coping with Climate Change', Economic and Political Weekly, 20 Oct., 2007.
7. Twelfth Five Year Plan, 2012-17, Govt. of India.
8. Economic Survey (various issues), Govt. of India.
9. Shukla, P. R., Rana, A., Garg, A., Kapshe, M. and Nair R., 'Climate Change Assessment for India: Applications of Asia Pacific Integrated Model (AIM)', Universities Press, Hyderabad, 2004.
10. Economic Survey (various issues), Govt. of India.
11. Human Development Report (various issues), UNDP.
12. Biodiversity and Climate Change: Ecosystems (http://www.unep-wcmc.org/climate /impacts.aspx)
13. Climate Change and its Impact of India (http://www.greenpeace.org/india/campaigns/choose-positive-energy/what-is-climate-change...).
14. Twelfth Five Year Plan, 2012-17, Govt. of India.
15. IPCC Assessment Report (Fifth Assessment Report, 2014).
16. Economic Survey, Govt. of India, (2015-16).

Chapter - 15

Religiousity, Environmental Strands and Social Justice: A Multi-Dimensional Analysis of *Kumbh Mela* at Allahabad City

—Ashish Saxena and Vijaylaxmi Saxena

In recent global era, there has been a spectacular growth in public consciousness about the forms of environmental degradation in India. With an amazing but welcome rapidity, this awareness is being translated on the one hand into substantial media coverage, and on the other into the creation of new government departments concerned with different aspects of environment management. All over the world people from local to global level have been directly victimised by the depletion of natural resources due to the short-lived developmental activities initiated by the modern forms of state apparatuses are organised themselves to raise the voice against the over exploitation of natural resources. Departing from the conventional categorisation of social movements based on ethnic, class, gender differences, these new social movements attracted voice of the people from different part of the world regardless of class, creed, colour or gender for a common cause called protection of our environment. The theory of Ecological Modernisation perhaps put forward a radical transformational phase as the way modern society grapples with the environment question. While coming down to Indian experience, religion is one of the most important facets of history and contemporary life. It may not be wrong to say that religion has been, and continues to be, a matter of absorbing interest for many in India still today. In former centuries no aspect of life was set apart from religion. All social relations were inevitably and legitimately suffused with religious ideas and acts. The possibility of religion in a modern world can be felt through altered functioning of religion. The marketisation of religion by religious gurus performing miracles and fascinating public, the involvement of religious organisations in the building up of hospitals and schools, working for the victims of natural disasters etc. and politicisation of religion by the outburst of fundamentalists reflect its altered character. Thus, in contemporary India, the impact of modernisation has led to the emergence of new religions, revivals, and reforms within the great traditions. In modern societies, with their complex fabric of social differentiations, not only among religion, but other groups and social activities, there appears a proliferation of rites. It is believed that during the auspicious astrological moment, the waters of the Ganges have the ability to wash away layer upon layer of karmic debt. Millions of Hindus have already started pouring into the northern Indian city of Allahabad for the Kumbh Mela *festival. Such a large-scale event poses unfathomable challenges for organisers, especially when it comes to sanitation. Even if enduring hardship is integral to the act of pilgrimage and even if such hardships do not deter pilgrims from attending these various circumstances - unsanitary conditions, severe cold, dense crowding and intense noise - are all those that would be expected to be bad for well-being. But are they? We ask if, in the light of social psychological research identifying associations between involvement in social group-related activities and well-being, participation in this mass gathering could impact well-being positively. Thus, against the dysfunctionality of crowd of '*Mela*' as source of nuisance, mismanagement and cheats, this work humbly tries to explore the critical functionality of historical 'Prayag* Kumbh*'. It is observed that 'religious* Mela*' has a spread-effect of maintaining sanitation through collective participation. It is emphasised that socialisation of good sanitation practices to the pilgrims can be instrumental in carrying it further at far flung areas of diverse India and making clean and green India. To this end, the Indian government set up a special administration body about a year ago that is responsible for the smooth-running of the festival. But the people who make it work are the cleaners. They're the lowest paid, and they're working round the clock. There are thousands of street cleaners, then there's a smaller group that cleans the water. Further, by going through the factors responsible for the failure of Ganga Action Plan (GAP), the parliamentary standing committee on science and technology, environment and forests has doubts if the Prime Minister's mission of cleaning Ganga by 2020 will be accomplished.*

Key Words: *Religion, Kumbh Mela, Environment, Sanitation, Social Justice, Allahabad.*

Background

In recent years, there has been a spectacular growth in public consciousness about the forms of environmental degradation in India. With an amazing but welcome rapidity, this awareness is being translated on the one hand into substantial media coverage, and on the other into the creation of new government departments concerned with different aspects of environment management. All over the world people from local to global level have been directly victimised by the depletion of natural resources due to the short-lived developmental activities initiated by the modern forms of state apparatuses are organised themselves to raise the voice against the over exploitation of natural resources. Although the voices were inaudible in the initial period, later on it got appreciation once the external agencies like media, civil society and social activists took this issue very seriously into the public discourse. Because of this combination of voices gave birth to institutionalisation of social movements by articulating the need for restoring our natural resources and adopting alternative views of development and modernisation. Departing from the conventional categorisation of social movements based on ethnic, class, gender differences, new social movements of this kind voyage new discourse in the public domain attracted voice of the people from different part of the world regardless of class, creed, colour or gender for a common cause called protection of our environment. Ecological modernisation theory perhaps puts forward a radical transformational phase as the way modern society grapple with the environment question. In so doing, the institutions of modern society, such as the market, the state and science and technology, need to be radically transformed in tune with the environmental crisis, but not beyond recognition.

Religion is one of the most important facets of Indian history and contemporary life. It may not be wrong to say that religion has been, and continues to be, a matter of absorbing interest for many in India still today. In former centuries no aspect of life was set apart from religion. All social relations were inevitably and legitimately suffused with religious ideas and acts. The possibility of religion in a modern world can be felt through altered functioning of religion. The marketisation of religion by religious gurus performing miracles and fascinating public, the involvement of religious organisations in the building up of hospitals and schools, working for the victims of natural disasters etc. and politicisation of religion by the outburst of fundamentalists reflect the altered character of it. Modern forces have certainly influenced folk culture and traditions in developing countries like India, but they have not as yet lost their vigor. References to modern objects, events and experiences find their way into folklore through the usual process of reworking traditional items, the composition of new pieces, and even the merger of new types. Thus, in contemporary India, the impact of modernisation has led to the emergence of new religions, revivals, and reforms within the great traditions. In modern societies, with their complex fabric of social differentiations, not only among religion, but other groups and social activities, there appears a proliferation of rites (see Saxena, 2009). It is believed that during this auspicious astrological moment, the waters of the Ganges have the ability to wash away layer upon layer of karmic debt. Millions of Hindus have already started pouring into the northern Indian city of Allahabad for the *Kumbh Mela* festival. Such a large-scale event poses unfathomable challenges for organisers, especially when it comes to sanitation.

Those pilgrims who stay for the whole month (known as *Kalpwasis*) live in conditions that are more difficult than those they experience at home. They live in rudimentary tents without heating, often without sanitary facilities, sleeping on the ground and experiencing night-time temperatures approaching zero centigrade. The event is also very crowded, and again this contrasts with life in the villages from which the pilgrims come. The crowds make walking to the bathing areas difficult and on days that bathing is judged particularly auspicious in terms of Hindu traditions, it can take several hours to walk a kilometre or so. Another striking feature of the event is its noise level. A vast array of competing loudspeakers broadcast religious discourses, songs, announcements and other administrative information throughout the day (and into the night).

Even if enduring hardship is integral to the act of pilgrimage and even if such hardships do not deter pilgrims from attending, these various circumstances-unsanitary conditions, severe cold, dense crowding and intense noise-are all those that would be expected to be bad for well-being. But are they? We ask if, in the light of social psychological research identifying associations between involvement in social group-related activities and well-being, participation in this mass gathering could impact well-being positively. Thus, against the dysfunctionality of crowd of '*Mela*' as source of nuisance, mismanagement and cheats, this work humbly tries to explore the functionality of historical 'Prayag *Kumbh*'. It is observed that 'religious *Mela*' has a spread-effect of maintaining sanitation through collective participation. It is emphasised that socialisation of good sanitation practices to the pilgrims can be instrumental in carrying it further at far flung areas of diverse India and making clean and green India.

Idea of Social Justice in Societal Framework

Sanitation and hygiene are critical to health, survival, and development. Many countries are challenged in providing adequate sanitation for their entire populations, leaving people at risk for water, sanitation, and hygiene (WASH)-related diseases. Sanitation is observed as an overall reform of any society including physical, social, psychological, economic, political and religious. It encompasses all spheres of human life which directly or indirectly affects the degree of freedom and well-being of the members of the society. It is based on the issue of justice and also removal of all forms of injustice leading to better life-chances and life-styles of human being.

Before linking the sanitation and justice, let us understand the notion of social justice as discussed by various social scientists. Plato (380 BC) said that justice was achieved when each person received goods they deserved based on their prescribed position in the social order. Aristotle (384-322 BC) said that justice was a principle that ensured social order by regulating the distribution of benefits. However, in Aristotle's view, equality and justice applied only to individuals who occupied the same stratum of the hierarchical social order. According to these ideas of social justice, unequals in the social hierarchy are to be treated unequally. These ideas did not challenge the social structures of society, but worked within them.

Utilitarians like John Stuart Mill argued that the distribution of societal goods should be for the 'greatest net balance of satisfaction' for society. Mill said that utilitarianism was actually a 'standard of morality' which used happiness of the greater number of people as its ultimate goal. In principle, although utilitarianism advocates for the greatest good for the greatest number of people in a society. Rawls' concept of social justice is probably the most influential. Rawls criticised utilitarianism as being able to be used to justify concentration of goods benefiting privileged classes of society on the basis that it was for the greater good. Rawls' conception of distributive justice provided that "all social values... are to be distributed equally unless an unequal distribution of any or all of these values is to everyone's advantage" (See Rawls; 1971).

To Amartya Sen, we might note at the outset, that we would choose to be governed by two principles of justice, the first guaranteeing fundamental individual liberties (of speech, association and worship, among others), and the second ensuring that social and economic inequalities are arranged to offer the greatest possible benefit to the worst-off in society, while upholding fair equality of opportunity.

The concept of social justice is an essential part of the broader concept of justice. In general, Greeks used the term 'justice' equivalent to 'virtue', while in modern times it is used as 'getting ones due'. The pertinent question here is how to determine what is a man's due and this brings us to the relationship between justices in general and social justice. In particular, social justice concerns the distribution of benefits and burdens throughout a society, as it results from the major social institution – property system, public organisation, etc. Thus, broadly distribution of power allocation of benefits, material as well as tangible such as wealth, prestige and self respect have to be the most important concerns of social justice.

Historically speaking, the birth of the concept of social justice coincided with shifts in human consciousness: the "death of God", the rise of science and the rise of the ideal of the "command economy" leading to scientific socialism i.e. reasons and intellectuals were supposed to rule. The roots of social justice thus lie in the thought process of enlightenment. The development of a scientific and rational viewpoint led to corresponding changes in the social thought process, which, in turn, initiated radical changes in the political and social structure of Europe, especially during the Renaissance. Thus, social justice, both as a concept and as a socially cherished goal, came into prominence during the French Revolution (1789) as far as Europe is concerned.

Significant philosophers had propounded there own ideas of justice. John Stuart Mill gave anthropomorphic approach by stating that-'Society should treat all equally well who have deserved equally well of it, that is, who have deserved equally well absolutely. This is the highest abstract standard of social and distributive justice; towards which all virtuous citizens, should be made in the utmost degree to convergence'.

J.J. Rousseau was a dreamer of an ideal just society. He wanted to build a genuine and humane community. He argued that men are equal by nature but the institution of private property has made them unequal and further perpetuated inequalities. Therefore, the perfection of man lies in the improvement of society that can be done by remaking man by cultivating natural feelings and sentiments which guarantee equality and social justice. He argued that the institution could be re-moulded in such a way as to realise a just and democratic society (Tilly, 2000).

For William Frankena, the concept of just society should emphasise on the principle and practical aspect of it. Therefore, he conceives social justice as part of political justice that emphasises to create just society. Charles Evans says that justice is giving every man his due and conceptualises justice as deserved treatment. For Robert Nozick historical entitlement is an important element of distributive justice where the society is aware of its wrongs and has an increased interest in compensation. Therefore, for him, backward-looking concepts are important that address the distribution of goods in society as social justice.

John Rawls conceptualise 'justice as fairness' where there is desirability of advantage for the marginalised groups in some respect. It includes the first principle that each person is to have an equal right to the most extensive total system of equal basic liberties compatible with a similar system of liberty for all; Second principle that social and economic inequalities are to be arranged so that they are both–(a) to the greatest benefit of the least advantaged, consistent with the just savings principle, and (b) attached to offices and positions open to all under conditions of fair equality of opportunity. To Rawls (Rawls; 1971), justice as fairness tries to uncover the latent ideas of freedom and equality, of ideal social cooperation, and of the person, by formulating two 'model conception', one of a 'well-ordered society and another of a 'moral person'.

There can be no single application of theory of social justice and no definite prescription of justice can be made. For Miller, therefore, a concept such as justice may possess sociological investigation awareness of cultural diversity and conceptual change (Miller, 1976).

Fundamentally, the basic premise of social justice remains to be the emancipation of the underprivileged, exploited, and oppressed section of society. Its main aim is to liberate mankind from traditional bondages of social and economic exploitation and discrimination. It postulates a social order which can guarantee freedom, mobility and equal rights to all section of society.

Social justice is a specific habit of justice that is 'social' in two senses:-

- The skills it requires are those of inspiring, working with, and organising others to accomplish together a work of justice.

These are the elementary skills of civil society, through which free citizens exercise self-government by doing for themselves what needs to be done.

- It aims at the good of the society and not as the good of one agent only.

Here Tocqueville rightly says that– "the principle of association is the first law of democracy, and then social justice is the first virtue off democracy, for it is the habit of putting the principle of association into daily practice".

In brief, Justice in broader sense includes: principle of equality; principle of utility; principle of compensatory justice; justice as fairness; social justice.

In opposition to Rawls' Theory of Justice, Robert Nozick has formulated the idea of social justice as entitlement. According to Nozick, individuals have a right to own property and of self-ownership, which gives them the freedom to determine what to do with what is theirs. The role of the state is that of a night-watchman, to protect individual property rights. Nozick regards any attempt by the State to (re)distribute resources, e.g. through taxation, as unjust. Miller's approach to social justice rests on the idea that the market is capable of giving individuals what they deserve. This theory treats individuals as responsible for their own actions and proportionately rewards (or punishes) them in accordance with their actions and efforts, insofar as the actions/efforts are the result of their individual choices. According to Sen (2009), the effectiveness of government action to improve social justice is judged according to an individual's capability to do things he or she values and the freedom of individuals to choose between different ways of leading their lives. Sen's approach to social justice focuses on assuring individual capacities to gain optimal wellbeing in their circumstances. He defines poverty as the deprivation of these basic 'capabilities' (such as being literate, being active in the community).

Idea of Hygiene

Hygiene is not just about cleanliness, but also about the conditions, activities and practices which protect health and prevent diseases. Hygiene refers to a procedure or system of procedures or activities used to reduce microbial contamination on environmental sites and surfaces in order to prevent the transmission of infectious disease (IFH, 2001). Thus, hygiene involves personal, domestic and community hygiene. In a developing country context, good hygiene practices might be particularly important in the presence of poor sanitary conditions. They include, therefore, perhaps most importantly, adequate hand washing, domestic cleaning, and removal of contamination in the outdoor environment, particularly where children are present.

The state of environmental sanitation influences both the infecting agent and any of the individuals exposed to that environment. The significance of hygiene becomes greater when environmental sanitation is poor and vice versa. Provisions, such as safe water supply, sanitary disposal of excreta and other wastes, good housing, genial climate, and pollution-free surroundings, provide effective barriers to the spread of infectious diseases. There are many human-related factors that determine whether a person is susceptible or resistant to an invading infective agent. Susceptibility to infection rests on lifestyle, behaviour and mind-set. Lifestyle factors that provide protection from infectious diseases include: positive health behaviour, healthy housing, safe occupation and work place, interest in health preservation and disease prevention, sustainable income, nutrition security, food hygiene, sanitary facilities such as for excreta disposal and safe drinking water, personal hygienic practices including washing hands before meals and after using the toilet, and good public health services. Protection has to be provided at the community, family and individual level.

On a personal level, hygiene consists of health consciousness, cleanliness, hand washing, safe drinking water, sanitary disposal of waste, freedom from addiction to tobacco and/or alcohol. Domestic and personal hygiene and the behaviour, habits and practices of its members determine the health of a household. Hygiene practice involves active efforts by every individual and family and is best instilled early on in childhood. Hygiene is largely a matter of human behaviour, which is determined by social traditions, customs and culture. Furthermore, health consciousness and awareness of factors injurious or conducive to health, and motivation and concern for taking steps to protect health and prevent disease, can change behaviour and promote a healthy lifestyle. Active efforts are possible only with the proper mind-set and if there is motivation to keep disease away. Habits such as defecation in the open are cultural. With urbanisation, modern housing, health development and national sanitation programmes, the use of sanitary latrines are on the increase. Such environmental adaptations at domestic or household situation result in variations in the degree of exposure to the risk of infection and other epidemiological factors which are locally significant and determine the state of familial and individual health or disease.

Life and behaviour of an individual who is health conscious will be quite different from that of another person who is indifferent to health or personal hygiene. An enlightened person acquires knowledge, seeks advice, and makes an effort to improve hygiene and health behaviour, while a person or family who is apathetic does not care about what happens to them or their surroundings. Every community has these two kinds of people and the magnitude of prevalence of infectious disease in any community depends on the proportion and distribution of these two types of people. Therefore, it is not uncommon to encounter unaffected persons or families, even in an event or outbreak of infectious disease in the locality. It is important to note that a community which observes simple rules of hygiene is more healthy and free from infectious disease than one which does not. Provision of a free water supply, immunisation services, sanitary conveniences, or health education, may not necessarily benefit people, if these facilities are used indifferently or not at all.

Many traditions and customs have become ritualistic or meaningless and the hygienic principles behind these practices lost. For instance, indiscriminate spitting is largely due to the lack of aesthetic and civic sense, rather than a deliberate act to pollute the environment or promote the spread of infection. Similarly, many people do not spit simply because they regard it as unstylish or a sign of backwardness, and not because of an awareness of the risk of tuberculosis. Merely telling people that the habit is unhygienic will have little impact. On the other hand, factors such as health awareness, knowledge of health and disease, and willingness to take steps to prevent diseases, do change behaviour. A good example is the increased use of bottled mineral water for drinking while on travel or eating out. This type of behavioural change helps to prevent alimentary infections.

Health behaviour is modified by a change of mind-set. An individual may use a particular health facility or follow a hygienic practice, but this does not guarantee that they will necessarily continue to use the available facilities. Many incidences of disease or their absence are due to differences in micro-ecosystems, human behaviour and lifestyles. Improvement in public health will certainly prevent infectious diseases in some families, but unfortunately this may not be universal for everybody.

For modifying a lifestyle and making it conducive to prevention of infectious diseases, current style of living should be studied in relation to hygienic practices. Elements which will have to be taken care of include:

- Regularity synchronises daily routines and habits to the body cycles and rhythms. Regularity prevents functional imbalance of various systems and enhances body defence mechanisms. Modern life has become hectic and irregular, especially in urban life, which makes people more susceptible to infectious disease.
- Moderation of food, work, recreation or rest is another golden rule of hygiene. Avoidance of extremes has even been advocated in Indian scriptures that advise *ati sarvatra varjayet* (discard excesses universally). The stresses the body is exposed to in modern life are due to immoderation rendering it vulnerable to infection and disease.
- Housing condition and the neighbourhood influence hygiene. This includes poor ventilation and overcrowding which facilitate the spread of airborne infections. Dampness in the home predisposes the occupant to rheumatic fever, while internal air pollutants such as dry sweepings, poor ventilation, and incomplete combustion of domestic fuels like wood, coal and cow-dung can also be harmful. In India, 80 per cent of households use solid fuel and about a half million

Indian children die annually from indoor air pollution, especially from acute respiratory infection (WHO, 2000).

- Cleanliness is a protective measure to minimise health hazards by providing an effective barrier against the risk of exposure to the disease-producing agents. Generally, the environment is full of the disease-causing germs. The hands, skin, body discharges and expired air should all be considered as potentially contaminated with harmful germs. Uncleanliness and dirty habits cause much morbidity and mortality, especially with respect to diseases of the digestive system. Washing feet or removing footwear before entering the house, washing hands thoroughly with water after using the latrine, and before cooking, handling or eating food, and cutting nails short to keep them clean, are all hygiene measures that reduce the risk of acquiring and transferring infections, particularly when used in conjunction with soap.
- Sanitation is a social and public responsibility. Faeces, animal excreta, urine and other kinds of waste often contain pathogens, necessitating proper modes of sanitary disposal. However, health authorities in India often give hygiene and sanitation a low priority. Most villagers, slum dwellers, and domestic servants, even those working in more affluent areas, have to resort to passing urine or defecation by the roadside or in open spaces. Efforts to discourage these bad habits and promote the use of sanitary latrines and urinals are worthwhile and necessary in the prevention of disease.
- Personal habits. Measures on a more personal level can be adopted. For example, regular use of proper footwear not only protects feet from injury, but also to a certain extent from diseases such as tetanus, hookworm and snakebites. Habits such as indiscriminate spitting and littering help in spreading diseases like tuberculosis and diarrhoea. Open defecation and tolerating dirt in the environment too are examples of negative health behaviour that should be eliminated as much as possible.
- Nutrition is essential for protection against infections. The immune mechanism of the body is dependent on an adequate and balanced diet. In order to avoid the risk of infectious diseases, observance of food hygiene is essential. Secondly, if the intake of food is just adequate or marginal, once infection is introduced and caloric requirement goes up, a vicious cycle of malnutrition and infection may become established. The effects are particularly serious in children aged between six months and two years of age.

- Positive thinking, attitude and mind-set are beneficial for health and social values. Worry and anxiety are non-productive, while optimism strengthens our power to defend against infections.
- Occupation is essential for health and livelihood. However, certain occupations expose people to infective agents that may lead to diseases such as leptospirosis, brucellosis and anthrax. Sewage workers, for example, and sweepers are exposed to pathogenic germs unless they use protective clothing and proper tools.
- Social factors including working conditions, family life and friends influence domestic and personal hygiene. A high tolerance to a dirty environment is an invitation to infectious diseases and vectors like houseflies. Vegetables, food, faecal matter and any other decaying organic matter provide all the material that flies require to breed, and are readily available because people are indiscriminate in disposal of these items. Breast-feeding provides immuno protection for the baby against diseases, while bottle-feeding on the other hand is frequently linked to contamination that causes diarrhoea in infants.
- Financial status has a significant impact on lifestyle and hygiene. Many cities and towns in India are without sewerage, and most municipal corporations discharge raw sewage without proper treatment directly into rivers thereby polluting the water. At the family level, economic status shows a direct relationship with health status (see Deodhar, 2003).

Hygiene Promotion

Improving access to safe water and sanitation facilities leads to healthier families and communities. However, when people are also motivated to practice good hygiene–especially hand-washing with soap–health benefits are significantly increased. Because the evidence on the importance of hand-washing with soap is clear, UNICEF has made it a programme priority. It helps to promote hand-washing and hygiene behavioural change by:

- advocating for increased funding for hygiene activities and the inclusion of hygiene in sectoral policies and strategies;
- supporting national and sub-national hand-washing campaigns;
- recruiting high-profile decision-makers and celebrities as hand-washing advocates;
- including strong hygiene components within its own WASH programmes in the field;
- ensuring that hand-washing and hygiene are components of emergency response programmes;

- developing strategies and tools to encourage hand-washing promotion by community health and outreach workers;
- Encouraging hygiene promotion in schools and the empowerment of children as agents of change within their families and communities.

Education and communication are important components of a hygiene promotion programme. All people have a right to know about the relationship between water, sanitation, hygiene and the health of themselves and their families. However, education alone does not necessarily result in improved practices. Knowing about the causes of disease may help, but new hygiene practices may be too unfamiliar, too difficult, or take too much time, especially for poor people. Promoting behavioural change is a gradual process that involves working closely with communities, studying existing beliefs, defining motivation strategies, designing appropriate communication tools and finally encouraging practical steps towards positive practices. Communities should be fully engaged in the process at all stages using participatory processes, and special attention should be given to building on local knowledge and promoting existing positive traditional practices. Behavioural change is necessary not only at the community level, but among decision-makers as well. All stakeholders–from politicians and government officials to field workers and people themselves–must be encouraged to recognise the importance of hygiene.

Sociology of Sanitation and its Association with *Kumbh Mela*

Present paper tries to develop an inter-linkage between environment, religion and polity. In Durkheimenian framework, one can observe 'sociology of sanitation' as a shift from profane to sacred elements. Locating the issue of sanitation L. Dumount rightly states that the Indian society is homo-hierarchicus resting on the religion with caste system having an element of 'pure' and 'impure'. Even M.N. Srinivas too speaks about 'purity and pollution', having bearing on caste interactions. His concept of '*sanskritisation*' has an inherent notion of sanitation for lower caste members. If one goes philosophically on the issue of sanitation of soul, one finds that 'secularisation' reflects decline in the religious intolerance and accommodation of diverse religious practices for healthy society. The doctrine of Hindu religion also focuses on sanitation with the purification of ones '*paap*' in the lifetime. Thus, sanitation of body and soul as a precondition for attaining *moksh* after death and for once re-birth. Even, performing once duties in the holy pilgrimage is deeply embedded in religio-philosophical matrix of Indian psyche. At this juncture the pilgrimage of '*Prayag Kumbh*' becomes crucial. The paper locates issues of 'sanitation' in the pilgrimage of '*Prayag Kumbh*'. Here emphasis is on 'power of sanitation' as an ideology and an instrument of maintaining sanctity and religious purity.

In the present paper an attempt has been made to observe the emergence of the environmental discourses and transition of sanitation issues owing to the famous *Kumbh mela* at holy *Sangam Nagri*, Allahabad. To refer MacLean (2003), historically speaking, the *Kumbh Mela* was applied to Allahabad's extant *Magh Mela* in the 1860s by *Pragwals* (river pandas [priests] of Prayag [Allahabad]) working upon and within the limits imposed by the colonial state and its discourses. This process was inadvertently aided by the British, and the resulting *mela* was affirmed by sadhus (Hindu holy men) and pilgrims. The "ageless" *Kumbh Mela* in Allahabad was therefore made by a combination of actors, responding to the aggrandizement and growth of the modern state, particularly its infrastructure, administration, and preference for well-controlled, predictable, orderly, and traditional manifestations of religion. In this sense, the making of the Allahabad *Kumbh* is not merely another example of an invented tradition; indeed, had it been suspected of being invented in any sense, it would not have been accommodated by the British to the extent that it was. The first phase of the understanding can be restricted to the colonial interventions wherein the *Kumbh* in Allahabad offers a complex illustration of how Indian actors, working with and reacting to British Orientalist assumptions, cast a major cultural and religious event. In carefully constructing a religious festival, they created for themselves a sphere in which they could enjoy some autonomy in the atmosphere of an increasingly repressive colonial state, despite post-mutiny promises of freedom (Oldenburg, 1989).

The first mention of a *Kumbh Mela* in British administrative reports that have been able to find, however, is in the closing discussion of an 1868 report about pilgrimage and sanitation controls. In this light, the application of the *Kumbh Mela* tradition to an existing religious festival-the Magh *Mela* can be seen as an attempt by *Pragwal*s to expand the fame of their tirtha. The environment of the later nineteenth century was not a favourable one for Allahabad's pilgrimage priests, a time when, recovering from an anti-*Pragwal* campaign after the rebellion, the *mela* was assailed with an aggressive missionary presence (Bayly, 1975, 106). The new government, despite promises of religious freedom, not only defended missionary labours at the *mela* but also voiced strong objections to pilgrimage on sanitary grounds, debating the wisdom of disallowing *mela*s altogether. In addition, there were optimistic predictions that pilgrimage in India would, "as it did in Medieval Europe," soon "die out or decrease as the minds of the people become more enlightened and as their information is increased, as other modes of education prevail and as trading customs alter" (see reference see MacLean, 2003). The demographic of pilgrims had changed in the nineteenth century from being princely and extremely wealthy to a more prosperous peasantry, with the result that, instead of relying exclusively upon princely patronage (which had, with the princes themselves, begun to decline), places of pilgrimage had to adapt to suit their new clientele. In 1868, the district magistrate of Allahabad noted that at the Magh *Mela* "the attendance consisted chiefly of the middle and lower classes of people and no Rajas attended this year as they generally have done and their absence has affected the profits of *Pragwal*s and the traders. For increasingly prosperous villagers, attending the *mela* was a means of expressing their status. Not only did pilgrimage still carry the aura of the elites, who, in former times, were the only ones who could afford to embark upon what was an expensive and dangerous enterprise, but establishing ties with a priest at a major pilgrimage centre gave enterprising peasants the opportunity to document their family and property. Lineages could be claimed and inscribed into *Pragwal* registers, as could claims to land ownership, which could be used as evidence in court cases should any dispute ever arise (Fusfeld, 1974, 20).

Hostility directed towards the minorities has been a feature of the *Kumbh Mela*, especially after 1966 when the VHP first appeared on the scene and was permitted to organise the 'religious conference'. In 1966, the main plank of the VHP had been the unity of the Hindus through the popularisation of the three cults of Mother India, Mother Ganga and Mother Cow. In 1978, the conversion of Hindus and the threat to Hindu ethos as posed by, for example, secular historiography were made the focus. And now in 1989 the VHP is flexing its muscles (See Navalakha; 1989).

Locating the Emergence of Environmental Sanitation and Health Issues

Although, the first mention of a *Kumbh Mela* in British administrative reports that I have been able to find, however, is in the closing discussion of an 1868 report about pilgrimage and sanitation controls. Contemporarily, The United Provinces *Mela*s Act, 1938 is vested with the power to impose tolls, taxes and fees under Section 5 in *mela* areas–tolls on any vehicle or animal entering, or person bringing goods for sale into such areas; Without prejudice the office-in-charge may allot sites for the following in particular - religious societies of persuasion, kalpbasis, market places, laterines, urinals and rubbish heaps, recreation and entertainments. Even the United Provinces *Mela*s rule miscellaneous, Oct. 16, 1940 says that a person suffering from plague smallpox or other infectious diseases shall not enter the *mela* area. The Officer-in-charge shall order any person found within *mela* araea suffering from an infectious disease either to leave the *Mela* or to enter the infectious disease hospital within a fixed time.

As reflected in local and national newspapers (*Times of India,* December 2012 and *Amar Ujala* December 2012), recently in 2013 *kumbh mela*, the Indian government set up a special administration body about a year ago that is responsible for the smooth-running of the festival. But the people who make it work are the cleaners. They're the lowest paid, and they're working around the clock. There are thousands of street cleaners, then there's a smaller group that cleans the water. There are lots of different camps of holy men, and they all want to take their dips first, because they want the water to be clear. People take dips in the water every day, but when the holy men take their dips it attracts big crowds-people want to dip at the same time as the holy men. The dips are staggered–there's always a half hour gap between each dip, so the cleaners and can go into the waters and clean. They don't use chemical products; they fish out any objects left behind, like the flowers people take with them to bathe. It seemed the weak links were water and sanitation-water leakage, not enough taps.

Recently, in the run-up to the festival, around 35,000 single-seat latrines, 340 blocks of 10-seat toilets, and 4,000 urinals on-site. They're linked by a 165 kilometre network of plastic pipes which carry the waste to pits, which themselves are reinforced by brick. It'll be interesting to see how many new latrines and pits the administration will have to build, as what they've built so far may not be enough. People do not always use the toilets, particularly children–they just go in the open air. There are 9,000 sweepers, whose job it is to sweep away faeces into the pits. Waterborne diseases and a cholera outbreak are real risks. We hope to carry out research that will help the administration prevent the impact of waterborne diseases. Even, the area of the *mela* is also on the rise: from 1,495.31 hectare and 11 sectors in 2001 to 1936.56 hectare and 14 sectors in 2013 (see official website of Kumbh *mela* 2013).

According to national newspaper reports, arrangements provided 5,000 gallons of purified drinking water every minute; 8,000 buses which shuttle pilgrims in and out of the festival area that spread over 3,00- acres; 16,000 outlets and 6,000 poles which provided electrical facilities; 6,000 sweepers and sanitation employees who worked around the clock to maintain health standards; nine pontoon bridges which spanned the Ganges at intervals. Although, the Indian government set up a special administration body about a year ago that is responsible for the smooth-running of the festival. But the people who make it work are the cleaners. They're the lowest paid, and they're working around the clock. There are thousands of street cleaners, then there's a smaller group that cleans the water. Further, agitated over high levels of pollution and shallow water in the holy Ganga, the Shankracharyas, seers and *Dandi swamis*, along with all the '*akaharas*', are all set to boycott the next '*Shahi Snan*' on *Mauni Amavasya* scheduled for February 10, 2013. These saints, on Friday, threatened that if the situation remained unchanged, they will not bathe in the next *Shahi Snan*.

By going through the factors responsible for the failure of Ganga Action Plan (GAP), the parliamentary standing committee on science and technology, environment and forests has doubts if the Prime Minister's mission of cleaning Ganga by 2020 will be accomplished. Our vision is that in 12 years' time, every camp at the *Kumbh Mela* will be green, and every pilgrim will be reminded that it is the sacred duty of every Hindu to protect the environment."

Conclusion

It is reflected that the role of religious ideology and socio-religious leaders too have become active players towards generating environmental sanitation. In conclusion it is urged that the "size and complexity" of the *Kumbh Mela* is inspirational for inter-disciplinary research in a number of complementary fields of urban studies and design, religious and cultural studies, environmental science and public health, technology and communications. There is a need to bring the issue of 'Right to sanitation' and also '*sulabhisation*' of pilgrimage sites. Needless to mention that environmental sanitation is the growing concern of the hour.

References

Bayly, C .A. 1975. *The Local Roots of Indian Politics, Allahabad, 1880-1920*. Oxford: Clarendon Press.

Deodhar, N.S. (2003). 'Epidemiological perspective of domestic and personal hygiene in India', *International Journal of Environmental Health Research*, 13:S1, S47-S56.

Fusfeld, Warren E. 1974. '*The Kumbh Mela in Allahabad: Networks of Communication in Nineteenth Century North India*' Master's thesis, University of Pennsylvania.

Ghurye, G. S. 1964. *Indian Sadhus*. Bombay: Popular Prakashan.

Gordon, Richards. 1975. 'The Hindu Mahasabha and the Indian National Congress, 1915 to 1926', *Modern Asian Studies*, Vol. 9, No. 2 (1975), pp. 145-203.

IFH. 2001. Recommendations for Selection of Suitable Hygiene Procedures for the Use in the Domestic Environment. International Scientific Forum on Home Hygiene.

MacLean, Kama. 2003. 'Making the Colonial State Work for You: The Modern Beginnings of the Ancient *Kumbh Mela* in Allahabad', *The Journal of Asian Studies*, Vol. 62, No. 3 (Aug., 2003), pp. 873-905.

Miller, David. 1976. *Social justice*, London: Oxford University Press.

Navlakha, Gautam, 1989. 'A Show of Hindu Power', *Economic and Political Weekly*, Vol. 24, No. 13 (Apr. 1, 1989), p. 658.

Oldenburg, Veena Talwar. 1989. *The Making of Colonial Lucknow, 1857-1877*. Delhi: Oxford University Press.

Rawls John, 1971. *A theory of justice*, Oxford: Oxford Univ. Press.

Sen, Amartya. 2009. *The idea of Justice*; London: Penguin books.

Sax, William.1 987. "Kumbha Mela." In Encyclopedia of Religion, edited by Mircea Eliade. Vol. 8. New York: Macmillan.

Saxena, Ashish. 2009. 'Religion, Caste and Community: Identity Substantiation through '*Maile*' Congregations among the *Dogras* of Jammu and Kashmir (India)' in '*Politics and Religion*' Center for Studies of Religion and Religious Tolerance, Serbia; issue no.1/2009 Volume III.

Tilly, Frank, 2000. *History of philosophy*, New Delhi: SBW publication.

UNDP. 1998. *Human development report 1998*. New York: United Nations Development Programme.

WHO. 2000. Press release, No. 56, 14th September 2000.

Chapter - 16

Globalisation and Environmental Sanitation: Health Implications in India

—*Sutandra Singha*

The study offers a conceptual framework for the health implications of globalisation and related degradation in environmental sanitation in India. The framework is developed by identifying the main determinants which deteriorate environmental sanitation and the ways these factors are getting affected by globalisation process. The resulting conceptual model explicitly visualises that globalisation impacts land use activities and thereby affects the environmental determinants of human health in terms of air, water and soil pollution. The paper intends to examine two main mechanisms– urban industrialisation and green revolution, through which globalisation can lead to ecosystem degradation and consequent health hazards. Industrialisation in India has resulted into unplanned growth of cities, congestion, unhygienic situation and health problems. The urban-industrial environment poses risk of water-borne, vector-borne, respiratory and infectious diseases and also the urban heat island amplification of heat waves. As the number of urban consumers and their material expectations are on a rise symmetrically cities keep on contributing environmental degradation in order to meet steep rise in consumer goods. In the agricultural sector, the Green Revolution has transformed India into a self-sufficient country; however it is posing serious threat to human health in terms of increased incidence of cancer and biological toxicity due to excessive application of chemicals and pesticides in farming. In this background, the paper provides an account of government strategies undertaken in the era of globalisation to safeguard and promote environmental sanitation. Further, it also offers some practicable policy measures that can be adopted to combat the existing environmental health hazards.

Key Words: *Globalisation, Environmental Sanitation, Pollution, Urban, Industrialisation, Green Revolution, Health Hazards.*

Introduction

Globalisation is the new buzzword that has come to dominate the world since the nineties of the last century with the end of the cold war and the break-up of the former Soviet Union and the global trend towards the rolling ball. The frontiers of the state with increased reliance on the market economy and renewed faith in the private capital and resources, a process of structural adjustment spurred by the studies and influences of the World Bank and other International organisations have started in many of the developing countries. Also globalisation has brought in new opportunities to developing countries. Greater access to developed country markets and technology transfer hold out promise improved productivity and higher living standard. But globalisation has also thrown up new challenges like growing inequality across and within nations, volatility in financial market, environmental deteriorations and related health problems among the living beings. Another negative aspect of globalisation is that a great majority of developing countries remain removed from the process.

Though the precise definition of globalisation is still unavailable a few definitions worth viewing, Stephen Gill defines globalisation as the reduction of transaction cost of trans-border movements of capital and goods thus of factors of production and goods. Guy Brainbant says that the process of globalisation not only includes opening up of world trade, development of advanced means of communication, internationalisation of financial markets, growing importance of MNC's, population migrations and more generally increased mobility of persons, goods, capital, data and ideas but also infections, diseases and pollution.

India opened up the economy in the early nineties following a major crisis that led by a foreign exchange crunch that dragged the economy close to defaulting on loans. The response was a slew of domestic and external sector policy measures partly prompted by the immediate needs and partly by the demand of the multilateral organisations. The new policy regime radically pushed forward in favour of a more open and market oriented economy. Major measures initiated as a part of the globalisation strategy included heavy industrialisation, urbanisation and in the rural areas there was the commercialisation and mechanisation of agriculture–the Green Revolution.

The implications of globalisation for a developing nation like India are many. It not only boosted and recovered Indian economy but also increased agricultural production manifold thereby making India a self-sufficient country. Along with these, globalisation promoted urbanisation, employment and education in India. However, there is the other side of coin also. Overcrowding, slums, squatter settlements, sewerage problems, thrash, pollution and health problems became evident in urban areas. Whereas, Green Revolution resulted in soil, water and air pollution in the rural areas followed by some health consequences. Both of these two factors: urban industrial development and Green Revolution have affected environmental sanitation which envisages promotion of health of the community by providing clean environment and breaking the cycle of disease.

Globalisation and Urban Industrial Development

Urban industrial development is a product of Globalisation. Globalisation generates new challenges in preparing strategies for urban development because globalisation threatens to exacerbate urban environmental pollution and natural resource degradation. Urban industrial environment encompasses the interaction of population, growth, city management and the built environment with the natural environment or ecological system in which city is located. Urban environment also links other parameters of the urban puzzle like health, energy, infrastructure and land use. However, the environmental problems of urban industrial areas that threat to people's present or future wellbeing, resulting in human induced damage to the physical environment in or borne into urban areas. Issues in urban industrialisation are raised by urban development initiatives and are related to environmental problems. These are inadequate potable water and sanitation facilities, air pollution, ground water pollution, excessive crowding, inadequate and inefficient waste disposal management, pollution of water bodies, loss of green areas, ecological disruption, resource depletion and emission of chemicals and greenhouse gases.

Impact of Urban Industrialisation on Environment and Public Health in India

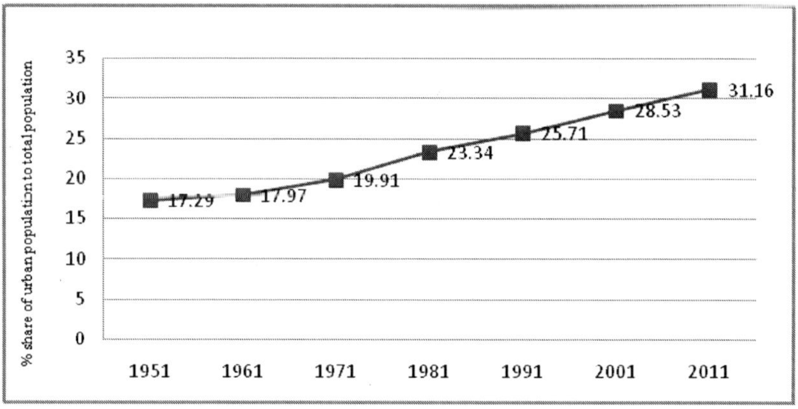

Data Source: Census of India, 2011.

Figure 16.1: Urban Population Scenario of India, 1991-2011.

There have been significant growth in urban population in globalisation period (Figure: 16.1) especially due to settling down of people near industrial and city areas of Delhi, Uttar Pradesh, West Bengal, Andhra Pradesh, Tamil Nadu and Maharashtra for employment, educational and better standard of living (Figure 16.2). The natural sequel of unchecked, unplanned and haphazard growth of urban areas results in the growth and spread of slums and squatter settlements which present a striking feature in the ecological structure of Indian cities, especially of metropolitan centres. With the advent of heavy mechanical industries began the chapter of the decline of Indian village cottage industries. Cities are constantly changing and growing. There is much pressure on the greenbelt. Mass migration from rural areas into town in search of easily commutable but cheaper living areas near the industrial centres and cities are making the available leaving areas congested followed by urban sprawl (Figure 16.3). Growing urbanisation is posing serious environmental concerns in India in terms of changing land use pattern, increasing carbon emissions, solid waste generation and disposal, pollution and poor sanitation amenities.

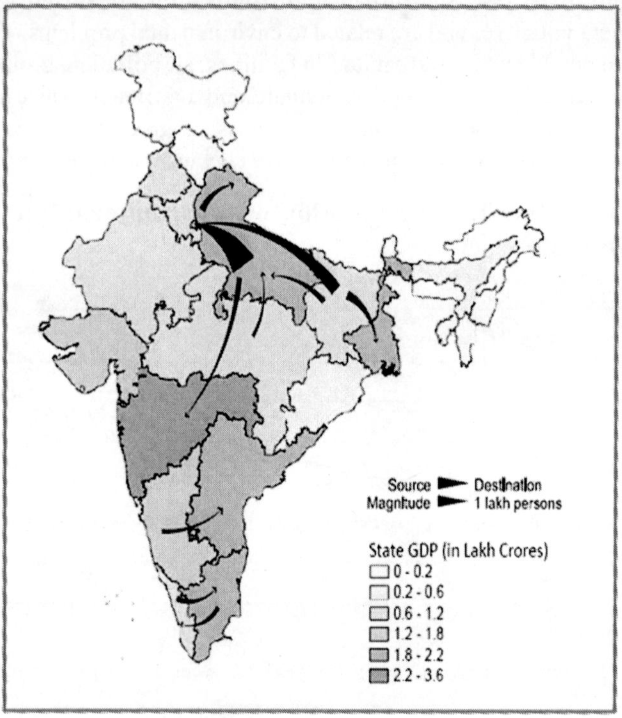

Image Source: Future Challenges Org. 2012.

URL: https://futurechallenges.org/local/news/a-dormant-volcano-inter-state-migration-in-india/

Figure 16.2: Estimated Major Net Rural to Urban Inter-State Migration Flow, 2001-2011.

Carbon emissions especially due to energy consumption have been increasing in India in recent years (Figure 16.4) and they are higher in urban areas.

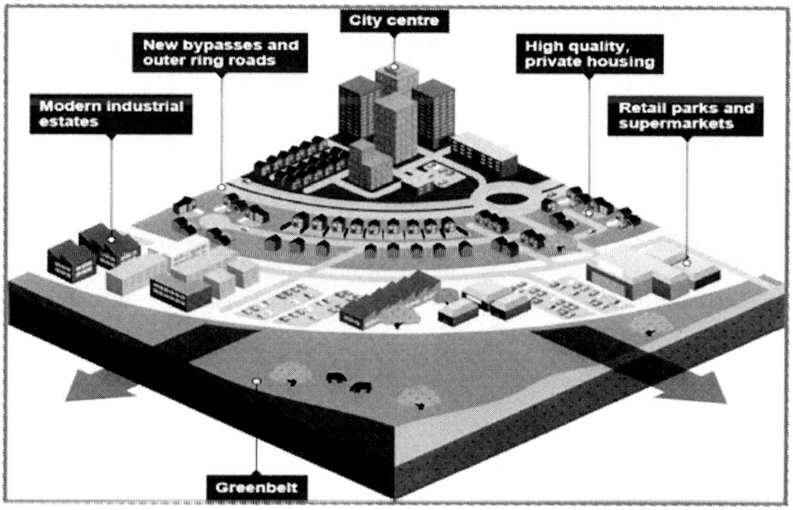

Image Source: BBC Bitesize

URL: http://www.bbc.co.uk/education/guides/zk32pv4/revision/9

Figure 16.3: Urban Sprawl and Green Belt Recession around a typical City Centre.

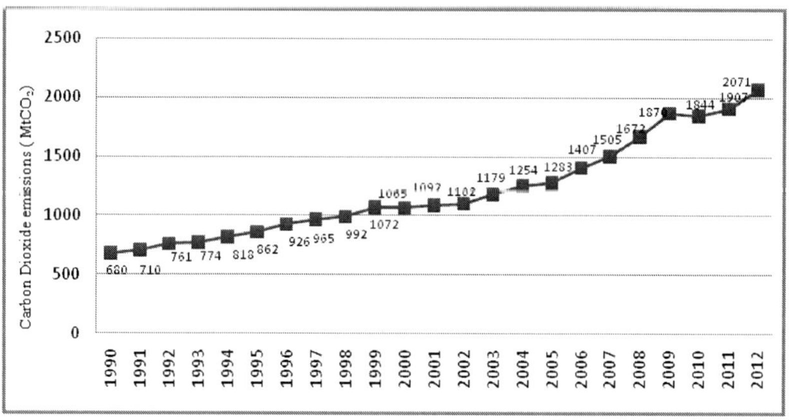

Data Source: Global Carbon Atlas, 2016.

Figure 16.4: Carbon Dioxide Emission from Energy Consumption, 1990-2012.

Average per capita carbon emissions are higher in the metropolitan cities of India (being 1.19 tons per capita as compared to only 0.90 tons per capita in the non-metropolitan cities), and the national average is 0.93 tons per capita. This is because larger cities have more polluting activity such as emissions from public and private transport. However, the corporation level emissions as a percentage of city-level emissions are much higher in the non-metropolitan areas than in the metropolitan areas because smaller city corporations lack the adequate technology to minimise their carbon emissions. Corporation level emissions include those emanating from street lighting, water supply and sewage systems, transportation, building and other facilities in the provision of various public services. The wastewater generated in these areas normally percolates in the soil or evaporates. The uncollected wastes accumulate in the urban areas, cause unhygienic conditions and release pollutants that leach to surface and groundwater. Inadequate discharge of untreated domestic/municipal wastewater has resulted in contamination of 75 per cent of all surface water across India. Mechanised, heavy and large-scale industries have negative impact which adversely affects the environment and human health. Due to industrialisation, there is constant depletion of natural resources. Many industries are powered by thermal power plants that consume coal. Large industries emit many harmful gases into the environment. The release of harmful chemicals into air leads to air-pollution and ejection of chemically treated waste water or effluents into water causes surface and ground water pollution. The noises that it produces leads to noise-pollution. Industrial pollutants, mainly discharged from various industries are the major source of soil pollution. These pollutants affect and alter the chemical and biological properties of soil. Hazardous chemicals enter into human food chain from the soil or water, disturb the biochemical process and finally lead to serious effects on living organisms. Lead paint, mining, foundry activities and vehicle exhaust release lead, mercury and heavy metals into the soil and pollutes it. Lead affects the nervous system and memory, growth and development, pituitary system, as well as cognitive development (lower IQs). Mercury causes itching, burning, pain, damage to brain kidney and lungs, Pink Disease, Desquamation, high blood pressure and hyper salivation. Consumption of plants and vegetables grown on hydrocarbons affected soils leads to auto immune system, eye irritation, nausea, vomiting, diarrhea, kidney and liver damage and, even Cancer. Volatile compounds can cause irritation of the eye, nose and throat. In severe cases there may be headaches, nausea, and loss of coordination. In the longer run, some of them are suspected to cause damage to the liver and other parts of the body. Air pollution is probably most dangerous to human health. Exposure to formaldehyde causes irritation to the eyes, nose and may cause allergies in some people. Oxides of nitrogen can make children susceptible to respiratory diseases in the winters. Carbon monoxide combines with haemoglobin to lessen the amount of oxygen that enters our blood through our lungs. The binding with other haeme proteins causes changes in the function of the affected organs such as the brain and the cardiovascular system, and also the developing foetus. It can impair our concentration, slow our reflexes, and make us confused and sleepy. Sulphur dioxide in the air is caused due to the rise in combustion of fossil fuels. It leads to diseases of the lung and other lung disorders such as wheezing and shortness of breath. SPM (suspended particulate matter). Suspended matter consists of dust, fumes, mist and smoke. The main chemical component of SPM that is of major concern is lead, others being nickel, arsenic, and those present in diesel exhaust. These particles when breathed in, lodge in our lung tissues and cause lung damage and respiratory problems.

Accidental releases of toxic substances into the atmosphere resulting in serious health risks are usually more common in developing countries. The reasons include inadequate safety planning, lack of skilled technical personnel to maintain proper facilities, and difficulties in obtaining spare parts and so on. One of the worst of such accidents occurred in Bhopal, India, in 1984, where leaking methyl isocyanides killed 2,000 people. Air pollution is now the fifth largest killer in India, says newly released findings of Global Burden of Disease report. Findings released by the scientists behind the study at a Dialogue Workshop organised by Centre for Science and Environment, Indian Council of Medical Research and US-based Health Effects Institute. In the wake of the GBD findings, CSE has analysed the latest air quality data available with the Central Pollution Control Board for 2010. Of the 180 cities monitored for SO_2, NO_2 and PM10. According to this finding, half of the urban population breathes air laced with particulate pollution that has exceeded the standards. As much as one-third of the population is exposed to critical levels of particulate pollution. Gwalior, West Singhbhum, Ghaziabad, Raipur, and Delhi are the top five critically polluted cities in the grip of PM10. Howrah, Barrackpore, Badlapur, Ulhasnagar and Asansol are the five top critically polluted cities in grip of NO_2. Maharashtra exceeds the SO_2 standard whereas moderate levels of SO_2 are noted in Jamshedpur and Saraikela Kharsawan in Jharkhand; Chandrapur, Badlapur, Ulhasnagar, and Pune in Maharashtra; Ghaziabad and Khurja in UP, Dehradun in Uttarakhand and Marmagao and Curchorem in Goa. The cities with critical double-trouble—particulates and NO_2 are Howrah, Barrackpore, Asansol, Durgapur, Sankrail, Raniganj, Kolkata (West Bengal), Badlapur, Ulhasnagar (Maharashtra), Delhi, Haldia, Bicholim, Jamshedpur, Meerut, Noida, Saraikela Kharsawan, Jalgaon and Raipur.

Green Revolution as a Product of Globalisation

Globalisation is an extremely complex phenomenon and it is the interactive co-evolution of multiple factors such as technological, cultural, economic, institutional, social and environmental. The commercialisation of agriculture in India through the Green Revolution led to the effects, which were far reaching and irreversible. The Green Revolution replaced indigenous agriculture with modern and technology intensive agriculture, led to the use of bio-engineered High Yielding Varieties (HYV) seeds that worked in conjunction with chemical fertilisers and extensive irrigation to increase crop yields. Green Revolution has influenced the economy and way of life in India to a great extent as is evident in terms of increase in agricultural production, prosperity among farmers, self-sufficiency in food grains, capitalistic farming, ploughing back of profits, agro-industrial growth and rural employment. The production of wheat and rice has produced the best results in fueling self-sufficiency of India. Along with high-yielding seeds and irrigation facilities, the enthusiasm of farmers mobilised the idea of agricultural revolution. However, poor farmers who could not participate in this capital intensive technology followed by widening income gaps between social classes. Heavy use of pesticides and chemical fertilisers caused some serious health problems as well as environmental degradation.

Green Revolution, Environmental Sanitation and Health Issues in India

The introduction of high-yielding varieties of seeds (hybrid seeds) and the increased use of chemical fertilisers and irrigation led to the increase in production needed to make the country self-sufficient in food grains, thus improving agriculture in India. Due to the rise in use of chemical pesticides and fertilisers there were negative effects on the soil and the human health. According to a report published in 1990 from the Environment Protection Agency (EPA), 50 per cent of the water pollution of streams and rivers occur due to leaching and mixing of chemicals from the agriculture practices- a non-point source of water pollution. Pesticides are those chemicals (such as insecticides, fungicides, herbicides, rodenticides, molluscicides, nematocides, plant growth etc.), which have been widely used throughout the world to increase crop yield and to kill the insect-pests responsible for transmitting various diseases to humans and animals. The trend of application of different pesticides in India radically differs from rest of the world. The 76 per cent of the total pesticides used in India is insecticide.

Water quality problems, thought to be caused in part by cropland runoff or non-point source pollution, affect drinking water and the nation's lakes, streams, and estuaries. When fertilisers, herbicides, insecticides, and fungicides are applied to cropland, some residues remain in the soil after plant uptake and may leach into subsurface waters, or the residues may move to surface water by dissolving in runoff or adsorbing to sediment. Spray drifts during application may carry pesticides to surface waters also. Chemical or physical processes transform residues into products that may also contaminate water. For example, nitrogen fertiliser or nitrogen from animal waste may be transformed first into ammonium and then into nitrates. Nitrates can turn into nitrites and both are detrimental to human health. A known human health risk from nitrate contamination is infant methemoglobinemia, a condition where nitrates are converted into nitrites in the digestive system, impairing the ability of infants' blood to carry oxygen. Concentration of nitrates or pesticides in drinking water may be below levels at which acute health effects have been observed. However, continued exposure may result in chronic effects (i.e., reproductive impairments, cancer, etc.) to humans. Impact of pesticides on human health is cyclic in nature (Figure 16.5). Pesticide dusts get mixed with the soil, water and air and, gradually enter human body through pesticide contaminated food (vegetables and dairy products), drinking water and polluted air followed by kidney, liver, eye and fertility disorders.

The main use of pesticides in India is for cotton crops (45 per cent), followed by paddy and wheat. The major part of the pesticides applied in any area for a specific reason (about 99 per cent) remain unused and it gets mixed with air, soil, water and plants which by several means causes harmful effects on human and animal health. Human health effects are caused by skin contact while handling of pesticide products, Inhalation of dust or spray and, consumption of pesticide contaminated food or water. Farm workers have special risks associated with inhalation and skin contact during preparation and application of pesticides to crops. However, for the majority of the population, a principal source is through ingestion of food which is contaminated by pesticides. After the death of about 100 people in India due to consumption of parathion contaminated wheat flour, Indian Council of Agricultural Research (ICAR) constituted a committee to suggest possible remedies to combat the toxicity caused due to presence of pesticides and their residues in the edibles.

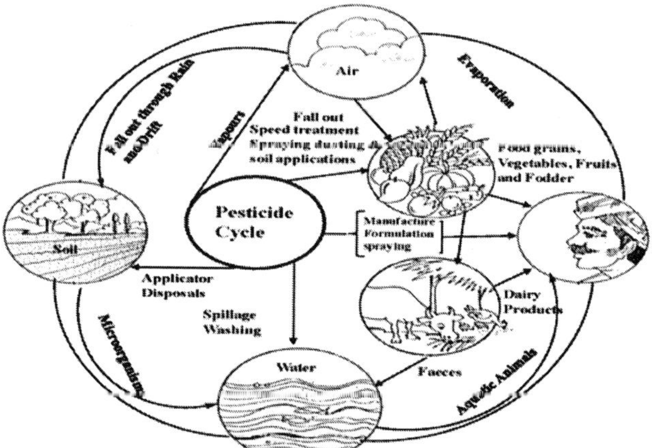

Figure 16.5: Pesticides Cycle in the Ecosystem (after Kailasa et al. 2013).

Indiscriminate use of fertilisers and pesticides for enhanced crop yield has caused the problem of air, water and soil pollution. The nitrous oxide (N_2O) produced by microbial action on inorganic fertilisers in soil causes depletion of stratospheric ozone layer, which serve as shield against harmful UV-rays emanating from the sun. Methane (CH_4) produced by methanogenic bacteria in the water logged paddy fields is a potent greenhouse gas responsible for global warming. India is often blamed by international community for global warming due to large scale paddy cultivation (Greenhouse gas methane is emitted from water logged paddy field).The inorganic fertilisers applied to the field are drained by rain water to rivers and lakes causing water pollution. The phenomenon of nutrient enrichment of aquatic bodies is known as eutrophication which deteriorates the water quality leading to death of fishes (Figure 16.6). There have been reports of ground water pollution due to the seepage of fertilisers and pesticides in Punjab.

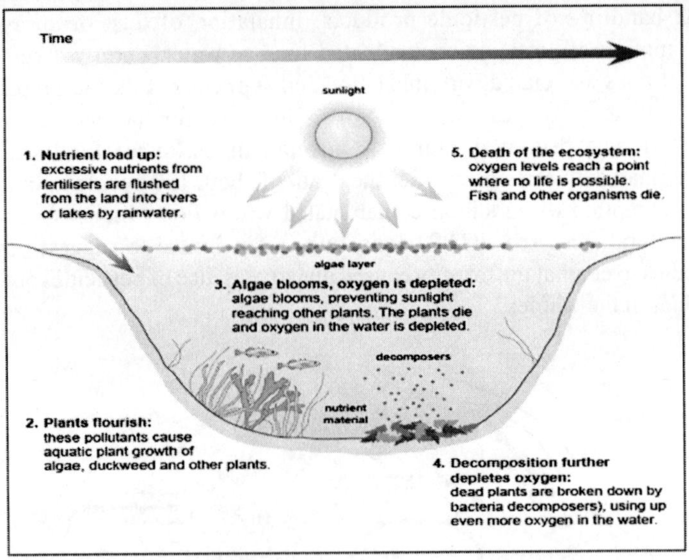

Image Source: BBC, UK 2014 URL:http://www.bbc.co.uk/schools/gcsebitesize/science/edexcel/problems_in_environment/pollutionrev4.shtml.

Figure 16.6: Eutrophication Process.

The construction of canals to boost the agricultural production under Green Revolution package technology has led to spread and outbreak of mosquito borne diseases like Malaria, Lymphatic Filariasis and Japanese encephalitis especially in states Uttar Pradesh, Bihar, Jharkhand and Assam. The Gorakhpur and adjoining Districts of Eastern Uttar Pradesh are worst affected from Japanese encephalitis-a viral disease spread by Culex spp. of mosquitoes. The West Nile fever-a viral disease spread by Culex Vishnui and Culex Fatigans species of mosquitoes, is another gradually emerging as a health problem in the state of Punjab.

Pesticides like DDT are non-biodegradable and are fat soluble which enter the food chain and reach the human body where they are deposited in adipose tissue. When oxidation of the fat takes place in body the pesticides are released in the system causing harmful effect to human health. The concentration of pesticides increases with increasing food chain and the phenomenon is known as biomagnification or biological amplification (Figure 16.7).

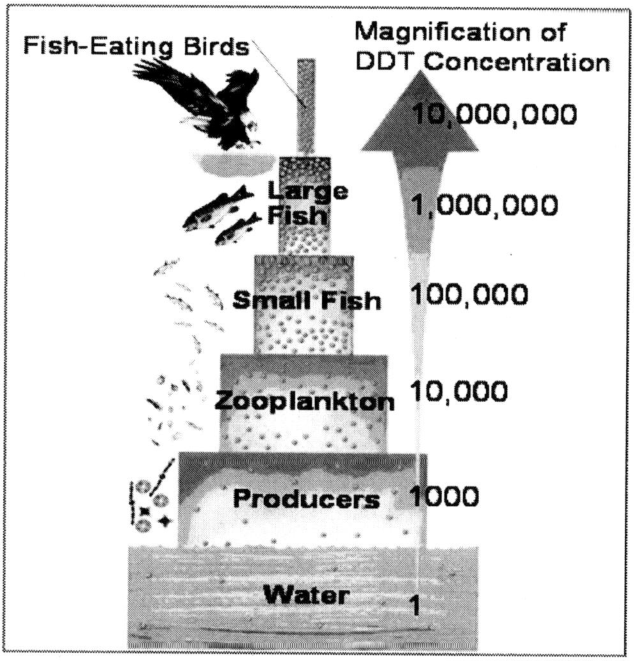

Image Source: Current Science Event, 2014.

URL: http://www.currentscienceevent.org/japan-wasted-contamination-water-and-biomagnification-process.

Figure 16.7: Biomagnification Process in a Food-Chain.

India's daily diet is reported to contain 270 μg of DDT. The concentration of DDT in Indians has reached to alarming proportions ranging between 13 to 31 ppm (parts per million). Delhi's citizens have the highest level of pesticides in their body fat in the world. There have been reports of cases of cancer, deformities, hepatic diseases and neurological disorders due to pesticide poisoning in cotton growing belts of Maharashtra and Andhra Pradesh. Throughout the era of Green Revolution, the use of Nitrogen (N), Phosphorus (P) and Potassium (K) have been increasing in India (Figure 16.8).

The excessive use of nitrogenous fertilisers decreases the potassium content of the food grains, which is important element to regulate blood pressure and averts the chances of heart attack in human beings.

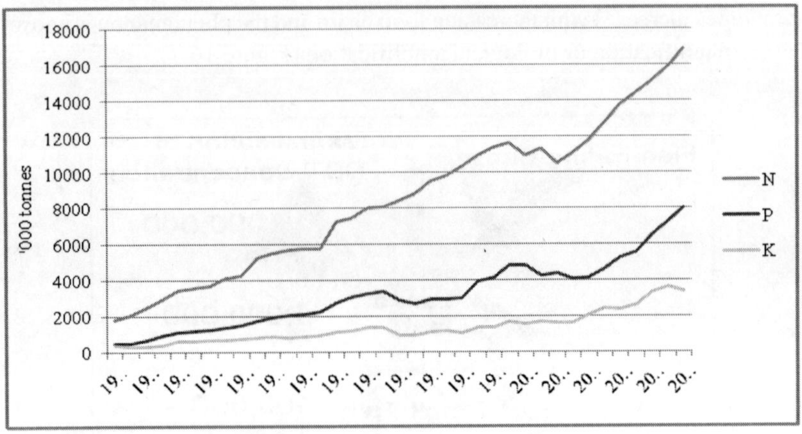

Data Source: Fertilizer Association of India, 2011.

Figure 16.8: Trend of Fertiliser Consumption (N, P and K) in India: 1974-75 to 2010-11.

The excessive potash and nitrate treatment decreases the proteins and immunity enhancer nutrients in foods, such as ascorbic acid (vitamin C) and carotene. Moreover, subtle balance of amino acids is disturbed within the protein molecule thus lowering the protein quality. Hence the escalating problem of cardiac disorders, hypertension, night blindness and other eye disorders, malnutrition and susceptibility to infectious diseases among Indians is due to the result of Green Revolution. In rural areas of Bihar, Jharkhand, Odisha, Madhya Pradesh and Chhattisgarh, Kwashiorkar and Marasmus are the common diseases caused due to deficiency of protein in children. Moreover, protein malnutrition in adults have made them susceptible to the diseases like pulmonary tuberculosis, which has emerged as a serious health problem among poor sections of the society of rural India.

Role of Government with regard to Environmental Sanitation

National Commission on Urbanisation (NCU) has, in its policy proposal of 1988, stressed the need for the Environmental Improvement of Urban Slums (EIUS) programme. Indian government's approach towards prevention and control of pollution has been mostly in the nature of legislation-based command and control measures while natural resource management has been largely carried out through programmes supported by allocations from the central (e.g., programmes of Ministry of Environment and Forests (MoEF), Ministry of Nonconventional Energy Sources, Ministry of Agriculture) and state budgets.

The use of fiscal instruments (other than expenditure policy) in environmental policy has been rather limited, even though the need to employ economic and fiscal policy instruments for the control of pollution and management of natural resources has gained steady recognition during the 1990s.

For greening cities in India, the Supreme Court has played a catalytic role. The Supreme Court identified critically polluted cities and suggested an action plan to reduce the level of pollution in these cities. In 1996, Delhi was the first city to order to develop an action plan, while the most recent action plans were mandated in 2003. To date, 17 cities have been given orders to develop action plans. In light of the Supreme Court's reputation as a driver of environmental reform in India, as well as the overwhelming approval of Delhi's CNG bus programme as part of its action plan. The Court mandated the use of catalytic converters in vehicles to reduce vehicular pollution. In 1995, the Supreme Court required that all new petrol-fueled cars in the four major metros (Delhi, Mumbai, Kolkata, Chennai) were to be fitted with converters. In 1998, the policy was extended to 45 other cities. It is plausible that this regulation could reduce the air pollution level in cities.

Task forces were constituted by the MoEF in 1995 and 2001 to evaluate the scope for market based instruments (MBIs) for industrial pollution abatement. In the last few years, the Government of India has expressed the desire to use markets for control of pollution in the country. India has levied a cess on coal at the rate of ₹ 50 (~US$ 1) per tonne, which is applicable to both domestically produced and imported coal. This money goes into a National Clean Energy Fund that is used for funding research, innovative projects in clean energy technologies, and environmental remedial programmes. To control the industrial pollution of NOx and particulate matters, the government is going to start the emission permit markets as pilot projects in three states namely, Gujarat, Maharashtra and Tamil Nadu. Similarly, to increase the energy efficiency in the energy intensive industries in a cost-effective manner, the Bureau of Energy Efficiency has launched the trading in energy efficiency certificate known as PAT programme. The Electricity Act 2003 together with the National Electricity Policy 2005 (NEP) and the Tariff Policy (TP) mandates promotion of electricity generation from renewable sources and encourage use of markets. Moreover, the Government of India has recently launched the National Mission on Sustainable Habitat (NMSH) under the National Action Plan on Climate Change (NAPCC). The NMSH would also help in greening the Indian cities.

Conclusion and Recommendations

Environmental sanitation is a major public health issue in India. Recent interventional studies on environmental sanitation in India highlighted the importance of prioritising control strategies. Research related to the appropriate cost-effective intervention strategies and their implementation in the

Indian context is a big challenge. India is still lagging far behind many countries in the field of environmental sanitation. Improvement in sanitation requires newer strategies and targeted interventions with follow-up evaluation. The need of the hour is to identify the existing system of environmental sanitation with respect to its structure and functioning and to prioritise the control strategies according to the need of the country. These priorities are particularly important because of issue of water constraints, environment-related health problems, rapid population growth, inequitable distribution of water resources, issues related to administrative problems, urbanisation and industrialisation, migration of population, and rapid agro economic growth. India's carbon emissions are currently are not alarming, given the low share of manufacturing in its GDP, but are likely to increase with the increasing role of manufacturing, urbanisation, rising incomes and the use of personal vehicles. The Government of India has resorted to a market-based approach to containing pollution. In addition, at the sub-national level, cities are also doing their bit to reduce carbon emissions, and increasing green urbanisation by making their buildings more energy efficient. The more immediate problems of India's cities relate to inadequate solid waste management, poor sanitation and sewerage which lead to pollution of the ground water aquifer. While a new National Urban Sanitation Policy has been drafted and innovative methods are being adopted by cities with respect to their solid waste management (e.g., waste segregation), the challenges that remain to be addressed relate to financing of the huge urban infrastructure backlog along with that for future requirements.

Bibliography

1. Agrawal, Anju, Ravi, S. Pandey, and Bechan Sharma. "Water pollution with special reference to pesticide contamination in India." *Journal of Water Resource and Protection 2,* no. 5 (2010): 432.
2. Chakravarti, A.K. "Green Revolution in India." *Annals of American Geographers* 63.3 (1973): 319-330.
3. Chaplin, SE. Cities, sewers and poverty: India's politics of sanitation. *Environment and Urbanisation*, 1999, 11: 145-158.
4. Dahlgren, G, Whitehead, M. Levelling Up: Strategies for Tackling Social Inequalities in Health. Venice, Italy: WHO-EURO Office for Investment for Health and Development; 2006.
5. Evenson, R.E., and D. Gollin. "Assessing the Impact of the Green Revolution, 1960 to 2000." *Science* 300.5620 (2003): 758-62. Web. 14 Aug 2009.
6. Garau, P, Sclar, ED, Carolini, GY. A Home in the City. Report from the UN Millennium Project. London: Earthscan Publ.; 2005.
7. Gopal, Singh. Socio-Economic Basis of the Punjab Crisis, Vol. XIX, No.1 1 Jan 1984, p. 42.
8. Human Settlement Management Institute (2000). *National Training Strategy for Urban Development and Management,* India, p. 54. 3.

9. Kailasa, Suresh Kumar, Hui-Fen Wu, and Shang-Da Huang. *Recent Developments on Mass Spectrometry for the Analysis of Pesticides in Wastewater*. INTECH Open Access Publisher, 2013.
10. Naik, N.T.K. and Rahman, S., Mansoor (2007): "Urbanisation of India",Serials Publications, p. 188.
11. Pathak, C.R. (2004): "Towards an Urbanisation Policy in India", *ITPI Journal,* p. 70. 2.
12. Report of the Working Group on Environment and Environmental Regulatory Mechanism (2007). *In Environment and Forests for the Eleventh Five Year Plan (2007-2012)*, Planning Commission, GOI, New Delhi, August 2007, pp.1-2.
13. Shiva, Vandana. The Violence of the Green Revolution: Third World Agriculture, Ecology and Politics. 2nd ed. London, UK: Zed Books Ltd., 1993.
14. Sury, M.M. (2008). *"India's Five Year Plans: I to XI (1951-56 to 2007-12)"*, New Century Publication, New Delhi, pp. 35-36.
15. UN Habitat. The Challenge of Slums: Global Report on Human Settlements. Nairobi, Kenya, UN: Habitat; 2003.
16. Utzinger, J, Keiser, J. Urbanisation and tropical health—then and now. *Ann Trop Med Parasitol.* 2006; 100: 517-533.

Chapter - 17

Dialectics and Dynamics of the EIA Professional Groups in Transnational Global Villages

—*Shital J. Tamakuwala*

Professionalism is a key concept in the sociologies of work, occupations, professions and organisations. The article considers different ways in which professionalism is currently being interpreted while taking special reference to the emerging profession in the era of globalisation. Wickenden elaborates six characteristics of a profession in the form of: (a) renders a specialised service based upon advanced specialised knowledge and skill and dealing with its problems primarily on an intellectual plane rather than on a physical or a manual labour level. (b) Involves a confidential relationship between a practitioner and compensates a client or an employer. (c) Is charged with substantial degree of public obligation by virtue of its profession of specialised knowledge. (d) Enjoys a common heritage of knowledge, skill and status to the cumulative store of which professional men are bound to contribute through their individual and collective efforts. (e) Performs its services to a substantial degree in the general public interest, receiving its compensation through limited fees rather than through direct profit from the improvement in goods, services, or knowledge, which it accomplishes. (f) Is bound by a distinctive ethical code in its relationships with clients, colleagues, and the public. Under the backdrop, the paper attempts to configure the methodological framework to analyse the profession emerging out on environmental impact assessment. In addition, attempt has been made to understand the formation of the profession of EIA in India and its dynamics in the discursive practices of the post-structuralist and postmodern sociological jargons. With the help of literature, an assessment is made as to how this profession has emerged so far and to what extent it fulfills the credentials as mentioned above. For the purpose of deriving empirical data, the study considered study of professionals in 10 institutions/institutes, 10 NGOs, and 10 EIA experts based at Surat, Gujarat. Data obtained was verified and compared with the blueprint of professional characteristics. Therefore, with the help of sociological imagination, the paper comes out with the interfaces of undercurrents that help enrich the discipline of environmental sociology.

Key Words: *Environment, Profession, Post Structuralist, Postmodern, EIA.*

Introduction

Environment Impact Assessment (EIA) can be defined as the study to predict the effect of a proposed activity/project on the environment. A decision-making tool, EIA compares various alternatives for a project and seeks to identify the one which represents the best combination of economic and environmental costs and benefits. UN/ISDR–UN Office for DRR (15 January 2009). EIA systematically examines both beneficial and adverse consequences of the project and ensures that these effects are taken into account during project design. It helps to identify possible environmental effects of the proposed project, proposes measures to mitigate adverse effects and predicts whether there will be significant adverse environmental effects, even after the mitigation is implemented. By considering the environmental effects of the project and their mitigation early in the project planning cycle, environmental assessment has many benefits, such as protection of environment, optimum utilisation of resources and saving of time and cost of the project. Properly conducted EIA also lessens conflicts by promoting community participation, informing decision-makers, and helping lay the base for environmentally sound projects. Benefits of integrating EIA have been observed in all stages of a project, from exploration and planning, through construction, operations, decommissioning, and beyond site closure.

Definition of Profession

A profession is a vocation founded upon specialised educational training, the purpose of which is to supply objective counsel and service to others, for a direct and definite compensation, wholly apart from expectation of other business gain. A professionalism is the conduct, aims, or qualities that characterise or mark a profession or a professional person for e.g., as athletics its aim is to gain or livelihood. It is the skill, good judgments and a polite behaviour that is expected from a person who is trained to do a job well.

Evolution of EIA as a Profession

Environment Impact Assessment is one of the successful policy innovations of the twentieth Century for environmental conservation. Thirty-seven years ago, there was no EIA but today, it is a formal process in many countries and is currently practiced in more than 100 countries. EIA as a mandatory regulatory procedure originated in the early 1970s, with the implementation of the National Environment Policy Act (NEPA) 1969 in the US. A large part of the initial development took place in a few high-income countries, like Canada, Australia, and New Zealand (1973-74). However, there were some developing countries as well, which introduced EIA relatively early–Columbia (1974), Philippines (1978). The EIA process really took off after the mid-1980s. In 1989, the World Bank adopted EIA for major development projects, in which a borrower country had to undertake an EIA under the Bank's supervision. Australia was the country which legislated EIA, and Canada and New Zealand took initiative to establish administrative procedures. Major public inquires helped to shape the process development. In the late 1970 and early 1980s more formalised guidance occurred. Other industrial and developing countries introduced formal EIA requirements i.e. France in 1976; Philippines in 1977 and Netherlands, 1978 began to use the process informally or experimentally and adopted elements such as impact statements or reports, as part of development applications for planning permission (German States [Lander], Ireland).

- Use of EA by developing countries (Brazil, Philippines, China, Indonesia).
- Strategic Environment Assessment [1] (SEA), risk analysis included in EA processes [2].
- Greater emphasis on ecological modeling, prediction and evaluation methods.
- Provision for public involvement.
- Coordination of EA with land use planning processes.

By the Mid 1980s to end of decade, in Europe, EC Directive on EIA established basic principles and procedural requirements for all member states. Not only that but increase in efforts to address cumulative effects and World Bank and other leading international aid agencies establish EA requirements.

Source: International Study of the Effectiveness of Environmental Assessment, final report, Environmental assessment in a changing world, Prepared by Barry Sadler, June 1996.

History of Environment Impact Assessment in India as a Profession

The Indian experience with Environmental Impact Assessment began over 20 years back. It started in around 1976-77, when the Planning Commission asked the Department of Science and Technology to examine the river-valley projects from an environmental angle. This was subsequently extended to cover those projects, which required the approval of the Public Investment Board. Till 1994, environmental clearance from the Central Government was an administrative decision and lacked legislative support. On 27 January 1994, the Union Ministry of Environment and Forests (MEF), Government of India, under the Environmental (Protection) Act 1986, promulgated an EIA notification making Environmental Clearance (EC) mandatory for expansion or modernisation of any activity or for setting up new projects listed in Schedule 1 of the notification. Since then there have been 12 amendments made in the EIA notification of 1994. The MoEF recently notified new EIA legislation in September 2006. The notification makes it mandatory for various projects such as mining, thermal power plants, river valley, infrastructure (road, highway, ports, harbours and airports) and industries including very small electroplating or foundry units to get environment clearance. However, unlike the EIA Notification of 1994, the new legislation has put the onus of clearing projects on the state government depending on the size/capacity of the project. Certain activities permissible under the Coastal Regulation Zone Act, 1991 also require similar clearance. Additionally, donor agencies operating in India like the World Bank and the ADB have a different set of requirements for giving environmental clearance to projects that are funded by them.

Importance of EIA

Reducing the burden of environmental impacts is necessary if development is to become sustainable. These impacts are more complex, larger in scale and further reaching in their potential consequences than thirty years ago when EIA was first introduced. As a result, EIA has become of ever increasing importance as a tool for development decision-making. This role is formally recognised in Principle 17 of the Rio Declaration on Environment and Development: 'Environmental impact assessment, as a national instrument, shall be undertaken for proposed activities that are likely to have a significant adverse impact on the environment and are subject to a decision of a competent national authority'. In practice, EIA is applied primarily to prevent or minimise the adverse effects of major development proposals, such as a power station, dams and reservoirs, industrial complexes, etc. This process is also used as a planning tool to promote sustainable development by integrating environmental considerations into a wide range of proposed actions. Most notably, Strategic Environmental Assessment (SEA) of policies and plans focuses on the highest levels of decision-making, when better account can be taken of the environment in considering development alternatives and options. More limited forms of EIA can be used to ensure smaller scale projects, such as dredging activities, road realignment and upgrading and housing subdivisions, conform to appropriate environmental standards or site and design criteria.

EIA and Globalisation

In its present form globalisation is a process, which has implications not only for social and cultural institutions of developed countries but is also transforming the social fabric of developing countries like India. At the most general level, globalisation refers to a process of change, which affects all regions of the world in a variety of sectors including the economy, technology, politics, the media, culture and the environment. According to Held *et al.* (1999; 2) 'globalisation may be thought initially as the widening, deepening and speeding up of worldwide interconnectedness in all aspects of contemporary social life, from the cultural to the criminal, the financial to the spiritual'. Anthony McGrew (1992) views globalisation as a process which operates as a global scale. He writes: Globalisation refers to those processes, operating at a global scale, which cut across national boundaries, integrating on connecting communities and organisations in space-time combinations, making the world in reality and in experience more interconnected. Globalisation implies a movement away from the classifiable sociological idea of a 'society' as well-bounded system, and its replacement by a perspective which concentrates on 'how social life is ordered across time and space'. Malcolm Waters argue that globalisation is basically a theory of social change. Sociologists have been studying social change through a variety of theories. Water (1995) writes such controversies as these are appearing to surround the issue of whether old Marxist or functionalist theories can be adapted to explain globalisation or whether we need to construct novel arguments. This may be because sociological theories of change have almost always implied the universalisation of the processes that they explain. Although, it did not arise without sociology, the concept has therefore found instant appeal across a range of intellectual interests. It remains for sociology to connect the concept with its own vital theoretical traditions. Water has not touched the emergence of social theory but the reality is that globalisation along with post-modernity has made conflict and functional theory irrelevant. McGrew concludes that globalisation dislodges society from its focal position in the discourse of modern sociology. The major positive aspect of globalisation is it has brought the awareness and consciousness for sustainable development which has further, laid strong foundations for the emergence of EIA as a profession. However, we find sustainable development is a key concept that has gained increasing international acceptance during the last two decades. A milestone in this process was the 'Brundtland' report, which defined sustainable development as 'development that meets the needs of today's generation without compromising those of future generations'. Five years later, the UN Conference on Environment and Development (UNCED), the Earth Summit, established a number of international agreements, declarations and commitments (refer below). Agenda 21, the global action plan for sustainable development, emphasises the importance of integrated environment and development decision-making and promotes the use of EIA and other policy instruments for this purpose. Gradually sustainable development changed its scenario and introduced the concept of Corporate Social Responsibility in the market. Thus, we can see the journey of it changed from social service and philanthropic to a law and legal compulsion. Hereby we state that the concept of CSR in world and India is not new, the term may be. The process though acclaimed recently, has been followed since ancient times albeit informally. Philosophers like Kautilya from India and pre-Christian era philosophers in the West preached and promoted ethical principles while doing business. The concept of helping the poor and disadvantaged was cited in much of the ancient literature. The idea was also supported by several religions where it has been intertwined with religious laws. "Zakaat", followed by Muslims, is donation from one's earnings which is specifically given to the poor and disadvantaged.

Similarly Hindus follow the principle of "Dhramada" and Sikhs the "Daashaant". In the global context, the recent history goes back to the seventeenth century when in 1790s, England witnessed the first large scale consumer boycott over the issue of slave harvested sugar which finally forced importer to have free-labour sourcing. The term CSR itself came in to common use in the early 1970s although it was seldom abbreviated. By late 1990s, the three concept was fully recognised; people and institutions across all sections of society started supporting it and they were Liberalisation, Privatisation and Globalisation. This can be corroborated by the fact that while in 1977 less than half of the Fortune 500 firms even mentioned CSR in their annual reports, by the end of 1990, approximately 90 per cent Fortune 500 firms embraced CSR as an essential element in their organisational goals, and actively promoted their CSR activities in annual reports (Boli and Hartsuiker, 2001).

Current Scenario of CSR in India

As discussed above, CSR is not a new concept in India. Ever since their inception, corporate like the Tata Group, the Aditya Birla Group, and Indian Oil Corporation, to name a few, have been involved in serving the community. Through donations and charity events, many other organisations have been doing their part for the society. The basic objective of CSR in these days is to maximise the company's overall impact on the society and stakeholders. CSR policies, practices and programmes are being comprehensively integrated by an increasing number of companies throughout their business operations and processes. A growing number of corporate feel that CSR is not just another form of indirect expense but is important for protecting the goodwill and reputation, defending attacks and increasing business competitiveness. Companies have specialised CSR teams that formulate policies, strategies and goals for their CSR programmes and set aside budgets to fund them.

Now, we shall study each characteristic which is mentioned and practiced in NABET Manual.

Characteristic 1: Renders a specialised service based upon advanced specialised knowledge and skill and dealing with its problems primarily on an intellectual plane rather than on a physical or a manual labour plane

(Page 47, 140, National Accreditation Board for Education and Training Quality Council of India June, 2015)

EIA team has a specialised category of qualification required. The experts are suppose to have adequate knowledge and skills in their own areas. For example, Minimum Educational Qualification for an EC is Bachelor's (graduate) degree or equivalent in technical subjects such as Engineering/ Architecture/ Environmental Planning/ Town Planning and the like from a UGC/AICTE recognised University/ Institution or Master's (post-graduate) degree in Science and other subjects - Physical/ Environmental/ Life Sciences/

Social Sciences/ Economics/ Management from a UGC/AICTE recognised University/ Institution. Even minimum seven years overall work experience related to EIA preparation is needed. Minimum Educational Qualification for FAEs is Bachelor's (graduate) degree or equivalent in technical subjects such as Engineering/ Architecture/ Environmental Planning/ Town Planning and the like from a UGC /AICTE recognised University/ Institution in specific disciplines as mentioned against each functional area or Master's (post-graduate) degree in Physical/ Environmental/ Life Sciences/ Social Sciences/ Economics from a UGC / AICTE recognised University/ Institution in specific disciplines as mentioned against specific functional areas. Minimum Experience for FAEs an expert should have a minimum three years overall experience in the concerned functional area(s).

Characteristic 2: Involves a confidential relationship between a practitioner and compensation a client or an employer.

(Page 23, point 9.5, National Accreditation Board for Education and Training Quality Council of India, June, 2015)

EIA Profession highlights a confidential relationship between EIA experts, EIA coordinators, directors of the company, management and the clients and even the state authorities are involved in it. Here in the process a trust and confidence is maintain and special care is taken that the information is not leaked in between the process. All information, documents and reports submitted by an AO/ACO to NABET are utilised by the NABET, assessors, members of accreditation and technical committees for the purpose of assessment and accreditation. These may also be used for research purpose or shared with MoEFCC, Govt. of India and other members of the International Personnel Certification Association. However, the identity of the accredited EIA consultant organisations would be masked for sensitive information related to business whenever it is called for/appropriate. In case an AO (applicant organisations)/ACO (accredited consultant organisations) wants the information to be kept confidential, a communication must be sent to NABET citing reasons for the same. NABET reserves the right to take appropriate decision in this regard. NABET also reserves the right of taking appropriate action against an ACO for deliberate breach of confidentiality. The ACO is required to have adequate arrangements consistent with applicable laws to safeguard confidentiality of all information provided by its clients. These arrangements are extended to include organisations or individuals acting on its behalf and as its representatives.

Source: QCI-Nabet Scheme for accreditation of EIA Consultant Organisations/ Version/ 3/June 2015, p. 23.

Characteristic 3: Is charged with substantial degree of public obligation by virtue of its profession of specialised knowledge

An EC should have an overall knowledge of the concerned sector/s and a clear understanding of environmental, biotic and socio-economic aspects related to those sectors. Minimum requirements of experience for an EIA coordinator are given in the below mentioned manual.

(Page 32, Appendix A, National Accreditation Board for Education and Training Quality Council of India June, 2015)

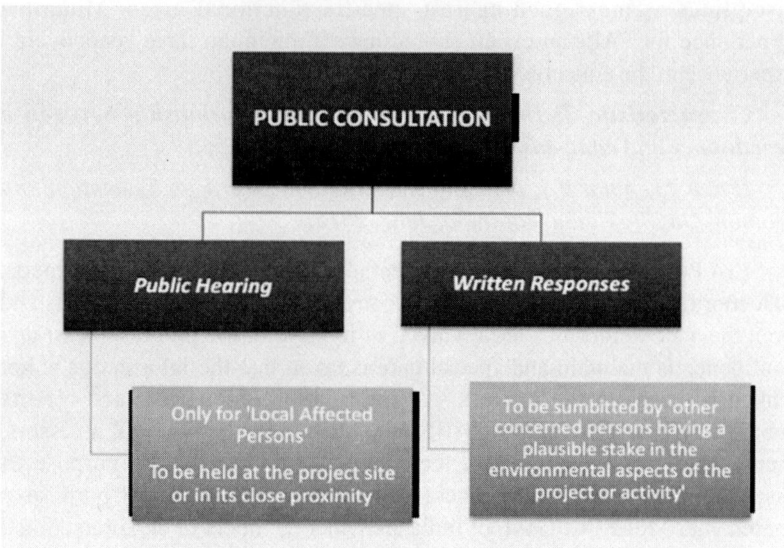

The main intention of EIA is that it is considered as a mandatory procedure for meeting the statutory requirements, it has many inbuilt advantages to the project proponent and to the society. Few of the advantages like major concern is to maintain environmental sustainability with better compliance with statutory standards. Public consultation is the corner stone of the Environment Impact Assessment (EIA) process. It is intended to ascertain the views of 'local affected persons' and 'others with a plausible stake in the environmental aspects of the project' on the environmental impacts of a proposed project.

Characteristic 4: Enjoys a common heritage of knowledge, skill and status to the cumulative store of which professional men are bound to contribute through their individual and collective efforts

(Point number 12.0, National Accreditation Board for Education and Training Quality Council of India, June, 2015)

The EIA profession includes the team of all expertise in their fields which collectively work for the preparation of the report on environment. The team members as mentioned in point 1 should have compulsory the required skills.

National Accreditation Board for Education and Training (NABET), a constituent board of the QCI has developed a voluntary accreditation Scheme with inputs from various stakeholders including experts in the field, regulatory agencies, consultants etc., and launched it in August 2007. Some of the leading consultants and professional men are bound to contribute through their individual and collective efforts for the welfare of the society. In fact, the profession has newly arose, we cannot say that it enjoys a common heritage of knowledge and skills and status, through generations compared to other professions. National Accreditation Board for Education and Training (NABET), a constituent board of the Quality Council of India (QCI) has developed a voluntary accreditation Scheme with inputs from various stakeholders including experts in the field, regulatory agencies, consultants etc., and launched it in August 2007. Some of the leading consultants in the field obtained accreditation under the scheme. The Ministry of Environment and Forests (MOEF) reviewed the scheme in 2009 and desired that the Scheme be updated incorporating the learning since launching of the Scheme. The Scheme was made mandatory by the MOEF through an Office Memorandum dated December 2, 2009. The Schemes Highlights of the EIAs are essentially multi-disciplinary activities where inputs are required from specialists having knowledge of the industry/sector for which EIAs are to be carried out as well as in functional areas like land use, air pollution control, air quality modelling, water pollution control, noise and vibration, ecology and bio-diversity, socio-economic aspects, risks and hazard management etc.

The 'Scheme for the accreditation of EIA Consultant Organisations' evolved by NABET identifies the following basic requirements of the EIA Consultant Organisation:

(1) Qualification and experience of EIA Coordinators and Functional Areas Experts,

(2) Requirements for field investigations and laboratory arrangement to ensure the quality of the baseline data,

(3) Quality management systems to be followed,

(4) Office facilities and other enabling factors to be provided by an organisation,

(5) Benefits of accreditation to EIA Consultant Organisation.

Apart from the fact that currently it is mandatory for organisations which prepare EIA reports for obtaining environmental clearance, to get accredited under the Scheme, some of the other advantages are–

(1) A system of yearly assessment by highly experienced NABET assessors providing valuable input for improvement.

(2) Listing in the QCI and the MOEF websites, which is an important database for prospective clients.

(3) Use of the QCI-NABET logo, a mark of quality in stationary, to improve the brand image of the organisation.

(4) Recognition in the international arena through the QCI which is a member of International Accreditation Forum (IAF).

Source: QCI-Nabet Scheme for accreditation of EIA Consultant Organisations/ Version/ 3/June 2015, p. 32, 34, 36.

Characteristic 5: Performs its services to a substantial degree in the general public interest, receiving its compensation through limited fees rather than through direct profit from the improvement in goods, services, or knowledge, which it accomplishes.

EIA consultant performs its services to a substantial degree in the general public interest and in return charges fees for the preparation of Report, TOR, No Objection Certificate (NOC) to receive (EC) Environmental clearance, etc. The team also drafts a report of Socio-economic baseline and CSR in consideration of the society which makes a compulsion for the company to contribute towards the benefit and welfare of the general public interests. The main intention of EIA report is it can very systematically understand the details of the project and its possible impacts on their environment. It enables public to visualise possible accidents, also to overcome the same with effective remediation measures. It can understand the economic development as against the natural resources depletion, and decide on project acceptance in their area well before project execution.

Characteristic 6: Is bound by a distinctive ethical code in its relationships with clients, colleagues, and the public

All ACOs are obliged to improve the standing of the consultancy profession by rigorously observing the Code of Conduct. Failure to do so may result in the suspension or cancellation of accreditation.

(Page number 27, National Accreditation Board for Education and Training Quality Council of India June, 2015)

In the EIA profession as such there is no such code of ethics to be followed in authorised documentation, but it is very necessary to have certain moral responsibilities towards the society which gives you ample of natural resources. It is our fundamental duty to protect and conserve our environment where we need to sustain. EIA profession tries to follow healthy relationships with its clients, colleagues and the public too.

Source: PDF CSR White Paper, page 7.

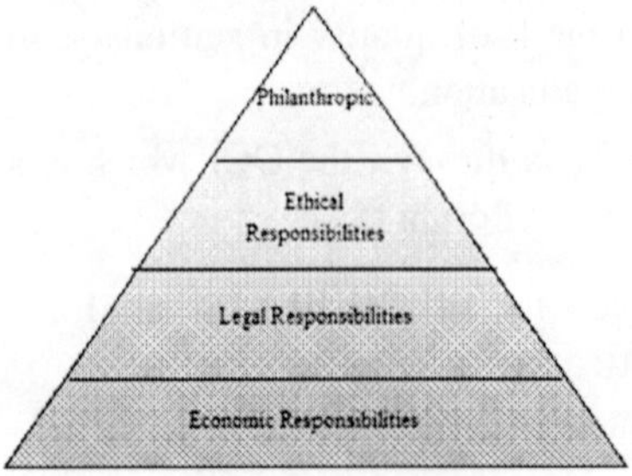

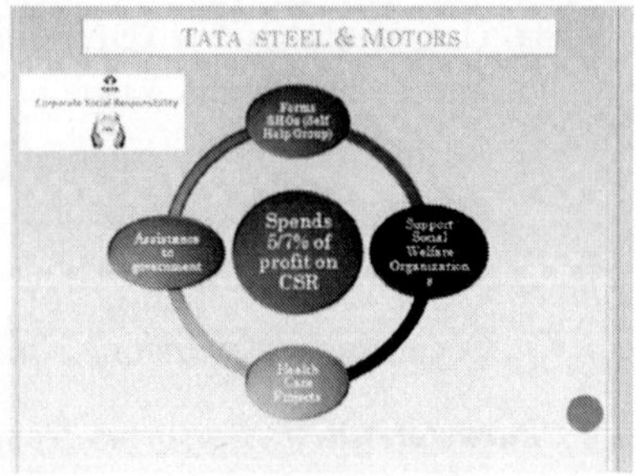

Conclusion

EIA study is a valuable tool for identifying the potential impacts on Environment and to source appropriate technologies for mitigating the impacts to tolerable levels. The effort put in by professionals in collecting as much technical details as possible about the project, the Baseline Data, Meteorological Data etc., can be of great use in defining a problem with better clarity for a realistic solution. EIA is a legal document and any attempt to provide wrong facts or down playing of relevant information is an offence. Many project proponents consider investment for an EIA study as a burden and settle for economical rates and ultimately end up with inordinate delays for want of factual data by the authorities. EIA Study is a protective weapon against vested interest groups and will defend scientifically and legally the right for existence of an Environment-friendly project. As per Carr-Saunders and Wilson in the year (1933) believes to be professional and was to serve the public interest. As Parsons later (1951) he expressed it in more theoretically sophisticated terms, the institutional forms of the Anglo-American professions embodied on implicit contract. Today most 'professionals' work in large organisations for a salary. But this transformation, we argue, is less significant than the mobilisation of concepts of professional values and self-identity by employers in pursuit of organisational goals which are not necessarily supported by their employees. Since the norms of new professionalism are shared by all consultancies and experts. The proponent prefers the EIA to find minimal environmental impacts to facilitate the development process and to avoid the imposing of potentially costly mitigation measures. The consultants preparing the EIS are contracted and paid by the proponent to find and assess environmental impacts. The consultants work with uncertain project data provided by the proponent and have to work on a fixed schedule and budget, which prevents them from doing their job properly. By using uncertainties in the results or using their expert judgement, an EIA professional can interpret his or her results with a certain level of subjectivity. As we have seen, the general framework for a professional order for EIA practitioners, with similar features to the Order of CPAs, is already in place: Public Trust in Profession, Qualification to Join, Code of Ethics and Professional Practice, Continued Professional Development, Enforcement and Penalties. EIA legislation would need to be amended to make membership in the Order mandatory for all involved in preparing environmental impact statements. This would ensure that EIS authors follow strict codes of ethics and best practice and that they are qualified for the task. At the same time, it is important that the codes of ethics and professional deontology are followed; thus, strict penalties must be in place and enforce to ensure that members of the order are fulfilling their duties and responsibilities to the client, the government, the public and the environment. Overall a professional order could improve the public's trust and confidence in EIA practitioners and more importantly, their environmental assessment work.

This paper, presents an initial idea to inspire thought about the topic and to encourage discussion about the EIA profession and the way it is organised. However, EIA profession can be concluded as an emerging profession as not all the characteristics have been found in it. Though the state and QCI team tries to imply its best efforts to make it a full fledge profession. Hence, we conclude by EIA as an emerging profession with lots of challenges in the globalisation era.

The Way Forward

For EIA to reach its full potential within the region, four key challenges need to be met, as outlined below.

Establish Conditions Conducive to EIA Consistent

EIA legislation and policy is required within each country and across the region. However, even with optimal legislation, the current perception of EIA as a 'green tool' must be reversed before EIA will be embraced and used to help meet critical priorities such as poverty reduction and improved socio-economic development. Ideally, this process needs to occur in the context of peace, stability, good governance and a healthy macroeconomic environment.

Improve Strategic Planning

EIA should be integrated into large-scale issues such as regional and transboundary initiatives, core national strategies, the African Union and NEPAD. To be fully effective, EIA should be linked with the full project life cycle.

Improve Human and Institutional Capacity

Inadequate expertise in EIA within the region is a severe limitation. Existing fragmented EIA expertise needs to be consolidated, and a strong culture of sharing best practice across the region promoted. A substantial effort is required to build and maintain human capacity, especially to reverse the 'brain drain' from government into private institutions, nongovernmental organisations (NGOs) and parastatals and, to a lesser extent, the exodus of skilled EIA practitioners from the region. Capacity can be optimised through adopting flexible institutional arrangements and diversifying approaches towards decision-making processes through, for example, forming partnerships between government departments, and between governments and NGOs.

Improve EIA Implementation

The implementation of EIA across the region could be enhanced through demonstrating the social, economic and ecological benefits of good practice and ensuring that existing policy is put into practice. Regular monitoring is necessary to ensure that developers implement the agreed-upon mitigation measures that result from EIAs, and to assess the effectiveness of these measures. Diversifying EIA to include strategic (including regional), cumulative, transboundary, and 'fast track' environmental assessment would ensure that it improves strategic planning, project implementation and the growth of Africa's small-scale and informal sectors.

Source: Innovate Journal of Business Management, Vol. 1, Issue 3, 2013, 6-10.

References

Adams, Bert N. and Sydie, R.A. 2001. *Sociological Theory*. New Delhi: Vistaar Publications.

Bauman, Zygmunt. 1989. *Sociological Response to Post modernity*. Thesis Eleven.

Bettelheim, C. 1968. *India Independent*, London: MacGibbon and Kee.

Degg, Richard. 2006. 'Change from Within: German and Italian Finance in 1990's', in Streck, Wolfgang and Kathleen Thelen. *Beyond Continuity: Institutional Change in Advanced Political Economies*. Oxford: Oxford University Press.

Fukuyama, Francis. 1992. *The End of History and the Last Man*. New York: Free Press.

Gajare, R.S. 2014. 'A conceptual study of CSR development in India'. D.B. Patil and D.D. Bhakkad, *Redefining Management Practices and Marketing in Modern Age Dhule, India*. Atharva Publications (pp. 152-154).

Giddens, Anthony. 1990. *The Consequences of Modernity*. Cambridge: Polity.

Gilpin, Robert. 2001. *Global Political Economy: International Economic Order*. Princeton and Oxford: Princeton University Press.

Jain, Sagar Globalisation and India (Lecture). University of N. Carolina.

Kastia, Ravi. Globalisation and India's Business Prospective (Lecture).

Ojha, A.K. August 2002. 'Globalisation and Liberalisation Prospects of New World Order'. *Third Concept – An International Journal of Ideas*.

Globalisation and Poverty: Centre for International Economics, Australia.

Globalisation Trend and Issues T.K. Velayudham.

Globalisation: Imperatives, Challenges and the Strategies.

Globalisation of Indian economy by Era Sezhiyan.

Heileiner, Eric. 2006. 'Alternatives to Neoliberalism?' in Stubs, Richard and Geoffrey Underhill. *Political Economy and the Changing Global Order*. Oxford: Oxford University Press.

Held, David and Anthony McGrew. 2009. *Governing Globalisation*, Polity.

Huntington, Samuel. 1996. *The Clash of Civilisations and the Remaking of World Order*, New York: Simon & Schuster.

International Journal of Management and Social Sciences Research (IJMSSR). June 2014. ISSN: 2319-4421 Vol. 3, No. 6.

Intimations of Post-modernity, London: Routledge, 1992.

"Executive summary and recommendations: CSR in India–Perspectives for Business". 1 May 2007.

"Implications of Companies Act, 2013 Corporate Social Responsibility". Grant Thornton India LLP. Retrieved 7 March 2014.

"Making Sense of Corporate Social Responsibility".

"The Flag Off of CSR Rules: India Inc.'s To-Do List for Compliance to Section-135". Forbes. 4 March 2014. Retrieved on 7 March 2014.

"Understanding and Encouraging Corporate Responsibility in South Asia". 2001.

Chahoud, Tatjana; Johannes, Emmerling; Dorothea, Kolb; Iris, Kubina; Gordon, Repinski; Catarina, Schläger. 2007. "Corporate Social and Environmental Responsibility in India–Assessing the UN Global Compact's Role".

Khanna, Parul; Gitika, Gupta. January 2011. Parul Khanna Paper_Corporate_ Social_Responsibility-1[1.pdf. "Status of Corporate Social Responsibility: In Indian Context".

Sathish, Ramya. "Corporate Social Responsibility in India–Putting Social-Economic Development on a Fast Track".

Rai, V.N. Repositioning India in the Globalised World (Lecture).

National Accreditation Board for Education and Training Quality Council of India. June, 2015.

Chapter - 18

Equity and Social Justice in Large Public Irrigated Command: An Analysis of Upper Ganga River Basin

—Ravindra Kumar

Land, Water, and Environment-the three pillars of ecological service providers, if degraded globally on the name of development, giving surge to rising temperature, pollution, no-flows in the rivers and poor health, what would happen to the concern of food security and poverty alleviation? While raising the most pertinent ecological issues, the paper further ponders into the question of water. The author assumes that the farmers are the best persons to provide the field view about the accessibility of irrigation water by delineating into questions of who gets water and who does not and; how water becomes accessible with what kind of instrumental means and ends. In view of this, a survey of farmers was conducted by WWF-India during Jan-Feb 2016 in Lower Ganga Canal and March-April, 2016 in Upper Ganga Canal command areas to overview 150 years old public irrigation system (UGC commissioned since 1854 with cultural command area of 9 lakh ha and LGC commissioned since 1878 having CCA of 11.2 lakh ha). The research finds a significant decline in both designed irrigated area over time to about 6 lakh ha annually against their created irrigation potential of 8.37×10^5 ha and 8.72×10^5 ha respectively. It is estimated that water input is three-times higher over evapotransmision (Et) requirements of crops. Excessive use of ground water in canal commands by 88 per cent (UGC) to 95 per cent (LGC) by farmers has been found due to water guzzling cropping pattern and unreliable canal supplies, leading to excess energy consumption and overdrawal of groundwater. Surprisingly, high crop yields have been seen in middle and tail ends of canal system during kharif and rabi respectively, but at increased cost of cultivation. Migration of young farmers from canal tail-ends in particular and from rural to urban areas in general is frequent in the area due to reasons of income and employment disparity. With the new land acquisition policy operative providing compensation @ 4 times higher than the market rate, most of the farmers would like to move out of agriculture for better incomes. At the same time, it provides an opportunity for intensive cropping and commercial agriculture with less land and water. On the basis of the findings, *the paper suggests that canal supply could be regulated in a better way to match the irrigation demand, i.e., for improving dependability while reducing the surface water wastage. Judicious use of surface and groundwater is essential to meet the irrigation demand and to ascertain adequacy. Proper utilisation of groundwater potential could help in improving the cropping intensity. Alternatively, canal supplies could be curtailed on head and used to meet the tail-end requirements, i.e., to ascertain equity and to avoid environmental degradation in command areas.*

Key Words: *Equity, Social Justice, Irrigated Command, Livelihoods, Ecosystem Services.*

1.0 Introduction

1.1 Equity and Social Justice

Public irrigation system aims to facilitate and ensure judicious, equitable and sustainable management, allocation and optimal utilisation of water resources for ensuring sustainable development and more inclusive growth in the state. Ending hunger through sustainable agricultural practices is one of United Nation's 17 Sustainable Development Goals-Vision 2030, could generate 22 million new jobs in India and 80 million worldwide by 2030 (Fraser Thompson, TOI, Nov. 2016). Two main sources of innovation to yields– when to plant seeds and informing of crop prices in the market by mobile internet to small farmers(<2 ha) and for large farms use of drone around improvement in soil health to precision farming techniques on application of fertilisers have been advocated.

1.2 Globalisation and Environment

Globalisation is where the key to modern world order lays superiority through technology. This open market economy affects the lives of the common man, natural resources, environment and fabrics of culture. Deprive the opponent of the latest technology and then dictate your terms in an unequal contest. Technology feeds on itself. These innovations of all kinds have made life more comfortable but at the cost of increased demands for natural resources. In 2015, global demand for natural resources has exceeded six days before of 2014, what the planet's ecosystems can renew in a year.

A policy study by D. S. Swamy (1994) concludes that, "the process of globalisation since 1991 continues and intensifies the anti-people process of development that has been going on since Independence. Its aims are neither to reduce poverty and unemployment nor to provide basic needs." What is most disconcerting is the fact that under the liberalisation process agriculture which is the backbone of the Indian economy has been further relegated to the background. Plan outlay on agricultural development, irrigation and flood control which accounted for 19 per cent in 1990-91 has been reduced to 12 per cent in 1997-98. Agriculture accounted for only 15 per cent of bank advances has come down to 12 per cent. Not only is that half of rural deposits routed to urban areas. Cooperative credit societies have also failed to meet the credit needs of farming population. Private investment in agriculture is also not likely to go up. Growth rate of food grains production which was 2.8 per cent during 1967-68 to 1992-93 has come down to 1.7 per cent during 1990-91 to 1996-97 and the myth of food self-sufficiency may exploded. The rural urban divide gets accentuated (Kripa Shankar, 1997).

With 330 million affected by drought, India urgently needs better water management. Mitigation measures must include reducing soil erosion, augmenting soil moisture, slowing rainwater drainage and improving the efficiency of water use. The State must involve communities in building and maintaining the water harvesting structures. Outside the water-rich Ganga-Brahmputra-Meghana (GBM) basin and the western coastline, India's water map is uneven. Just 29 per cent of water resources service 64 per cent of its land area and rest depend on rains. India needs a time bound plan for controlled irrigation- privileging water for basic needs. Recognising right to water signals that how water governance is politically and legally held responsible, enabling those who are denied water to have means to contest and struggle for water (Jay *et al,* 2011, Water Conflicts, 2015).

1.3 Canal Modernisation and External Donors

The withdrawal of financial support in 'Modernisation of Upper Ganga Canal Project' in 1982 by World Bank and now financing Water Sector Restructuring Project, Uttar Pradesh since 2002 (phase-I, 2002-11 for Sarda Sahayak Irrigation project) and since 2013 (phase-II) for modernisation of Lower Ganga Canal Irrigation project by improving PLGC capacity from 4000 to 8900 cusec to increase kharif irrigation intensity to 46.5 per cent, annual 82.5 per cent, improving water and soil productivity through farmer water school at outlet command areas where improvement in irrigation water availability and timely support to water user associations will be integrated with improved agriculture production and on-farm water management practices under ongoing UPWSRP -II (2013-20). The analysis underlines the critical importance of converging rehabilitation investments with investments in agriculture and institutions below outlet levels to realise the optimum returns to rehabilitation investments. Inclusion of benefits from such interventions coming from agriculture intensification (71 per cent) substantially improved the ERR from 7.7 per cent (irrigated area expansion by 20 per cent only) to over 19 per cent (PAD, World Bank, 2013).

1.4 Water and Welfare

This paper presents farmer survey conducted in Ganga Canal Commands (UGC and LGC) extended from Haridwar to Allahabad to map the mood of farmers in saving water for the sake of Restoring the Ganga- Healthier Rivers for safer water and more productive agro-ecosystems, a research undertaken for IWMI led CGIAR project executed by WWF-India and partners.

The national river Ganga is revered by millions of countrymen. This reverence is not only for socio-cultural reasons, but also for providing valuable resources for food production in the Indo-Gangetic plains. The silt-laden water used for irrigation makes the land fertile and provides much required watering for the crop fields. Therefore, in true sense, the river Ganga is a lifeline for the country. Resource intensive farming has been seen all along the Ganges River Fig. 18.1 (Astad Pastakia, 2014). UGC and LGC network between Ganga-Yamuna doab is shown in Fig. 18.2. The water balance study in UGC command shows that water INPUTS = 9752 MCM and OUTPUTS = 2702 MCM (Crop ET). The overall irrigation water use efficiency being 27.7 per cent (Fig 18.3). The water allocation, roster for distribution is shown in Fig. 18.4 (Ravindra, 2008).

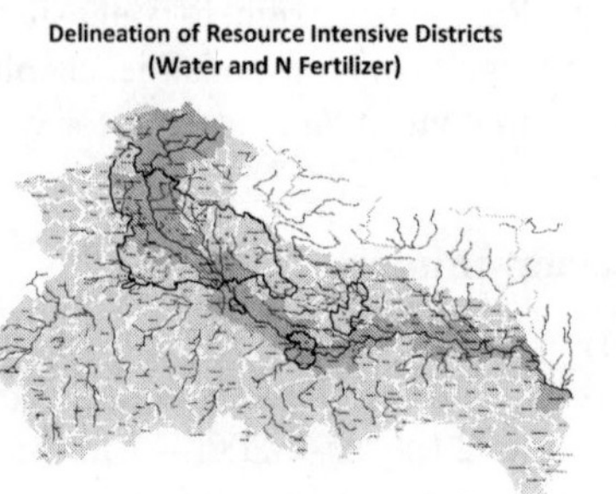

Figure 18.1: Credit: WWF-India, 2014.

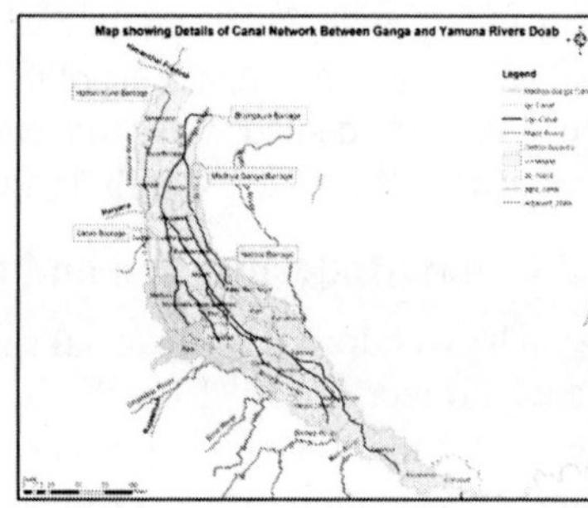

Figure 18.2: Main canal network in UGC and LGC command.

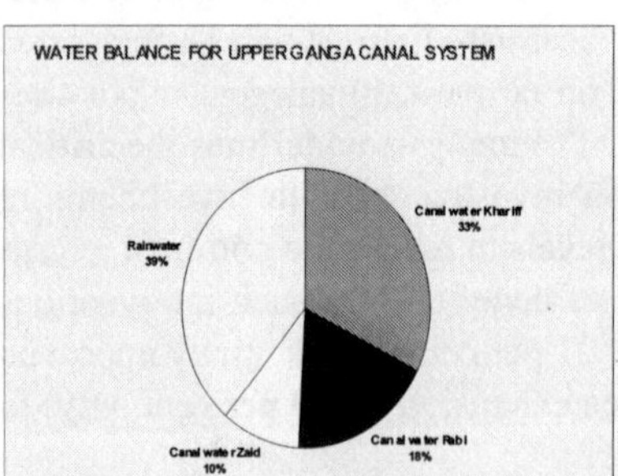

Figure 18.3: Water balance for UGC.

SERVICES

Allocation: Sufficient during kharif - Insufficient for rabi
Initial design Kharif (66% of CCA) (April to September) & Rabi (40% of CCA) (November to March)

Scheduling: Roster at distributary level based on availability of water during previous year KHARIF : 3 weeks ON 1 week OFF - RABI 2 weeks ON 2 weeks OFF

Service to farmers : Proportional system
Deliveries of discharge in distributaries (based on ratio of land) and proportional sharing along disty and minors.

Figure 18.4: Water Allocation and Scheduling of water.

2.0 Survey area

The project area defined as Upper Ganga river basin means the stretch of Ganga from Haridwar to Allahabad; mainly taking into account the river stretch and perennial irrigation systems-Upper Ganga Canal (UGC) taking off from Bhimgoda Barrage and Lower Ganga Canal (LGC) taking off from Narora Barrage. These diversions have critical implication onto the flows and water levels in the downstream stretches of Ganga. Farmers' reaction for saving water in agriculture and to leave some water to see Ganges ever flowing, survey data is analysed and compared for LGC and UGC commands.

Survey Geo-Locations: All the farmer survey locations were geo-tagged. Based on geo-referencing; following maps (Fig. 18.5 and Fig. 18.6) were created to show the locations, where surveys were conducted; in addition to that, the Main canal plus Branch canals of the system were also overlaid for easier understanding.

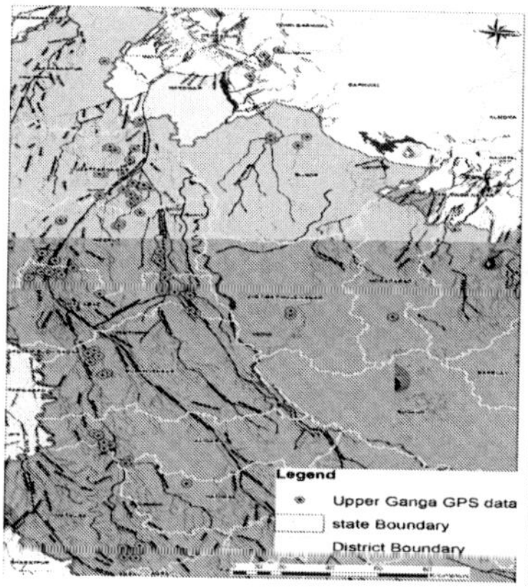

Figure 18.5: Farmer Survey locations on Upper Ganga System.

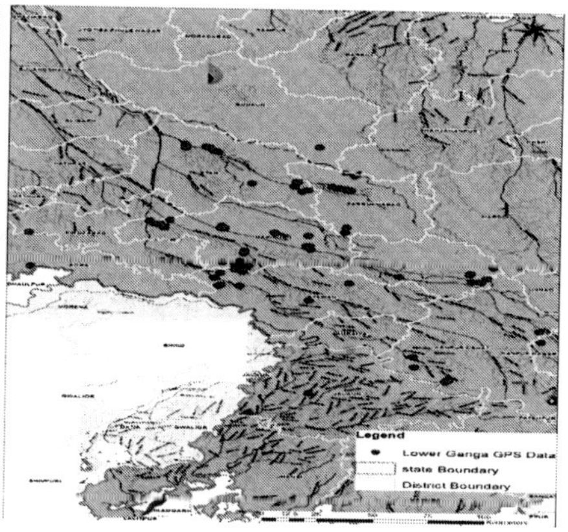

Figure 18.6: Farmer Survey locations on Lower Ganga System.

The performance on these canal systems in terms of irrigated area over the time is given in Table 18.1.

Table 18.1: Irrigation by UGC and LGC system in lakh hectare

Canal System	*Head Discharge (in Cumec)*	*CCA lakh ha*	*Proposed Irrigation in lakh ha*		*Max. Irrign/ Potential Created, lakh ha*	*1399 Crop Year (1991-92)*		*1409 Crop Year (2001-02)*		*1418 Crop Year (2010-11)*		*Average irrigated area*
			Kharif	*Rabi*		*Kharif*	*Rabi*	*Kharif*	*Rabi*	*Kharif*	*Rabi*	*Kharif Rabi*
UGC	297.3	9.02	4.27 (47.3%)	4.11 (45.6%)	6.96 (77%)/ 8.38 (93%)	3.53	3.33	2.88	2.29	3.23	2.82	3.21 2.81 = 6.02
LGC	240.7	11.27	4.67(41%)	4.06 (36%)	6.54 (58%)/ 8.73 (77%)	3.03	3.50	2.58	2.28	2.61	3.38	2.74 3.05 = 5.79

(*Source*: UP Irrigation and Water Resources Department)

Note: After modernisation post Tehri dam irrigation intensity in UGC (due to PUGC enhanced capacity of 13500 cusec) for kharif is increased to 66 per cent and thus annual106 per cent and for LGC is 82.5 per cent.

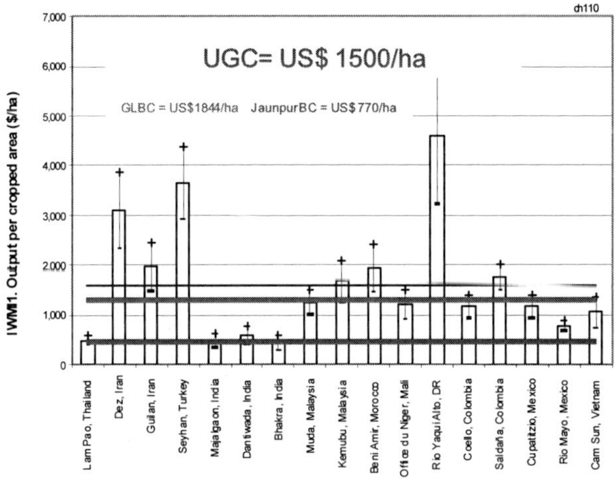

Figure 18.7: Production per cropped area in UGC, GLBC, JBC and others.

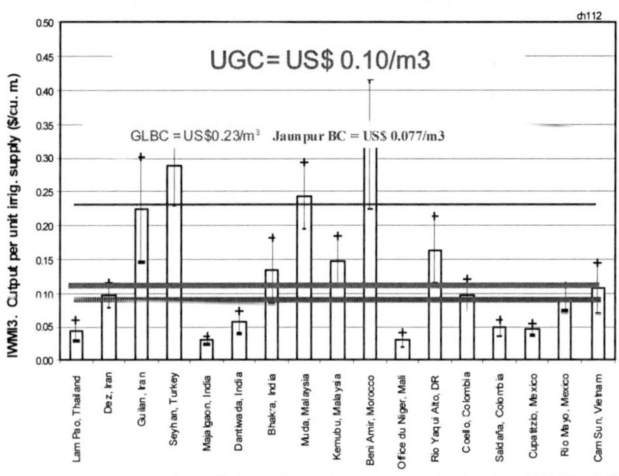

Figure 18.8: Productivity of Water in UGC as compared with other system.

As compared to best practices of irrigation in the world, performance of UGC in terms of output /crop area and output / unit water supply rank below other system even one in Karnataka state but far above than Sharda Sahayak Jaunpur branch canal system as shown in Fig. 18.7 and Fig. 18.8 respectively (*Ibid,* 2008).

3.0 Objectives and Time Period for Farmers Survey

WWF-India conducted farmers' survey in LGC and UGC command for "Restoring the Ganga-Healthier Rivers for safer water and more productive agro-ecosystems". These results are tabulated below as comparator for LGC and UGC farmers's willingness to change in improving water and agriculture productivity and sacrifice for cleaner and healthy Ganges. The survey team conducted farmers' survey during Jan-Feb 2016 in LGC and March-April, 2016 in UGC command areas.

3.1 Sample Size

270 farmers is the sample size for each of the canal system, so a total sample size for canal farmers is about 550. This number has been proportionally divided as per the head-middle-tail reach of the canal systems. Additionally, farmers from 'near-to-canal' and 'far-from-canal' are also included in the survey.

3.2 Findings of Farmers' Survey

The summary of farmers survey output is given in Table 18.2.

Table 18.2 Results of farmers' survey in UGC and LGC command

Activity	*UGC*	*LGC*	*Remarks*
Water allocation: heavy use of GW in command	88 per cent farmers use GW to supplement canal irrigation	95 per cent farmers use GW to supplement canal irrigation	UGC have adequate water supply from canal Tehri reservoir
Rabi crop irrigation, nos. of irrigation	758 farmers have GW support in irrigation	936 farmers have GW support in irrigation	UGC follow one week off and LGC Two week off roster
Zaid crop, nos. of irrigation	713	247	GW supported
	4 per cent farmers share	2 per cent farmers share	
Capacity of Pumps for GW use			
3 -5 HP >5-10 HP >10-20 HP > 20-40 HP	11 per cent 80 per cent 4 per cent 5 per cent	5 per cent 91 per cent 4 per cent -	Mostly depend upon GW table, location of aquifer and capacity required.
Life of bore >10 years	65 per cent	76 per cent	Often more
Depth of bore> 160 m, nos.	60	10	Governed by geology
Diesel, nos., per cent	103, almost 50 per cemt	70 per cent	Rural electricity quality being poor
Institutional support, nos.	Agri-43, Pvt firm 10, health 6	Agri-29, Irrig, 2, Pvt firm 03, others 2-3	Poor extension service
Need of farmering	Modern Agriculture-253 Farm Demonstration-229	248 180	Willing for moderntrain-ing agriculture Farmer Water School

contd...

Don't get water	25 per cent	26 per cent	Inequity a social issue
Warbandi	59 per cent	26 per cent	If water supply is assured
Canal supply-major Low discharge	Siltation, poor M&R.	Do	Low capacity problem
Gender gap in agri-decision making, nos.	Men-256 Women-1	257 Women 3	Major social issue, land is not in women's name
Level of education Up to high school, nos.	302	317	Educated opt for better service
Land market price, ha, nos. of respondents	Varies from 5 to 190	3 to 45 times of market price	For Lucknow-Agra lakh/ Expressway UPGOV purchased land @ 4
Annual income from culture (INR lakh), respondents	< 0.70, 141 farmers >0.70-1.30, 60 farmer >1.30-2.0, 36 farmer >2.0-4.0, 19 farmer	198 35 20 2	Most of the farmers agri-like to move out of nos of agriculture
Land holdings Marginal < 1 ha Small 1-2 ha Normal >2-5 ha Big > 5 ha	Distribution pattern, 42 per cent 27 per cent 28 per cent 3 per cent	 61 per cent 27 per cent 12 per cent -	Agriculture is the main source of livelihood for 89 per cent and next as farm labour
Main crops	Wheat in rabi 98 per cent Rice in kharif 85 per cent	86 per cent 57 per cent	Sugarcane belt in Muzaffarnagar, Meerut
Soil testing, nos. of respondents	Done 30 Not done 256 Fertiliser application based on soil testing 24	22 238 15	Government is encouraging soil health card
Age of respondents, nos.	>50-60, 134 >40-50, 66 20-40, 52	90 41 128	>50 per cent are above 50 years age and young are moving out agriculture
Irrigation application	Flooding 95 per cent	96 per cent	OFD required
Mode of water conveyance from outlet to field, nos.	Earthen FC, 210 Lined gul, 10 Polythene pipe, 28	155 10 87	High water losses in field application
Pressure irrigation, nos	Nil	4	No sprinkler/drip in canal command
Storage of produce Traditional, 59 per cent	Modern, 41 per cent Na by day	Na is increasing day	Nos. of cold storage
Marketing of produce	Krishi Upaj Mandi, 61 per cent, Local middlemen, 39 per cent	Mandi	West UP farmers use NCR market opportunity
Visit to river Ganga festivals for bathing	97 per cent visited on	89 per cent sentiments prevail	Religious/cultural
Cleanliness and depth	Unsatisfactory 56 per cent	49 per cent	Low flow, low depth
Pollution level change in last 20 yrs	Slight degrada, 72 per cent High degrad.,18 per cent Worst degrd., 2 per cent No change, 8 per cent	50 per cent 11 per cent 8 per cent 21 per cent	Untreated industrial, municipal and agri cultural wastes drain directly into river

contd...

Trouble perception in bathing	Inadequate depth, 62 per cent No problem, 38 per cent	64 per cent 36 per cent	Channel multiplication
Transfer of canal water for Ganga	Agree, 94 per cent Don't agree, 6 per cent	80 per cent 20 per cent	Religious sense of sacrifice for Ganga largely prevails.
Use of additional water created through improved WUE, nos.	Sacrifice for E-flows, 103, Change in CP, 132	127 60	People could be easily motivated for Aviral and Nirmal Ganga.
Perception on aquatic life in Ganges	Decreasing, 89 per cent Increasing, 2 per cent Constant, 2 per cent No opinion, 7 per cent	73 per cent 5 per cent 21 per cent 21 per cent	People like to see aquatic life in Ganga as religious sentiments
Support to water allocation for maintaining aquatic life in Ganges	Agree, 97 per cent Disagree, 3 per cent	81 per cent 19 per cent	People are concerned with restoration of aquatic life in Ganges

4.0 Discussion on Findings

4.1 Crop Productivity HMT wise t/ha in UGC as compared with LGC

It has been observed that in case of wheat highest productivity in both the canal system has been obtained by tail end farmers whereas paddy productivity is maximum in middle command, not in head canal command where water is always available (Fig. 18.9 and Fig. 18.10). This may be due to degradation soil health due to waterlogging and salinity due to often more application of water.

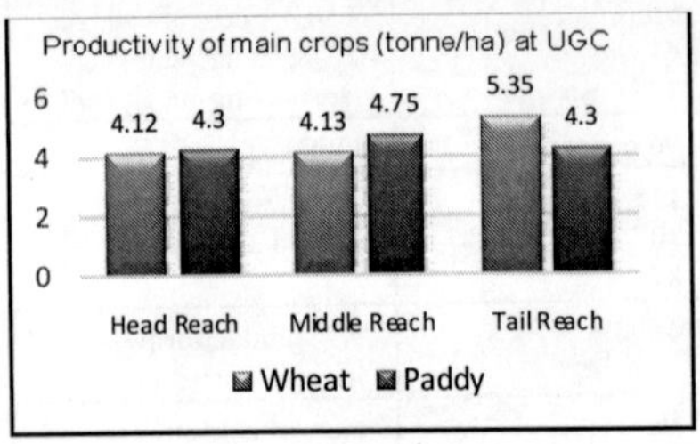

Figure 18.9: Productivity of wheat and Rice crops in UGC.

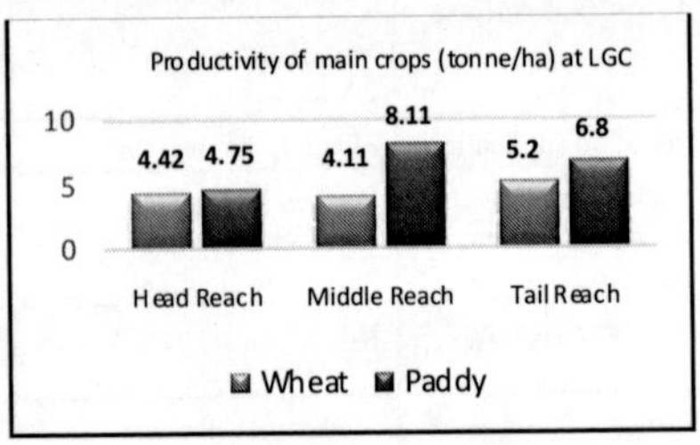

Figure 18.10: Productivity of wheat and Rice crops in LGC.

4.2 Cost incurred Rs/ha in UGC as compared with LGC

Table 18.3: Crop production cost in UGC

Head		*Middle*		*Tail*	
Wheat	*Paddy*	*Wheat*	*Paddy*	*Wheat*	*Paddy*
7250	7171	6252	5020	11378	9139

Table 18.4: Production cost in LGC

Head		*Middle*		*Tail*	
Wheat	*Paddy*	*Wheat*	*Paddy*	*Wheat*	*Paddy*
8187	7218	8349	9233	6351	11686

It is concluded that cost of produce is higher in LGC than in UGC. Paddy cultivation in tail end is more costly due to more energy consumption.

4.3 Number of Average Irrigation by Source

Table 18.5: Number of average irrigation by Canal and Tubewell UGC vs LGC

Season/Source	*Head*	*Middle*	*Tail*	*Source*	*Head*	*Middle*	*Tail*
Rabi							
Canal	2.4	3.1	2.5	Canal	1.9	1.8	2.4
Tubewell	3.7	2.9	3.7	Tubewell	3.6	4.3	3.4
Kharif							
Canal	4.0	4.4	4.3	Canal	3.5	2.5	3.8
Tubewell	5.9	4.2	3.6	Tubewell	3.5	3.5	3.1
Zaid							
Canal	4.6	5.5	5.0	Canal	1.5	1.3	3.5
Tubewell	6.0	3.5	5.4	Tubewell	3.4	6.2	4.2

It could be concluded from perusal of Table 18.5 that due to more water availability number of irrigation is more in UGC than LGC. Tubewell irrigation is more dominating and reliable than canal supplies.

4.4 Migration: Migration is Greater in Middle and Tail Reaches

5.0 Presentation of Results of Farmers Survey in UGC Command

The Head Reach Branch is Deoband and Tail Reach Branch is Mat from which Hatras branch also taking off; however, the direct distributaries are across all the reaches in the UGC. The Branch Canals selected by the team for the purpose of Baseline Surveys are as follows–

(a) Deoband Branch Canal (head)
(b) Anoopshahr Branch Canal (middle)
(c) Mat Branch Canal (tail)
(d) Direct Distributaries off main canal

The responses of all the 270 respondent farmers from UGC were fed-in a excel-sheet for analysis.

5.1 Findings from the Field–the Current Scenario

This subsection is organised in a manner, where key thematic statement is made which is supported by a figure and then a short narrative to substantiate the finding.

Heavy Use of Ground Water in the Canal Command Area:

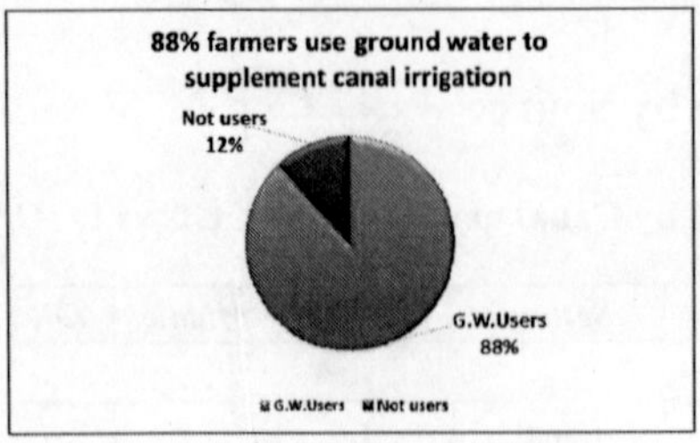

Figure 18.11: Use of GW in canal command.

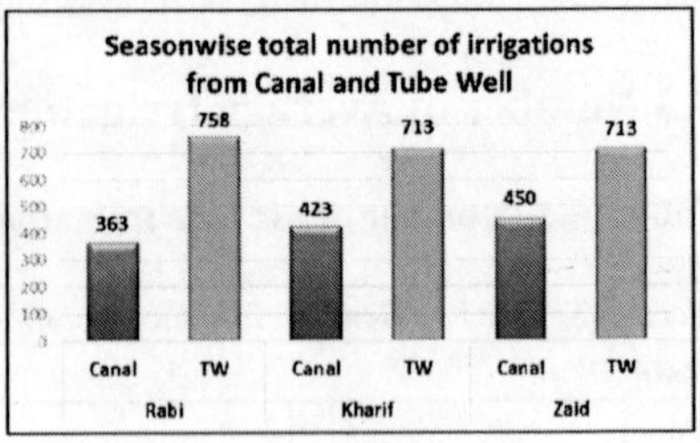

Figure 18.12: Source-wise total number of irrigation.

It was found that 88 per cent of the farmers in the canal command use ground water to supplement canal irrigation. Besides, the use of ground water in comparison to canal water is very high. In rabi season the number of irrigations provided by the tubewells are more than 2 times than canal water. In zaid (hot) season the number of irrigations provided by the tubewells is more than 1.5 times than canal water. The heavy reliance of the farmers on ground water may be attributed to (i) designed partial coverage of command area for irrigation by the canal and (ii) unreliable canal water supplies. This leads to avoidable extraction of ground water and consumption of fossil fuel and energy. This situation offers an opportunity to switch over to better and scientific methods of irrigation, namely piped conveyance, drip and sprinkler technology, promoting better water distribution methods like turn-fixation (warabandi) and improving rosters of canal.

A strong case for scientific conjunctive use of surface and ground water also emerges from this scenario. An institutional mechanism is needed to implement the conjunctive use of surface and ground water which calls for development and strengthening of Water User Associations in the area.

Farmers have Excess Pumping Capacity, Yet Don't Share

Only four per cent farmers share water though they have excessive pumping capacity to meet their own demand (Fig. 18.13). Well capacity is on decline (Fig. 18.14). Mostly use Diesel pump set (Fig. 18.15) and low extension support provided (Fig. 18.16).

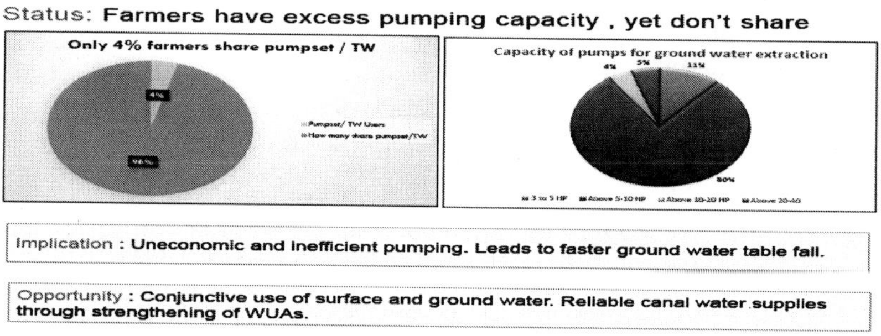

Figure 18.13: Not sharing of resources to other farmers.

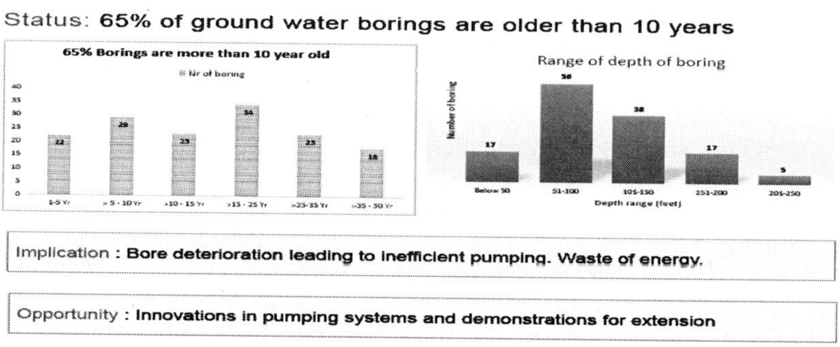

Figure 18.14: Capacity of well on decline.

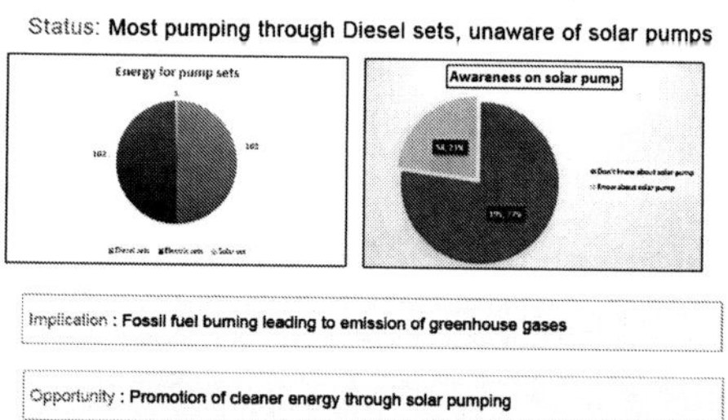

Figure 18.15: Not interested in alternate use of pumping energy.

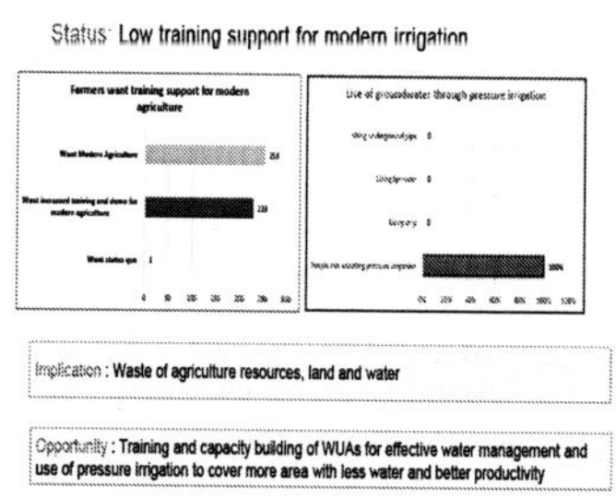

Figure 18.16: Poor Institutional support.

Gender Gap in Agriculture Decision Making and Poor Education amongst Farmers

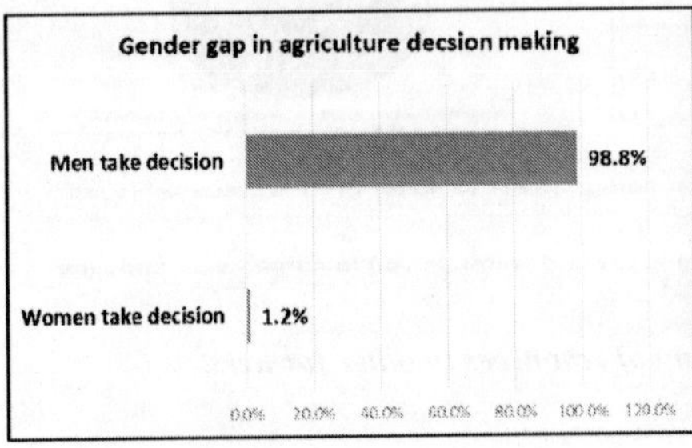

Figure 18.17: Gender gap in agriculture decision making.

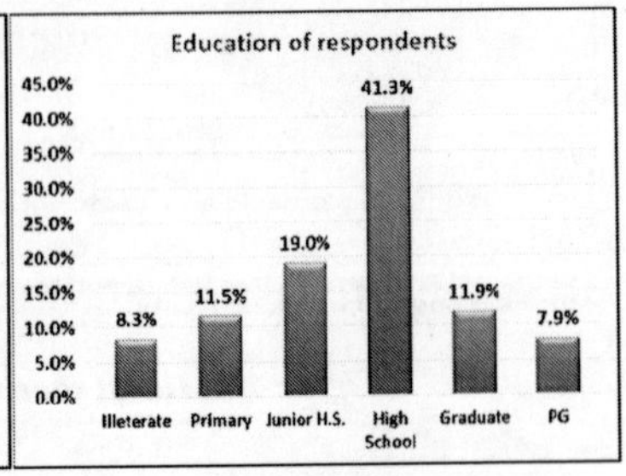

Figure 18.18: Poor education of farmers.

It was found during the Survey that only 1.2 per cent of women take part in agriculture related decision making (Fig. 18.17). Generally, the land is not in the name of women. This becomes a great disadvantage when membership is based on land holding. For example, under UP-PIM Act, a member of WUA must be a land holder. Since the land is not in the name of women, they are not entitled to be the members of WUA. It is suggested that the name of husband and wife, both should be recorded in the land title. Madhya Pradesh has amended its PIM Act to include wife of landholder as a member of WUA.

It was also found that the level of education of respondents is quite low. More than 8 per cent of the farmers are totally illiterate while another 30.5 per cent of the farmers have primary/junior high school level village education (Fig. 18.18). It suggests that the communication and extension strategies should be based on audio-visuals and demonstrations and the use of handouts and pamphlets should be minimised.

Small Land Holdings and Reluctance to Join Contract Farming

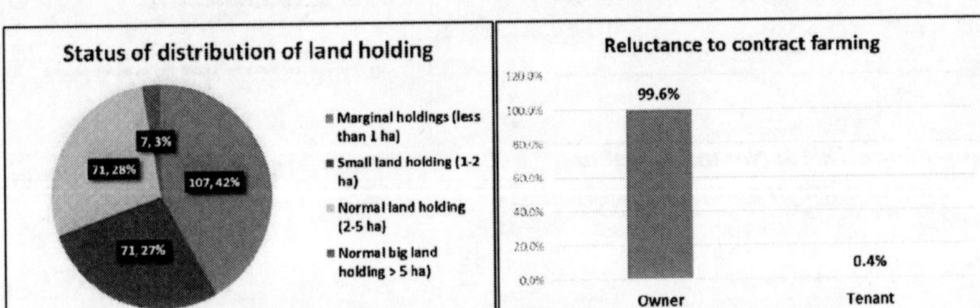

Figure 18.19: Marginal holdings with 42 per cent farmers and hence reluctant to contact farming.

Low returns from agriculture as land holdings are not commercially viable.

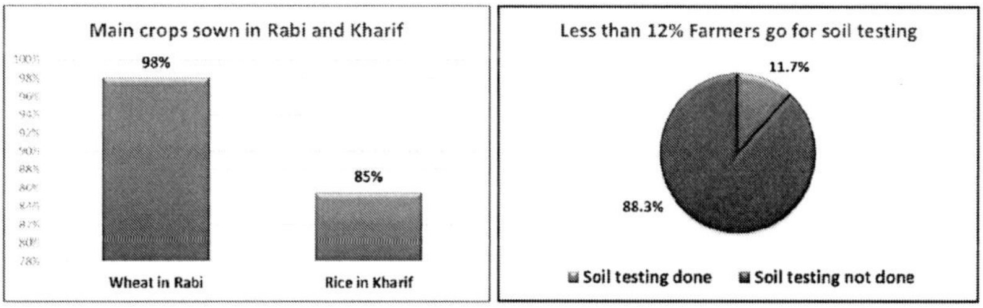

Figure 18.20: Livelihood based cropping pattern without scientific input management.

It was found during the Survey that the wheat -rice cropping pattern is predominant in the command. About 98 per cent farmers sow wheat in rabi season and 85 per cent farmers sow paddy in kharif season (Fig. 18.20). For small and marginal farmers, this cropping pattern ensures food security more than income. The productivity of both these crops is around 4 tonne / ha which is quite low seeing the potential of land productivity. The poor productivity may be attributed to the unscientific thumb-rule input management without the soil testing. Less than 12 per cent of the farmers got their soil samples tested and only 9 per cent farmers applied the fertiliser doses based on soil testing recommendations.

There is a lot of scope for improvement in productivity and change to more remunerative and less water consuming crops.

Poor conveyance and irrigation application methods causing heavy seepage and water losses at field application level

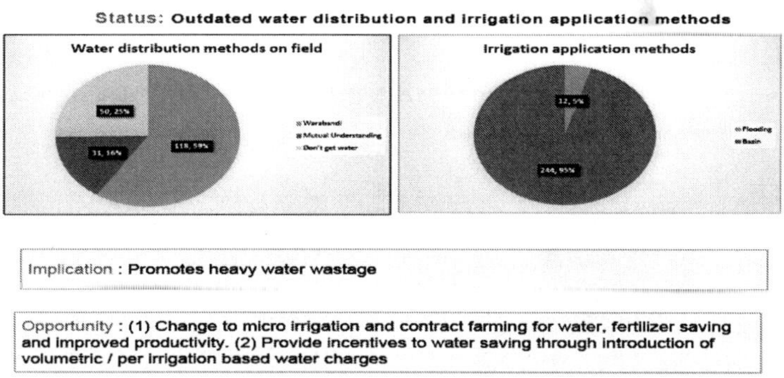

Figure 18.21: Kind of water distribution system and irrigation application methods.

There is lot of seepage loss in conveyance of water from outlet to the fields since 84.7 per cent farmers still use earthen channels to convey water to their fields (Fig. 18.21). In addition to it, field application methods are outdated causing a lot of water wastage during irrigation application. Farmers largely use basin method for applying irrigation while modern irrigation application techniques like drip and sprinkler irrigation save a lot of water and ensure better productivity. There is an opportunity to adapt micro irrigation for water, fertiliser saving and improved productivity. Policy level changes are also required which provide incentives to water saving through introduction of volumetric/per irrigation based water charges. Although the UP Government has introduced per irrigation based water charges, but the charges are paid by the government on behalf of the farmers. It acts as a disincentive to save irrigation water.

Perception of Farmers

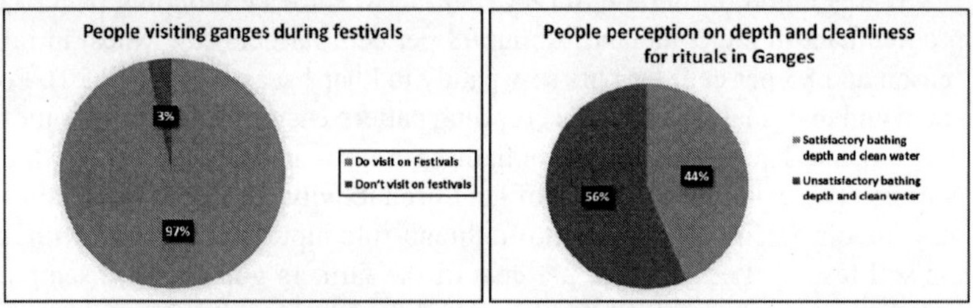

Figure 18.22: People's perception on Ganga is led by religious sentiments.

It was found during the Survey that 97 per cent of respondents visit the Ganga during religious festivals and ceremonies (Fig. 18.22). Only 56 per cent of the respondents found the water depth in Ganga is unsatisfactory for bathing. 44 per cent of the farmers found that Ganga provide satisfactory bathing depth.

Only 8 per cent of the farmers feel that Ganga is severely polluted (Fig. 18.23)

Status: Only 8% people feel that Ganga is severely polluted

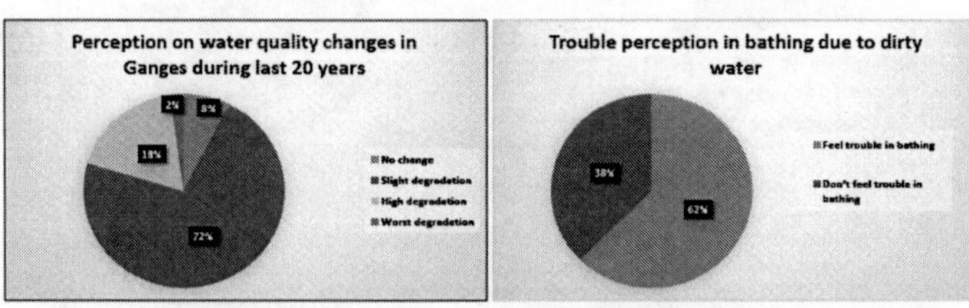

Implication : **Religious sentiments prevail when a decision is taken on Ganga**

Opportunity : **(1) People can be mobilized to work for cleaner Ganga and aviral Ganga, once it is clearly communicated that Ganga is deteriorating fast.**

Figure 18.23: People's perception about water quality of Ganga river.

About 8 per cent of the farmers feel that there is no change in the quality of water in the Ganga since last 20 years. Seventy-two per cent farmers feel that there is only slight degradation in the quality of water in the Ganga since last 20 years. Only 2 per cent of the farmers said that Ganga is severely polluted (Fig. 18.23). When asked about trouble in bathing due to dirty water in the Ganga, 38 per cent of the farmers said that they don't feel any trouble. It shows that the perception of water quality of Ganga is largely guided by the religious sentiments. There is an opportunity that the people can be mobilised to work for cleaner Ganga and aviral Ganga as they are religiously attached to the river.

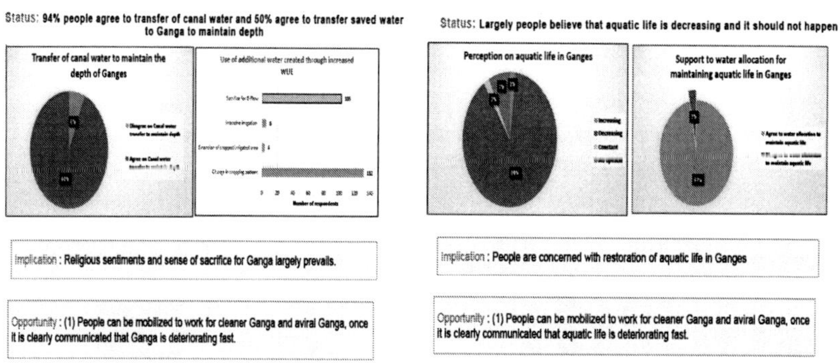

Figure 18.24: Most of the farmers are prepared to transfer canal water for good health of Ganga ji and are concerned with restoration of aquatic life in river Ganga.

But it has to be clearly and convincingly communicated to mobilise them that the Ganga water is deteriorating fast in terms of quality and quantity.

6. Lower Ganga Canal

The Branch canals selected by the team for the purpose of Baseline Surveys are as follows–

(a) Farrukhabad Branch Canal (head),

(b) Kanpur Branch Canal (middle),

(c) Bhognipur Branch Canal (middle to tail),

(d) Etawah Branch Canal (tail).

6.1 Findings from the LGC

No Awareness of PIM Act and Little Institutional Support

PIM Act has not been taken up with required pace and attention in the LGC command area which is mandated by project. Ninety-seven per cent of the farmers' who were interviewed said they have never heard about the PIM Act. Only three per cent admitted that they have heard about the Act but nothing beyond that (Fig. 18.25). If the Water User Associations are established as per the mandate of UP PIM Act, a mechanism of mutual accountability of line agencies and WUAs can be made functional which will greatly encourage the efficient and economic canal water management as the mandate of UPSRP-II.

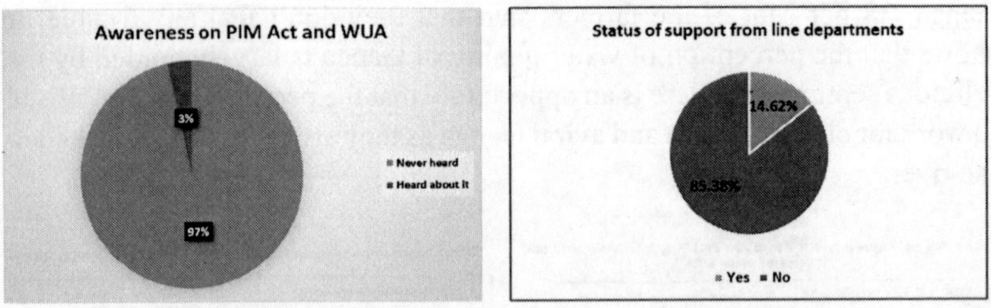

Figure 18.25: Awareness on Participatory Management Act and Functions/Responsibilities of WUAs.

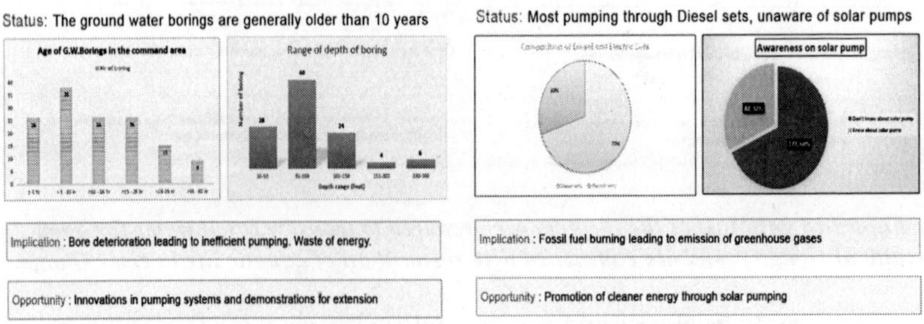

Figure 18.26: Most of diesel driven pumps have outlived their life. Use of cleaner energy improves health.

Land Acquisition Policy of Uttar Pradesh and its Impact on Agriculture

The Government of Uttar Pradesh model of Land acquisition from farmers at a rate 4 times higher than market price though have succeeded in Lukhnow-Agra Express Way Construction without any opposition from land owners and Government of India is adopting this model for Road Construction, this has adversely affected selling of agricultural land to generate money to move away from low gain agriculture sector to do business. This phenomenon has brought many projects unsustainable due to financial burden of increased land cost. The main livelihood is dependent on agriculture (Fig. 18.27) but due to the lucrative market price of agricultural land most of the younger farmers would like to move out of agriculture for the better income (Fig. 18.28).

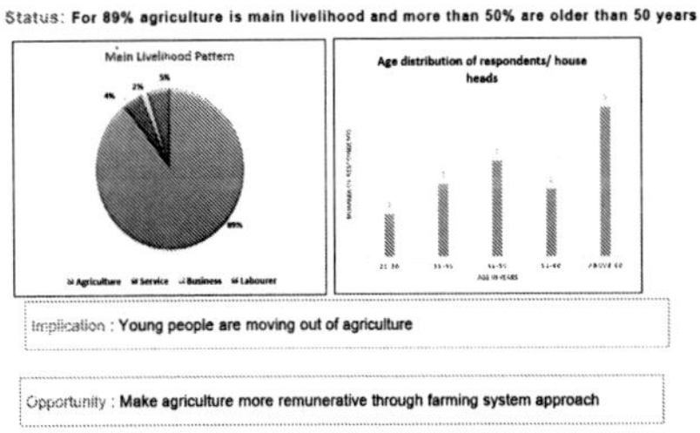

Figure 18.27: Main sources of livelihood of farmers.

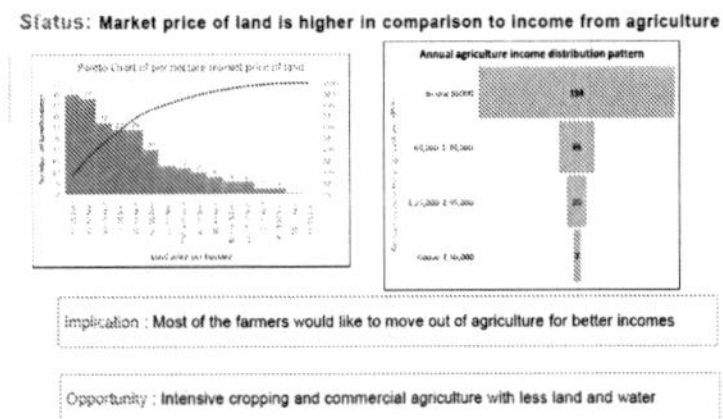

Figure 18.28: Agricultural land market price

The other aspects of survey were the same as found in UGC except for variation in responses as already given in Table 18.2.

7.0 Perspective of Departmental Field Colleagues-Based on Primary Surveys

With a view to understand the perspective of field officials and functionaries from Executive Engineer to Junior Engineers and from Ziledars to Seenchpals; detailed open-ended interviews were conducted in the division and sub-divisions of UGC and LGC. Total number of field colleagues interviewed is thirty-five. For this purpose separate visits to their offices in the fields were undertaken during the month from February to April 2016.

Analysis

A comparative analysis around key aspects which were discussed with the field colleagues was done and the same is presented in following table.

Upper Ganga Canal System (UGC)

The questionnaire captures large set of information regarding canal operation and policies. It also captures the perception of field staff and issues they face on the field on various aspects. A overall summary of various locations along UGC system is mentioned below with respect to head/middle and tail portion.

Aspect	*Head*	*Middle*	*Tail*
➢ Operation of Canal as per irrigation demand schedule fixed in roster	• Yes, but it largely depends on availability of water at head and schedule fixed in roster	• Yes, but it largely depends on availability of water at head and schedule fixed in	• Yes, but it largely depends on availability of water at head and roster **Not getting water as per roster, supply is low**

contd...

<table>
<tr>
<td rowspan="2">➢ Evaluating demand
➢ Delivering, monitoring and measurement accuracy of canal water</td>
<td colspan="3">• Overall water demand for a Minor/Distributaries/Branch command is calculated based on PPA (Proposed protected area) and traditional cropping pattern(Generally overall demand in a command remains constant and change due to change in PPA)·
• Based on PPA, crop water requirement overall demand value is calculated Demand may fluctuate if there is change in PPA
• 15-20 per cent conveyance loss is added to calculated demand
• Demand at minors are added subsequently to get demand at distributaries and then at branch level.
• Seenchpals after field surveys compiling info on type of crop and area sown and time of sowing with interactions and feedbacks from farmers, provide information to division about the water applied, area sown for any dynamic demand and for revenue related records
• Water is delivered as scheduled in roster and may vary according to availability at head
• Monitoring is done through gauge levels marked at regulators (which provides decent accuracy of 90-95 per cent) on Branch/DY and sometimes minor heads
• Gauge register is maintained by "Taar Babu" of a division (info collected from all Branch\DY and minors under command) where water accounting is done
• Seenchpal interacts with Farmers on continuous basis and provide information to division (through Tar babu) for any dynamic change in demand (More or less)</td>
</tr>
<tr>
<td>• Water is delivered to a minor if its demand exceeds 50 per cent (i.e. demand is generated from 50 per cent of the area under minors command)·
• Gauges at most of minor heads are damaged or not present</td>
<td></td>
<td>• Discharge at minors not measured.</td>
</tr>
<tr>
<td rowspan="2">➢ Water supply at head as per roster
➢ Delivering correct volumes to lower reaches
➢ System allowing designed deliveries and improvement required to ensure reliable deliveries</td>
<td colspan="3">• Based on PPA and estimated water availability at head, a delivery schedule is fixed (roster)
• The water is distributed against the schedule set in roster, but amount of water delivered depends on actual water available in the river and subsequent supply at branch /distributaries heads
• Schedule of delivery may change from roster, based on real time demand (feedback from farmers and seenchpals) which is prerogative of in charge of the division
• Gauge levels at head regulators are observed to check amount of water delivered
• Monitoring by field staff till minors and feedbacks from farmers
• Water at non-gated minors are indirectly assessed by looking at gauge levels at Dy's and sometimes water reaching at particular kolaba</td>
</tr>
<tr>
<td>• No continuous supply at tail reaches, but its mandatory to give irrigation atleast once in six
• Rice cultivated areas in tail reaches face water shortage
• System allows design deliveries
• Improvements needed:
  • Canals should be cleaned regularly
  • Funds and staff crunch</td>
<td>• Canal operates as per design delivery
• System allows design deliveries but cleaning months by any means out regularly which decreases canal capacity
• Improvements needed:
  • Staff crunch issue needs to be addressed for reliable deliveries on field</td>
<td>• Canal can operate as per design but to meet the growing demand the design of canals not carried discharge is required which is not the case at present (supply reduced to one third at times)
• Improvements needed:
  • Being tail end</td>
</tr>
</table>

contd...

	a big issue • Water use in Sugar-cane cultivation should be checked. Low water use variety should be used • Sprinklers and drip irrigation should be used to save water • Awareness drive from agriculture department should be carried out on low water use crops	• Canal repair and maintenance to be done regularly	water supply is low, assure design discharge so that demand can be met • Staff crunch issue needs to be addressed
➢ Interferences in canal running ➢ Problems faced in running canal for ensuring reliable deliveries	• Yes, interferences in canal like obstacles, breaches, direct pumping • Size of pipes at kolabas are modified for high intake of water • Case is registered against accused in extreme cases but most of them are resolved amicably with farmers • **Problems faced:** • Political influence is making operation and management very difficult (to assure reliable and equitable supplies) • Heavy usage of pesticides should be avoided, uses too much water • Too much wastage of water from farmers side is observed, being free water • Staff crunch on fields, shortage of funds for maintenance of canal and unauthorised use • No authority of sanctioning funds for local repair work, delay in payments make contractors refuse to work • Farmers dumping agriculture waste in canal • Gates at minors damaged	• **Few instances** of canal interference Case is registered against the accused and fine (Tawaan) imposed • **Problems faced:** • Political influence is making operation and management very difficult • Staff crunch on fields, for shortage of funds maintenance of canal and unauthorised use • Shortage of funds • No authority of sanctioning funds for local repair	• Yes, interferences in canal like obstacles, breaches, direct pumping • **Registering and pursuing the cases and tawaan is difficult in majority of situation. Only extreme cases are pursued** • **Problems faced:** • Political influence is making operation and management very difficult • Staff crunch on fields, shortage of funds for mainte-nance of canal and unauthorised use • Shortage of funds • Free water system should be removed

contd...

➤ Canal water being used for other persons/institutions and other stake holders	• Yes, Drinking water to Delhi and Noida supplied (370 and 50 cusec respectively) from Muzaffarnagar branch		• 150 cusec water to agra drinking water supply, but only after the irrigation demand in command is met
➤ Groundwater usage and implications on command area	• 10 per cent-30 per cent, that too in rice growing season (Kharif) •	• Heavy usage • Private tubewells operating in area • Overuse of Ground-water made several areas in dark zones In past 15-20 years groundwater levels gone down from 25 feet to 250 feet	• Excessive usage from private tubewells in absence of ample canal supply • Water levels going down, increasing operation cost • 60-40 ratio of groundwater: canal water
➤ Status of un-authorised water use and measures to check and most powerful lobby	• Unauthorised use mainly in tail ends • Unauthorised use like inserting bigger pipe in kolaba than govt. installed one to access more water • Farmers lobby is strong and field staff face lot of political influence due to which offences are ignored under pressure • Law and order situation not good	• Very high • Farmers/Politicians lobby	• Moderate
➤ Conflicts in a month and how it is resolved	• Few conflicts, that too happens in summer season • Resolve them amicably with farmers by proper dialogue. • Inspections by survey teams, seenchpal • As farmers are well politically connected the situation is handled carefully • Penalty, FIR in extreme cases	• Few • Regular survey by field staff • Penalty and FIR on complaint but it remains a formality • Police inaction • No support to field staff	• Few conflicts, that too happens in summer season

8.0 Conclusion

1. Survey data in both LGC and UGC command suggests farmer's willingness to adopt modern technology in agriculture and irrigation best practices provided demonstration at their doorstep or elsewhere is shown to them.
2. Farmers appear to sacrifice use of canal water in agriculture to maintain easy-flows in Ganges for *aviral-nirmal* status and are concerned with restoration of aquatic life in Ganges.
3. Issues of Equity and Justice are central to feudal society. Until and unless HDI is improved or might is right concept disappear by live

and let others live in peace with tranquility comes with right to water. Recognising right to water by UP PIM Act 2009 empowers stakeholders that how water governance is politically and legally held responsible, enabling those who are denied water to have means to contest and struggle for water.

4. Canal supply could be regulated in a better way to match the irrigation demand, i.e., for improving Dependability while reducing the surface water wastage.
5. Conjunctive use of Surface and Groundwater is essential to meet the irrigation demand, i.e., to ascertain Adequacy.
6. Proper utilisation of Groundwater potential could help in improving the Cropping Intensity.
7. Alternatively, canal supplies could be curtailed, and used to meet the tail-end requirements, i.e., to ascertain Equity.

Acknowledgement

The author is thankful to Sri Ramujagir Verma of Arthik Vikas and Jan Kalyan Sansthan, UP for conducting survey work, Sri P.K. Sinha, Consultant to World Bank for data analysis along with Mr Suresh Babu, Mr Nitin Kaushal and Mr Aerjit Mishra-all from WWF-India Team with whom the author himself was part and parcel in the field survey and finalisation of report. Dr Sejal Worah, Programme Director and Sri Ravi Singh, Sec. General and CEO, WWF-India draws special thanks for extending support and guidance. The Financial support given by IWMI led CIGAR project is also duly acknowledged.

References

Astad Pastakia, 2014, Identifying Hotspots of Resource Intensive Farming in Ganga Basin, WWF-India and WWF-Germany Report, New Delhi.

Dalip S. Swamy, 1994,The World Bank and Globalisation of Indian Economy, PIRG, Delhi.

Forum for Policy Dialogue on Water Conflicts in India, 2015, Water Conflicts, Pune.

Fraser Thompson, 2017, Report of Business and Sustainable Development Commission.

K. J. Jay et al, 2011, Life, Livelihoods, Ecosystems, Culture: Entitlement and Allocations of Water for Competing Uses.

Kripa Shankar, 1997, Fifty Year of Indian Independence, Arthik Anusandhan Kendra, Allahabad.

Ravindra Kumar, 2008, Mapping of Canal Services, UPID/FAO Training Workshop on Irrigation Management Modernisation, Upper Ganga Canal, Sept. 16-25, Meerut.

World Bank, 2013, Project Appraisal Document, Report No. 73422-IN.

WWF-India, 2016, Farmers Survey under Rejuvenating Ganga-Healthier Rivers for safer waters and improved agricultural productivity, IWMI led research project sponsored by CGIAR, New Delhi.

Index

H

I

N

O

P